KW-409-356

KOSOVA

PRELUDE TO WAR 1966-1999

KOSOVO

MARY MOTES

REDLAND
PRESS

UNIVERSITY OF PLYMOUTH

Item No. 9004528802

Date 1 5 JAN 2001 Z

Class No. 320.9497 MOT
Contl. No. 0850364922

LIBRARY SERVICES

© Copyright 1999 by Mary Motes

Library of Congress Catalog Card Number: 99-95675

All rights reserved

ISBN: 0-9674343-0-0 (hard cover)
0-9674343-1-9 (soft cover)

Published by Redland Press
25000 S.W. 162nd Avenue
Homestead, Florida 33031
http://www.redlandpress.com

Edited by Jan Fehrman

Jacket Design by Paula Munck

Cover Photo by Ethon Winslow

Map by Alice Motes

Book Design by WordRunner
Petaluma, California

Printed in Singapore

Errata
pp. 14/299 "Dusan" to "Lazar"
p. 286 "Ibrahim" to "Sali"

E very person in *Kosova Kosovo* is real: only the names have been changed except, of course, for President Tito and Gregory Peck and one other, Fehmi Agani, shot dead.

This book is to be returned on
or before the date stamped below

2 3 NOV 2001

−5 DEC 2001

2 8 FEB 2002

2 8 FEB 2002

2 8 MAY 2002

1 6 JAN 2003

− 1 MAY 2003

1 3 APR 2004

UNIVERSITY OF PLYMOUTH

PLYMOUTH LIBRARY

Tel: (01752) 232323
This book is subject to recall if required by another reader
Books may be renewed by phone
CHARGES WILL BE MADE FOR OVERDUE BOOKS

WITHDRAWN
FROM
UNIVERSITY OF PLYMOUTH
LIBRARY SERVICE

nent in

n could

ina and

ere sud-

orld she

he night

wearing

Comrade

'Kosovo

a, one of

er school

got to be

smoker's

students,

partment

ng for the

of Kosovo

n ear for

has long

lived there.

90 0452880 2

Ethon Winslow

Mary Motes taught in Kosovo at the Faculty of Philosophy, Pristina, from 1966 to 1971, establishing Pristina as a British Council post. While researching for a Ph.D. in Albanian studies at London University she was recruited by an unsuspecting BBC to become an entirely unsuitable Albanian and Serbian translator. She returned to Kosovo and two more years teaching at the fledgling University of Pristina from 1974 to 1976. Since then she has lived in Homestead, South Florida.

The author returned to Kosovo and Belgrade in 1988 during the turmoil over the "Kosovo Question," then in the winter of 1994 during the Bosnia war and again in the spring of 1997 when fighting had ceased in Bosnia and in Kosovo everyone was wondering when it would begin.

Acknowledgments

"Long-suffering" is the word that comes to mind: my dear, departed, long-suffering mother, who understood that before commonsense kicked in, I had to hitch-hike round Yugoslavia or die, who years before had become 'Mama Rosa' to Milena and Nada and, later, their children and who became Emina's 'Second Mum.' To my long-suffering South Floridian husband whom I actually met in Kosovo — a kind of Balkan blind date plotted by Emina and her brother Suleiman — and to my long-suffering children who knew that if the words *Yugoslav*, *Serbian*, *Albanian*, *Kosovo* or *Balkan* occurred singly or together, on radio or TV or from the ice cream van in the street, they were to shout immediately for their mother or shut up if she were already there, even if it were only to listen to a lanky Croatian basketball player giving a monosyllabic interview on MTV.

To my friends in the UK who endured years of my Yugo-fever, right back to school days and learned to ignore my pointed comparisons between the dynamic world of the Yugoslav Republic and the moribund society of old south-east England.

To my friends in the US who, for nearly 24 years now here in South Florida, have given me that warm, open friendship that I thought was copyrighted by Yugoslavs, especially Serbians.

To my long-suffering Serbian friends who had to put up with me falling in love with the most wayward corner of Yugoslavia and with unfailing love and wonderful food and drink looked after me whenever I came up from the province to Belgrade, always ready to pick a fight over Kosovo.

To all the friends with those electronic 1999 skills but also with the age old ones of patience and reliability: to Jan, Janell, and Jo-Anne, to Paula and Peggy and Ethan and Amy; definitely Without whom....

To so many of my former students in Kosovo who despite missed assignments and continuing problems with the definite article, fulfilled their promise: becoming the teachers and leaders of that first generation in Kosovo to learn English and to the new generation they have taught and all the young Kosovars, still in exile or beginning to rebuild, who need to reinvent the old concept of 'Brotherhood and Unity' and remember when Kosovar was used by Tito, he meant both Serb and Albanian.

Above all, acknowledgment is due to the long-suffering people of the former Yugoslavia; to the Croats, the Bosnians, Serbians, Macedonians, Albanians, Hungarians and all the rest for whom the description 'long-suffering' is hardly adequate but is still preferable to 'age-old-Balkan-enemies.'

"....the emnity that rages between Slav and Albanian in the districts both claim....This is the first of the great Balkan hatreds."

— Edith Durham, *The Burden of the Balkans*, 1905

"All I want to do is finish my exams."

— Vlaznim, Albanian student
Pristina, Kosovo, January 1999

Kosova Kosovo — the Albanian form and Serbian: only one letter divides them.

Contents

Introduction

When I first spent a summer in the Federal Peoples' Republic of Yugoslavia travelers were advised: Take your own razor blades and toilet rolls, be careful what you say and remember there will be probably be no hot water, which in fact had sounded about the same as going to stay with my grandmother. That had been far back in the mid-fifties but by 1963 things had smoothed off considerably and the Yugoslav National Tourist Office came out with a great travel poster aimed at the Western European holiday maker:

> Discover Yugoslavia before everyone does! SEVEN frontiers, SIX republics, FIVE nationalities, FOUR religions, THREE languages, TWO alphabets… AND ONE gloriously warm climate!

I hadn't liked that at all. By then I was deeply in love with Yugoslavia and didn't want to share it with anyone. Not the mosques and wild mountain rivers of Bosnia nor the Venetian palaces and tiny orange trees of the Adriatic. Not one fiord, alp, limestone cavern, waterfall, Roman temple or Byzantine church, not even a branch line railway station or old bus and certainly not the faces; the strong bones of the Slav, the velvety dark of the Latin, the cool blonde of Northern Europe. I'd fallen in love with Yugoslavia because of the faces.

Yugoslavs were good looking because they were a mix, Nada's father had declared. Nada was still a school girl back then, someone who had started off as my pen pal from Belgrade. "We are Germanic! Slav! Italian! Greek! Turk! Magyar!" he said. "You are an island, you English and my god, look at your faces!"

Yugoslavia had been called, like America, a melting pot. And by that year of the celebratory ad, 1963, Marxist rhetoric had eased up and many Yugoslavs with a blithe disregard of ideology were declaring under the picture of Tito or Lenin hung behind the bar or over the mirror in the hairdressers, "We will be a little America!" adding cryptically, "We have to be!"

Certainly all the boys Nada knew had looked like Americans. Some had crew cuts, because of the army, and as it was always summer when I went, they were always suntanned. Everyone was 'Comrade' and with me fresh from England there were always jokes about doomed Imperialism or cold-blooded Capitalists, but they were so friendly, so American with their energy and thick bouncy tennis shoes, playing basketball down in the old Turkish fort.

There had been Turkish soldiers in that old fort overlooking the Danube and Sava, a Turkish garrison, right up to the eighteen sixties. Serbia as part of the old Turkish Empire had, according to the travel books, "...existed for centuries in primitive isolation on the fringe of Europe." Still, I knew the French always said that about the English.

Yugoslavia was "a patchwork of peoples" cobbled together from the old frontiers of the Turkish and Austrian empires and then under Tito, the Communist guerilla leader from the Second World War, claiming the precarious spot "between East and West" once again. No longer the frontier between Orthodox Christian, Catholic and Moslem, but the East and West of Communism and Capitalism. Tito had broken away from Stalin and, according to sympathetic observers and the Yugoslav Tourist Office, with a bravado and grand disdain for what should be possible and with a dose of what would be called in the States plain old Yankee ingenuity and pragmatism, was trying to turn the Peoples' Socialist Republic of Yugoslavia, the rag tag edges of warring empires, into a new world and a tourist paradise.

Tito, in fact, was one of the few Communist leaders invited to America for a State visit. He was the last head of state ever to be received by President Kennedy.

That fall of 1963 I was on my grand trip round Yugoslavia and hadn't got back to Belgrade until November, on the afternoon of the 22nd. The big winter stove was lit; Nada was hemming a skirt ready for a party on Saturday. But in a few hours we were to hear that President Kennedy had been shot and Yugoslavia came to a halt. Saturday was a national day of mourning. The mother of Nada's friend canceled the party. People gathered in silence outside the American reading room, some in tears and took flowers inside. Nada, who always said she would never cry was in tears too: "There is so much lawlessness and violence in America!"

It was Yugoslavia which used to be called Land of Assassins. Her most notorious assassin, of course, was the young Bosnian who shot Arch-Duke Ferdinand in Sarajevo, in 1914. The last head of state in Europe to be assassinated was King Alexander of Yugoslavia, a Serb, shot by a Croat in 1934.

Like Yugoslavia, America was always described as a volatile mix, full of people from other places. That was what we were told in England, the explanation for the higher level of violence and mayhem in the States; the price paid for all that energy and vitality. But the dynamic mix was the whole point. Americans, so the story went, were all refugees too, like the inhabitants of the new Socialist post war Yugoslavia, from the old world craziness of religious wars and old imperial quarrels, all the ancient savageries of Europe. But so many citizens in Yugoslavia were not there from choice but by historical accident or rearrangement of frontiers; the parent countries were right there on her borders. It was impossible for Yugoslavia to leave the old world behind.

In the Second World War the Austrians with the Germans, the Italians, Hungarians, Bulgarians and Albanians had all invaded and claimed pieces of the Yugoslav pie. Yugoslavia had been devastated not only by a war of occupation but civil war between Serb and Croat, Orthodox Christian, Catholic and Moslem, Royalist and Communist, the memory of which for most Yugoslavs transformed the tired slogan of those postwar years, 'Brotherhood and Unity' into more of an unspoken vow: "Never Again!"

It was just after Kennedy died, and just before my visa expired in December, that Nada managed to get me an interview with the head of the English department at Belgrade University. "If you love Yugoslavia so much you should try and work here. Besides, it would be fun." Nada, like Tito, had a Slovene mother and a Croat father and had always been relentlessly good at organizing. She lent me a winter coat to wear for the interview and would have lent me shoes but my feet were much bigger than hers. It didn't matter anyway; there were no positions teaching English available.

That had been the year, 1963, when I'd first visited Kosovo, called Kosmet back then, and met the Albanian band.

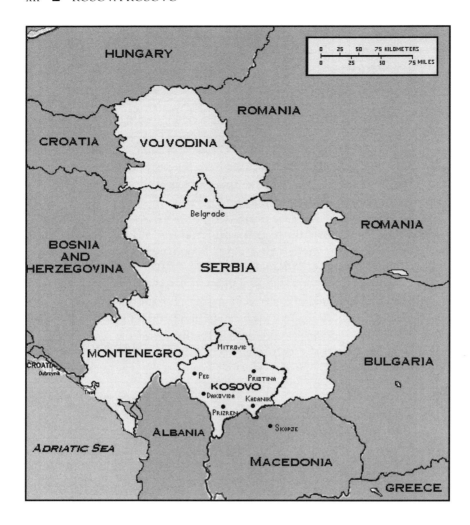

Notes on Names and Places

As I started working in Kosovo when Serbian was still the dominant language, all names appear in their Serbian form. Albanian equivalents are given when they play a part in the narrative. Kosova also appears in its indefinite form: Kosovë.

Pronunciation differences can mostly be eliminated by adding an 'h': Serbian names requiring an 'h' are pretty familiar: all the 'son of' names: Petrovic, Petrovich; Milosevic, Milosevich; and the town of Pec, Pech.

And add an 'h' to the occasional 's': Milosevic — Miloshevic, Dusan — Dushan, Siptar — Shiptar.

The Start

1966

"They need a *lektor* for English down in Pristina with your 'nice' Albanians — remember?" Nada had written in August from Belgrade. She meant my Turkish-Albanian band. "I have suggested you for the post. It's at the *Filozofski Fakultet*. All you need to bring are boots."

Nada had been down in Pristina that spring, teaching at the Peoples' University. "I never saw so much mud in my life."

I remembered the dust, the donkeys' hooves sinking into it like sand along the side streets.

"Pristina's Faculties are part of Belgrade University. Teachers go down twice a month but they need someone there. For now, you could come up for the weekends and their University year is very short."

So, as a university town, Pristina, capital of Kosovo and Metohija, (Kosmet) Autonomous Province of the Yugoslav Socialist Federal Republic of Serbia, had that much in common with Oxford and Cambridge.

"You know, if it were any of my other friends I would never suggest it," Nada concluded "but you are different." I wondered what Nada could mean by that.

Part I

Liberation

1966–1968

1966

ONE

∎

Situation Vacant

Suleiman, the Albanian assistant from the Pristina English department, was on the platform with Nada when the Tauern Express pulled into Belgrade at six in the morning. Dark and quite handsome, he looked about in his mid-thirties, a few years older than us. He was wearing a charcoal grey suit and a pale grey satin tie. I was wearing my-two-nights-and-one-and-a-half-days-on-the-train-sitting-in-a-corner-seat-if-you're-lucky look. Nada, still tanned from an Adriatic summer, was cool and chic as usual, in sandals and sun-dress. It was early September and hot. The shouting passengers racing past us were shiny with sweat. They were shoving huge suitcases randomly through train windows in the classic Yugoslav manner. Under the bright blue sky I had to remind myself that I'd not come to Serbia for another long summer holiday but, at the start of a new academic year, to try and get a job.

Home in Nada's flat, where Fowler's *Modern English Usage* still propped up *Rat I Mir* (War and Peace) on the shelf above the couch, Suleiman explained over his coffee cup how he'd first met Nada. Not sloshing through the springtime mud of Pristina apparently, but years ago, on a British Council English course. Pristina was a young, pioneering department he announced, the youngest in Yugoslavia. Plenty of scope for new ideas. Of course, text books were always a problem. And qualified staff. He turned to me graciously. Nada wanted his opinion of a new English grammar. Amid the talk of verbal phrases and new approaches to the problem of the indefinite article, I started to nod off.

"— And what is *your* field, Miss Mary? Your prospective area of research?"

This was going to be worse than I thought. Surely the whole point of traveling from one end of Europe to the other, especially to the rough end, was to get away from that kind of question. My English degree of six years ago might be getting a little faded at the edges but I'd hoped it was serviceable enough for the academically lightweight role of 'lector.'

"Mary likes the old Yugoslavia," Nada said smoothly. "That's her 'area of research.' She's a romantic. That's why she doesn't mind going down to Kosmet."

"Yes!" Suleiman exclaimed. "When Nada told me there was an English girl with a degree in English willing to come to Pristina — I didn't believe it!"

Certainly even the fact that I knew some Serbian and as a 'Native Speaker' spoke something called "R.P." ("Received Pronunciation! BBC English!" Suleiman murmured reverently in his own impeccable accent) seemed completely overshadowed by the fact that I had not only been to Pristina but was prepared to go back.

Two

■

The Balkans and the Beale Street Blues

1963

I hadn't noticed any Faculty of Philosophy when I'd been down in Pristina three years before. Not that I could honestly say in a place like Pristina I would really be on the look out for one. Kosmet was Southern Serbia. Macedonia lay to the south, Bulgaria to the east, Albania to the south east and Montenegro over the mountains. It was the heart of the Balkans and I'd been in the classic Balkan traveler mode, wandering about bemoaning five hundred years of Turkish occupation while delighting in the world it had left behind. As our bus trundled into Pristina down Marshal Tito Street we passed three gypsy carts, each one towing a large brown bear. And at the bus station a shoeless gypsy knee-deep in children was leading a pink-bottomed monkey through the market on the end of a piece of string.

Pristina's more permanent attractions according to Putnik, the Yugoslav travel agency, were the Imperial Mosque, the Sultan Bayazit Mosque, the Turkish Baths, the Partisan Memorial and the Nineteenth

Century Clock Tower with Roumanian Mechanism. The Turkish Baths should be struck off the list, confided the boy at Pristina's Putnik because they'd been turned into a cheese factory. And that was it for Pristina. Even Putnik, famed, if not notorious, for its optimism and powers of positive thinking could only manage for the capital of Kosmet in 1963 "...not before long an oriental village."

Until 1912 Kosovo and Metohija had been part of the Turkish Empire. The local Albanian workmen still wore slightly raffish turbans made of grey scarves or what looked like tea towels wound round white skull caps. Packed into a bus with a load of them coming up from the station I felt I was further east than the Balkans. In their mix of old lounge suit jackets and untidy turbans they looked less like Socialist workers in Tito's Yugoslavia than pictures of Yemeni irregulars or Kurdish rebels. The fact that many of them were fair with blue or grey eyes under the turbans made them somehow the more striking.

I'd been nearing the end of a marathon impulse trip round Yugoslavia. Having started off from a tiny seaside place on the northern Adriatic, just to see Zagreb, and leaving most of my stuff behind, I'd been looking increasingly scruffy and out of place till I came south to Kosmet where noone else looked like they had many changes of clothes either. It had been October, and a beautiful Indian summer. How right the word seemed for Kosmet with its water buffalo, turbans and ox carts, the gypsies with their dark Indian faces, the mosques, the buses jammed to the roofs and children everywhere and to the west and north west the great mountains blocking off Albania and Montenegro; the Northern Albanian Alps. Kosmet had been the Ottoman Empire's wild North West frontier when the fathers of the workmen on the bus were young men.

The plain of Kosovo was nearly 600 meters above sea level. As the sun went down it grew cold. The loaves being sold in the bread kiosks were steaming in the twilight. The soldiers and police were already in winter great coats nearly down to their ankles, the gun belts riding up over the top in an oddly innocent way, like a toddler's harness. I'd never been in Yugoslavia in cold weather. The young soldiers in their great coats with the red star on their caps looked as though they should have been off guarding Lenin's tomb.

In the October chill I'd been almost as down at heel and cold as the barefoot gypsy children pushing their fists against my legs. ("Come on, Aunt! Give me ten dinars! Only ten dinars!") So down at heel, in fact, that the man on the door of Hotel Bozur, the new hotel in the center of Marshal Tito Street, didn't even want to let me in on Saturday night. It was a dark, slim young waiter with an exact blend of deference and personal interest who had sized me up, ushered me in, brushed the crumbs deftly off the table cloth and brought me a strong Turkish coffee.

Like all the waiters in Yugoslavia back in the early sixties he still gave the impression of just playing the part but he was playing it very well. When he discovered I was English he announced grandly, "Then you will be our guest."

"I" he said with a significant pause, "am... Albanian!"

He was the first Albanian I'd ever met.

"You're the first Albanian I've ever met," I said.

"Oh, we're *all* Albanian round here!" he declared with a flourish. "It's only the peasants who wear the white cap."

I had read a lot of books on Yugoslavia, especially Serbia, my favorite Republic. I knew Albanians were the black sheep of the Balkans. They were in Kosmet in great numbers because they had driven the Serbian Christians out. They were the Balkan Christians who had 'turned Turk.' But that evening I was to discover if the waiter and the band were anything to go by then Albanians had all the proverbial charm of the black sheep, too.

Outside the gypsy children on Marshal Tito Street had pressed up against the glass, gesturing to their mouths, till the man on the door chased them away and my Albanian waiter drew the thick red curtains. He was bringing out free saucers of the management's potato chips which he called 'krips' and frowning at the men sitting nearby who kept going Psst! at me.

"If you like," the Turkish drummer suggested tentatively, "you can sit at our table. Here it is not good for a girl to be alone."

The band had started at seven thirty when the lights went up. They played *St. Louis Blues, Beale Street Blues* and *Sixteen Tons* and never once the miserable music that had been following me all round Yugoslavia that summer, the wan selection from *The Merry Widow* with its tinny, unheeded climaxes on stringy violins, the sort of music that made me wonder why Yugoslavia had had a revolution at all.

When the band stopped they came down to sit with me and 'make the joke' as Nada used to call it before her English got almost better than mine. All except the piano player, the oldest, who had been their biology teacher. He stayed up on the bandstand marking a pile of biology books behind the lid of the grand piano. They were all Turks and Albanians; saxophone, electric guitar, trumpet, and the Turkish drummer, fair with freckles. In fact, there was nothing exotic or Balkan about any of them. Two had degrees in physics, one was a vet. We played matchbox football on the table top and told bad jokes. At eight two singers had arrived; one very dark and quiet who spoke a little English and so became bashful and tongue-tied. He sang *Granada* and *Be My Love*. The other fair one, ("I am NOT Turk! I am ALBANIAN!") belted out *Beale Street Blues* and *Let's Twist Again*. He was a boxer, he announced and "The Champion Non-stop *Tvister* of Belgrade." When I wrote down the words of *Hit the Road, Jack* he went off and did it right away as 'Heathrow Check.'

The packed Saturday evening crowd talked uproariously through the music and applauded uproariously every time it stopped. All Serbs and Montenegrins said the band. All men, smoking and drinking hard. No! said the drummer there are so many *women* here tonight! I'd counted four and that included me. The band drank lemonade and didn't smoke. "We are *Muslimani*."

About eleven some of the Serbs and Montenegrins began to smash their glasses on the floor. Though Bozur was new it had the sign up on the wall usually seen only in the smaller, rougher *kafanas: For the breaking of glasses, 1,000 dinars*. Soon a ragged line of men formed, arms round each others' necks, stumbling over the broken glass. The band played on, switching to a Partisan song and then the *kolo*, the Serbian national dance. When they came down to sit for their last break round about midnight they asked me, "Are you having a good time with us, Mary?"

"Yes" I said. "My nicest evening in Yugoslavia."

They found that very funny. The Champion Non Stop Twister of Belgrade nearly fell off his chair. "— Then tell your friends in Belgrade!"

So as I had a post card of Pristina, taken from the new end, all new blocks and flower borders, I did.

THREE

Belgrade Maneuvers

Suleiman had arrived very early the next morning. "We must strike while the iron is hot!" he announced through the bathroom door.

Nada had just left for her first class. Her mother was at the market. When we got back the water melon would be cooling in the bath and there would be fat Yugoslav grapes on the coffee table. After lunch we would all retire for a nap enveloped in the cosy smell of ironing as the drawn curtains baked in the windows against the hot glass.

Suleiman was talking about work permits. It was suddenly dawning on me that much of the charm of Yugoslavia resided in the fact that it had always been a place impossible to imagine ever working in. Most Yugoslavs had the same problem, confiding disarmingly, "We don't like to work, you know!" with a touching innocence that anyone could even stand in the doorway of most Yugoslav shops or offices and not realize that immediately.

Nada's family lived in an old flat that had survived the war, right in the center of Belgrade so it only took Suleiman five minutes to march me along to an office on the ninth floor overlooking Marx-Engels Square.

The Serbian woman who interviewed us wore a *tvinset* and pearls and spoke better R.P. than I did. In keeping with her *tvinset* and pearls she seemed obsessed with the British Council. Had they advertised the post? Had I been there? What did they have to say? Without official backing from the British Council, the cultural branch of the Embassy, the idea of a foreigner just going down to Pristina and wandering into the Faculty was, for *Tvinset*, quite out of the question.

Down below Marx Engels square was jam-packed with cars. I could remember when it was just a building site. That was where I'd first seen Albanians, probably, men in white caps with barrows and pickaxes. I could remember when there were no cars in Belgrade at all, when it had been like Pristina.

"Of course," Suleiman was saying blandly. We were, of *course*, just on our way to British Council but as a courtesy, had called on *Tvinset's* government department first.

The British Council offices were on a noisy corner of Marshal Tito Street over a book shop. Suleiman led the way up the stairs past dove grey photographs of British poets and composers, through the outer office policed by Serbian secretaries ("Good morning, Comrade colleagues!") and straight into a room where a fair young man was kneeling among piles of books and what looked like an inexhaustible supply of posters of Westminster Abbey.

"This is Tony, our English Language Officer," Suleiman announced, gazing down at him benignly.

Before I could stop him he'd introduced me as the new English Language teacher who had traveled across Europe *specifically* to seek Council backing for the new Pristina post.

The head of the British Council was even less encouraging than *Tvinset*.

They had no money for an extra post! And they were certainly not empowered to contact any lady up on any ninth floor. And, frankly, Kosmet was a very difficult area. If I should succeed, well, I would be welcome to borrow books and things. Met Tony?

We found ourselves back on the pavement again and it wasn't even nine a.m. We did have a lot of posters of Westminster Abbey. Suleiman was starting to look hot in his dark suit and tie. The peasant women selling flowers on the corner were already sprinkling them cool with water. The thing to do said Suleiman, thinking hard, was to leave no stone unturned.

What we needed was someone interested in Kosmet. Someone who saw the importance of opening up the province to foreign teachers, of aiding Albanians at this dynamic stage of their development. Someone with vision. Someone, that is, with more clout than *Tvinset*.

I was told to be ready by seven again the next morning. Suleiman was going to try to get me an interview with the Secretary for Education in Serbia. He was an Albanian.

The Minister was seated alone at the end of a conference table, three ash trays along. Dark as Suleiman, a little weary and remote, he still had that un-English spark of appraisal and appreciation when faced with a female, even at eight in the morning, which never failed to surprise me. In England only men who dug up roads or worked on building sites were allowed to react to the presence of women which was why I'd never quite lost the feeling once across the Channel that almost every man in sight was leaning on a shovel watching me go by.

The Secretary ordered coffee and started to question Suleiman in Serbian about the Faculty and the closing of the English department in Prizren. Suleiman told him Prizren students could come to Pristina.

"Do you think I care about *town* students?" the Minister broke in scathingly. "Prizren is the center for a *mountain* region. And you destroy *that* because you teachers are too 'tired' to travel there twice a week!"

Suleiman looked at the ministerial carpet. I counted the ashtrays. Coffee arrived and Suleiman began again in what must have been Albanian. The Minister was beginning to look amused. There was a definite twinkle. He was probably hearing about my 'nice' Albanian band.

"Yes, of course, it would be very good for us if you went." He was talking in Serbian again. "But —" dryly — "aren't you scared? It seems you know the conditions in Kosmet but haven't you heard what they say about us Albanians? ...That we sell girls in our villages? Hmm..." He was leaning on his shovel again. "...Your father could get quite a good price for you..."

■

FOUR

South with Suleiman

The train for Kosmet still left at 8:20 a.m. from Bay 1. Passengers were already taking off their shoes and placing their feet carefully side by side on sheets of newspaper. The man opposite me, fitted out for life in scratchy, durable homespun, had just shoved a smelly bucket of cheese overhead, squashing the posters of Westminster Abbey.

"You will come up every weekend!" Nada commanded from the platform.

There were two routes south through Serbia from Belgrade. The international expresses took the broad Morava valley, swaying through to Sofia, Thessalonika, Athens and Istanbul. The 8:20 a.m. for Pristina, stopping at every station and often in between, chugged down into the Ibar gorge and out onto the Plain of Kosovo by about half past one every afternoon. It was the only daily train which under the circumstances was prudent as the whole railway network when faced with the Ibar gorge dwindled into a single line track.

A gypsy band started playing in the end compartment and soldiers and boys began drifting past to listen. They would be going to play at a wedding, Suleiman remarked, Autumn was the season for weddings, and the passing boys looked down at us speaking English with slow, unhurried stares.

"You'll find almost no-one speaks English," Suleiman said gloomily, "not even at Faculty level. I don't know what you would do without your Serbian, poor as it is."

The band had all spoken Italian and French but my foreign language at school had been German. That had always been a useful language in Yugoslavia as all the older Yugoslavs knew some German, because of the Occupation.

"Yes, then after the war first it was Russian in schools and then French and now suddenly it must be English. — Just like that!" Suleiman grumbled. "Where are the teachers? — And then they wonder why nobody can speak nothing!"

Suleiman obviously found like Nada that, however perfect your English was, sometimes nothing less than a double negative would do. He had studied at Belgrade University too and was in fact the first ever Albanian from Kosmet to graduate in English. Suleiman said the situation in Kosmet was so rare in the post-war world that the province had the dubious distinction of a line to itself in a UNESCO report as one of the few areas in the world where English had not been taught at all in schools.

"When the Minister called you a *pionir* he was not exaggerating."

Nothing had been taught in the Albanian language till after the Second World War. According to Suleiman all education was a novelty for Kosmet Albanians. "Under the old Kingdom of Serbia and then the Yugoslav Kingdom we were as backward as under the Turks!" It was the first time I'd seen Suleiman roused. He said the only schools for Albanians had been the Islamic religious schools where instruction had been in Turkish. The word Albanian had not been recognized at all, let alone the language.

But in the Turkish Empire, at least, Albanians as Moslems had been the most privileged class. That was why their lot had been so hard in Kosmet after the Balkan Christian states had re-conquered the peninsular.

"Ha! All the Christians had their schools at the finish, under the Turks. And Great Powers to support them! Only the *Albanians* were forbidden! Our teachers were imprisoned or exiled. They were even killed — by the Greeks too! The Turks wanted us only as Moslems and fighters!"

When the train stopped we could hear the roar of the Ibar. Children and their mothers hurried along below the carriage windows selling mugfulls of plums until the guard chased them away. At each tiny station the man on duty, the station master himself probably, stood stiffly to attention, red flag clamped under his arm, strong-boned Serbian face handsome and serious under his peaked cap.

Our train was being pulled by one of the little kettle engines still running in Yugoslavia; small and black with rounded sides and a big funnel belching lots of smoke. Watching one of them made you think not of inventing a steam engine, but inventing a kettle. The train was shrieking as it chuffed into one little tunnel after another, all the able-bodied rushing to close the windows against the smoke and sparks, an operation just completed as we chugged out into the sun whereupon there was a rush to open the windows and let out all the smoke again.

Down by the river below us were cottages and patches of garden, a little hay stack and row of maize, a cow and some sheep. Turning a bend there was a sudden glimpse of a pale stone soldier by the road across the water. Behind him rose the cliff of the gorge. Through the other window scree dotted with bushes turning gold and crimson climbed up almost against the glass.

This was the route of the Serbian retreat in 1915; the army, the King, priests and the people, fleeing south from the Austrians, Germans and Bulgarians. They had crossed the hostile mountains of Albania in midwinter. The Albanians had attacked them. But then the Montenegrin king had instructed his people, fellow Slavs, not to help the Serbians. The Austrians had bombed the columns of refugees on the plain of Kosovo. It was the first aerial bombardment of civilians in history.

"You know much more than I do," Suleiman commented. "I don't know any Serbian history."

Near the end of the gorge massive iron buckets crossed overhead, tilting and dripping over the line. The great lead and zinc mines of Trepca, of sacred memory to pre-war British shareholders: TREPCA MINES LTD. owned by us. Here the Albanians came piling in, clothes patched, faces unshaven and gaunt under white skull caps, many falling asleep as soon as they sat down, leaning against each other.

Then we were into the flat, the plateau of Kosovo, rattling towards the battlefield of Kosovo Polje, the Plain of Blackbirds, of sacred memory to every Serb where Sultan Murad defeated the Serbian Czar Dusan in 1389. On the wall of the hotel where the band had played, the Bozur, were the outlines of three knights, caparisoned for battle, lances upright, gallant pennant flying, riding out to Kosovo. *Kosovski Bozur* was the Kosovo peony, said to bloom on the battlefield every spring, like the Flanders poppy, from the blood of the fallen. It was not until the First Balkan War of 1912 that Serbians bore arms again in Kosovo, invading from the north with their Mannlicher and Mauser rifles. They tiptoed over the sacred ground it was said so as not to disturb the sleeping heroes.

The tomb of Sultan Murad was still on the battlefield outside Pristina, and the tomb of Gazimestan with the bodies of his commander, standard bearer and shield bearer.

"You haven't been to see them yet?" The band had demanded solemnly. And I'd been so deep into the somber Balkan drama of it all that until The Champion Non-Stop Twister of Belgrade laughed I hadn't realized they were joking.

The Plain of Kosovo was still so uncluttered and unspoilt that for half an hour under the limitless blue sky there was nothing much taller than a telegraph pole and nothing larger than a village: clusters of low, red-roofed, whitewashed houses away over the stubble, many behind high, sunbaked mud walls, marked by a line of poplars or a modest minaret.

There were the water buffalo I remembered, noses in air. Two girls in Turkish trousers were chasing a cow out of the stubble. The trousers bil-

lowed as they ran and as they stopped and frowned at the train, fell back
into the classic tulip shape. As they moved, the tulip divided into two, each
ankle a stem. How graceful Turkish trousers were when you were slim-hipped.
How graceful anything was when you were slim-hipped. Small boys, still
sunburnt, their shaved heads growing out into downy crew-cuts like Easter
chicks, capered along beside the track, making faces up at the train. The larks
still hovered high above the stubble and the stacks of mud bricks baked on in
the steadfast autumn sunlight. Away in the distance the mountains were
pitched low on the horizon in a light haze, like the tents of Sultan Murad.

The train didn't stop at Pristina but 10 kms away, at Kosovo Polje. The
Moslem Begs had not allowed the railway anywhere near Pristina when it
first came in 1874, Suleiman said, so fittingly enough, it was 'Kosovo Polje'
and not Pristina in all the railway timetables just as it was not Pristina but
Kosovo Polje ("battle of, epic of, legend of,") in all the history books.

There was the wooden station hotel where I'd stayed, against the
law; it was, understandably, out of bounds for foreigners. The low wooden
fence, the water trough, the unspeakable Turkish lavatory we could all smell
from the train, several kiosks and rising up behind, the grain silo and a
canning factory.

Suleiman refused to join the desperate race for the bus. We walked
through women squatting on the ground suckling their babies, gypsies,
bundles and buckets and past travelers standing about wolfing grapes out of
newspaper, like fish and chips. All the young girls were wearing trousers
under their skirts.

We were lucky. The single decker bus was already jammed with the
most able-bodied and quickest off the train but the Faculty car had come to
pick up a visiting Serbian professor and Suleiman and I squeezed in too. It
swerved round the large crowd of passengers left milling about, overtook
the bus and the line of carts strung out along the narrow cobbled road that
cut straight to Pristina, through fields of withered maize fronds and stubble;
the soil rich, almost purple.

Ibrahim, the Albanian chauffeur, with his thin, mobile face and dark
eyes, his deft, easy manner, reminded me of the waiter in the Kosovo Peony
hotel three years before.

"I hear you've come to help us Albanians!" he called over his shoulder in Serbian. "Ha! Did they tell you in Belgrade that we have tails?" That
was what the Minister of Education had said.

"So! What do you think of Albanians?"

If I went by all the books I'd read the answer would be not much. For me it was gallant little Serbia versus the unprincipled Albanians who had sold their souls to the Turks in exchange for land and a gun. It was the monastery church of Gracanica just outside Pristina, with the Patriarchs and warrior saints round the walls; King Milutin and his Queen Simonide in a rich, heavily jeweled head-dress like a Cleopatra; Christ gazing down from the central dome, hand raised in blessing and then five hundred years of dust and donkeys and empty servitude. The martyrdom of Serbia had lived on like a fresco of the flight into Egypt, burning all the brighter for being in the dark for five hundred years. The image of the stubborn, Serbian Christians with those burning, intense Byzantine faces, abandoning Kosovo and Metohija rather than their faith, trudging north behind their bearded Patriarch and golden cross, guarding a few sacred relics from their monasteries and churches, those walls of saints and eyes, left staring steadfastly across the cold flagstones for five hundred years while behind them the shaggy overspill of mountain men, the newly converted Albanian *Muslimani*, poured down across the painted wall into the rich, deserted plain.

I couldn't remember having read anything positive about Albanians at all. Well, I told Ibrahim who was still waiting for an answer, "I really don't know. I haven't met many yet," adding a little archly, "I'll have to wait and see."

Ibrahim seemed to find this very funny. "Ha! 'Not many!' 'Not many.' Well, you've come to the right place to find out! There are enough Albanians round here!"

FIVE

Staying with Mrs. Petrovic

The gypsy children still made a beeline for me in Marshal Tito Street, bumping my legs with their knuckles. They curled their fingers over the palms making a nest for coins, showing the patchy red varnish on their small nails. They still called after me, Aunt! and Girl! in their urgent, husky smokers' voices. The donkeys in their red and blue plastic harness still trotted out of the yard by Radio Pristina, sacks of flour across their backs, flour on their eyelashes. But my band had gone. As the hum of *korzo* died away the sound of one of those *Merry Widow* trios seeped across the terrace of Hotel Bozur. No, not from Croatia or Slovenia, Suleiman said and certainly not Albanians.

"Albanians do not play instruments in cafes" he announced with the haughty air of a Balkan Lady Bracknell.

Most hotel music in Kosmet was performed by Bulgarians, Suleiman explained because Serbians would never play for Albanians. But that hardly mattered, he said, as it was extremely rare for any Albanian to frequent those kind of places. In low class cafes gypsies made the music. I wondered who was playing in *The Belgrade* opposite Hotel Bozur. The music there was wonderful. It sounded like something coming through from North Africa intermittently on the short wave. *The Belgrade* was popularly known as 'Texas.' I'd had a meal there three years before. Suleiman looked dumbfounded. He refused even to slow down as we passed Texas on *korzo*.

"I teach at the Faculty!" he hissed.

Suleiman had been escorting me round Pristina. He had taken me to the Faculty, he had accompanied me on *korzo*, the evening promenade, twice but when I stopped to check out *Texas* he abandoned me.

It was still hard to get through the wedge of riff-raff in the doorway. There was the same clarinet player with hooded eyes and two-tone shoes: the waiters with emphatic black moustaches, swaying through the tables, loaded trays under their ears and up on the platform the two singers in long dresses sitting behind a rickety wooden table. I didn't know if they were the same girls but I recognized the dresses under the cardigans. The unforgettable pea green brocade and the pink velvet. Suddenly an old man in a ragged sheepskin jacket and magnificent moustache clambered up to the girl in the pink dress and stuck a 1000 dinar note to her forehead with a dab of spit and a yearning "OOOF!" The girl stuffed the money down her front. The nearby tables cheered. If it hadn't been for the cardigan she could have been in a cowboy film. They all could.

When I caught up with Suleiman halfway back to Mrs. Petrovic's, he'd received these fascinating details in icy silence.

Yes, it was true. I was no longer the summer traveler, gone tomorrow. I'd been to the Faculty and shaken hands with the Dean. I'd shaken hands with everyone. I was a guest now with Family Petrovic and I'd said I wanted to teach at the Faculty too.

Staying with Family Petrovic had been Nada's idea. Mrs. Petrovic was teaching English at elementary school but was also one of a group of teachers who were mature students in the English Department. Everyone was hungry to learn English in Kosmet now Suleiman said. Mrs. Petrovic's best friends, a Montenegrin headmistress and a Slovenian teacher, were all struggling with English too. The Slovenian, married to an army officer, organized an afternoon tea with the General's wife. They both lived in the best block of flats in Pristina, the one housing the officers of the Yugoslav Peoples' Army. The General's wife was very gracious and we all toasted my application and read the coffee cups. No-one saw the Faculty in my cup, but lots of lovers and journeys.

"What about the job?"

"See? Here is a snake. That's bad. We will have to wait."

The Faculty of Philosophy was just down the road from Family Petrovic's flat. Three stories high, long and low in the front with a few tiles falling off, it had been opened since 1960, Suleiman said. Below the steps a brief stretch of parched grass sloped down to Marshal Tito Street, just as it shed its last greengrocer and shoe-mender's and became the open road heading south for Macedonia and Greece past the new flats. On one side, among a few goat-bitten trees, was a tiny barracks with dirty pink plaster walls where three or four young soldiers washed socks and watched the girl students go by. Sheep and cows grazed round the Faculty, their bells ringing. They wore strings of blue beads across their foreheads, against the Evil Eye. The first morning we went to meet *Administracija* and the Dean there were four goats as well, up on their hind legs demolishing the last of the newly planted trees in front and an old man with two water buffalo. There was more livestock round the Faculty than students.

"The students come up in about ten days," Suleiman announced in his best academic voice as we sidestepped the sheep.

Mrs. Petrovic didn't have a spare key and had the habit of rushing off to school at odd hours, locking the door behind her. I was sleeping on the couch in the best room where the blinds were kept down against the beautiful October sunlight, the Indian summer of Kosmet. Below I could hear the shouts of the peasants selling logs for the winter. On the balcony opposite a young gypsy girl was always hanging out washing, under necklaces of drying scarlet peppers. The classic Yugoslav smells of roasting coffee beans and sweet peppers swirled up every morning. In the constant twilight of Mrs. Petrovic's best room the plastic flowers in their navy and gold pot perpetually bloomed on the piano below the picture that had taken a year and a half of her youth to embroider: a floppy Arab slumped in the shade of a palm. The shade alone must have taken a month.

Nada phoned. They'd got tickets for the theatre that weekend. Suleiman advised me not to leave. "In case of ...*developments*." He had no idea how long I would have to wait for a decision.

"You know nothing is done anymore in Yugoslavia without meetings."

At some point my application would have to go before a full scale Faculty Workers' Council, self-management session, when the cleaners and caretakers could consider it too. Well, they'd all been very friendly; everyone had. Suleiman shrugged. I certainly had no right to look impatient. Who was it who'd left her birth certificate at home?

"Meanwhile...read the papers," Suleiman said. "Improve your Serbian."

That was the last thing I felt like doing, to settle down in the gloom of Mrs Petrovic's flat with *POLITIKA* in the Cyrillic alphabet and *BORBA*, aptly named "Struggle." Tackling the Russian alphabet for any length of time had always held about as much appeal for my eyes as fighting through a privet hedge. The only daily paper in Pristina in the Latin alphabet was the Albanian *Rilindja* which meant Renaissance. When I passed the newspaper kiosks words like *reform*, *argument* and *incident* jumped into focus off its front page, making me feel international and intelligent but Suleiman was surprisingly adamant.

"I am Albanian but I say concentrate on Serbian. Not only because of Yugoslavia as a whole but because of Kosmet. Most Serbians here speak no Albanian and every Albanian knows Serbian — well, every Albanian you're likely to meet. Besides, I expect you will be more with Serbians. And if you find Serbian grammar hard, remember Albanian is worse."

Suleiman said there was very little work at the Faculties in Albanian. "Even though we teachers are supposed to be here for Albanians. Anyway, the number of qualified Albanians is still so small. It can be very hard on our students from country areas whose Serbian is poor. Of course, I've never had any problem. I speak Serbian excellently."

Mrs. Petrovic had already confided, "Suleiman's Serbian is very good, you know. He's a very cultured Albanian."

Parched, threadbare hills rose close round Pristina and the dust still drifted like sand along the side streets. The carpenters rolled out their low, round wooden tables for sale every morning, past the three legged stools and cradles. Down by the bus station near the market a row of rickety fiacres along one wall was the taxi rank. There was the oriental bazaar sound of metal being hammered in dark doorways, but in Pristina it was not for tourists, unless they were interested in stoves, watering cans, washing troughs or a souvenir length of pipe.

Pristina had a theatre with a new season beginning in Serbian and Albanian and three cinemas: *Yugoslav Peoples' Army*, *Brotherhood* (known as the Fleapit) and *Youth,* one small department store called *The Bushes* and an incredible number of barbers and cafes. In the evening there was *korzo,* the evening promenade.

"If you want to *walk* anywhere," Suleiman told me, "you can walk on *korzo.*"

But the pace of *korzo* was so leisurely, seemingly based less on a slowing down of legs than on some mysterious law of flux governing moon and tides. Suddenly at about a quarter past seven it would be flowing strongly along Marshal Tito Street, Serbs on one side, Albanians the other, spilling out into the road, everyone drifting along the pavement past the little acacias and silver birches with the black edged death notices pinned to the trunks and the beautiful weeping willow that hung down low outside the Headquarters of the League of Communists. Boys were in rows, arm in arm, the few girls arm in arm too. Sometimes men strolled by or a pair of young conscripts, holding hands; it was affection for the opposite sex that wasn't on display. The deep hum of *korzo* had always been one of the most exciting sounds in Yugoslavia. You could hear it well away down Pristina's side streets as everyone passed by to slow and wheel when they reached the steps of the theatre, like ships turning, and begin the drift back the other way.

There was no traffic to be stopped for *korzo,* as in Belgrade and bigger towns up north. About once a day a lone car might be seen to slow down behind a truck which was being reduced to a crawl by a bullock cart. An authentic traffic jam, it was the signal for some youth to raise the ironic cry, "Oh Look! LON-don!"

Milovan, the Serbian head of the English department, had asked me cautiously how long I might be prepared to stay, "Continuity is so important for the students."

I felt like saying till they ban horses and carts from Marshal Tito Street. After my first Monday evening I'd have said till there were no more strings of ponies being ridden in bareback, at dusk, ready for market on Tuesday.

Pristina was jammed with carts on market day. The Serbians drove in, husband and wife side by side, the men often wearing the grey army cap, the women in sensible short skirts and black head-scarves. In the Albanian carts turbaned and white capped men and boys sat tight-packed, facing inwards, often steadying a sheep or calf in the middle of their knees. The only time I saw an Albanian woman in a cart was outside the hospital. The Albanians were still coming in at ten or eleven, white caps set at jaunty angles.

Mrs. Petrovic, back herself from the market by half past eight, sniffed:

"They get up very late, you know!"

The main meeting place seemed to be the short cobbled street leading to the bus station and market. The Albanians squatted easily on their heels in a circle or with their backs to the wall, sticks or black umbrellas held between their knees. The older they were the more tough and assured they looked; their eyes often deep set and slightly hooded, screwed up a little as though they were facing into a cold wind. A surprising number were in costume, even young men, the traditional black and white homespun. The older men wore watch chains across their waistcoats and clamped sticks under their arms like colonels' batons. They would often lean forward and coolly blow their noses between finger and thumb, reminding me of the riddle my grandmother used to pose: "What does the rich man put in his pocket that the poor man throws away?"

It had been Mrs. Petrovic who first told me there were no Albanians in Kosmet. The Albanian name for Albanians was 'Shqiptar,' pronounced 'shcheeptar.' It meant 'son of the eagle' and Albania itself was 'Shqiperia' — Land of the Eagles. In Serbian the word had been modified into Siptar ('Shiptar') which had a nautical ring to it and was certainly easier to say.

Mrs. Petrovic had taken pains to make it clear. We were talking mostly in Serbian, as her English was even more erratic than my Serbian, and as I had no pretensions to be a teacher in Serbian, it was less embarrassing for me to air my mistakes.

"You see, Albanians live in Albania," she explained, which sounded reasonable "but here in Kosmet we've got 'Siptari'!" She'd lowered her voice making it sound like a complaint.

"You mean Albanians who live in Kosmet are called 'Siptari'?"

"No! No!" Mrs. Petrovic had got quite upset. "What Albanians? I told you! There ARE no Albanians in Kosmet!" But she ended on a note of triumphant logic: "How *can* they be 'Albanians' here when they've never been part of Albania!"

Bits of Kosmet were, in fact, in the Second World War; tacked on to make 'Greater Albania,' part of Mussolini's brief, ramshackle empire. But Albania itself had only been an independent state since the end of the First World War so you could say Albanians themselves had only recently become Albanians. If Mrs. Petrovic wanted to play those kind of games the Balkans was full of them; it had practically invented them.

What about 'Yugoslav'? It couldn't be used to describe anyone before 1929. That was the year the Kingdom of the Serbs, Croats and Slovenes became the Kingdom of Yugoslavia, the Kingdom of the South Slavs. So there were no 'Yugoslavs' before 1929. Some observers said there were no

'Yugoslavs' still. And just like Albania, here in Kosmet, in Macedonia too, and Northern Greece until just over fifty years ago no-one had been part of anywhere except the Ottoman Empire for over five hundred years.

Mrs. Petrovic had looked a little dazed. I should have warned her I got much more excited about Balkan history than English grammar. I should have let her win. It was obviously very important for her. And I was a guest in her house, at home with the traditional warm Serbian hospitality that was so easy to take for granted. And it was true that Albanians in Kosmet had never been part of Albania. Perhaps I just didn't like the way Mrs. Petrovic lowered her voice when she said, "'Siptari!"

Six

■

The Second Liberation

Ilija had "popped in" to tell me there was a good film on. He would persuade Suleiman to go with us. It would be *fun*. Ilija was the other young bachelor in the English department. Mrs. Petrovic was very fond of Ilija. Like 'Mr. Suleiman' he was still young and *not married!* No-one in Mrs. Petrovic's circle could decide who was the better catch: Suleiman was handsome but Ilija cooked and played the piano. I'd first met him when we'd had a musical evening round Mrs. Petrovic's piano, Ilija enchanted because I knew all the words of all the songs from *Oklahoma!*

Neither Ilija nor Suleiman were Slav at all. They marked the extremes of Serbia, like a pair of ethnic bookends; Ilija from the northeast near the Roumanian border, his mother Austrian, his father Roumanian and Suleiman from the southwest, the Albanian border, his mother Turkish, his father Albanian. Both their mother tongues imperial legacies of the empires that divided Yugoslavia; Ilija spoke German at home, Suleiman Turkish. Both proud of their Roumanian and Albanian blood but not speaking Albanian or Roumanian well; their language for work and life outside the home, Serbo-Croatian. And the language they spoke with such relish and precision, with a delight in perfection that never ceased to amaze me as I struggled with my Serbo-Croatian, was English.

Ilija with his hearty smoker's cough was very bracing: everyone was looking forward to me working at the Faculty! He'd heard his students boasting about me over at Law and Economics!

But it was almost the middle of October, the students all back, swelling *korzo*. I'd heard nothing from the Faculty and 'Uncle' in *Administracija* and a chill wind had begun to blow. I couldn't go on indefinitely drifting up and down *korzo*, unemployed, though according to Ilija and Suleiman that was not only a perfectly acceptable way of life in Kosmet but in fact the goal of many of the students.

It was pouring when we left for the cinema, Ilija tucking me under his big black umbrella, Suleiman following under his. As the tickets were sold directly onto the street, the crowd of boys and young men milled around in the downpour, clashing umbrellas, Suleiman and Ilija being greeted continually: "Good evening, Comrade teacher!"

"Half the English department here as usual!" Ilija remarked.

We were outside the *Yugoslav Peoples' Army* cinema and it was the Yugoslav Peoples' Army who finally let us in. A young soldier unbolted the door and inside two more soldiers in the grey-green army uniforms took the tickets. The crowd poured in, looking like a set of young conscripts themselves, banging their way along the wooden seats. A scuffle broke out and a soldier paced down over the creaking boards to sort it out.

"We Albanians are a mountain people still, even here on the plain. We all know which tribe we belong to" Suleiman had told me proudly, obviously laying claim to all those highland qualities of keen intelligence, energy and independence that are supposed to fade the nearer one got to sea level. In the half light of the cinema, surrounded by all that uniform vitality and exuberance I had the odd impression that everyone was from the same tribe, the Albanian tribe and had just swept in not off a rain drenched *korzo* but in the classic image of their arrival in Kosmet, in a tribal flood down from the hills.

Nada had said she could always tell an Albanian by the way he walked, "Somehow, not lazy but easy. Really, one has to say like a panther. It is always an Albanian when someone walks so."

She had been commenting on a student crossing the street ahead of us in Belgrade and the old Albanians in Pristina walked that way too. Thin and rangy, none of them looked like they'd grown fat yet down on the plains. The Albanian costume stretched them out even more; the thick white trousers starting perilously low on the hips with a cummerbund above wound round at least a foot deep. It was the cummerbund that made them look like lanky cowboys wearing gun belts and when they squatted against the walls down by the mosques and bus station on market day, their hands hung over their knees from the wrist, languid yet aware, like gunfighters' hands.

I still didn't really know what an Albanian should look like. Like Yugoslavs there seemed all sorts, from tall and fair to short and gypsy dark. There were even some with red hair and sandy eyelashes. Ever since that first summer, Nada and I school girls in Belgrade and at the Adriatic, I'd been obsessed with Yugoslavia; always ready to attribute all that was best and brightest in human nature to Yugoslavs, especially Serbs. Seven years later, on my last visit when I'd met the Albanian-Turkish band I'd been studying faces and everything else so intensely; brooding about national characteristics and the common denominator that made a 'Yugoslav' out of the mix of peoples inhabiting Yugoslavia. Drawn to the edges, preoccupied with definitions of nationality rather like Mrs. Petrovic. It was a wonder I hadn't been arrested on suspicion of spying. I had gone to every frontier region: Italian, Austrian, Hungarian, Roumanian, Bulgarian, Greek and Albanian, as though I expected to see an immediate transformation of people on the other side. Partly it was no more than an islander's fascination with frontiers; in Britain you were either on it or in the water.

And here I was behind the blinds with the cut crystal from Czechoslovakia and the plastic flowers and the handmade lacy crocheted mats that caught in everything, on the most dramatic frontier of all: the only one of Yugoslavia's still totally closed, the Albanian. Between Yugoslavia's smallest neighbor and her largest minority. The total number of Albanians in Yugoslavia according to Suleiman was forty percent of Albania's population and growing all the time. Yes, Mrs. Petrovic said, Albanians have so many children but she had added generously, Albanians make wonderful fathers. They love children so much. Maybe a reason she and her friends had said slyly, to marry an Albanian.

The film showing that night was *The Ipcress File*. Everyone packing the wooden seats, the tribal family, was relishing Michael Caine; the dead-pan bloody-mindedness, his frank interest in food and women, that peaky, independent working-class style. Something new. It made one quite proud to be British.

"Too many of our students are studying English now just because it's fashionable," Suleiman had commented. "There's a craze at the moment for everything English."

Up on the imperfect screen of the Yugoslav Peoples' Army cinema that sagged a little like an old sail, were the red buses and rolled umbrellas of Whitehall: top civil servants standing about with straight backs and keen eyes like old Albanians on market day but gradually *The Ipcress File* turns dark. Michael Caine is caught and imprisoned. We discover at the end of the film that he is actually staring at the wall of a North London warehouse as he lies on his prison bunk but he is tricked into believing, and so are we, that he is in Albania. The audience knew it right away. A hiss went round the Peoples' Army cinema and the creaking of the wooden seats suddenly stopped. In the silence, Suleiman murmured to Ilija and me that the signs tacked up on the warehouse walls were, indeed, in Albanian.

And then someone said something in Albanian. Admittedly it was the villain, described as someone who had an Albanian mother, as though that explained his villainy. He spoke the one curt word of interrogators everywhere: "*Mjaft!*" "*Enough!*"

Soldiers began to pace slowly, then faster down the aisles. Kosmet would be the only place in the whole world where *The Ipcress File*, where just that one word, would get such a reception. The 'real' Albanians, who, as Mrs. Petrovic had pointed out, lived in Albania, would never have the chance to see Michael Caine in their austere, forbidden corner of Europe, one of the few forbidden corners left anywhere. A mystery too, for every Albanian in Kosmet only a few miles away. The word must have spread that someone was saying something in Albanian up on the screen and out everyone had poured, the young men and boys of Pristina, through the rain. But Pristina did that for every film. Last week they'd been doing it for Randolph Scott and Doris Day; no reason to read heavy Balkan drama into everything.

But this year, 1966, had indeed turned into a year of heavy Balkan drama for Yugoslavia and especially Kosmet. It was of such importance for Albanians in Yugoslavia that they were calling it The Second Liberation. (The end of WW II was the First Liberation.) It was the fall of Aleksander Rankovic, the Vice President and Tito's head of State Security Police since the war, a Serbian. The Brioni Plenum as the whole affair had come to be called was the greatest political upheaval to hit Yugoslavia since the 1948 break with Stalin. The English papers had been saying it heralded a new era of liberalization in Yugoslavia, unprecedented for any of the Socialist countries. Tito was dismantling the power and structure of the secret police and the Communist party.

Suleiman had been surprised and pleased that the Brioni Plenum had been in the English papers. There had even been reports from Pristina itself, most about current investigations of ill-treatment and murder of Albanians, especially teachers and intellectuals, under Rankovic ten years ago. "Brioni is so important for us" Suleiman said. "We can hardly believe it. There are Serbian police locked up now in the Pristina police station instead of Albanians." Suleiman said he'd been taken to the police station himself as a teenager, for having the temerity as an Albanian, to practice his English by talking to foreigners.

He said Rankovic's name was so feared among Albanians that the children would be shooed off to bed with "Go to sleep or RRRrrankovic will get you!"

Hearing about Rankovic made sense of the abrupt, obscure comments of the Turkish and Albanian band in Bozur, all of them 'intellectuals' and teachers; their puzzling, bitter insistence that Turkey was a more 'progressive' place than Socialist Yugoslavia, their adamant: "There is NO place in Yugoslavia for... *people like us!*"

Suleiman said he remembered the band; they'd been very popular.

I wondered how many had gone to Turkey. When the drummer had first said they were 'Turks' I thought he'd been using the word like Bosnians did, in the sense it was used throughout the old Turkish Empire, meaning simply 'Moslem' but then they'd mentioned relatives in Izmir and Istanbul. Thousands of Albanians had left from Kosovo and Macedonia because of political pressure Suleiman explained; that was why almost every Albanian could say he had relatives in Turkey. Suleiman's own brother, his eldest brother, had gone, living in Istanbul now. "None of them were Turks" he said of the band. "It is only in Macedonia that you find many ethnic Turks. They were Albanian."

The band would had missed, by just three years, The Second Liberation for Yugoslav Albanians. And Yugoslavia would have lost not just a great band but two physicists, a civil engineer, a teacher of French, a vet, not to mention the Champion Non-Stop Twister of Belgrade.

Quite by chance I had arrived at one of the most dramatic moments in Kosmet and postwar Yugoslav history. It certainly made sense of the fact that Mrs. Petrovic and her friends could not see any news about my application in the coffee cups. This was obviously not the moment to try and persuade any *Administracija* to embrace a foreigner for the first time at such a politically turbulent moment even though, ironically, it might be the very fact of the Plenum that made my application down in Pristina, a possibility. Suleiman had looked blank at this and then laughed.

"We don't take women THAT seriously here! I hardly think you are considered in a political category! Opposition to your appointment, *which I foresaw*," he added darkly, "is far more likely to be coming from within the department! From *someone* who fears that you as Native Speaker will show up the poverty of his English!"

SEVEN

Good Morning, Dear Listeners!

No-one at Radio Pristina seemed to think much of the English department at the '*Fil. Fak.*' or the current crop of students. While waiting to hear from the Faculty I was going down to the radio station by the market every Friday morning with Suleiman to help record an English language course. Radio Pristina had borrowed one from Radio Sarajevo and Suleiman had translated the Serbo-Croatian bits into Albanian.

Nik, our producer on Radio School told me I ought to be in Albania, in Tirana.

'Education is serious in Albania! Not like here! Students must work there or they are OUT!" And as a bonus, Nik added: "Albania has the best beaches in Europe!"

I didn't think I'd be let into Albania. I didn't think anyone was let in, except the occasional plane load of Chinese technicians. Since the 1948 break with Yugoslavia Albania had broken with Russia too and was now linked fraternally with China, a convenient distance away.

"Oh, the English can go! It's only the Americans and Yugoslavs who aren't allowed in!"

Everyone down in the buffet at Radio Pristina had found this combination irresistibly funny. "Yugoslavs! and —" Violeta, the announcer I worked with, made a noise that I thought at first, with her perpetual cold was a sneeze "...Tsseeeyah!" The CIA.

It was the CIA which had been involved in the abortive attempt to overthrow Enver Hoxha and Communist rule in Albania. That was the operation the British spy Kim Philby had betrayed to the Russians causing the death of many Albanians. As for Yugoslavia, the Yugoslav-Albanian border remained one of the most hostile in the world. I'd seen the gunboats cruising the Macedonian-Albanian lakes and already heard of the deaths of the odd naive or desperate soul who plunged into the mountainous countryside beyond the border, going home to Albania. If the Yugoslav guards didn't shoot you, the Albanians would. "Of course!" Abdylla, the recording engineer, cupped his hands. "Albania is so *small* she has to be careful of *everyone*!"

Certainly Albania was so small that every neighbor was a threatening Great Power: the whole of the country could fit into the Republic of Serbia.

But far from being intimidated surely Radio Tirana was one of the most hostile radio stations in the world: all that classic invective about the running dogs of imperialism, the bandits, fascists and renegades of Moscow, Washington and Belgrade.

The Albanian engineers, announcers, writers and reporters down in the buffet at Radio Pristina, the Serbians too, just grinned.

Every Friday morning Nik would come down the steps of the small villa which housed the radio station, arms outstretched between the last chrysanthemums and autumn roses, smiling broadly. Suleiman and I had to wait by the glass booth at the gate till the guard had phoned him. Behind us the donkeys trotted by from the miller's yard, red and blue pom poms bouncing on their foreheads. Nik was a new sort of Albanian, very short with a quizzical, crumpled, cockney face. Abdylla, his engineer, was just as short. "Don't worry about us, Mary," Nik confided with a wink. "We are just half men. *We* won't give you any trouble!"

Suleiman would sort out the tapes with him on the other side of the glass while Violeta and I sat at the green baize table in the recording studio talking about men in Serbian, while the sun grew stronger behind us, shining in the window over the garden wall, past a stubby minaret. Suddenly the light would change, Nik would raise his eyebrows at us through the glass, chop down his hand and Violeta would swallow a sneeze and start off in Albanian: "Good morning, dear listeners!"

All I had to do, said Nik, was to wait for each English word to crop up and say it loud and clear into the microphone. The English words stuck out alright, in the middle of Suleiman's Albanian script: the problem was knowing when Violeta had reached them. It wasn't just the impenetrable look of Albanian with its clots of consonants; it was the sheer speed. Suleiman said No, Violeta was NOT gabbling; she was the best woman announcer in Kosmet. Albanian *should* flow. The flow included none of the reassuring international words from *Rilindja*, like 'problem' or 'incident' but the stubbornly alien Albanian for pen and pencil, question and answer. Even Mrs. Brown ('Zoti Braun') looked odd in Albanian. So many words put out an extra consonant and tripped you up at the start, like the familiar 'shqiptar'; small, everyday words like 'mbi' (on) or *ndaj* (towards). There was something familiar about them, but not from a European language. They reminded me of words I'd heard from African languages like the names Nkrumah or Mboya and I upset everyone who asked me eagerly what I thought of Albanian, by saying so.

Nik knew his job. In spite of the pauses and false starts while I caught up or Violeta sneezed, exactly at nine she would have left the Browns behind and be heading for "Goodbye, dear listeners!" and a good blow of the nose.

At nine Ibrahim arrived for the next recording. Twice the size of Nik, with a deep velvet voice, he was an old friend of Suleiman's.

"We learnt the quick step together in the shed at the bottom of his father's garden," Suleiman had said, introducing him, 'when we were young and scared of women."

That must have been a long time ago.

Like Nik and Suleiman, Ibrahim was from Prizren, the chief town in the plain of Metohija and the historic capital of Kosmet. They all spoke Turkish together. Turkish was so much the town language of Prizren, Nik told me, that even the Serbs in Prizren understood Turkish.

Violeta didn't speak a *word* of Turkish, she announced proudly. "I come from Djakovica. In Djakovica even *Serbs* speak Albanian!"

But Djakovica was only about half an hour away from Prizren. "It's an almost completely Albanian town" Nik explained. "All our best announcers come from Djakovica."

We were talking Serbian together; Nik disappointed I didn't know Italian. ("Albanians are like Italians! We love women, we love children! *La Dolce Vita!*") Violeta with her derogatory sniff, not happy with my lack of Albanian. If I were in Djakovica she said I'd HAVE to learn Albanian. With the borders of Albania so firmly closed Kosmet would certainly be the place to come to study language, and Albanians too.

"Oh, they all do," Nik told me airily; "Linguists, anthropologists. The Americans, Germans, French..." Though the only foreigners in Pristina I had heard about were a small group of East European engineers on loan to the local power station and leading wealthy, secluded lives clogged with non-convertible dinars.

Violeta began to tell me the name of everything in Albanian on Friday mornings. She had a brusque, ironic, wary manner, like the Albanian typist in *Administracija* at the Faculty. With her grey eyes, hair like straw and that perpetual sniff, Violeta looked a bit of a cockney too.

"*Shkreps!*" she would say sharply, jiggling a box of matches under my nose. Yes, you scraped a *shkreps*. "*Muri!*" — the wall. Yes, 'mural.'

Suleiman told her to stop confusing me; I would soon be mixing Serbian and Albanian. "Mary should learn Albanian!" Violeta snapped. "Why do you think she came to Kosmet? — And why don't YOU learn Albanian? Ha! You two can learn together!"

I noticed when Suleiman handed over his translations on Friday morning Violeta would go through the Albanian changing endings and sometimes whole words.

"The first Albanian teacher of English at the Faculty and you can't speak Albanian properly!" The trouble was she said, Suleiman was "too much of a Turk."

Violeta made 'Turk' sound as bad as Serbs made '*Siptar*!' It certainly angered Suleiman. But it was true he'd brought back a dictionary and grammar from his summer in Istanbul. He'd shown me them when his sister Emina had invited me to tea. And he said he was determined to learn standard Turkish, obviously still smarting from some kind of reaction in Istanbul, some Turkish Violeta perhaps, who'd sneered at his Turkish.

The Turkish of Kosmet was left over, like so much else in the province, from the days of the Ottoman Empire. It would be pre-revolutionary Turkish, untouched by the reforms of Kemal Ataturk, full of old Arabic and Persian. Perhaps that was why it sounded so beautiful. But for Suleiman, bright young graduate and man about town in his dark grey suit and satin ties, it would mean that when he opened his mouth in Istanbul he was talking a quaint, archaic, provincial dialect.

The Turkish I heard on Radio Pristina was quite different from the Turkish everyone spoke. It was tight and constricted. The girl reading the six o clock news sounded as though she'd got a clothes pin on her nose.

"*Tamam*!" Exactly! Violeta had cried triumphantly, using the neat Turkish word still current in Serbian and Albanian too. The announcer was a local girl, she explained, tying herself in knots trying to speak the Turkish of Istanbul. "— Like Suleiman!"

Walking back from Radio Pristina one Friday morning Suleiman, still smarting from Violeta's sarcasm as she corrected his Albanian, commented bitterly, "Now you see why I say concentrate on ONE language here! Don't get into our mess! Every five minutes we switch languages."

That was what fascinated me; that effortless switch between Serbian, Albanian and Turkish. It wasn't effortless at all, Suleiman said.

"Yes, most educated Albanians here speak three languages and not one well! That is why it is not good to be a member of a minority! — I speak as a linguist," he added dryly.

"You see with me, the language I know best — Serbian — is neither the language of my nationality nor my mother tongue. My mother tongue — Turkish — is not even standard enough, in its Kosmet form, to be written down! And the Albanian here is not standard either. Everyone makes mistakes, even Violeta. I won't be interested in learning Albanian properly till we adopt the standard Albanian from Tirana. All the scholarship and research is being carried on there. We are completely cut off here in Kosmet. Western scholars get more than us. We cannot get books or any materials. They have excellent scholars and linguists in Albania; men who studied in Rome and at the Sorbonne. They are very serious. — If you wanted to learn good *Albanian* then you are in the wrong place. You should have gone to Tirana."

EIGHT

Czar Dusan's City

I t was on the third Saturday stuck in Mrs. Petrovic's best room away from the sun that I decided to play truant. The day before I'd finally gone for a real walk, very tamely and correctly, just along the side of the main road up to the excursion spot outside Pristina, a wooded slope with a restaurant and picnic tables. Students on their break at the teachers' training college had lined up, laughing, to watch me pass: "Where are you going, girl?"

"Well, do you see women here just *walking about?*" Suleiman had asked scathingly when I complained. No. Even the Serbian girls were never alone but always in pairs like police in rough areas. Women only walked to the shops and the market and most Albanian women weren't even allowed to do that. It was the Albanian men not only in the market but in the *Self Serviz* chucking sugar and soap into their metal baskets. Suleiman's sister, Emina, didn't know the price of anything. Her husband did all the shopping.

That third Saturday morning, finally deciding I'd never get the job at the Faculty anyway and, all things considered, it was probably a good thing, I resolved at least to see Prizren before I left Kosmet. 'Czar Dusan's city,' Mrs. Petrovic and Nada called it. One of the most beautiful places in the Turkish Empire, Suleiman announced. And I resolved to hitchhike, *auto-stop*, just once more; leave Kosmet in a defiant blaze of western disreputableness just as I'd arrived last time, scruffy and down at heel, to be looked after in the hotel by my waiter and the band.

I told Mrs. Petrovic I was going to take the bus to Prizren and we had a coffee before I left. ("I see a journey in the cup, Ha ha!") But I started walking the other way from the bus station, up the hill out of Pristina on the road to Macedonia. Large letters began to appear in front of me; it took five minutes to trudge past the words: K O S O V O K O M B I N A T. The sky was sullen and heavy and after a while so was I. Big black crows kept taking off and settling back along the verge in front of me in an aimless and rather unpleasant way. There was no traffic to disturb them. After an hour the tally was two early morning lorries and miscellaneous carts. After the second hour the tally was one traveling salesman in shirts and socks. By which time I no longer cared if the only people in mechanized transport with a seat to spare were all serial killers.

The traveling salesman turned out to be a solid family man. He kept suggesting we pull off the road in a secluded spot so he could show me pictures of his wife and son. He left me reluctantly in a tiny village outside a blacksmith's. Two young men were shoeing a donkey in the gloom. Their eyes showed up like miners' eyes under the low roof; white caps set straight across their foreheads like miners' helmets. There was that hard, cold, Albanian stare. Behind me the empty, poplar-lined road led back across the dusty plain of Kosovo; ahead dark storm clouds were building up over the hills, that authentic navy blue which always meant trouble. It was becoming clear minute by minute that I'd finally thrown aside Mrs. Petrovic's blinds and shutters only to be swamped by the first of the autumn rains.

No, no buses stopped on Saturday, said the waiter in the little *kafana*, they were always too full. An occasional donkey pattered past the open doorway, hurrying home before the rains came, the old man in turban and ragged clothes sitting sideways on its ridgy back kicking it routinely in the ribs.

I started walking up through the Crnolevo hills, the divide between Kosovo and Metohija, just as Kosmet's Indian summer came to an end. Everyone sitting on the carts that passed studied me for long periods of time from under their big black umbrellas, sacks, strips of polythene or their own coats pulled up over their heads. I should have remembered: when everything moves at walking pace there is nothing dashing or wild and free about hitchhiking.

"FOR GOD'S SAKE WHAT ARE YOU DOING?"

A van had stopped but deafened by the rain bouncing off the rocks I hadn't even heard the driver.

"I'M WALKING TO PRIZREN!"

"YOU CAN'T DO THAT, GIRL! GET IN!"

The van had been packed with old Albanians. It was like squeezing in with a bunch of elderly army officers, if not actually up before a courts martial. All stared straight ahead, shirts spotless white and dry, sticks held between knees, backs ramrod straight.

So that was how I'd arrived in Prizren of all places, being chased up

side streets by the van which had immediately decanted all its old Albanians and was bumping over the cobbles after me, beeping its horn. In the
end I'd dived up a tiny alley which turned out to be a gypsy street, with
bright periwinkle blue walls and disrespectful children and ponies coming
down from the mountains above laden with brush which nearly knocked
me over.

Prizren, miraculously, was bright and sunny and bone dry but the
sound of water was everywhere; as Putnik said it was "criss-crossed with
mountain streams." The river Bistrica, the clear and shining one, raced down
through the center of the town, a line of young poplars along its bank through
which you could see the old town, green with trees and gardens, climbing
up in white walls and rose red tiles to the crumbling fort. Halfway up a
ruined white church grew more glowing white, like the minarets, as dusk
fell and *korzo* began; the word TITO appearing, picked out in light bulbs
high as the moon up on the old ramparts.

Korzo in Prizren was tight-packed and inexorable, moving at the pace
of a slow regimental march past the Turkish fountain and the Orthodox
church, up the steep cobbled street to the bread kiosk where it wheeled,
four abreast, and paced slowly back — no U turns — following me with its
collective eye. Retreating down the hill past the Sinan Pasha mosque I'd
made for the second bridge only to find myself between the knees of all the
young men perched up on the rails above the river. The mountain water, so
loud it drowned the hum of *korzo*, raced below us, falling over itself to get
across the valley and into Albania. There were the great Albanian Alps in
the distance. Prizren was a perfect frontier post; no stranger could cross the
border without the whole of Prizren knowing.

I knew everyone on *korzo* knew how I'd arrived in Prizren. The boys
on the bridge knew and the shoe-shine man outside the hotel and the re-
ceptionist handing me my key. As I climbed upstairs away from all those
eyes, up the typical death trap stairs of old Yugoslav hotels, the stair rods
coming adrift underfoot in the same old reassuring way, I'd told myself it
didn't really matter; I wouldn't be staying in Kosmet anyway.

For if there were no prospect with the authorities in Pristina, there
could certainly be no help forthcoming from British Council in Belgrade,
ever. Over our Nescafe at the Council the young English Language Officer
had confided:

"You know, you'd never get that post through us anyway. The Council would never send a woman down there. Kosmet for us counts as the
Middle East."

NINE

■

Health Station Number One

Mrs. Petrovic sounded excited. Suleiman was on the phone. Even he sounded excited. "You are to go for an X-ray" he told me. "That will be Health Station Number One, opposite the Yugoslav Peoples' Army cinema."

Of course. When you were accepted for employment as a teacher, you had to get an X-ray.

I stood leaning against the wall with a row of workmen waiting for X rays too. Health Station Number One would be my local surgery. The concrete floor was wet and muddy, the benches crammed. On the wall were Health Hazard pictures hard to see in the light from the low watt bulb. A pair of dirty, work worn hands: WASH YOUR HANDS! An alcoholic slumped across a table top. The women there were mostly Albanian, wrapped up like downtrodden nuns, faces blank, their babies and toddlers with runny noses and white faces, knots of blue beads on their shoulders and in their hair. The Albanian country girls all dressed the same in long rusty black overdresses gathered in at the waist, worn over trousers, and shapeless old black shoes with thick woollen socks. Their heads were muffled up in big woollen shawls, always brown. Even the town women's scarves overshadowed their pale faces like visors, looking ready to fall and snap shut. They seemed to have adopted light green or fawn poplin macs as a standard costume for the street, their Turkish trousers hitched up underneath, leaving their legs surprised in thick woollen stockings.

A couple of Serbian women were at the surgery in scruffy coats and hennaed hair. In the middle of the floor two very pregnant gypsies, knuckles on hips, Turkish trousers crammed into the tops of their wellington boots, stood talking loudly in *Rom*, the fourth language of Kosmet. Every few minutes a man with a terrible cough pushed his way out to spit into the wet November dark.

It was Violeta who'd told me TB was still a problem in Kosmet. "Everything is" she'd said angrily. I knew Kosmet was called the India of Yugoslavia. "Worse!" Violeta cried. "Because in India you were there, the English, but here we had the Turks!"

The band had blamed everything on "bad *kanalizacija!*"

" — The drains!" the vet who played guitar had explained.

There was ignorance, illiteracy and superstition in Kosmet, the band had admitted.

"It's the drains!" insisted the vet.

This last summer, in fact, just before Nada had written to me, cholera had broken out in Pristina. When it came to the capital of Kosmet, Serbs and Albanians were agreed. "It's the *water!*" Mrs. Petrovic said darkly, just like the band. Pristina had no real river. "How can you have a town without a river?"

The vet had explained. "Pristina has no mountains, so no mountain rivers — no *running water!*" The basic idea of sanitation it seemed was medieval; left over from the Ottoman empire. Nature, not man, created running water.

The new Communist regime had made Pristina, 'not before long an oriental village' on the wind bitten plain of Kosovo, the new administrative capital of Kosmet in 1945. It was the plain of Metohija with its orchards and vineyards, 'the garden of Metohija,' where the real historic towns of Kosmet were, like Prizren and Pec, built on the banks of fast flowing, cleansing rivers pouring down from mountains where, the Putnik brochure said, lynx and bear still roamed.

Mrs. Petrovic insisted that in spite of Pristina's shortcomings, Kosmet was, of all the six Republics and regions of Yugoslavia, the best place to live: "Because this is old Serbia where the old ways of hospitality have stopped the longest."

"We are very poor here," the band had told me "and so here you find the best friendships and good times in Yugoslavia. Here we are all 'Comrade.' In Belgrade everyone is 'Mister' now."

The government booklet in the English department library said in Kosmet there were only 417 doctors for nearly one and a quarter million people. Kosmet had a phenomenal birth rate; the fourth highest in the world. The average number of children in an Albanian family was between six and seven. The province had the highest infant mortality rate in Yugoslavia and the lowest life expectancy. "And here," Violeta had announced one Friday morning glaring at Suleiman, Nik and Abdylla, the inoffensive radio engineer, "is one of the few places in the world where women not men die first!"

I wondered how long the *hamals* lived, those dark-skinned men bent double under planks or mattresses or wardrobes, half-running through the streets of Pristina, peering up from under their eyebrows like dogs. Now they often passed carrying a fridge or electric cooker a sign of progress hardly likely to raise their spirits as they obviously weighed more.

Nik said "Just look around. Albania is not so poor as this."

Mrs. Petrovic and her friends had told me Albania was so poor that "After the war we did everything for them even though we had nothing ourselves!" She'd lowered her voice. *"We built them their first railway!"*

Perhaps that was part of the early plan by the new Yugoslav Communist regime to incorporate Albania into Yugoslavia, together with Kosmet, as the seventh Republic.

Nik had explained the current situation. "Albania is poorer than most of Yugoslavia but NOT Kosmet!"

And just like the urbane professors from the Albanian department, courteous and soft-spoken in their dark suits and conservative ties, Nik insisted "We Albanians in Kosmet are *much* more primitive than Albanians in Albania!"

"We are northern Albanians," explained the senior Albanologist, "traditionally more backward than the south. More independent of the Turks like the Montenegrins but we were so tribal and isolated in the mountains and here, in Kosmet, well, at the end of the Turkish Empire it was anarchy we can say."

The name for Northern Albanians and their variant of Albanian was Geg; for southern Albanians which included Enver Hohxa and the majority of the ruling Communist Party it was Tosk. Tosk was the standard Albanian now, Suleiman explained, the Albanian he wanted to learn, and Tosks, who lived nearer Greece and in the lowlands had always been the more civilized Albanians. The dividing line between Geg and Tosk came in Central Albania at the Shkumbi river. So if Mrs. Petrovic and her friends wanted to draw any line between Albanians, it should have come there.

From one of the surgery rooms came the sound of raised voices, Albanian then Serbian. One of the Serbian women caught my eye, grinned and shook her head. A Serbian male voice was insisting: "Tell him I've got to examine his wife!"

Mrs. Petrovic had said Albanian peasants would not allow their wives to see the doctor or else would walk right in, and refuse to leave. "And then they threaten the surgeons, '— If my child dies I will KILL you!' and then they wonder why they don't have enough doctors here!"

Byron wrote that his life had been saved by his two Albanian servants who frightened away his physician, threatening to cut his throat if their master were not cured promptly. Suleiman had pointed out the two copies of Byron's *Childe Harold's Pilgrimage* in the English department library; two slim volumes complete with Albanian footnotes. Suleiman knew many of the lines off by heart:

'Fierce are Albania's children, yet they lack

Not virtues, were those virtues more mature..."

He'd made me look up the English and check he was right. There was the famous portrait of the poet at the front: "Byron in Albanian Dress."

I could do a class on Byron for the Albanian students. And one on Tennyson for the Serbians and Montenegrins, the *Ode to Montenegro*: "...rocky throne of Freedom, Beating back the swarm of Islam for five hundred years..."

I'd have to see how good their English was. Lined up under the picture of Tito in his uniform as Commander of the Fleet, the little English department library had all the old favorites: *Peregrine Pickle, Romeo and Juliet, Moby Dick, Sons and Lovers*. Up there on the third floor with open farmland through the corridor windows where cows were rooting through the withered maize stems and carts rattled by, were the *Times Literary Supplement* for the last six months and *The International New York Herald Tribune*. None of them had been opened. They were all waiting for me.

TEN

Oral Exercises

Back in the staff room on my first morning after my first class Ilija was waiting to take me down to the buffet for a brandy. He was already reporting initial reactions. One distraught Albanian First year apparently had rushed out of the class to confide to him in the corridor:

"But Comrade teacher Ilija, she isn't *speaking* English!"

"Isn't it wonderful?" Ilija exclaimed gleefully, in his perfect accent, "They've never heard *real* English before!"

I'd been preparing for all kinds of problems in the teaching of English as a foreign language but hardly to be accused of not even speaking it.

"We need you," Milovan, the Serbian head of the department, had said, "for Oral Exercises."

That was what I being paid for. It was up on the notice board. It was why they'd finally issued me with a visa valid for one year down at the police station.

Ilija was down for some Oral Exercises too, but he was no help.

"Oh, I tell them jokes, teach them rhyming slang, songs. Just talk about England! Madame Tussards! So-ho!"

Ilija had spent the last year in England, on post-graduate studies. It was his giant PAN AM calendar on the staff room wall.

Suleiman's advice was to teach everyone proverbs. Write one up on the board. Make them all recite it, translate it, write it down, read it back; say it all together, one at a time, in twos and threes, this side, that side, Serbs then Albanians, boys then girls. Close their books, shut their eyes. It was surprising, he said, how quickly three quarters of an hour could pass like that.

But some of the students were over twenty-one. There was even an old man, a Serbian, well into his sixties, who came from a remote village at exam times and sat for the first year exam, Ilija said. He'd been doing it for years. Everyone called him Grandad.

"You won't understand a word he writes," Ilija told me, "but you'll *love* him!"

Somehow I had the feeling that whatever method I chose to employ, conducting Oral Exercises was probably going to make me look a lot more silly than the students. I'd already had a taste of the incidental oddities of English language teaching at Radio Pristina with Violeta and Mr. and Mrs. Brown and where they put their pens and pencils.

That was a beginners' course and it was beginners I started with my first morning at the Faculty. About twenty Serbians, Albanians and Montenegrins. As I came in they all stood up. It was like Hotel Bozur on Saturday night. I could only see three girls. Over the blackboard behind me, President Tito in his uniform as Supreme Commander gazed sternly yet humanely out of the window at the Geography department.

"Do sit down."

As the murmur of translation died away they sat down and I saw that no-one had a book. Comrade teacher Suleiman had ordered them from Belgrade but they hadn't come. The student who was telling me this had obligingly sat at the front, by the window. Outside down below I could hear sheep-bells and what sounded like the mad old man with the water buffalo who shouted not at his animals, but at us.

The student by the window who spoke English was called Muhammed. Muhammed was to get me through the year. He was from an Albanian village near Kacanik, scarcely more than a village itself at the entrance to the Kacanik gorge leading south into Macedonia. Muhammed was cheerful and charming. His manners were perfect and he had a dry sense of humor. Above all he spoke English, simple, basic, grammatical English.

How had *he* managed it?

"I went to Belgrade and bought a book," he said simply, a little anxious he had done the wrong thing.

Milovan had emphasized that all my classes should be conducted in English. Thinking of my Serbian, all those leading articles in *Borba* still undeciphered, I wondered what else he could have had in mind. Suleiman said it was enough for the students just to hear the language from a Native Speaker: "Something we can't give them," he added, in his faultless English.

Certainly if Suleiman were anything to go by or Muhammed in the first year, all this was totally unnecessary. Muhammed had just bought a book and Suleiman had taught himself, long before English was a subject in Kosmet schools, listening to the *Voice of America* from Thessalonika.

"Just talk," Suleiman insisted "and the effort of listening will be enough."

I soon discovered this was true. After five minutes those fresh faces and shining eyes were dulled. Jaws had dropped and brows were knotted. Along the back row here and there veins were standing out. I probably looked like that every Friday trying to follow Mr and Mrs Browns' adventures in Albanian. However depressing or alarming the sight might be, I came to recognize it as the sign of success. The students were trying. It was a bright and relaxed expression on all but the best of the Fourth year that meant the struggle to understand had been given up entirely and the student was just sitting back like I did with Turkish, letting the beautiful, alien syllables roll by.

Certainly it was easy enough to talk. That had never been a problem but I knew the real job was to get the students to talk to me and that meant questions: What is your name? How old are you? Where do you live? After all those years of interrogation myself on Yugoslav buses and trains, park benches and beaches, struggling with Serbian to answer Why wasn't I married and How much did my watch cost, finally, in Yugoslavia, I was asking the questions.

"Remember, they are very shy," Ilija said.

It was a novel experience to see Yugoslavs being shy, too.

I was determined to steer clear of Mrs. Brown and her pens and pencils but we could have, "What is on at the pictures?" the old standby, "Where are you from?" and "Who will clean the board?"

Some questions I was soon really going to need an answer to, like:

"Is it true the nearest dry cleaners is in Macedonia?"

One question I didn't have to ask was "Are you Serbian or Albanian?" It was the Albanian students who had such good English accents. Albanian, unlike Serbian, was full of English sounds. For a start it had the omnipresent "er," as in "Er...Sorry er'm late." And it had 'th," the bugbear of all foreign language students, and both sorts: English 'th' as in 'the' and soft as in 'thistle.' It even had 'ng' though not at the end of a word but at the beginning. So it was the Serbians, mostly a few girls in their new autumn suits and fresh nail varnish who were the ones to sound like Brooklyn gangsters, like Nada had in her younger days, grinding out her dis and dat and dese and dose while the Albanians, sunburnt wrists shooting out of ill-fitting jackets, hardly ever had to be corrected. They never 'sank a sonk' or "sought somesink" or had dat problem. The Serbians were mystified. If anyone should be corrected for anything, you could see it was expected that it should be Albanians, the *Siptars*.

Milovan had asked me to do more than my 'norm' of twelve hours a week. There were only four members of the department living in Pristina; Milovan, Suleiman, Ilija and a Bosnian I almost never saw. None of them wanted extra classes. Milovan was deep in postgraduate work and so were Suleiman and Ilija, or were supposed to be. There was not much else to do in Pristina and the students were the best company anyway, so I said yes and got to tackle Essays as well as Oral Exercises, something that could be just as daft but after a slow start produced some enchanting results.

Most of the students didn't seem to know what an essay really was let alone had ever written one but Essays were on the Belgrade syllabus and we followed Belgrade. Up on the board went the old formula, the classic command:

"Choose ONE of the following:"

The students would study the list of subjects with extreme caution. It was not just a question of the language. They were wary of committing themselves openly and obviously considered their opinions their own affair, that if they should believe that "Travel Broadens the Mind" or "Too Many Cooks Spoil the Broth" they would be most unlikely to blurt it out to the first person who came along. On the other hand they could be completely open and frank, entrusting me with the most intimate facts of their lives:

"My father is bigamist. His first wife was dry so he married my mother and for now we are ten."

"I am betrothed and must to marry. What is the life?"

"My father is drunkard and my mother cry."

Many of the essays lacked grammatical perspective and were as lopsided and vivid as the famous Yugoslav naive peasant paintings, fresh and unspoilt as the students themselves:

"For the Day of Liberation we got into the forest, make fires and dance."

"We were to fetch the bride with horses. We went forty."

"I live in a small house near one great forest. My brother is a bus conductor."

Eleven

Filozofski Fakultet, Room 47

I soon got to know the Faculty of Philosophy very well, from the clang of the cleaners' buckets at six in the morning to the rattle of the chains as the night-watchman checked the doors just before midnight. I was not only working at the *Fil. Fak.* I was living there in a small room ('Room 47') on the ground floor opposite the Physics department. The housing situation in Pristina was just as dire as everywhere else in Yugoslavia. There was at least a two year wait for Faculty flats and Ilija had suggested that if I were there, in Room 47, literally under the nose of the Dean, a constant reproach, foreign and homeless, then something would be done — Right away!

Getting Yugoslavs to reproach themselves about anything I considered a losing battle but I didn't want to move in permanently with a school teacher like Mrs. Petrovic or a respectable widow who would plunge me back into the genteel gloom among the crocheted mats and plastic flowers.

My initial idea had been to find a room down one of Pristina's cobbled side streets where my landlady in cosy Turkish trousers would tend the flowers and chickens in her little courtyard under a spreading vine. I'd seen those places from the balcony of Emina's flat.

"None of those houses have running water," Suleiman said, " Where would you wash?"

I had that problem in the *Fil. Fak.* Behind the door marked Room 47 was a space just big enough for a wash basin and waste paper basket. Two rooms led off from there. The larger one with six beds and chairs was an overnight dormitory for visiting academic staff, the small one was a room with one bed and a chair which until I arrived must have been for the lucky visiting professor who got there first. We took that over one morning, Jovan, the Bosnian caretaker and Ilija's drinking companion, bringing along two student desks, more chairs and an old electric grill from one of the labs. He presented me with a large bottle of home-made Bosnian brandy as a room-warming present and he, Ilija and I sat on the bed and toasted good friends and good times.

Jovan was also living at the Faculty, in a miserable two rooms at the back, with his wife and two young sons. He was waiting for a flat too. With lots of space for my suitcases under the sturdy iron bedstead, its metal top and bottom stenciled with pale blue flowers, the heating due to come on at the end of October and Branka to give me clean sheets when she changed the professors' next door, I thought I was doing quite well. And when I went to Belgrade for the November 29th holiday, I bought a large plastic bowl garlanded in pink roses to use as a bath.

However I put it to Nada and Milena, it was hard to present Room 47 or my bit of it in a way that met with their approval. Milena was even more appalled than Nada.

"They should be down on their KNEES to you!" she'd cried. "You don't understand the mentality of these people! — These 'Siptari.' O.K! — The Serbians down there too — And up here," she added gloomily. "All of us! We are all Balkan. That means first everyone will despise you for living so especially as you are a woman. Your students will be ashamed for you! And this way you won't get not nothing to live not nowhere never!" and Milena reverted to Serbian, in order to gnash her teeth, Serbian style, over a string of negatives all 'n's like ours.

The whole Kosmet escapade had been news to Milena. She was my other Belgrade friend from schoolgirl days. Back then she'd been a fervent Marxist. ("You can't just BE a Communist!" she'd said, quite shocked, "You've got to be good enough!") Milena's opinion carried a lot of weight with me. She was one of the true children of Tito's revolution; idealistic, outspoken and a lot of fun.

But this time Milena was as adamant as Nada. Nada, of course, saw Pristina merely as the first step to a job in Belgrade. But both insisted now I had signed my contract I stayed put in Belgrade until the Faculty provided me — their first foreign lector — with a flat.

"An *English* woman" Milena kept repeating, "willing to *live* and *work* among them!" making me sound more and more like one of those Victorian ladies at large in the Balkans with a string of ponies and a saddlebag of bibles.

Everyone in Belgrade had been toasting me as a "missionary" for having gone down to Kosmet. It's our 'Vild Vest,' they all said. Even though it was a highly competitive market for English Language graduates, no-one was prepared to live in Kosmet.

But to refuse to live in Pristina because conditions were 'primitive' was to behave just as the Dean had said I would. "You'll think it is interesting, *egzotik* for a month," he'd said, "maybe two and then you'll find it too hard and go home telling everyone how *primitiv* it is here. Oh yes! It's happened before. And we don't want that."

The Dean, like everyone else, didn't understand that what was getting me down in Pristina was more the prim than the primitive. Anyway, I told Milena, the Dean had said he knew I would leave and I had promised I wouldn't. That's why I got the job. And anyway, everyone was waiting for a flat. How could I jump ahead of Jovan? He had two young boys and no flat.

Milena had breathed in very, very slowly like a French policeman. She had initially been intrigued by the idea of me in Kosmet, and, unlike almost everyone else in Belgrade, had been very positive about "'Mary's *Siptars*."

"They are a very good people," she'd said, with an air of moral authority and certainty I could never aspire to, "good as the primitive are, very true and honest. Even Serbs will tell you stories of that. If an Albanian gives his word, the *besa*, he will be true to death. But life is so cheap with them because of the blood feud. They will kill for a word and say they must for it is pride and revenge. And they are very private. No-one knows them. But that is Moslem too."

But now Milena, casting a baleful eye on my large plastic bowl, declared:

"Even with a four room flat you should not be there! Not just because you are a woman in a Moslem place but because you have this very English, open character. I blame Nada. She should *never* have suggested it!"

I liked living at the Faculty. Apart from the obvious advantage of being able to leave for classes a minute after they should have started and still be on time, it certainly satisfied my English hunger for privacy. Not only my own room but at the weekends a whole three storey building to myself.

The English department was up on the third floor of the language wing. Below us was the Albanian department and on the ground floor, round the corner from Room 47 was the Russian department. And at the end of the Russian department were the lavatories, Turkish style.

If I left it too late in the morning, there they were: the early risers, the neat and efficient among the students of Russian arriving far too soon for their eight o clock class. A particularly obnoxious lot I soon decided. Boys lounging against the radiators, backs to the windows, girls about as informal as a wedding group. And there I was, sometimes with my nightgown hitched up under my coat, usually barelegged, and the long walk down the corridor. I could never decide which was worse; to hear the question, "Who is *she*?" or even worse, "Here she comes!"

Next door the occasional visiting professors behaved with impeccable formality. If surprised at the communal washbasin in pyjamas, toothbrush in their mouth, they nodded gravely and politely. For Serbs and Macedonians they seemed a remarkably withdrawn and quiet lot though Milena and Nada would no doubt have said they were just stunned. No-one can have complained about the foreign woman living permanently next door, emptying her big plastic bowl with the pink roses down the sink every morning. Perhaps they said to themselves, this is Kosmet, a backward area.

The only time there was a disturbance in Room 47 came one night when the short, round professor from Skopje with the big black moustache snored so loudly that the two other visiting teachers sleeping there pushed their beds out and round to the Physics department at two in the morning. The professor from Skopje snored through it all even though the beds didn't have wheels. The other two never came back. Neither did the beds.

Living in the Faculty was really the right decision after all. It was an oasis. Even though there were no other female assistants or teachers at all. But inside were my students and chemists, historians, Albanologists, *Doonesbury* and *Peanuts* in *The International Herald Tribune* up in the English department, *Paradise Lost* and *Pride and Prejudice*. Inside, there was always a bottle of homemade brandy in a desk drawer round in the Chemistry department or Biology, always time to go down to the buffet for 'elevenses' with Ilija or Jovan the caretaker. Or to make coffee in my room on the electric ring, if the buffet were closed.

Outside was a world of which Suleiman said cuttingly: "Do you know what is said about you, because you smile so much?" Outside, in Pristina, the Albanian historians and linguists so unfailingly courteous and charming in the Faculty corridors as we stood discussing the Treaty of Berlin or Latin roots and Turkish borrowings, looked straight through me in Marshal Tito Street, whether I smiled my bright Home Counties smile or not. Albanian colleagues would ignore me when I was with Ilija too. Ilija found it all very funny.

"You are walking with a *man*. They don't want to make me jealous!"

"But they know it's you!"

"Ah, but I'm a *man*. That's the rule!"

Ilija's favorite story from his days of Oral Exercises over in Law and Economics, arose over the phrase, 'Give my regards to your wife.' All the future Albanian lawyers and economists had warned him as man to man, *never* to say that to an Albanian.

"They told me that any Albanian would demand, 'What's been going on between you and my wife?'"

In the afternoon the Faculty was deserted. Classes began anew at four, the same hour the shops re-opened and at seven the Faculty emptied again, the last students singing as they left, their voices echoing down the stairs and along the corridor past my room. Students from the Russian department sang Serbian songs and gloomy Montenegrin ones. Only one lone Albanian was taking Russian, Ilija said. Albanian and Turkish songs came from the Albanian department and from the English students on the top floor, a real Kosmet mix of Serbian, Turkish, Albanian and Montenegrin would flood down the stairs.

Now, after the Brioni Plenum, Albanians would be able to have their own songs again. "It was twenty years for singing a nationalist song," Suleiman told me. But there was still no open talk of the Plenum or what it had changed. "Albanians have learnt to be very … cautious," he said.

The Montenegrin and Albanian male students, their voices high, hard and sing song, usually burst out into a few lines of traditional epic at night; chants for heroes who'd fought the Turk, celebrations and laments of death and honor. Radio Pristina played half an hour of these mountain epic Albanian songs every day. I listened dutifully because it was the living Homeric tradition but they were dry and stony as the Montenegrin landscape. The haunting, lyrical Albanian songs I loved were not authentic, Suleiman announced disapprovingly. They were just turned out by modern song writers. There was certainly no tradition of romantic love in Albanian society. Sometimes at night one of the very few Albanian girl students at the Faculty would begin to sing, suddenly unconstrained in the darkened corridor. The boys would join in for a moment until they reached the brightly lit entrance, banging out of the main doors, to the student dining hall or over the muddy grass to Marshal Tito Street, the girl's voice dying away.

Every department held a "Comrades' Evening" during the Fall term in their largest classroom, with all the lights on and a record player up near the blackboard. Ilija and I organized ours with beer, lemonade and some of those awful Yugoslav wafer biscuits. The boys all wore dark suits though not many of them had ties. There were only about six girls present, all Serbian. Suleiman opened the proceedings by dancing a quick step with me. He then danced with the two prettiest girls which left five for the remaining forty odd males. Ilija did the Charleston, egged on by rowdier members of the Second year. Milovan left early, so did Suleiman. The Bosnian hadn't come. The girls soon disappeared. Some of the boys started a *kolo*, linking arms and pacing round rather than dancing, a martial Montenegrin one, with an abrupt "Ho!" at the end of each line as though the marching feet had been trodden on. I requested a Serbian *kolo*, then an Albanian one and just as we were getting warmed up a student arrived with an invitation to join the Biology department who were having their "Comrades' Evening" too.

There were no girls left there either. Almost all the lights were off but I could see bottles of slijvovica on the tables. The budding young biologists, Albanian, Serbian and Montenegrin, were singing. Murad, head of the Biology department, and his assistants were in the middle, singing too, and waved Ilija and me to join them. Ilija and I had seen a lot of Murad and the biologists because they were waiting for their new laboratory to be finished and Murad's big fridge to arrive. He needed a very big one, Ilija told me, to freeze his white rats, those standard victims of the enquiring scientific mind.

"It's all to do with astronauts and the Red Army!" Ilija had explained. Ilija was very proud of Murad, everyone was. Son of an Albanian blacksmith, he'd become the youngest Ph.D. in Yugoslavia and, still in his midthirties, had done research in Russia, at the Pavlov Institute. Murad loved Russia, the first Albanian I'd heard say that. Ilija, who would slap the back of his neck like a Russian after each gulp of brandy, loved Russia too. He said, to my amazement, that his Russian was *much* better than his English.

Murad poured me out some brandy. He knew I couldn't stand the Yugoslav vermouth which Albanians thought the only appropriate drink for women.

"So how do you like our Biology department?" he yelled in Serbian through the singing.

Murad was the only person in Pristina who'd said from the start that I would stay and knew the reason why.

"— Because you'll never find such a crazy mix anywhere else!"

Murad said the only other region in the world like Kosmet was the Caucusus.

"I went down to Azerbaijan with colleagues from Leningrad for a *piknik*." It sounded a long way to go for a picnic.

"They said, 'This will be something authentic but very strange for you.' I was the only one to feel at home. They'd taken a Turkish dictionary but I translated. It was just like Kosmet."

One of the biology students stood up, pulling the next student up too and the whole row unwound off their seats and into an Albanian *kolo*, arms round each others' necks, heads low then flung back, frowning a little, concentrating, singing in those hard, high, challenging voices and in the near dark, answering the sound, the Montenegrin and Serbian biology students straightened up, raised their arms to shoulder height, reaching out to make a line. They broke into song and our students stood up and peeled off, Albanians to the Albanian *kolo*, Serbians and Montenegrin to the Serbian. And there was a sudden scuffle, a spat as the Albanian line tangled with the Serbian and the Biology staff stood up, Albanian and Serbian, sorting it all out deftly, arms on shoulders, heads low:

"Comrades! Brothers! Come on! Let's go!"

And everyone started to drift away, knees sagging here and there, past the other caretaker, the Serbian, standing in the doorway. I knew he was Serbian because he always wore the grey army cap, badge of the Serbian peasant. He was jingling the bunch of Faculty keys in his hand, waiting to unlock the main doors and let everyone out except me.

TWELVE

■

Christmas and Ramazan

It began to snow just after the Day of the Republic on November 29th. A week later the peasants began driving sledges, the home-made wooden runners hissing down Marshall Tito Street. All the stray dogs that had been shot at the beginning of the cold and not removed were frozen in the snow where they fell. I could see the leg of the one caught by the boiler room from the window of No 47. Stojan told me to ignore it; it would be there until the spring thaw. So was Pristina's last innocent snow fall which had frozen on every path and pavement into a wicked, dirty, deadly yellow ice. Throughout the town people were creeping, clutching, laughing, falling, breaking legs and doing everything except put down gravel.

The flow of *korzo* was more pronounced than ever as rows of boys and girls slid by arm in arm, as though skating. I was arm in arm too, whenever possible, edging over to people whom I'd completely ignored when it had only been a question of a light ground frost and tucking my arm tightly in theirs. The reason for the small trees along Marshal Tito Street became clear: from December to March they were there to hang on to. Ilija declared he wasn't going out again until it thawed and Suleiman who'd bought a pair of galoshes that turned out to have plastic bottoms, said he fell over so many times just trying to turn round and get back inside, he was seriously thinking of spending the winter break taking the waters at a spa.

All the English department were wearing something on their heads; Ilija a sinister homburg, the Bosnian a fur hat with flaps and buttons while Suleiman and Milovan, the head of the department, jammed berets so far down that their foreheads disappeared entirely, lending credence to the low opinion held of the intellectual capacity of the English department. Most Albanians had dismantled their turbans and tied the scarves over their white caps, knotting them with a flourishing big bow under the chin. Driving by in their sledges, rugs over their knees, they looked like a particularly formidable selection of early suffragettes in motoring headgear. The Albanian women, already covered from head to toe, needed nothing more; they were always muffled up, no skin showing, heads down, as though everlastingly facing an unending bitter wind. I wore a woolly head-scarf, too tied, like the Albanians, firmly under the chin. Branka advised me I was looking like a peasant, and when told our Queen wore one the same way, said firmly then *she* was dressing like a peasant too.

It was Branka who changed the sheets for the visiting staff next door and washed them, hanging them up round the back of the Faculty by Jovan's flat where they were looking very grey now against the snow. She made coffee and lent me the Faculty iron and answered the phone, the only one in the whole Faculty, outside the Dean's office.

Branka, tall and strong, dressed all in black, with an open air face that would have been beautiful if it weren't so worn out, was for me a typical Serbian. She was a 'Kosovo Serbian,' Suleiman said, that is born in Kosmet not a *kolonizer*. Between the wars the Serbian government had settled poor peasants from other parts of Yugoslavia in Kosmet, giving them land, in an attempt to counter the predominance of Albanians. Branka was waiting for a flat too. She had three children Suleiman said and no-one thought much of her husband.

"*Dusa*" she would call softly through my door — *Dusa* meant soul or spirit, "I've got a letter for you. Perhaps it's from your mother."

Christmas cards began to arrive for me. Branka brought them down from the Dean's office. With the cards she gave me instructions on how to get to the Catholic church. And there was a convent too, she said, the sisters came from Croatia and worked in the hospital. Yes, there were Catholics in Kosmet, they were Albanian. As soon as Branka heard that my Christmas was the 25th December she classified me as a Catholic. Orthodox Christmas, celebrated by the Serbians, came in January, on the 8th. It was always the first question of older Yugoslavs, or the second, after "Where is your husband?" "— What is your religion?" And like everyone else in Kosmet, whether Orthodox or Moslem, member of the League of Communists or gypsy shoe-shine man, Branka didn't understand the Church of England and Protestant bit at all. That was brushed on one side and I was asked slowly and clearly,

"But when do you celebrate *Christmas?*"

"But that's the *Catholic* Christmas!" And I was told gently but firmly that I was a Catholic. In fact, I wasn't anything at all, but had been brought up in the standard low key Church of England way which meant I was unnerved to be lumped together with Catholics who took everything so much more seriously. It always seemed important to get this clear so I would launch into the Protestant break away from the Church of Rome in my primitive Serbian and, to judge from the expressions of my listeners, making it sound as though our religious wars like the ones in Yugoslavia were only a generation away.

The only official holiday in Yugoslavia between the Day of the Republic and the First of May was New Year. But in mid-December the balconies of the minarets were suddenly lit up with strings of electric light bulbs. Emina, Suleiman's sister, said they were for Ramazan, giving the signal that the daily fast was over as dusk fell. The Moslem festival "Little Bajram' was going to fall at Christmas this year, Catholic Christmas, she explained.

Emina was quiet and shy with her hair in a stubborn brown bob.

"What a shame Suleiman got all the looks in that family," Mrs. Petrovic had observed.

I knew I'd get on well with Emina even before I met her as soon as Suleiman had said she flatly refused to go to the hairdressers. That made two of us in Pristina, at least.

Emina, unlike Suleiman, was a worrier. "Some of the smaller children in class are so white and tired this Ramazan," she told me anxiously, "and the others laugh. I don't like them to laugh and I don't like for others to fast, especially in the cold. As teachers it is our duty to say them not to fast but I don't like to do *that* either."

None of our Albanian students were looking white and tired.

"They're all good Socialists," Ilija commented dryly. "Fasting is against their principles."

In the staff room on Christmas morning Milovan apologized because he'd forgotten. "Well, I'm not really a Christian anymore," I said. No, said Milovan firmly, it's your holiday and you're far from home. But I'd been looking forward to Oral Exercises on Christmas morning and stayed anyway. Two of the Fourth year Serbian girls gave me cards and Muhammed from

Kacanik made a short speech from his seat by the window on behalf of the First year and Ilija took me off to *Bozur* for "Christmas Dinner."

Every lunch with Ilija was like Christmas dinner and breakfast down in the Faculty buffet was pretty festive too with its inevitable brandies "to keep out the cold." Then there were 'elevenses' as Ilija called them when we slid down the snowy bank to *The Three Hats* opposite where the waitress in a little frilly apron and cap plonked down brandies and Turkish coffees in front of the men in sheepskin coats and astrakhan caps. Outside, the winter coats of the waiting bullocks and ponies showed up in little jagged outlines against the dazzling snow. Even in the sun they had icicles on their muzzles. With the sledges gliding by in the sunshine, the sound of sleigh bells and jingling harness and the sky a brilliant blue over the snowy roofs, Pristina had been a Christmas card all month. In that bright sunlight no-one looked cold anymore, not even the crippled gypsy boy dragging his bad leg to and fro in the snow by the Faculty steps.

"Don't give *him* anything," Ilija said as we sloshed back from *The Three Hats* on Christmas morning, "he'll only spend it on drink."

Ilija went home for New Year just as the greengrocers began to look festive with things we hadn't seen before: bananas, oranges, lemons and dates. Portraits of Lenin and Tito began to appear in shop windows or were moved down to the center front and strips of cotton wool snow were laid along the tops of the frames. And one afternoon, two gypsies walked slowly up and down Marshal Tito Street in a freezing wind, noses running, holding out paper hats.

Pigs and fir trees were being brought home from the market on children's toboggans, the pigs with their trotters tidily together. Small pigs, some pink, some black, were squealing down Marshal Tito Street, twirling slowly above the icy pavement by one leg, first one way, then the other. Anyone carrying a pig you knew was Serbian, or anyway Christian. The raising of pigs had been a Christian tactic of survival under Moslem rule in the Balkans. If a pig were an unclean animal then it wouldn't be stolen.

Mrs. Petrovic had bought half a pig and invited me for New Year but I'd already accepted an invitation from Emina.

"They won't eat pig, you know!" Mrs. Petrovic had warned me in a low voice.

I'd already seen what we were going to have, tied by the leg to the lavatory pedestal, a cockerel.

There were splashes of fresh blood everywhere on the stairs up to the flats and down below women in winter boots and an odd assortment of tea gowns and house coats were squatting in the snow killing hens and cockerels with small kitchen knives.

It was Agim, Emina's husband, who'd killed the cockerel, plucked it and now, on New Year's Eve, was keeping an eye on it in the oven. We were over at Suleiman's flat. They always ate together. "My brother is not married yet," Emina had explained, "so I cook for him because he is my brother."

Agim was fetching up wood and lignite for the stove and found time to start peeling the potatoes. He was dusting off the glasses for the Yugoslav Vermouth and making tea. Yes. Emina said, everyone told her he was the perfect husband — and in Kosmet of all places. Even more incredible he was from a village. Agim was an Albanian Albanian. He'd come over the frontier as a refugee with his parents and brothers when he was a small boy in 1948 like the first Albanian I'd ever met, my waiter in Bozur. That was the year of Tito's break with Stalin, when Albania closed her frontiers. It would have been interesting to have talked to Agim about it but Suleiman always said,

"Why do you have to bring all *that* up?" and Agim usually stayed in the kitchen.

"He is ashamed he doesn't speak English," Emina told me.

Emina taught at the Albanian primary school down by the market and her English was quite good but she was overshadowed, like we all were, by Suleiman and his English.

Suleiman's contribution to the evening was the entertainment. He was playing Turkish music he'd taped in Istanbul that summer. "Listen to the words" he commanded. "With Albanian songs it's the melody, but with Turkish it's the *words*. Now, this is the Istanbul taxi driver with a hangover praising the girls of Istanbul. This one, the girl is dying of T.B. — Listen! You can hear her coughing. It was banned because people were too upset by it."

Suleiman was lying low. If he invited a girl to *Bozur* or anywhere else for New Year's Eve Emina explained then the whole of Pristina would have him engaged by morning. She said he hardly went on *korzo* anymore. When I first arrived he'd escorted me a few times, hearing the increasing number of "Goo deevenings!" I was getting.

"You already know more people here than I do" he'd commented with gloomy relish. It was Suleiman's ambition to get from one end of Pristina to the other without being greeted by anyone.

After dinner Suleiman played old tapes he'd recorded from the BBC Overseas Service. Agim, understandably enough, had fallen into a deep sleep. Like Emina, he was immediately familiar not only because his coloring was a straightforward Church of England low key brown but because his voice was too. Like most people in Belgrade, Mrs. Petrovic, her Serbian family and friends, had dramatic, demanding voices. There could be a fierce, tireless quality to them that in low moments always made me want to plead in the words of the classic cartoon:

"Most men lead lives of quiet desperation — Why can't you?"

With Suleiman, Emina and Agim I felt at home on some deep inarticulate level; not understanding a word when they all spoke Turkish together but basking in the tone, as ignominiously dependent on the pitch of a voice as a dog or a baby. With them, with Nik at Radio Pristina, with the soft spoken Albanian professors in the corridors of the *Fil. Fak.* I didn't feel I was in the Balkans at all.

At half past eleven Suleiman decided we should see the New Year in properly and woke Agim up. He poured out Vermouth for everyone but Agim fell asleep again so he drank his too. Soon after that his face turned red and he showed Emina and me how to do the Hokey Kokey. The Hokey Kokey reminded him of the belly dancers he could just remember in Prizren just before the war. When the Italian soldiers had arrived they wanted to know where the belly dancers were. Suleiman did a little dance to show us what they'd been after and Emina, who'd drunk nothing at all, began the Albanian wedding dance by herself, humming the tune and using Suleiman's tie as a scarf.

Suleiman wanted real Turkish music to usher in a brand New Year but after all the Vermouth he had a job finding the right tape.

"Advanced English Intonation" a voice suddenly announced at one minute to midnight and into the brand new Balkan year through the open windows and over the snow came a bright, familiar, undemanding voice:

"Melanie's had a catastrophe with the meringues!"

1967

THIRTEEN

Sons of the Eagle

The Faculty was deserted. The voices in the corridors had thinned and died away and the heat had too. It was the middle of January, the winter break. Not only was the Faculty of Philosophy stone cold but Pristina routinely suffered power cuts. Most evenings the moonlight shone brightly in the windows reflecting off the snow but when the night sky was cloudy I had to make my way down to the lavatories at the end of the Russian department by the light of a guttering candle. The only sounds were the rattle and creak of the doors straining against the wind, an occasional crash and tinkle of broken glass as one of the double windows broke loose and smashed into its twin and outside the howling and snarling of dogs round the frozen dustbins. Inside I took my candle up to the English department harvesting old copies of *The New York Herald Tribune*, *The Observer* and *The Times Literary Supplement* and with the electric ring glowing faintly towards the high, cold ceiling in Room 47, sank lower and lower under the blankets in my winter coat, fumbling the pages with my gloves on.

Mrs. Petrovic's friend, the Montenegrin headmistress, had invited me to stay with her as long as the cold lasted. Ilija had said I should go home to Vojvodina with him. Emina wouldn't invite me to her parents' house in Prizren because "Turkish houses are so cold in the winter."

We'd stayed there in November when Emina had taken me to a wedding. The three-legged little black barreled stove had glowed almost red hot, spilling out scarlet ash onto its tray. The walls had been so thick, the warm, wooden ceiling so low and Emina had brought the *mangal*, a brazier heaped with hot charcoal, and placed it at my feet like a big glowing chalice apologizing all the while for the uncomfortableness of old Turkish houses.

As the Faculty was closed and Jovan the caretaker gone back to Bosnia for the holiday, I was often locked out and would have to wade through the snow past the leg of the dead dog sticking up and bawl down to the boiler room: "LET ME IN! I LIVE HERE!"

At night I'd become aware of the dogs behind me pacing first one way then the other across the snow, swinging round suddenly with an abrupt lift of the head, as though in cages. The Montenegrin headmistress had told me never to go out at night without stones to throw at them. "These are not your English dogs! These are the wild ones coming in close now because of the cold."

I'd watched them from the Russian department corridor, crouching in a wide circle round the flock of dustbins in the moonlight while the leader leapt on a bin, rocking it till it tipped over and spilled out its frozen rubbish. Agim said most of the strays would be shepherd dogs turned out because they were too old to work.

Killing a sheepdog in the Northern mountains always started a blood feud. There was a whole chapter on dogs in *The Unwritten Law of Albania* which I'd borrowed from the Albanian Institute with the solemn promise I'd have it back right after the winter break. It was a 'must' Suleiman said and very scholarly — published by the Cambridge University Press in 1954. The Law recognized four categories of dogs; chained dogs, that is house dogs, sheep dogs, hunting dogs and pet dogs and there were detailed rules about each one mostly about the penalties for killing them. The *Kanun* of Leke Dukagjini, the fourteenth century Albanian leader who codified "Albanian customary law," was the code of conduct still followed by the northern Albanian tribes. The establishment of the vendetta had been "an instrument of social survival and cohesion" from the period of Icelandic sagas and Homeric epic in a tribal mountain world innocent of police or law courts. "*Siptars* are not scared of the police!" Mrs. Petrovic told me. "If they believe a man has wronged them they just go after him and *kill* him!"

There in the pages of the Cambridge University Press, no less, in 1954 the northern Albanians were compared to native Americans, the Pathans and the head hunters of Borneo and Assam. Not surprisingly politeness and individual dignity were at a very high level among the northern tribes; incivility led to death.

In Albania itself, the Unwritten Law had disappeared but among the mountains in the north and among those tribes "unjustly incorporated into Yugoslavia in 1912 and 1913" said the Introduction, the Law still survived.

The Unwritten Law of Albania was by an Englishwoman who had lived in Albania during the thirties, Margaret Hasluck. There was another English woman, Edith Durham, who had championed Albanians before the First World War. The two had devoted their middle and declining years to Albanians, especially the Albanians of the North. "They loved the more primitive, exotic and backward ones!" Nik had explained, his cosy cockney face beaming with pride. "US!" The Albanians who lived in the Northern Albanian Alps and Kosmet, lands of the blood feud.

Rules differed among the tribes, Margaret Hasluck wrote, but, however poor, a man always owned his land and the rule at tribal councils was democratic: one man from every household. Superstition was rife but no-one feared priests. As they carried no guns they were classed with lunatics, gypsies, women and children but were sometimes allowed to keep the minutes at tribal meetings as they could read and write.

In many ways the tribesmen of Northern Albania sounded just like everyone else. Literacy was considered useful only in so far as it helped in attempts to avoid taxation, a woman 'rarely murdered any other man than her husband' and the Law said only a man who has built a house or married off a daughter can know what trouble is.

Nik was pleased I was finally reading Margaret Hasluck. He had mentioned her as soon as he'd met me at Radio Pristina. I knew there'd always been a great tradition of inquisitive and eccentric Victorian and Edwardian women riding off to the Balkans. Margaret Hasluck was obviously the last of an indomitable and slightly dotty line.

"Until you!" Nik had said with typical Albanian gallantry.

Suleiman had lent me an Albanian English dictionary too. There wasn't one available to buy. Ilija said he could hear similarities between Albanian and Roumanian: both had borrowed from Latin right back at the start during the Roman period. Many words sounded as though the Albanian borrower had been drunk at the time and as *fron* (throne) would suggest and *mik*, (*amicus* — friend), had a strong cockney accent. *Shen* was a saint and *shok*, (*socius*) comrade. Sometimes the borrower sounded not so much drunk as victim of a severe speech impediment: *imperatur* had become *mbret*, *hospitium* (house) had turned into *shtepi* and *fqin*, (neighbour), Albanian colleagues assured me, was straight from *vicinus*.

There was often an expectant pause after I was told the meaning of an Albanian word. The pauses were most polite among the soft spoken and dignified members of the Albanian department, those elder statesmen of Pristina's academic world who never came down to the buffet. After a while I realized, as we stood in the corridor, they were waiting for my keen cry of recognition as I recalled the original Latin. It was a courteous gesture and a civilized pastime but rather a strain. Given a long enough pause and a few hints I could turn something like *qen* (dog), back into *canus* but the fact that when you raised your glass and cried *Gezuar!* you were toasting your colleagues with a *Gaudiamus!* that would have kept us in the Faculty corridors all day.

It was when I'd still been at Mrs. Petrovic's, when I'd first arrived that I'd got fascinated by Albanian, working out where the words came from. "I see you've noticed!" Mrs. Petrovic had commented. "Albanian is so poor. It's just made up of words from other peoples' languages!"

"It sounds like English, then."

"No! No! It's so poor it *steals* words!"

Flutur was of course butterfly and *huti* an owl. *Thumbi* was the thorn and *thimth* the thting. *Shkrumb* meant to be charred and *grope* was a mine while *hurp* (to sip) was exactly how Albanians drank their tea. On the other hand *gurgulim* was uproar, *turbullim* a gathering and *grumbullue* to heap up. There was *shkrupull* as in shkrupullously clean and *shkaterrim* destruction and of course, *zbokth* had to be dandruff.

I wondered where Albanian had stolen *pshtjell* from: "a kind of apron worn behind" and *shkarrezyhet* a word for a horse which was sprawling and then scratching itself against the ground and *sokellij* "I call for dog to pursue wolf" and the verb which meant to stuff pieces of rag into small holes in the wall.

Mrs. Petrovic had insisted that Albanian was not a *language* at all. But in my student days Albanian had been allocated a whole branch of the Indo-European language tree to itself: "Only surviving representative of the Illyrian group."

The professors from the Albanian department had winced at such unguarded labeling from the other side of Europe. In the absence of written records they explained, theories could flourish but Albanian was indeed a paleo-Balkan language. That meant for purposes of practical argument, Mrs. Petrovic didn't have a leg to stand on. Albanian, like Albania itself, was hanging on, a tiny archaic branch, stealing words from here and there perhaps, but unique, irreplaceable, whereas if one really wanted to play the game of one upmanship, it was Serbo-Croat that was merely a sprig, an orthodox twig together with a crop of others on the thick Balto-Slavonic branch.

Nada and Milena had been expecting me for the winter break. I hadn't been to Belgrade since the November 29th 'Day of the Republic' holiday. Walking up from the station I'd heard Albanian as I passed a squad of men hosing down the deserted night-time street. All those sounds so handy for the student of English: "This is er dustbin. That is er hose." The group hanging around at the top of Nada's street with their axes and handcarts weren't from Kosmet. They were from Macedonia. I'd asked them.

"You are meeting the intellectuals," Nada's husband told me. "Here they sleep twelve or fourteen to a room. It's cheaper and warmer that way. They have come to earn enough money to buy a wife."

Milena had a party on the evening of the 29th. I bought a bottle of *Johnnie Walker Red*, to celebrate regular employment in Yugoslavia, no longer a tourist. Only tourists drank plum brandy in Belgrade now. I had my green medical card and my surgery: Health Station Number One.

A lot of Milena's friends I hadn't met before.

"Yaah! Kosmet!" All the girls reacted in the same way, the slap of the open hand to the face, taking two steps back and transferring the hand from the cheek to the top of the head: "Yow, Meri! *Kosmet!*"

One of the girls asked me whether I'd noticed yet how bandy-legged Albanian women were. It came from sitting cross-legged all the time.

But Albanian women never sat cross-legged. It was considered improper. Even young men couldn't sit like that if they were with older men. It would be disrespectful.

"You see," Milena had laughed. "You already know more about your *Siptars* than we do!"

"Well, *Siptars* are our blacks," someone else explained crisply. "When your lavatory needs unblocking you say 'Get a *Siptar!*'"

Kosmet was certainly the poor south.

"They are *all* primitive down there!" one of Milena's friends exploded. "*Siptars* and Serbians! Perhaps the Serbians even more! It was so hard for them all those years and the best have always been killed or left!"

That was under the Turks, till the Balkan Wars. But "the ruthless oppression" between the wars in Kosmet, according to the official government booklet up in the department library, intended to "change the national composition of the area" was "a product of pan-Serb chauvinism." That was when the Serbs had dominated the Kingdom of Yugoslavia.

In the kitchen Milena apologized. "People are upset from the Plenum. All we heard about for so long were bad things from Kosmet. That was because of Rankovic, we know that now. But now we suddenly hear of more terrible things that were going on there."

But it wasn't Albanians who'd been doing the terrible things.

Back with the cashew nuts and the *Johnnie Walker Red* the girl who knew why Albanian women were bandy-legged, was announcing, "Well, I could never, *never* live among such a people after what happened in Kosmet during the war!"

In *that* case, I heard myself replying tartly, she must find it impossible to live *anywhere* in Yugoslavia — after what had happened in the war.

■

FOURTEEN

Visits to the Battlefield

Suddenly there were workmen everywhere, painting, tacking up and tearing down, kneeling along Marshal Tito Street in ones and twos, filling in gaps among the cobbles, all in a bitter March wind. One gang was planting fir trees along the verges, up to our Faculty steps and down again, and another gang was knocking in stakes round each new tree to keep off the goats. A column of men with pickaxes and shovels tramped slowly past the Faculty one morning. Ilija said they were prisoners. Opposite *The Three Hats* the muddy crater in the paving round which we all automatically curved was filled in so quickly that most of us had made several more curves round the spot before we noticed. Going down to the market on Tuesday, I discovered that the annexe to the Tas mosque on Brotherhood and Unity Square had been painted a color my family had always referred to as 'underwear pink.'

Jovan the caretaker was having the time of his life supervising the Faculty work force out at the front, paving the muddy path between the new fir trees and on one epic morning raising three shiny metal flag poles that began straight away rattling in the wind.

By then it was obviously no longer a joke when people said, "Tito must be coming!"

"Yes, Tito *is* coming," Ilija told me finally and I heard it on Radio Pristina that night. Ilija was a member of the League of Communists and had been busy with meetings all the week. I'd heard them all leaving the Faculty council chamber one night, coming down the stairs at eleven, voices low. Agim had been coming home late too. He worked at the League of Communists Headquarters. Agim said that this was a historic moment for Kosmet — and for Tito. Tito had never been to Kosmet. Tito, who so often made tours in the six Republics. It seemed incredible that he'd never been to us, only six hours away, much less on his special 'blue train.'

Down at Radio Pristina the Albanian journalists said Rankovic had been to blame. As head of the security police, the story went, he'd told the President that Kosmet was the one place in the world where he could not guarantee his safety. This, they'd all agreed, had been a great shame most of all for Tito, who'd been denied the best hospitality in Yugoslavia.

Tito was coming on the last Saturday in March, sometime in the afternoon. We were all to assemble as though for classes and each department come down in an orderly fashion, students and staff, over the newly laid paving, to line the road in front of the Faculty. It was the first time I'd seen the whole Faculty together; boys and men in their dark winter coats and grey scarves like a uniform, the girls still in their winter boots and an assortment of tamoshanters and berets all walking four abreast down the Faculty steps. Above us a banner proclaimed in Serbian and Albanian:

"LONG LIVE COMRADE TITO OUR DEAR CONSCIENCE AND LEADER OF THE LEAGUE OF COMMUNISTS!"

A sepia cloth portrait of Tito, as big as a King-size sheet, which had taken Jovan and the others more than an hour to fix up, billowed out over the Dean's window while down below the flag of the Yugoslav Peoples' Republic, the Red flag and the flag of the Republic of Serbia streamed out side by side as the March wind rattled the new shiny poles.

When we reached our space behind the fir trees we all craned our necks down the road though it was much too early. Opposite us were children from the school where Mrs. Petrovic taught. Emina said her school was getting the prime spot outside Hotel *Bozur* where Tito was staying. It was bitterly cold. The police still in long, grey winter coats were pulling their cuffs down with their fingers, and hunching their shoulders as they walked up and down, sometimes tidying us back behind our fir trees, sometimes talking. No, they didn't know when Tito would arrive, either.

Flags were billowing out deep as bed spreads from the windows of the top floor flats. One of Nada's cousins from Slovenia was living there, up on the fifth floor. She had married an Albanian. I asked her afterwards whether they bought their own flags that size and she said no, the caretaker always brought them along when it was a day for hanging out flags.

Just behind where we were standing was a powdery square in the grass that had been a tiny two-windowed house in the corner of the Faculty grounds till that morning when some workmen, not from the Faculty, had knocked it down after breakfast, the plaster walls so soft they'd done it in a few minutes with pick axes. The Serbian family had watched, a woman and three children, beside their belongings on the grass. They'd had a table, a roll of carpet, some pots and bedding dusty from the plaster blowing in the cold wind. I knew they were a Serbian family because they owned a table.

It was about four when, following the police, the black cars finally swept by, Tito and his wife Jovanka looking the other way, of course, at the school children.

The next morning, Sunday, we all re-assembled at the Faculty, the ranks of the English department noticeably thinner, and marched into Pristina under the banners stretching across Marshal Tito Street, in Serbian, Albanian and Turkish; the students singing Partisan songs and chanting "Teee...TO! Teee...TO!" Tito was going to address a big meeting in Brotherhood and Unity Square.

Our student contingents arrived early enough to be near the platform. There was the swathed fez of the Imam, the black beard and black habit of the Orthodox bishop, men in dark suits and several motherly, middle-aged women. They always turned out to have been teenage Partisans, like Milena's first husband, who'd been off in the forests and mountains with Tito and like all the ex-Partisans I'd met, suffered badly from humdrum rheumatism. Behind them all rose the Tas mosque with its underwear-pink new paint, built soon after the Battle of Kosovo and now situated next door to the *self-servis* with the biggest selection of wines and spirits in Pristina.

Brotherhood and Unity Square was almost full, contingents still streaming in. Around the edge were the tiny shops hung with donkeys' harness, eider-downs in pinks and purples, gold and silver wedding sandals and satin slippers with turned up toes, the ice-cream and lemonade sellers and the jewelers. Each had a flag dropping down from the low lintel to the ground. One of the few level surfaces in Pristina, the square was usually deserted, the smooth paving used only by young boys playing marbles with walnuts or some Serbian child wobbling his rare bike round and round.

Soon the harness and slippers disappeared from view and only the tops of the big flags and the tiles of the roofs were visible. The soldiers from their barracks on the Kosovo Polje road had marched up behind the students. Peasants and workers from the surrounding communes were starting to press forward. In the middle of us the three pronged symbol to the people of Kosmet soared above the banners and flags into the cold blue sky. Suleiman said the three represented Serb, Albanian and Turk. Mr. Petrovic had said Serbian, Montenegrin and Albanian, but the word 'Serb' was used for Serbian, Montenegrin and Orthodox Bosnian. Like Albanians Montenegrins still had the blood feud. Miroslav, one of Nada's old friends in Belgrade, a Montenegrin said "of course" he knew which tribe he came from. He'd added, "The blood of Montenegrins and Albanians is very mixed."

You could see it in the faces; those quizzical, down-turned eyebrows, the receding hairline; the craggy, quirky features often common to both Albanian and Montenegrin, nothing broad and Slav. The face of Milovan Djilas, the famous Montenegrin writer and dissident, one of Tito's High Command in the war and after, was a typical Albanian face. "One reason for the mixing was there were always so many fleeing to another place to escape the blood feud" Miroslav said "but of course none of them like to be told that their blood is mixed!" It was Djilas who wrote that not one of his male relatives died peacefully in their beds.

There was a relentless pressure forward. This was going to be the biggest *miting* of Tito's first-ever visit to Kosmet. I was being pushed into a close up thicket of scratchy Albanian costumes, spotless white caps and turbans, watch chains across fronts, eagle eyes forward. I saw Murad over on the left, swaying backwards and forwards in a group of his Biology students, face shining, great lopsided beam because Tito had come.

Murad had said I was like Lenin. Or to be accurate he'd said he himself was a democrat "like Lenin" and then he'd said "and you are a democrat too. People don't understand it here." He was referring to me living in Room 47.

"In Kosmet you must behave as though you are important or be patronized. It's our oriental characteristic. You and I are patronized."

But Murad's students loved him. And my students were saying "Dear teacher, thank you for coming to us" and "Please stay, Comrade teacher, Meri."

Everyone was starting to sway. It was coming in waves through the crowd, like a vast slow breaker. Banners were being dropped and suddenly there were stakes and plywood around our legs. I'd got my forearms pushed against the back of an upright old Albanian in front but I knew with the next wave I was going to go down. Just before it hit three of my students appeared, fighting their way through the swaying backs, three Albanian Second years led by Bashkim, meshing their arms and holding me up like the stakes round the fir trees. We spent the whole of the rest of the *miting* like that, the students less embarrassed by the fact of having to prop me up than the burden of having to comment on it all in English.

Tito's accent was distinctive, a reminder that he was Croat by birth. It was always the Serb-Croat polarity that was referred to first, when the nationality problems of Yugoslavia were discussed. Talking about favorite towns during their Oral Exercises, Albanian students always put Zagreb, the Croatian capital first, then Sarajevo, never Belgrade. The best Albanian students I was told, or the ones with more money, were studying at Zagreb and many of our staff were Zagreb graduates. Several Albanian graduates had Croat wives, met while studying. There were some Hungarian and Slovene wives too, like Nada's cousin but I didn't know of any Serbian-Albanian marriages.

Suleiman said there were quite a few among the older generation. That would have been the young men and women just after the war in the new Socialist Yugoslavia. But 'mixed marriages' Suleiman explained always failed for one simple reason.

"Almost without exception the parents, Serb or Albanian, refuse to have anything more to do with their daughter. Now," he added dryly, " how can any marriage work if the wife can't go home to her mother!"

Tito was recalling the plight of Albanians before the war, barefoot in the old bourgeois kingdom of Serbia and then the war, the War of National Liberation. According to the booklet in the library, the Socialist Autonomous Province of Kosmet had been established "... as the best way of mitigating national antagonisms and eliminating national claims to this region."

Tito spoke of the 'transformation' of Yugoslavia since the Brioni Plenum, still less than a year old. He warned us teachers against chauvinism. A steady murmur of Albanian had begun. The Albanians round me, spruce and dignified even in the crush, didn't seem to be deliberately uncivil. It seemed the Serbian, literally, was going over their heads.

"If you come from a village where there are no Serbians, then you don't speak Serbian," Agim had explained.

I was willing Tito to say something in Albanian, something quite simple, the kind of thing that triggered such beaming goodwill toward me in the shops and Faculty corridors, just "Good morning, Comrades" or "Long live Brotherhood and Unity!"

There would be such a deep roar of approval and welcome. But then it would set a precedent. There were so many mother tongues in Yugoslavia, there was Turkish here, for a start.

"It has been a mistake to speak of 'national minorities,'" Tito was saying, "we in Yugoslavia must give an example...that it is not possible... 'majorities' and 'minorities' but producers, working people, equal citizens of Socialist Yugoslavia."

The Montenegrin headmistress said how charming and natural Jovanka, Tito's wife, was. She'd sat next to her at the dinner in Bozur. No-one was allowed to walk on the side of Marshal Tito Street where the hotel was, while Tito was there. There'd been some surreptitious talk in Oral Exercises with the Second year about the taking into temporary custody of some Albanian school boys along the route of the blue train. But commenting on the security precautions for Tito's visit, one of the journalists at Radio Pristina had said for the first time ever Serbian extremists had been taken into custody.

"What they have to worry about from now on, after Brioni, are the Serbs here — the Serbians and Montenegrins — not the Albanians."

It had been Tito the Croat who had dismissed Rankovic, the Serb, the head of the Secret police and with the Brioni Plenum had ended Serbian supremacy in Kosmet.

On Monday we all had to line up outside the faculty again. Tito was taking the road south, to Metohija. It was at Pec that he would eat with the Albanian tribesmen of Rugovo, sitting cross-legged on a blanket out in the mountain air and be offered "Bread, salt and our hearts," the traditional Balkan welcome. This time as they passed Tito and Jovanka were standing up in the back of an open car, looking our way and waving in the freezing wind, smiling and suntanned.

Ilija had invited me home for the First of May. His parents lived in a small town northeast of Belgrade, near the Roumanian frontier. I was struck by the sight of so many old women out of doors. And so many bicycles. Even old women on bicycles. I'd forgotten how well off the rest of Yugoslavia was compared to Kosmet. People were wearing glasses. Even the gypsies wore glasses. There was the Mother Goose world again of the old rural Austro-Hungarian empire; freshly painted walls in creams and yellows, deep arches and wide, empty streets, broad as football pitches where men cycled slowly past with flowers and vegetables tied on their handlebars, ringing their bells at friends and neighbors and Ilija.

Ilija's mother took me to see all the churches because it was Easter.

"When is your Easter?... *Ach! Ilija! Maria hat die Katölische Östern!*"

The church doors were open wide at night, banks of white flowers at the altars, the candles lit. At the Orthodox church Ilija's mother had a long talk with the priest about someone who was ill. I found her Serbian very easy to follow. That's because she spoke it like I did, Ilija said, with a grand disdain for the intricacies of decent grammar. Like Kosmet, the languages changed so often, sometimes in mid-sentence, that it was hard to remember which language had started; not Serbian, Albanian or Turkish here but Serbian, Roumanian, German and Hungarian.

We went visiting and were visited. We drank and watched television, sang songs round the piano and played cards and one evening a game that took over the whole of the dining room table called KASINO but mostly we ate. That was what people were famous for in Vojvodina, Ilija said. We ate everything except the Moslem speciality of Kosmet, lamb. There was cebabcici and siskebab, roast pork and goulash, fried chicken, wiener-schnitzel, sauerkraut and salami, red cabbage and veal, beans and bacon, potato salad and pumpernickel bread, baklava and torte, apfel-strudel and pretzels, a kind of plum dumpling made with flour and potatoes, pita and pilaf, chicken soup with noodles, herrings in vinegar, pickled paprika and cucumbers, roasted peppers and yoghurt, every kind of cheese, pancakes with honey and walnuts and sour cream with everything.

Hardly able to walk, we puffed up the hill to look at Roumania beyond the vineyards and wobbled off on bikes with no brakes to the river, tributary of the Danube that marked the frontier. Ilija said the frontier was open and when he got his car he was going to make trips over the border. He did, coming back triumphantly to Pristina with Chinese brandy and cigarettes, wooden boxes with the names of Roumanian towns burned into their lids, *Three Men in a Boat* with Roumanian footnotes and a big box of Kellogs Corn Flakes which he swore he bought in Temisvar.

It was during the First of May holiday that Ilija began to buy a car and just before the end of term on 25th May, an uncle of his drove it down from Belgrade. To celebrate and practice driving and show Uncle round, Ilija drove out to the Kosovo battlefield and invited me too.

We took the Belgrade road north, Ilija driving carefully past Obilic, the village outside Pristina dominated by the gleaming pipes and cylinders, cat walks and high smoking stacks of *KOSOVO TERM-ELECTRAN* — Mining, Power and Chemical works, the biggest postwar cluster of technology in Kosmet. So contrary with its sudden blackouts; this morning belching hard-worked smoke into the blue sky. With every power cut came talk of sabotage; with any disaster came talk of sabotage. The cinema called *Youth*, the largest in Pristina, had just burned down but no-one said it was an accident. 'They' had done it. Who 'they' were depended on who you were.

Nada had remarked dryly on my last visit to Belgrade, "It's got even worse trying to follow your use of pronouns. Now I see it was quite a simple thing in previous years to decide when you said 'we' if you meant the 'we' of you and England or the 'we' of you and us and Yugoslavia or Serbia. But now we have this third or fourth 'we' cropping up, which is for you and everyone in Kosmet."

That elusive 'we.'

"Kosmet belongs to the people who live there." That was the policy of the Yugoslav League of Communists, that was us: Serbs, Albanians, Turks, Montenegrins and Others as the census put it. Did anyone in Kosmet say 'we' like that? After nearly nine months there, what about me?

Ilija's new car overtook the carts, leaving behind those frowning, white-capped workers who wanted to cadge a lift home from Obilic. We passed another knot of people scowling by the side of the road, waiting for a bus. The Kosmet scowl was as much a trademark as the white cap.

No-one except a sleek Serbian child or two, wobbling round Brotherhood and Unity Square, rode a bike in Kosmet, and no-one smiled. Very few people wore glasses either. Perhaps that was one reason for the scowls; half the population needed their eyes tested.

Obilic receded behind us like a model on a tray, three diagonal streams of smoke surging up from three chimneys. Obilic, named for Milos Obilic who killed Sultan Murad, the Turkish leader, stabbed him to death in his tent before the battle had even begun. That was why the Serbian king was not taken prisoner. Both leaders, Christian and Moslem, died on the battlefield.

"All those white caps!" commented Uncle cheerily. I wondered what nationality he was. He even gave a wave. It was Milena who said there were no more Yugoslavs in Yugoslavia. Half Serb, half Croat, she'd never called herself anything but Yugoslav.

"But NOW," she'd exploded, "I go for a new passport and put down Nationality — 'Yugoslav' and they send back the form: 'Incorrectly filled in!'"

"I am NOT 'Serbian.' I am NOT 'Croat.' I am typical bloody Yugoslav mix! This is very bad. And very stupid. And very bad message for our people."

The memorial on the battlefield was a short, square tower with slit windows and shrubs and wind bitten iris round the base. On slightly rising ground, it stood dark and solid against the sky. Two curved knives, like scimitars, faced us on the wall over the famous words addressing all who were true Serbs to Remember Kosovo. The very word brought forth a scowl for centuries: the password whispered under the Turks: "Remember Kosovo!"

How Serbian the brooding vitality of Kosmet suddenly felt. Even Uncle shook his head and drew in his breath.

The doors were locked. We walked round the tower, a tower without church or battlements. It was warm near the walls.

"Ah!" exclaimed Ilija, "Here he comes!"

An older man in a long, dark raincoat and white fez was walking towards us unhurriedly.

"He's a Turk," Ilija told Uncle and me. "His family look after the monument and you listen, when he describes the battle he'll say, 'Here were the Serbian armies and here were ours!' — That is the Turks!" and Ilija nearly doubled over laughing.

The custodian picked the key to the tower out of a clump of iris.

"Ah! Now I'll know where it is!" Uncle exclaimed in a loud, jovial way as though the man were deaf.

"It will be in a different place next time." the custodian replied smoothly.

He led us into the dark well of the tower. On every turn of the stair we were confronted with an engraved verse from the epics of Kosovo, the greatest poetic cycle in Balkan literature, that begins "There flies a grey bird, a falcon, From Jerusalem the holy..."

At each bend we all paused behind Ilija while he read the lines in a strong, teacher's voice. At the top the custodian led us out into the strong May breeze and over to the bronze engraving of the battle array that June morning. He pointed to where the Serbian and other Christian forces were. It was all open country still but there was no red yet. We were too early for the poppies. Ilija nudged me, waiting for the moment when the custodian would say, "— and here were ours!" but he didn't. He said " — and here were the Turks," and Ilija was disappointed.

Uncle asked the custodian whether he was a Turk.

"No," he said, leading the way down the stairs again, "I am Siptar."

"Oh, really? Are Siptars and Turks the same?" asked Uncle with polite interest.

I wondered how Uncle could be so ignorant. Did he just think it sounded more North of the Danube and civilized not to know? And why was I so sharp, anyway?

The old man didn't seem to mind. Maybe he'd been chosen for his public relations qualities.

"We have the same religion," he answered mildly. "That is all. We are Moslem too."

In fact, I'd really been like Uncle, always lumping the Muslimani Albanians together with the Turks. Albanians fought with the Serbs and other Balkan contingents at Kosovo. My students had told me that, Serbian students. The Serbian King Tsar Lazar had formed a Balkan coalition to fight the Turks and Albanian Catholics had joined him, an early example of Brotherhood and Unity. How stirring it sounded, Albanian Catholics riding out to Kosovo. Perhaps one of the three knights on the wall of Bozur was Albanian Catholic. And look at Bosnians: how many became Moslem for the same reason as Albanians, for the right to citizenship and the right to bear arms.

"Come on, Mary!" Abdylla at Radio Pristina had said, with a typical sly Albanian grin. "How could we fight the Turks if we didn't have guns?"

"Do you know how many times Albanians rebelled against the Turks?" Suleiman had asked in exasperation once. "The trouble is, you don't know any Albanian history!"

"What is with Serbs?" Bashkim the second year had asked loudly in Oral Exercises one morning. "Serbs talk only Kosovo, Kosovo always! Why? It was DEFEAT! NO Albanian ever talks for defeat!"

Serbs had found it hard to govern Albanians in Kosmet between the wars, like the Turks had before them. It was said they posted the expendable politicians there: people they wanted to get rid of. But the biggest death toll had always been from Albanian killing Albanian.

The gun and the rifle were the weapons of the blood feud. Every week *Rilindja* and often the national press, were reporting blood feud killings.

"There are always deaths on market day," I'd been told.

The worst year of the post-war Rankovic period, every Albanian agreed, was 1956, the year of "collecting of arms." That was the year of the massive exodus of Albanians to Turkey, the year when Suleiman and Emina's elder brother left, the year of the 'worst excesses' by the security forces brought to light after the Plenum. Every Albanian household was estimated to own a gun and from each house the police demanded that a gun be handed in.

Back at the bottom of the tower again, Uncle who must have been reflecting on the answer that Albanians were *Muslimani* too, watched the custodian lock the door and declared brightly,

"...Ah! You don't drink and you don't eat pig!"

"How could we live without *raki?*" exclaimed the Albanian suddenly, in a loud and jovial way too, and Uncle was pleased.

"You see?" he said to me.

I wondered whether the Albanian said that because he knew it would please Uncle. I wondered why I had to be so truculent about everything. I wondered if Ilija was right, and I ought to leave.

This was the end of the academic year. Ilija was saying I wouldn't stay another year and even though he would miss me I *shouldn't*. For once, he was really serious:

"Mary, dear. It's too hard for you here and not just living in that room."

The body of Sultan Murad was back in Turkey but Kosmet had the coffin. The tomb was nearby in a little walled paddock where a gypsy woman was fanning a fire in one corner and another was beating sheepskins against a wall. Rose red tiles and bags of cement were piled up outside the tomb. There were nice china door knobs on the doors and over the coffin a green cloth with gold lettering, Arabic one side, Albanian the other. The hereditary custodian, a rather testy old Turk, told us the cloth was new, "It's come from Belgium."

Belgium?

"Yes," said Ilija. "Albanians in Brussels like ...Croats in Cleveland. Some group lives there and they've donated this."

"*Tamam!*" That's right said the old man in Turkish.

He followed us out into the sun, pausing by the tiles and cement.

Perhaps they'd been donated too.

"Here it all sits!" he told us, "and here it will stay! No-one wants to do any work here! The rain will fall," he intoned, looking up at the beautiful Kosovo May sky, "and the cement will go hard..."

Uncle looked sympathetic. Uncle really was the perfect visitor. The gypsy who'd been beating the sheepskin had sat down on it, legs straight out and wide apart like a child.

"That's Kosmet for you!" the custodian declared, "What's wrong with the people here?"

I wondered if Uncle was going to ask him if he's Albanian, or Turkish or, from the way he was talking, Serbian. Uncle didn't.

Fifteen

■

Kismet or the Special Soap from Bosnia

June was *Qershor* in Albanian, cherry month. We sat up in the library eating cherries as we marked exam papers, the cicadas noisy outside and down below the last spring lambs still plaintively losing their mothers between the boiler room and the Geography department. Ilija was busy reading out gems from the First year: "Comrades! Listen to this one! What's the plural of 'penny'? — 'Penis!'"

We were getting ready for the head of the Belgrade English department who came down at exam time to adjudicate the Finals for the Diploma year. As Nada had hoped, I certainly knew the head of the department very well now. She thought I was invaluable. But, as I explained to Nada and Milena, she thought I was invaluable in Kosmet.

"It's far more important to have our best people here. I wish more would come. Albanians are so quick-witted and have a real talent for languages and they are learning English — learning everything — for the first time. They are *tabulae rasae*, so receptive and open, not like our students in Belgrade."

She was not at all surprised I was going to stay another year. "It is much more rewarding for you here," she said during the June exams. "Everything is at the beginning. You are setting standards for education in Kosovo, nothing less."

After the exams I went to the Adriatic with a big family group from Belgrade; Nada, her husband, parents, Uncles, Aunts and friends. They all found it funny, except Nada, that it was obvious now I was from Kosmet as soon as I opened my mouth. It was not just that I was using Turkish words that were becoming obsolete elsewhere but when I spoke Serbian my voice was going up at the end of sentences. I'd noticed that with Mrs. Petrovic's family when I'd first arrived, they slipped into a strong, rhythmic Serbian when they got excited or angry, the end of each sentence turning up like the tip of a Turkish slipper. Albanian was like that too.

"And you repeat your verbs," Nada observed, "like 'Sit! Sit! or See! See! Eat Eat!"

That was what Turkish speakers did. And that's what I did with my Turkish, too. It certainly helped make my one or two words go further.

Emina's mother would greet me like that: "Meri! Meri! *Dobro! Dobro!*" coming out on to the verandah of the old house in Prizren when she heard the courtyard door open. She'd turn her back to us for a moment as her feet slid out of slippers and searched for the wooden pattens lined up below the step then she'd clack up the courtyard over the cobbles, hands tucked into her sleeves, half swamped by her Turkish trousers and shawl. And as she hugged Emina she'd smile over her shoulder at me: "Ah! Meri! Meri! *Dobro! Dobro!*"

And Agim behind us would give a snort of laughter and she'd flash a bright, impish grin over which she'd immediately clap a delicate hand. I thought it was a reflex of the generation growing up wearing the veil but Emina said it was just because she was ashamed of not speaking Serbian. That was why Agim laughed because *Dobro!* '— Good!' was the only Serbian she knew. That, and *majka* — mother. So Emina's mother taught me my first real Turkish too: "*Bilmem! Bilmem!*" I don't understand. I don't understand.

Serbian itself was full of Turkish: the words for food and utensils in the kitchen, for sheet, slipper, window and attic, bird cage and well and enemy and nightingale, cobblestone and tower.

By Kosmet standards Emina's mother was an educated woman. She could read and write, something many men, even much younger than she, still couldn't do. Her parents had sent her to a religious school in Thessalonika when she was a child and Thessalonika still part of the Ottoman Empire. She had learned Arabic and to read and write in Turkish but in the old Arabic script so she couldn't write to her son in Istanbul or read his letters. She would shake her head slowly over her eldest child exiled in Istanbul, over Suleimen not being married, over Emina, childless still and go slowly up the steps inside to read the Koran.

Suleiman and Emina's father was a very quiet, calm man with an excellent sense of humor, not to say an uncanny one, always laughing in the right places even when we were talking English. I'd met him first in Pristina at Suleiman's when he'd been on his way home after visiting his son in Istanbul. We'd talked for a long time in Serbian, smoking his Turkish cigarettes till it was time for him to pray. He was the first older Albanian man I'd met who didn't give me the feeling I was being sized up and, inevitably, found wanting. He'd given me a pair of scarlet and gold slippers from Istanbul for Christmas.

"Yes, he likes you very much." Suleiman told me, mystified. "I don't know why."

I had been invited to stay in Prizren whenever I wished. Emina had protested that I shouldn't be their guest till they'd had a bathroom put in, and bought some tables and chairs.

"I thought this way I might make my father make changes, but he said, 'Is Mary to be shown a tap and a table? That's to show our peasants. Why do you think she came to Kosmet? Our house is very old and she will like it, *a la turka*."

Prizren was famous for its old Turkish houses, hidden behind high, courtyard doors with ornamental knockers. Suleiman and Emina's house looked like one of the oldest to me, oriental in the Chinese not Turkish way. The set of the roof over the one-storey house was like a pagoda. Emina said it was indeed very old and very awkward. The first thing she did on getting home was to put on her roomy Turkish trousers because all her work would be done squatting on the floor or in the yard by the tap. There was no bathroom and no kitchen in the house in Prizren, just one tap with cold water, exactly like my household arrangements in Room 47.

"The women are very lucky now," Suleiman observed, "and should not complain. Ten years ago they had to fetch all their water from the street fountains."

The sound of mountain water pouring down into water troughs could be heard all over Prizren, day and night, as loud as in the tiny village I'd visited years ago in Bosnia.

Emina always worked very hard in Prizren because her mother did very little. She'd lost all interest in life, in the house and cooking, during the harsh Rankovic years when her eldest son had left for Turkey.

The house consisted of just four rooms, linked by a cool hall with a loft overhead full of corn cobs and cats. The two small rooms at the back lined with shelves were full of drying seeds, metal dishes and old water pots. The two bigger paneled rooms had beautifully carved centers to the ceilings.

One was the best room with the dismal best room smell where Emina would lay out a mattress for me. High up on a narrow shelf all round the walls was a collection of old long handled Turkish coffee pots and little tea pots and porcelain plates and bowls which Emina said her grandfather had brought from Austria. Verses from the Koran hung below, in black, dark green and gold and in one corner was a gilt mirror that needed re-silvering, draped with a runner of white lace and gold strands of tinsel which were worn by brides at weddings. Stuck in the frame were curling photos of the eldest brother, dark and handsome, and his family in Istanbul.

Emina had been worried about me sleeping on the floor. So was I when I saw her plumping up four inches of lumpy mattress with a mound at one end that looked more like a doorstop than a pillow, even harder than the polythene-covered embroidered cushions on the window seats. But I slept better there than anywhere else. Not so much because of the serene lack of furniture but the very fact of being on the floor. There was no further to go. It was as though all my life I must have been lying down at night with a vague feeling at the back of my mind that perhaps this time I'd fall out of my bed, stuck up on its legs, or, somehow, fall through.

Strangely enough it was in Prizren staying with Emina and Suleiman's parents that I got to enjoy that most un-Yugoslav of pleasures, my own separate room. Across the courtyard by the covered passageway leading to the street door was a small whitewashed room over the old kitchen, up a rickety flight of stairs. Though nearer the busy street the only sound to be heard was the call of the *muezzin*. It would float down over the poplars and the jackdaws on the roof, from the minaret just across the road, rising and falling as though battling a strong wind.

The room had been Suleiman's and before that, the eldest son's. There was a kitchen table by the window, covered in oilcloth and one wobbly chair. The bed was western, high off the floor on metal legs and with springs that sagged just the right amount. There was still a pile of old *Life* magazines dating from the late forties under the bed and a 1955 calendar on the wall from Istanbul, torn off at the month of *Kasim*, November. Behind a square of gingham on the wall was a small niche, like an empty shrine, a little Turkish cupboard. And on the floor in the corner a large radio that didn't work anymore, perhaps the one that Suleiman had started to learn English on, listening to *The Voice of America*.

Before the exams began in September I went back to Prizren for a few days but found someone was in my room. It was a Moslem priest, a *hoxha* from Bosnia.

I took an instant dislike to the *hoxha* not only because he had my room with the pile of *Life* magazines under the bed but because of the way he sat on the verandha in his new, long raincoat, one hand on his knee, one arm on the table and the way he asked Emina's father questions, nodding his swathed fez solemnly at each answer.

Emina's father was a very devout man. He prayed five times a day, washing his forehead, face, feet and hands at the water tap before crossing the road to our mosque opposite.

I was interested to see *hoxha's* reaction to Kosmet, the most Moslem part of Yugoslavia, of the Balkans, the last stronghold. Emina said the old people still spoke Turkish in Thessalonika and Suleiman had mentioned that his mother used to listen to the programmes in Turkish from Bulgaria, on Radio Sofia, but nowhere else could compete with Kosmet where Albanians and Turks made up almost seventy percent of the population and ninety-five percent of that seventy percent were Moslem, or, at the very least lived *a la turka*. Surely a flock indeed and a flock mostly uncorrupted by the West. In Kosmet most people were still too poor to alter the way they had lived under the Ottomans.

Sarajevo might be the center of the Moslem church in Yugoslavia, the 'City of a Thousand Mosques' in old travellers' tales, but the fact remained that the Austrians had taken over nearly a century ago in Bosnia. After Kosmet, Sarajevo seemed about as oriental as Oxford Street. I'd heard a lot of Albanian, though, in the bazaar area round the great mosque.

The *hoxha's* white fez was nodding graciously at each answer Emina's father gave. How many *hoxhas* were there in Prizren? Mmmmm. And did they have a *medrese?* — a religious school. And how much were their *hoxhas* paid? And did they have any supplementary income? And was there a mosque nearby?

The mosque was so close you could see the muezzin above the poplars, cupping his hands as he called the faithful to prayer. Emina's father politely reminded *hoxha* of the mosque they'd passed as they came in. I went off to sit with Emina and her mother, who never came out when there were visitors. Emina agreed with me, *hoxha* was being rather grand.

While the *hoxha* was staying with us in Prizren an invitation arrived for the ladies of the house to take tea with an old acquaintance. Emina's mother never went out so Emina asked me to come instead. We had tea in an idyllic *cardak*, a Turkish verandha up on the first floor of one of the old Prizren houses, surrounded by the leafy branches of the courtyard trees.

When I commented on how delicious the pastries were the mother of the house, a widow, sighed deeply. Her daughter had made them herself. She had brought us tea. She had embroidered the scratchy gilt cushions I was leaning against. Her daughter, she said, could do anything. She had a well paid job, too, in an office in Prizren. She was still pretty her mother said mournfully. She was, with a mass of energetic black hair. But we could all see the problem. She was at least forty and not married. That was why, the mother told us when her daughter went downstairs for more tea, they needed the help of our visiting *hoxha*. She wouldn't ask a local one; there'd be too much talk.

Of course, the mother told me, they wouldn't have needed *hoxha's* help at all if the neighbors hadn't been so jealous of such a daughter, and over the years turned away prospective suitors with lies and worst of all, told spells. But then she checked herself, lifting her hand palm outward like one of the women about to dance, turned the hand in towards her forehead and drew a finger across it with a graceful gesture of resignation:

"Kismet! If it has been written here that my daughter will never marry then so it shall be!"

Even so, she added as she dropped her hand, please persuade *hoxha* to pay them a visit.

Emina reported later what happened. *Hoxha* had indeed taken tea with the widow and daughter. He'd asked some shrewd questions and apparently told them a few home truths. In fact, Emina said, he'd made them cry. But he'd promised to send the daughter some special soap from Bosnia which she must wash in, and he would write something down for her.

"You mean a spell?" I asked.

"Oh dear," Emina looked embarrassed. "I suppose."

And she must stop worrying, *hoxha* said, and everything would be alright.

And the funny thing was, it worked. A few months later the forty-year old woman married a handsome young man who was nice, no mean feat anywhere, let alone Prizren. Then a few months later we heard she was pregnant. From then on of course we exhausted even Agim's patience with our everlasting jokes about sending for the special soap from Bosnia.

I had wondered about *hoxha*; the way he'd looked me up and down, the way he'd asked me, lingering on the word,

"So, you're not married...You're still a...maiden?"

And then, "Do you sleep on a bed or a couch...? Mmmm. A bed is much softer don't you think?" and he'd squeezed my upper arm.

"If he hadn't been a *hoxha*," I'd commented to Suleiman later, "I'd have said he was a dirty old man."

Suleiman had laughed. "Ha! You don't know them! He was no doubt a *hoxha* AND a dirty old man!"

■

SIXTEEN

Number Five, North Africa Road

On the first afternoon of the new academic year only two students showed up. The Indian summer sun was shining in along silent corridors. I could hear the larks singing high over the farmland as I came up the stairs. Neither Nezir nor Mehmet, the two Fourth years who'd come, knew the word for lark in Turkish, Serbian or Albanian. But if I *wished* for one bird, Mehmet said, frowning hard to reconstitute his English after the summer, he knew a student who could catch me a singing one.

Our voices were echoing in the empty classroom. I heard myself say we could either cancel the class or talk English just as well out of doors. So we went for a walk up into the farmland above the Faculty, past the newly opened five-storey student hostel.

Flanked by the clattering, withered maize, cicadas leaping out from under our feet, we passed the mad old man with the water buffalo and Nezir described how when they were small in Prizren there used to be a 'cowboy' who collected all the cows in the morning from each house to take into the valley. At night the cows all made their own way home, knocking their horns on the wooden doors to be let in. "And we would ride our own cow back sometimes. The cows did not like it so then it was 'rodeo.'"

We followed the farm tracks until we found ourselves beyond the market, on the long road I was always to think of afterwards as the 'North Africa Road.' It ran high above Pristina and the sun going down had tinged the clouds of dust pink and gold as they rose round the cart wheels and horses' hooves. Two barefoot girls had been swinging along ahead of us, one with a tray of bread on her head, one a water pot, their Turkish trousers lilting along above the white dust round their ankles.

Not Turkish trousers, Nezir and Mehmet said, but *dimi*, Bosnian trousers, the narrower and more practical ones for work, and more graceful; the fullness swirling round the ankles not bunched up on the hips in Elizabethan profusion. *Those* were the Turkish trousers, usually white and gold, worn to weddings with all the gilt and tinsel finery.

"Yous peak Ingerlish?"

Three small schoolboys, exercise books in their hands, trudging up through the dust behind us, their close cropped heads making them look all neck and eyes, those shining Albanian eyes that belied all the ugly Kosmet statistics on disease and infant mortality. They must have been at least seven, the year when Yugoslav children began school, so there were three of the very first generation of Kosmet school children to learn English right from the start — the future hope of our English department.

Mehmet explained who I was: the teacher from England who was teaching them, at the Faculty! Both Nezir and Mehmet were going to be teachers and had already taught in village schools for a year. The boys looked sceptically at my sandals and bare legs. One of them gave an uncertain giggle that was cut short by Mehmet cuffing him round the ear. Both he and Nezir were showing the absolute authority of an Albanian male when faced with a child and also the high seriousness they attached to being a teacher. There had been eighteen doctors in Kosmet in 1945 and six tractors I'd read, but not one Albanian teacher. "We have only a thousand graduates now in 1967," Nezir said. "*That* is the Albanian 'intelligentsia' of Kosmet."

One of the boys asked if we would come home with him and be his guests. Mehmet had to leave. Nezir announced reluctantly, that if, indeed, I wished to see the house of this boy then, of course, he would stay and accompany me.

The boy led us down a dusty lane with high wooden fencing and high wooden gates on either side. He suddenly disappeared through one of the gates, shutting it after him. Two minutes later it opened a crack and I saw a pale, hollow cheeked face, and the standard cotton scarf down over the forehead. Nezir began speaking in Albanian and the gate stayed open just that fraction till he'd finished. Then it swung wide and there was the yard, just hardened dry earth that would be mud when Kosmet's Indian summer came to an end. The woman latched the high gate behind us. She was in *dimi*, the workday Bosnian trousers, made of the same tough tartan cotton as Emina's. An aluminum trough for washing was upended against the fence and there were a few pot plants in oil cans. I couldn't see any water tap. They must have had to go to the tap at the top of the lane where it joined North Africa road.

It was twilight. The boy's mother led the way to a dim doorway and beyond a small, dim room. Halfway across the beaten earth floor our feet came to a shallow wooden border where we left our shoes. Beyond that was a layer of straw covered with old blankets. The light bulb was so feeble that at first I didn't see the old man with his back to the wall, staring ahead, a wrist resting on his drawn up knee, the hand itself hanging free, in the typical Albanian way; drawing attention to the hand as a fine, intricate instrument at rest.

The woman prodded a bundle on the blankets which immediately rose up, clutching an old eiderdown round itself and went and laid down beside another bundle nearer the wall. The old man raised a hand from his knee to point out the space made, with just his finger tips, turning only his eyes to us. The boy who'd brought us was hovering in the doorway, overwhelmed at what he'd done. He knelt on the dried earth floor behind and to one side of his mother who was kneeling too, resting an elbow on a knee as she laid her cheek along her forearm in a weary gesture that tilted her head at a quizzical, enquiring angle as she gazed at us.

The old man threw Nezir and me cigarettes across the blankets and the boy got up to fetch another tin lid ash tray, walking backwards like the girls did when they waited on guests. Near the door was an earthenware water jar, the big round metal dish, the *tepsija*, for eating and halfway up the wall behind our heads a battered transistor radio hanging lopsided and silent on a nail.

The woman was apologizing because she had no tea or coffee and then began the standard set of questions: How old was I? Was I married? How many brothers did I have? Then the old man roused himself to ask the other set of questions, about my religion.

"But when do you celebrate Christmas?" he asked, brushing aside the Church of England like everyone always did. Then came the nod; same day as the Catholics. I found myself once more struggling in Serbian to disentangle myself from the Catholic church. Maybe I'd do better in Albanian; Albanian had the same word, protest, as in Protestant; *me protestue*.

"He won't understand a word like that," Nezir muttered angrily, "that's a word for the Faculty."

When the grown ups had finished their questions the boy went to fetch his English book, laying it in front of us under the miserable light bulb swinging just over our heads. Nezir, cross-legged on one side, read, listened and corrected. I couldn't decipher one word in any language.

"How is his English?" asked his mother in Serbian.

"*Dobro! Dobro!*" I said, sounding like Emina's mother.

"They should eat supper now," Nezir said. "We will say we have eaten but remain because it is not polite to go just before. We should have gone by now."

Supper, as usual in Yugoslav households, seemed to be what was left over from lunch: this time vegetables cooked in a little oil scooped up with chunks of bread. The *tepsija* was placed near the grandfather, the boy bringing in a basin and towel and tipping the water pot for his grandfather to wash his hands before and after the meal, rising each time in one swift movement and slewing around as he did so, facing the doorway when he'd stopped unwinding. The two bundles slept on, the coal mine light a blessing. I thought of Mrs. Petrovic's youngest son every evening tossing and turning on the couch in the brightly-lit kitchen when I was sleeping on his couch.

Nezir had stood up and was saying goodbye. He turned to the old man giving a slight nod and put his right hand to his heart. The mother came with us to the gate still looking uncomprehending not so much about my foreignness I felt, but about my position as Nezir's teacher. That made me the teacher of her son's teachers; more exalted than that, in fact, because they taught in elementary schools and didn't have a degree while someone like Nezir, if he passed next June, would be a graduate and entitled to work in a high school.

The boy shook hands at the top of his lane where the water tap was. The Wednesday evening lights were shining below in Pristina, all that electricity. The drifts of dust were cool over my sandals and between my toes. It was like being on a beach in the dark. The road here was so high we could see the pattern of squares of red roofs and courtyards below and one little mosque of what looked like whitewashed mud, with a stubby little pagan minaret, set down among the one-room houses of baked mud bricks with their mud floors, mud bowls and water pots — earthenware.

"Pristina exports mud!" That had been the first joke I'd heard from the students. Pristina had a special, self-willed mud that could catch you off balance and pull you over. It had sucked shoes off my feet going down to the Faculty and it was like quicksands round the new flats. Well, people used what they had. In Metohija there was stone. Men drove their carts down into the rivers and levered out stones and boulders from the river beds. In Kosovo we had mud.

'Goodbyethankyou!' said the boy suddenly and there was that startlingly clear English accent, an accent that even after all these years Nada would have given her eye teeth for.

As we walked down toward Pristina I remarked to Nezir how lucky Albanians were with that accent. He had it too. What a head start Albanians all had over Serbians for example, when it came to learning English.

Nezir didn't answer for a while. Then he burst out, "Yes, having seen how it is with us Albanians, how we live, you still think to wait for this boy to join us at the Faculty?"

Seventeen

■

Playing the Game

One Wednesday morning in November Ramazan knocked on the door of Room 47 and presented me with a shoe box full of roasted chestnuts.

"We cannot come today," he murmured, the shyest of the Fourth year. "Today is the football."

A combined Kosmet side was home to Yugoslavia, the national team, that very afternoon in Pristina, the winner to go on to meet Albania on Sunday in a friendly match to be held in the Red Army stadium in Belgrade. Ramazan doubted there'd be *anyone* in the Faculty that afternoon.

In that case, I suggested for Oral Exercises: 'The Football Match.' Ramazan and the other five up at the new student hostel called for me after lunch and we took along the chestnuts. There was Nezir from Prizren and Ramazan, Idriz and Ali from Pec, all town Albanians whose mother tongue was Turkish and Fran, Catholic Albanian from a village whose first language was Albanian.

The bare patch in front of the stadium was packed with coaches and cars. I'd never seen so many Kosmet number plates. The upcoming match in Belgrade would be the first with Albania since 1948 and the closing of the border.

Gypsies were selling tickets, each one engulfed in a circle of men and boys waving money. The men from the cinema queues were out in full force; the sunflower and pumpkin seed, peanut and chickpea sellers, gravel-voiced and sunburnt, with their small tin measures and twists of paper, baskets slung demurely over their arms.

The stadium was filling up fast. Everywhere you looked there were able-bodied men sitting about doing nothing, a common enough sight in Pristina during working hours. In Albania the students said they were called "Istanbul loafers." I saw Jovan, the Bosnian caretaker, with a group of assistants from Chemistry and Physics, the Secretary of the Faculty, men from accounts and 'Uncle' from *Administracija*. The workmen and cleaners were there, the people I saw more than anyone, those Albanians who made a point of greeting me in Albanian: "Oh! Meree! Long life to you!"

Two of the cleaners were text book Albanians. Lean and lithe they loped down the corridors with big, beautiful smiles. The other two were short with toothbrush moustaches and timid expressions. One was always telling me he was worried about his wife's back. The Montenegrin dean, no longer dean now, was buying peanuts, *Politika* and *Borba* under his arm. Everyone had bought newspapers to spread out on the cold, concrete ledges: *Borba* and *Politika*, *Rilindja* in Albanian and *Jedinstvo*, 'Unity' the Serbian bi-weekly for Kosmet, and those popular papers and magazines flourishing in Yugoslavia's liberal climate with their familiar headlines: "IS HITLER DEAD?" and "FORTY REASONS FOR FRIGIDITY IN WOMEN." And their strip cartoons: *Donald Duck* and *Dennis the Menace*, *Rip Kerbi*, and *Vajt Erp*.

Whenever Kosmet scored someone in the stadium released pigeons and when Yugoslavia missed an open goal they were sent off too, in ironic thanksgiving, beating up into the chill blue sky and wheeling away over the Moslem cemetery on the slope behind the score board. The final score was three all so it would be a combined side which would meet Albania in the Red Army Stadium in Belgrade.

"The stadium will be full with ...*Albanians!*" Bashkim declared eyes shining. Bashkim, one of the Third year now, had an Albanian name, not a Moslem Arab-Turkish one. 'Bashkim' meant Unity. It was an easy one to remember, because of the phrase Brotherhood and Unity.

There would be all those Albanians pouring north from Kosovo, Macedonia and Montenegro, the students from Zagreb and Sarajevo and Belgrade itself, the aristocracy of the Albanian student world that we never saw in Pristina; those with more money or opportunity and academic drive. Higher education in Kosmet was still considered, and not just by Serbians, to be a joke. On Sunday they'd all be mingling with the Albanians like the ones at the top of Nada's street, "earning enough money to buy a wife," chopping wood, laying bricks, emptying dustbins. But the students were earning their brides as well.

"You need diploma for any job now — even in Kosmet" Nezir had said. "No girl wants to marry you if you haven't finished the Faculty."

Bashkim, on his return from the Red Army Stadium, seemed to have put such frivolities as football behind him.

"Albania," he informed the class in Oral Exercises, "has been far too serious to bother with football."

Albania had been annihilated four: nil.

"They haven't played in Internationals for so long!" the Fourth said.

But when I asked in Oral Exercises, "Who won?" everyone said, "We did!"

My Albanian students, Albanian-Yugoslavs, Yugoslav-Albanians, giving a wry grin as they asked, innocently, "How can *we* lose?"

There were only about a dozen or so regular Fourth year students all well into their twenties, the boys all facing military service before long. Tom, at nearly twenty-six, was right up against the student deadline. Tall and broad-shouldered, with a blond crew cut and piercing blue eyes Tom looked even more like Paul Newman than that type of Albanian usually did. The feeling that he'd wandered into Kosmet from some other world was intensified by his leather brief case, smart chunky sweaters and white trench coat which he wore with the collar up. The others made fun of his finery. He had a brother in Australia who sent him money and another brother running a silver filigree jewelry business in Prizren and on the Adriatic. His English was good too.

"I practice it every summer at the seaside," he told me, with his slow, Paul Newman smile.

Tom always sat next to Duska, one of the three Serbian girls in the Fourth. Duska's husband, on Pristina's football team, was doing his military service somewhere deep in Bosnia. Duska's hair was hennaed in the Serbian fashion, her eyebrows finely plucked. Her legs needed no outside help. The best pair in the Faculty, Ilija confirmed. He swore that one young lecturer in Sociology refused to hold classes if Duska didn't show up. Duska had just returned from England where she'd been an au pair, causing havoc in some Wimbledon household. I could hear her laugh when I was still only half way up the stairs. "And does she swear!" Mehmet confided later.

Albanian students always swore in Serbian or maybe I just recognized those familiar phrases coming out loud and clear in the middle of the Turkish and Albanian. Nezir said they started when they arrived at the Faculty and were ashamed to be out-sworn by the Serbian girls. We had just one Albanian girl in the Fourth, bright but very bashful. The only other Serbian speaker was Nikola, a Montenegrin from Pec. He looked the oldest, dark and already worn out around his eyes, probably the result of heavy drinking, the brandy for breakfast like a cup of tea. In third year Oral Exercises he'd explained why he had five brothers: "So no-one makes quarrel with us! If one dies there are four to revenge" he said with a big grin. "That's Montenegrin way!"

I liked Nikola because when the Serbian girls weren't there he always spoke Albanian with the others.

Fran was the only one of the Albanian Fourth whose mother tongue was Albanian. He was a charming, handsome and shy young man whose university career, like so many others, had obviously been based on sitting next to the right people. Last year, Fran had always managed to sit next to Nezir. "My name is Fran," Nezir would hiss out of the corner of his mouth in Oral Exercises. "I am betrothed to one girl from my village... I come from a

Catholic tribe."

Fran, unlike Tom, was very poor. When I said Fran should move for tests, the other Albanians in the Fourth pleaded with me. "Fran has problems because his Serbian isn't very good" Nezir explained defensively.

All the Albanians in Kosmet historically had Catholic, not Orthodox roots. Another division between them and the Serbs. Nik, who rattled away to Suleiman in Turkish at Radio Pristina, had told me, "Yes, I'm from a Catholic tribe."

"We can all trace our line back to our Catholic roots," one of the Albanologists had said. "Ask any old Moslem round Pec, for example, to recite you his family line and he'll say a string of Moslem names and after four or five generations you'll find he's reciting Catholic ones."

Those short, stubby, one syllables among the Moslem and the Albanian: Mark, Fran, Pal (Paul), Prenk (Peter), Tom, Nik: stubborn saints' names. The women announcers at Radio Pristina must have been Catholic too: Maria, Susannah and my Violeta.

Murad, head of Biology and now the new Dean, had said last Christmas Day when we'd been celebrating "Mary's Christmas" with Ilija that conversion had happened to his family round about the beginning of the nineteenth century, from Catholic to Moslem. He said it as breezily as someone explaining that their family used to live in London till they moved to Leeds.

It was as though suddenly the whole brooding, Balkan epic of martyrdom, of exodus and exile under the Christian banner, could seem a little unnecessary. Here were Albanians skirting the Balkan black hole of the Turkish occupation with brisk pragmatism. Agim had told me that sometimes in an Albanian family, some children would have Christian names, some Moslem. He'd looked surprised that I should find that strange. "Well, they like it that way," he explained.

But the Albanian Fourth were very proud of Fran. Unlike them, it was Albanian that he spoke best. His Serbian was poor, his Turkish nonexistent. He was from the countryside, not the Moslem town.

"Fran is a *real* Albanian!' they declared. "His family never gave in to the Turk!"

I'd pointed out that Fran then was just like a Serb. That was why they were so proud; all those Serbian Frans holding on to their faith for centuries, poor peasants helpless before their Moslem overlords. That was the force of the historic grudge of Balkan Christian people against the Albanians, against any one who 'turned Turk.' And I was favored with a look I was coming to recognize in Kosmet and in Belgrade too:

"Come on now, whose side are you on?"

Eighteen

■

Enver Hoxha and the Thrifty Pig

The collected works of Marx and Lenin were taking over front and center in all the book shop windows. This November would mark the fiftieth anniversary of the 1917 Russian Revolution. Stojan and the workmen were building a plinth and shallow steps in front of the three new flag poles by the *Fil. Fak.* entrance. Ilija said a memorial would be unveiled on the Day of the Republic to those who had died there in the Second World War. The Faculty, just outside the town, had been the site of a German SS concentration camp. The grim one-storey barrack-like student dormitories stretching between the *Fil Fak* and Law and Economics were part of the original camp and the gentle slope in front of our Faculty had been an execution spot for Yugoslavs and Albanians in 1944. According to *Rilindja* Pristina had been one of three internment centers for Communists and political prisoners from Albania: the other two Buchenwald and Mathausen.

When Yugoslavia was occupied in 1941 Italy claimed most of Kosmet. The province, together with Western Macedonia with its large Albanian population, and Albania itself, became "Greater Albania' under Italian protection. Bulgaria got a slice of Kosmet along the eastern border and, until Italy's capitulation in 1943, Germany's zone began just north of Pristina. Germany made sure no-one else got Trepca Mines, Ltd. still the lynch pin of Kosmet's economy. They had inherited the only tennis courts in Kosmet, too. Our students from Trepca told me proudly, "We have tennis courts! The British made them at Trepca and left them behind!"

Well, they'd hardly have taken them away.

Suleiman's father, reflecting on how the Germans had taken Prizren, told me they were very brave. The soldiers had gone through the town by the little connecting gateways used by the women and children which linked one courtyard to another. "They never hesitated!" His neighbor said the Germans were disciplined. People didn't just disappear when the Germans were around.

"AllAH!" they were dirty!" Mehmet said of the Italians. "People could take along any chicken from being ill or just dead out of the road and sell it at the barracks in Prizren. They never ask how it died!"

On the Day of the Republic we had the unveiling ceremony in front of the Faculty. Everyone had grown curious since a swathed object had appeared on the new plinth. Several men in dark suits, bareheaded in the cold, made speeches, veterans of the National War of Liberation. An Albanian actor from the regional theatre declaimed something and then there was the unveiling and laying or rather propping up of large artificial wreaths wrapped in cellophane and crossed with declamatory ribbons. And as they pulled off the wrappings, right in the middle sitting hunched and hollowed out, frail and spidery from suffering was a sculpture of concentration camp man. All the students loathed him instantly.

But by the time the dark green wreaths had faded a little in the winter sun, the figure had become the focus for meetings and end of term photographs; the girls parking their bottoms beside his bony metal buttocks, tossing their hair back and smiling at the camera.

Tom, the Fourth year with the brief case and the chunky sweaters, told me his father had the distinction of being the first man shot in Prizren when the Partisans entered the town.

"He was the richest man in Prizren before the war." Tom shrugged, paused and with perfect timing added "He went on making money during the war."

Under the Italian occupation Suleiman said Catholic Albanians had been welcomed back into civilization — Mussolini's new Roman Empire — as 'Latins' and 'Romans.' Certainly Italian seemed to be the first and favorite foreign language of the older generation of Albanians. There was a Catholic church in the middle of Prizren which had been full the Sunday morning I went and on the outskirts a graveyard laid out like a woodland glade with a gravel path, solid headstones crowned with angels and crosses, little verses in Albanian and photographs and to look after it all, a man with a barrow and rake. On market day among the incredible mix of costumes in Prizren and Pec were the Albanian Catholic women, some in long dresses, some in trousers but many down from the mountains in trim, sensible short skirts, swinging along like Serbians. The famous filigree craftsmen of Prizren had always been Catholic and Suleiman said there were Albanian Catholics all along the Adriatic.

Nik, whose mother tongue was Turkish, was proud to be named after the favorite saint of the Northern Albanians. It was Northern Albania that had been Catholic; the south Orthodox. And then there were all the converted Albanian *Muslimani*, the Northerners like Murad, quite unabashed at their Catholic ancestors 'turning Turk.' It seemed Albania within its tiny territory had suffered all the contradictions and tensions of the old Yugoslavia, split between Catholic, Moslem and Orthodox. That was why unification was so hard for Albania, Suleiman said, and came so late.

One of the Popes was Albanian, Nik had announced. "Of course," he said slyly, like Bashkim, a real son of Albania in the new Third year, "*all the Popes wear our white cap...*"

According to Suleiman there were about a quarter of a million Albanians in Southern Italy, descendants of those who fled to Italy when Albania finally fell to the Turks.

"But long before the Turks came we were fighting the Slavs here, I am afraid," one of the Albanologists had explained. "We were all Catholic then and they Orthodox and so when the Serbs had their powerful kingdom under Dusan, Albanian Catholics were *not given the vote* we can say!"

So the battlefield of Kosovo had seen that older conflict too; not between Moslem and Christian but Christian and Christian.

The Albanian students up at the new Fourth year hostel had invited Ilija and me for Christmas Eve. They wanted to celebrate my festival Ilija reported and also show off the hostel. Though I'd gone walking with Nezir and Mehmet at the start of term and off to the football match none of the Fourth had ever once behaved in class as though any of that had ever happened; pretty miraculous anywhere let alone Kosovo where the ability to make *veze* (connections) was considered far more vital to survival and success than good looks or brains.

Making connections with me however, was not going to do anyone any good any more. This Christmas Eve would be my farewell. This was my second Christmas in Room 47 and I had had enough. Murad was the new Dean so I had delivered my ultimatum to him. No more Room 47. No more of those awful early morning walks down the Russian department corridor to the lavatories, the Turkish lavatories. Branka had brought us coffee and brandy across the carpet of the Dean's office, giving me a wink and listening hard.

Murad still hedged. Maybe it was more difficult for him because everyone in the Faculty knew we were friends. Maybe people really believed the joke going around: "Mary, to live like this with us — You must be a spy!" Maybe I was totally naive as Nada and Milena said adrift in a strange Balkan sub-culture. Maybe I should take more seriously the fact that I was, as many people reminded me back in England 'Living In A........ COMMUNIST Country!' But that was something many Yugoslavs didn't seem to take very seriously either.

"It's just we are Balkan people," Murad had said with an infuriating grin. "Until you throw us in the water we won't swim." Well, I threw Murad in the water, alright. I cried. I cried about having nowhere to live and no-one to listen. I cried in the Dean's office over my brandy and coffee and I cried in the Biology department where I cornered Murad with his rats. I knew Branka was waiting for a flat too. But I didn't care anymore. I didn't care if every widowed Albanian mother of six and crippled Serbian veteran was waiting. I didn't care anymore if they were all standing outside in the snow. I was going home to England for the winter break. And if there was nothing more for me in the New Year than the old Balkan shrug and Room 47 then I would never return. Though I would have to, if only to clear all my stuff out from under the bed.

What had been the final straw was to find out that after all this time, I was not even *on* the list for flats at all. I never had been. Suleiman had just discovered it. Apparently because everyone had been waiting for me to go home "any minute" my application had never been taken seriously. That was why every time I'd come back from Belgrade, or Skopje or that time to Sofia, Branka had been so surprised. She'd heard the radio through the wall again while she was ironing, or met me at the sink, emptying my big plastic bowl, and she'd always exclaimed, "Oh! I thought you'd gone home!"

After all this time it was as though I'd only just arrived. Even Suleiman seemed nonplussed. The former Dean, he reported, was shocked to discover I had not had a bath for a year. Far from being a constant reproach and reminder down on the ground floor as Ilija had promised, no-one official had apparently registered I was there at all. 'Uncle' in *Administracija* it seems had never even known I was in Room 47 until this December. "She can't do that!" he'd yelled, "She's breaking the law!"

Nada and Milena had been right. I was behaving in a bizarre, crazy way and living in a bizarre and crazy world.

It was Ilija's comment that was the last straw. It was Ilija of all people, Ilija who offered me hot meals and baths — and now I saw why — It was Ilija who was saying I should never have stayed in Room 47 in the first place.

"I would never have stayed there and I am a *man!*"

"*But you suggested it!*"

"*Yes, but I didn't think you'd do it!*"

Ilija called for me on Christmas Eve, stamping off the snow in the corridor outside Room 47. For once we really needed a brandy before leaving. Ilija suggested another one too, "Just in case." We weren't expecting any alcohol not because most of the Fourth had a Moslem background but because our English students, unlike budding young engineers and scientists, got no scholarships, only *kredit* of about six pounds a month.

Outside the wind hit us with such force as though it had swept in from Bulgaria over our low eastern horizon with nothing to stop it till it smacked up against the wall of the hostel and us. Students were trudging back up the hill from the dining hall, heads down, slipping in the deep, icy cart ruts. But inside the heating was so powerful that many of them were wandering about in pajamas.

The Fourth did have alcohol; a bottle of Skenderbeu Albanian cognjac, named after Albania's national hero. "Even the Serbs say it's good!"

There were quite a few things being imported now from Albania; the cognjac, mastika, bottled paprika and gherkins, tobacco, even pickled onions. And Ilija pleased everyone by announcing that his father judged the tobacco as good as prewar and *that* was known as the best in the Balkans.

Idriz, Ramazan and Ali were there from Pec, we were in their room, and Nezir and Mehmet and Fran, the shy Catholic student. Ali unwrapped processed cheese triangles for us and put on *Three Coins In A Fountain*. It was Ali who sat us up under the hard light of the reading lamp to eat our wafer biscuits. Ali was the one Fourth year I could have done without. Then Ilija got things going doing tricks with a pack of cards and a piece of string mystifying no-one but Fran and me. And Nezir put on the records that we could buy from Tirana, now, Albanian songs. There were the lyric love songs: *When I held the flower in my hand...* and *The violet in the flower pot*, the shepherd's song and the chilling legend of the fortress of Scutari and the high reedy girl's voice on *Our Brigade* singing "With joy I go to work!"

Gradually the room filled with other students who sat cross-legged on the three beds and began to sing. Nezir translated. Most of the songs from Albania were serious, he said. One about the graduation of the first woman in agriculture, one about the girl killed helping to build Albania's railway. "When something happens, they write a song."

A young Albanologist had told me about the Albanian peasant, the old man who'd come up to the hostel to find a student to write down his song. How wonderful, I'd said — the oral tradition. No, the young academic had said gently, the *end* of the oral tradition.

Nezir was starting the classic which the students always sang with a grin: "Who gave bread and salt to the Albanian people? The Albanian Workers Party!" and then the singing got louder.

"This was one song banned before Brioni. You can't imagine what it was like to hear our songs freely for the first time in twenty years!"

Nezir said he'd been in Hotel Theranda in Prizren the night the group from Djakovica, the most Albanian town in Kosmet, had played their first concert since the Plenum.

"We broke half a million dinars worth of glasses that night! The manager could do nothing! When I *die* I shall remember that night!"

The same group had performed in Pristina, in the spring, wearing the black and red colors of Albania, banned under Rankovic. Long before the concert started the theatre was wild with cheering and stamping. There were no glasses to break but men had thrown their coats in the air, cigarettes on to the stage and burned handkerchiefs, whirling them round their heads as they blazed. One man set fire to his newspaper.

Ali, who had given up trying to get his Frank Sinatra records played, was talking seriously to Ilija in the corner with Idriz. Idriz was like Emina and Agim; grey eyed, low key, brown hair. I could never see him as foreign at all. It sounded like Ilija was quoting dirty bits out of *The Canterbury Tales*.

One of the students unraveled himself from a cross-legged position, opened the window and snow drifted on to the windowsill. Ramazan was telling a new arrival it was almost *Krishtlindje*, Christ's birth; Christmas Day. The student laughed and said something in Albanian.

"He is reminding us that Albania is the first atheistic state in the world — for one month now!"

The November Decree; all churches and mosques in Albania could legally be closed. Nezir raised his glass. "No more bloody *hoxhas*! You don't understand the power of these people in the villages! *Look* at Kosmet! So backward — *Look* at the women! Look at us bloody students so poor in English!"

It seemed *hoxhas* had a lot to answer for, I remarked. "You see how she jokes!" Nezir pointed out.

The newly arrived student began to address me sternly in Albanian.

"Speak Serbian!" Nezir cried.

"This is Kosmet! She should speak Albanian!"

"She speaks more Albanian than anyone else in the department!"

"In Albania" the student began reluctantly in Serbian, "power is gone from *hoxhas* and priests. Women are free; they are in factories and offices. The Albanian Workers Party has electrified the villages. No, there are no cars but *Enver Hoxha* does not have a car! *That* is real Communism! And there is a doctor in every village!"

How did he know?

There are books, the radio. "It is known," he said stubbornly. And Enver Hoxha had ended the blood feud.

"Even though our people are so stubborn and refuse to change!" Nezir declared.

And yet apparently in Albania, even the stubborn, independent northern Albanian had just handed in his gun and the Moslems had begun to eat pork.

Albanian *agronoms* and economists had recommended the introduction of the thrifty pig to Albania I had read, an animal which needed no grazing and had few food fads. Enver Hoxha had ordered pigs in large numbers.

But could our students start eating pig? Nezir had been telling us a Mehmet story from the summer. At the seaside his group of students had bought a melon to go with their loaf of bread and a small tin of meat *konzerv* for lunch. They'd put the melon at the water's edge to cool and while they'd been playing football on the sand it had rolled out to sea. Just as they sat down with the loaf and *konzerv*, Mehmet had idly read out the ingredients on the side of the tin: "including pig fat."

"And though we were SO hungry," Nezir said, "no-one could eat. The throat closes." So one of the students had thrown the tin out to sea after the melon. And then they all went after Mehmet.

So what would happen to all the pigs?

Nezir paused and said something in Albanian. "I am telling him you are *always* sarcastic and ironical. Albanians hate that! You know if any other teacher spoke to us as you do, then we would never again come to the class! But we know you wish to make us learn and so we put up with it!"

To put up with — Very good, very idiomatic. But they wouldn't have to put up with me much longer.

Idriz wanted to know what Murad had said about a flat. It had been a bad time to try and get his attention. He'd been so full of the historic trip he and other Faculty members had just made to Albania, to Tirana University.

"So many books! So much scholarship! We were like children! Peasants! They are doing so much work!"

When they came back he said, they all piled into the first car and just filled the second up with books.

A protocol had been signed in Tirana and there would be more visits and exchange of books and scientific material. "It will be a historic year!" Murad declared. "There are so many important Albanian anniversaries in 1968 and for the first time in a generation we will be celebrating them together!"

Most important was the five hundredth anniversary of the death of Skenderbeg, Albania's national hero. A delegation would be going to Tirana for an international symposium and scholars from Tirana would be coming to the symposium to be held in Pristina, in May.

"It's all just beginning for us in Kosmet! To co-operate, to make links

— And *we* are the ones to do it! The Faculty people!"

Well, there were those importers of brandy and pickled onions but obviously the Faculty, our '*Fil Fak*' was at the center. I'd arrived at the beginning of a new era after the Brioni Plenum and it looked like I'd be leaving just as it all gathered momentum.

"It will take a year at least to see how real the changes are," Suleiman had commented when I'd first arrived. The changes were obviously very real. The *Siptars*, the lavatory cleaners and laborers of Yugoslavia, were on the move. Mrs. Petrovic and her friends could only shake their heads and stand back. The Albanians of Kosmet were enjoying their Second Liberation.

1968

NINETEEN

■

Rilindja — Renaissance

Faruk, actor, film-star, grandson of an Albanian Beg, swept across Marshal Tito Street, arms wide. "Mary! Where have you *been?*"

He was the actor who had reaffirmed our revolutionary values at the unveiling of concentration camp man. Faruk lived in the same block of flats as Ilija. They exchanged recipes, two gourmet bachelors. I'd brought him back some English mustard. He strolled round me and my new winter coat. "Mmmm! *Elegant-na!*"

Faruk congratulated me on getting a flat. It was Faruk who'd been intrigued by the way I cooked cabbage on my electric grill in Room 47. Yes, I put it in water and then? Then I boiled it. And then? — Then I ate it.

"Ugh!"

"Thank goodness you're getting a flat!" he boomed. "Every time I pass the Faculty I smell cabbage!"

Faruk took me along to a dress rehearsal for *Othello*, a brand new production in Albanian. He was playing Iago and said the whole thing was a disaster. The producer, an Albanian actor in his own right, was sunk in gloom in the darkened stalls. Above us Othello clumped backwards and forwards swinging his arms, not knowing, apparently, how to express jealousy. Strange for an Albanian. No-one seemed physically at home. They should all have been dressed as Pashas, Turkish generals, Albanian tribesmen. Othello the proud Albanian lord hired by the Venetians to fight the Turk, Desdemona in the gauze and brocade of the harem; then every gesture would have been instinctively right like the finesse of the local Balkan shrug.

In two recent Albanian student productions I'd seen gestures and movements that would have required English actors, even Royal Shakespearean ones, to retire for special training. Learning how to rush in with a message and touch their foreheads to the floor in one fluid movement without braining themselves; how to hold a scimitar and shift their weight with a terrible impassiveness. Hardest of all would have been the heroic style that still came so naturally to most Albanians whether on stage or off. They could all declaim without a hint of self parody, like the lithe, soft-footed tribesman in white and black before the serene cruel fatness of the Pasha:

"There is nothing so sweet in all the world as when an Albanian dies for Albania!"

The grand robes of the Turkish officials, their plump turbans, might be long vanished but the white and black braided costume, the white cap were worn still, the cummerbund like a gun belt. The student actors, friends of Nezir, Idriz and the others, assembled on stage, their gunfighter hands hanging loose over the knee at the cross-legged council of war. They left their weapons at the threshold, hanging their rifles up, tidily in fact, on a row of pegs behind the door. Every movement still there, the hand to the heart, the nod, the lack of fuss.

At the first night of *Othello* even with the elegantly dressed wives of local top Albanians present the atmosphere was like a football match, with the outcome of the action for most of the audience equally uncertain. Everyone was there to cheer on every player; this was in *Albanian*. There was a sharp hiss at the unbelievable villainy of Iago — Faruk having a great time — and a sad yell of protest from the back, a real Albanian "Aaaaooh!" when Ophelia fell victim and no-one could save her. It really *was* the first night of *Othello* in Pristina I remarked to Faruk afterwards, who winced. "Provincial" and "small town" were words he reserved for his enemies.

That very same week came another premier; *Wolf of the Accursed Mountains*, the second ever film to be shot in Kosmet. The Accursed Mountains are the Northern Albanian Alps, home of the Rugovo tribes and 'Wolf' is an Albanian patriarch in the magnificent snow white headdress of the Rugovo tribesmen. He was played by a Serbian but the most respected actor in Yugoslavia so the students didn't mind. Pec, where Idriz and Ramadan came from, was the town at the mouth of the Rugovo gorge, one of the most majestic corners of Yugoslavia. In the film it's a background to the Second World War action sequences; Albanian tribesmen ambushing Italian convoys, picking off occupiers from behind rocks, dwarfed by the towering limestone cascades of the gorge, that cowboy canyon. Strange to see Kosmet up there on the screen under Italian occupation and people I knew but everyone in the *Brotherhood* cinema greeted them too: there's Faruk, the villain as usual; there's the producer of Othello and Desdemona being the leading lady as usual and there is Prizren.

I'd watched them filming *Wolf* in Prizren one evening in the summer, up a steep cobbled alley between overhanging timbered houses where locals leant out shouting ribald comments to other locals being filmed below. Handsome young Albanians and Serbs in the uniforms of Germans, Italians and Partisans grasped rifles and peered round corners. There was the resolute profile, the sudden dash, heels of their boots slipping on the cobbles, the wounded comrade.

In one scene Wolf rides down into Pec from the Rugovo gorge with his armed retinue, all in the muffling white headdress that makes them look like regal desert tribesmen. The film also has an orgy; Italian soldiers gulping grapes and sweating in the Prizren *hamam*, the Turkish bath, with tousled girls, the local bad lots. Very daft and steamy. The Prizren *hamam* was known as the finest piece of oriental architecture in Kosmet, soon to be opened as an art gallery. The whole film was really *The Second World War Meets the Kosmet Tourist Board*.

The most moving moments come at the beginning and end when the old tribal chief, upright and resolute, takes an axe to the young trees he planted on the birth of his sons. As the film opens he is felling one for his older son, killed in the Occupation; at the end for the young son he himself has killed, because in avenging his brother's death the son has transgressed the Unwritten Law.

Radio Pristina was expanding. The old barracky student buildings where the smell of the lavatories dominated until the cold came and the students would be crunching across the snow with buckets of lignite and bits of broken chairs to feed their stoves, those remnants of the concentration camp were finally being demolished. There was going to be a nine-storey radio and television center near the Faculty.

Nik said there would be a whole new English Language series on television in Albanian next year.

"Stay around, Mary," Faruk promised, "and we'll make you a star!"

Having a flat was like being a star. After more than a year in Room 47 I was amazed that so many doors and lights and areas could be considered essential for the well-being of one person. A kitchen with its own walk in larder which had its own light and pretty soon its own mouse from the farmland outside; the large room that made this a bachelor "one room flat" with its own terrace, where I could hang my washing and dry my peppers like everyone else, a bathroom and a hall. It was all brand new: covered in builder's dust with delivery labels on the boilers from Slovenia and brown paper still wrapped round the lavatory pedestal. A Western lavatory. After the Turkish one at the end of the Russian department, it was like an armchair.

For the Lector in English Language the location was perfect: two and a half minutes down hill over the ruts to the backdoor of the Faculty and the language wing. That estimate was for dry weather. When it rained and the paths winding down the hill dissolved into mud, then it could take any length of time depending on whether you lost your footing entirely and had to struggle back up to change out of everything and start again. It was no good looking for a paved path. There wasn't one. My small block of flats faced the other way, to open country where beyond the row of dustbins there was just a farm track and by itself among the maize, the new Fourth year student hostel.

Some of the students were wearing lapel pins commemorating the centenary of Karl Marx's birth in 1868 but most of the Albanian students wore the ones for Skenderbeu, the Albanian commander who died, undefeated by the Turks, in 1468. "One of the greatest tacticians the world has ever known": not something claimed by Albanian students in Oral Exercises but stated by Gibbon in *Decline and Fall of the Roman Empire*.

It was for Skenderbeu that the sleeves of the Albanian jacket were cut short in perpetual mourning. The name was Turkish for Lord Alexander. The Turks had acknowledged their enemy as such a great soldier they called him after the Macedonian Alexander.

According to Bashkim in the Third year Alexander the Great was Albanian too and so was Kemal Ataturk, the founder of modern Turkey, or at least his mother was. Agim said old men in Prizren, veterans of the Turkish army, talked of how they'd heard Kemal Ataturk speak Albanian. Suleiman and Emina's father had pictures of Kemal Ataturk and Skenderbeu in the hall of the house in Prizren, together with the standard black and white one of President Tito as Field Marshall. Skenderbeu was sitting astride a mighty medieval charger, sword raised, like Richard Coeur de Lion outside the Houses of Parliament. He was bearded, his helmet crowned not with an eagle but a long horned wild goat. Beside him was a colored print of Kemal Ataturk riding in triumph through what looked like a crowd of elderly boy scouts who had strewn his path with roses.

As a prelude to the May symposium on Skenderbeu in Pristina, Albania sent over the film *Skenderbeu*, a Russian-Albanian co-production. It began in Constantinople, Russian actors with grand Bolshoi gestures getting the film underway on broad, imperial steps, the young Skenderbeu standing a little apart from things in a Byronic way. Gibbon strongly disapproves of his betrayal of his Turkish overlords. As a brilliant young commander he deserts the battlefield to raise the flag of revolt in Catholic Albania. The film takes flight as he gallops back to Albania, cloak flying. As he reins in his horse, his band of trusted warriors round him and feasts his eyes on his native land, those glorious aloof peaks seen across the valley from Prizren, everyone in the *Youth* cinema feasted their eyes too. Then comes the moment recorded in one of the songs when a young peasant looks up from his plough, in the white cap, the white and black jacket, its sleeves not cut yet, and in that fresh, breeze-blown landscape cries: "Where are you going?"

"To free Albania!"

And he leaves his plough to follow Skenderbeu.

There are battles and sieges and incredible Albanian victories against the invincible military machine of the Turks at the height of their power. The smallest Balkan country impoverished by the annual devastating campaigns of the Imperial Ottoman armies fights on, defender of Christendom, prayed for and blessed by a grateful Pope. Overhead streams Skenderbeu's coat of arms, the double headed eagle, now the flag of Albania, instead of a gold crown now a gold star.

The grainy black and white film with its little cracks and joins give the shots of the flag flying the look of an old newsreel as though we are witnessing the raising of the flag again at the Declaration of Independence in 1912. But the music was not Albanian. The one film that could have surged forward on a wealth of native-born Homeric epic or the current celebrations of Skenderbeu that the students sang in the Faculty corridors or the swelling choruses that broke out spontaneously in the cinemas when there was a power cut. Instead the soundtrack throbs with a thousand Russian violins. And worse, Skenderbeu's young wife, revered as one of those legendary Albanian women who fought beside their husbands, frolics around a blossoming fruit tree with a lot of Swan Lake bending of elbows. Then, adorned with Teutonic earphones of braided blond hair, she smiles coyly at the mighty Skenderbeu. And, even worse, he smiles coyly back. Traditionally an Albanian wife, like a Montenegrin, never even raised her eyes to her husband in public.

By the time we had reached that moment it was clear that most of the audience were considering that this film alone went a good deal of the way in explaining why Albania had switched her allegiance from Russia to China.

Elegant paper backs were starting to pour off the presses from Pristina's printing house *Rilindja*. Many were reprints from Tirana with titles like *History of the Albanian Alphabet* and *Towards a Purification of the Albanian Language* which, in Kosmet, made them instant best sellers.

In April *Rilindja* brought out the classic *Serbia and Albania* by Dimitrije Tucovic, published in 1914. Even Suleiman, who like the other Albanian members of the Faculty, had obviously cultivated an urbane, low-key attitude to controversy and ideas as a survival tactic during the Rankovic years, couldn't hide his excitement. Published in 1914, *Serbia and Albania* condemned Serbia's imperialist policy in newly conquered Kosmet and Northern Albania. Tucovic, one of the great early Serbian Socialists, had tried to make his Serbian readers see Albanians as real people, Suleiman said, and not 'men with tails.' So that was where the expression came from. And if Albanians had, under the Turks, 'usurped' the Serbian lands of Kosmet, Tucovic wrote, then who had the Slav tribes usurped when they first arrived?

Albanians, much to Serbian chagrin, traced themselves back to the Illyrians who were in the Balkans before the Romans. "Lirim" was certainly an Albanian boy's name: it meant Freedom, and Illyria land of the free. One of our new Albanian First years was called Liria, a grey-eyed girl with corn-colored hair. Another first year was named after an Illyrian king: Agron.

It was Bashkim who told me Kosmet was the Illyrian province of Dardania. The Illyrian tribe of the Dardanians had fought the Romans for centuries *here* he announced, tapping his desk while the Serbian girls rolled their eyes. Here was the old Roman-Illyrian capital of Ulpijana. We were on one of the great trade routes; the Via Aegnatia.

Remembering my corridor conversations with the Albanologists I knew it was unscholarly to claim Albanians actually *were* Illyrian, though many writers did. We were dealing with six hundred years BC — back from *Nasa Era* ('Our Era') or *Nova Era* (New Era: A.D.) and battling through waves of invasion and assimilation. But it seemed pretty certain that if anyone had the right to be called an Illyrian it was an Albanian and that Albanians had definitely been in the Balkan peninsula for centuries before Slavs. And that made sense of the argument that Albanians saw themselves as having reclaimed Kosmet under the Turks not stolen it.

That grand perspective from the antique world was summed up neatly by an old Albanian I'd got talking to at Health Station Number One.

"Now," he'd said gently, referring to the Slav invasions of the sixth and seventh century and then, centuries later, the Turkish, "if you found two thieves in your kitchen, would you stop to ask which one came first?"

Suleiman had got his wish; Kosmet had adopted the Albanian of Albania, the Tosk dialect. There was no more excuse for him not to learn Albanian properly. Especially now poor Mrs. Petrovic and all the other Serbian teachers had to struggle not only with their English, but Albanian too. Albanian speakers now had the right to education in their own language so every teacher in Kosmet, of whatever nationality, must now know some Albanian. The only consolation for the Serbians was that it was a problem for most of the current Albanian teachers too, educated as they had been, in Serbian. Like Suleiman, like the Fourth up at the hostel, most of them spoke Turkish and then Serbian; their Albanian came a bad third. I had a similar problem. Students like Bashkim were starting to ask why did I speak Serbian and not Albanian. Well, when I was with my Albanian friends all I heard was Turkish. Bashkim obviously considered I had the wrong friends.

Serbian children in Kosmet were supposed to learn Albanian too. I was buying their text books. Having got somewhere with Serbian, I was rolling back to the bottom with Albanian, back to the world of 'This is a table: That is a book.' Last year the school books said on their cover *"Let's Learn Siptarski!* This year, 1968, it was *"Let's Learn Albanian!"*

Albanians in Yugoslavia were to be called *Albanci*, the word with a fresh, white international ring to it, well away from the local Yugoslav *Siptar*.

But it was hard to break old habits. As most Serbians were saying: "Ha! They'll always be *Siptars* to me!"

April 24 was Students' Day and the group of Fourth year, about to leave, invited me to the concert at the Faculty where students and *Shota*, Kosmet's leading dance company, were performing.

The amphitheater was packed, students sitting on the edge of the balcony, in the aisles. They greeted the Albanian student performers with cheers, the Serbian and Turkish with indifference. Even when *Shota* began the Albanian wedding dance the students seemed to be holding aloof, waiting. It was when the last of the brocaded, slippered girls disappeared behind the curtains and the deep beat of a drum was heard, growing louder, that the audience erupted into cheers and incredibly piercing whistles. We all knew that was how the dance of the Rugovo tribesmen always began; an empty stage and in the distance, the beat of a drum growing louder.

The drummer entered walking backwards luring the dancers out, their arms on each others' shoulders, legs in unison looking oddly like a row of chorus girls, legs stepping high but ominously precise as a stalking cat. Raising the right leg very slowly, pivoting on the left heel, the body made a menacing pounce as the leg came down to the beat of the regimental size drum. Now we could hear the spidery pattering of the small stick on the other side as the foot slithered forward, and then silence and in the stillness the martial throb began again, like a call to arms.

To present the dance as Duel over the Girl was wrong according to one academic in the Faculty. The Rugovo dance he wrote is a tribal preparation for war on the eve of battle. The two young warriors swing out into the center making small jumps, legs wide apart and close to the ground, bottoms out — that's what gives the African and Native American look. Their heads and necks are muffled in white, like Arabs in the desert. Suleiman told me the head-dress is a shroud, like Arabs wear: nine meters long, enough to bury a man. "Because a warrior must at all times be ready to die."

Arms stretched wide above their heads they draw forth their sabers, their feet in moccasins making no sound. The weapons are real. As the duel is fought to the beat of the drum their blades ring and strike sparks. The dance is ended by an elder who comes forward to make peace. Suddenly the two warriors have leapt back into the line which becomes a circle again, arms on shoulders, heads together like a rugger scrum.

By this time the drum had been drowned out in a crescendo of whistling, stamping and clapping. Students were throwing cigarettes on the stage, whirling blazing handkerchiefs around their heads and setting fire to newspapers. Coats were flying: one thrown so high it caught on a beam near the ceiling. The warriors don't come back to take a bow. Nezir and Idriz are apologizing for the noise, bending low and shouting to make themselves heard. The concert is over, stuck high on the climax of the Rugovo warriors' dance, like the coat on the beam.

We were reprimanded in *Riljinda* for the nationalist tone of our manifestations. Students, the intelligentsia of Kosmet, should set an example. But how hard it was to remain unmoved, to fail to respond to the Rugovo drum in that eve of battle ceremony for Albanian mountain warriors before their skirmishes and battles against the Turks, against their hereditary enemy, the Slav.

TWENTY

Summer of '68

"A report from the south!" yelled Milena as I came in the door. "— Our own 'Special Correspondent'! Now, the students sent the telegram to Tito of course, but what's *really* going on at the Pristina Faculties? Where do your Albanians stand?"

In Belgrade students were encamped in front of the University buildings and over the Sava at the big new campus in Novi Beograd.

"It's wonderful!" Milena said. "They are discussing all questions about our society with the people who go by!"

The students had closed down the university. The first open student unrest for ten years had hit Yugoslavia, part of the world wide revolutionary fervor of 1968.

For the first time the head of the Belgrade English department had been free to come down to Pristina when it suited us. The upheaval among the students in Belgrade had ended all thoughts of examinations.

"It's good to see some work still being done somewhere," she observed dryly.

"Has there been *nothing* down in Pristina?" Milena was baffled.

No demonstrations, no philosophical debates, no Trotskyists, no anarchists, no long hair — no jeans. Hard to imagine student upheaval when the girls all went to the hairdressers and the boys wore suits. Our students strolled down from the hostel in the early morning sun for yoghurt, jam and bread. They sunned themselves on the windowsills, joking and haggling with the peasants selling peaches and cherries below. In the afternoon they scuffed around, barefoot, with a football until the ball got lost in the maize. One boy played a violin and the other students would join in, both Serbian and Albanian songs and sometimes people from our block of flats opposite would join in too.

There had been the Student Day concert with its "nationalist manifestations" and, according to the Fourth, a big fight in the student dining hall when all the chairs got broken that arose from the age old philosophical dispute between Montenegrins and Albanians over being Montenegrins and Albanians.

But as Milena said, the questions being raised by the students in Belgrade were of particular importance to Kosmet: the shameful inequalities within a Socialist society. In a sense, the demonstrations were for us, in the deep South. And I was lucky. Milena had to work but I was free to go down to the *Fil. Fak.* on *Studenstki Trg*, Student's Square, our parent faculty, and see it all happening. She thought that was why I had come up.

I wanted to go shopping. I wanted to run amok among the tinned goods, grab anything that wasn't goulash, spam or sardines. Buy *Nescafe* and Worcester sauce and stack up on paper bags. In Kosmet when we bought anything it was shoved into a cone or square of old *Rilindja* or *Politika*. I had to admit, it was less philosophical debate I was missing in Kosmet than paper bags. Most of the students could have done with some big paper bags too. Leaving after Finals, many of the Fourth year ('the future intelligentsia of Kosmet') were making off down the hill towards the bus station with their belongings wrapped in newspaper.

Agim said it was the worst August for years. All over Kosmet the piles of bricks stacked to bake dry melted into each other in the heavy rain and half-completed walls slid back into the mud at their base. The house in Prizren was miserably cold. Agim sat hunched over his transistor radio he'd brought from Pristina, or talked to Emina's father, his Turkish low and urgent. The talk was as much about Bulgaria as Czechoslovakia. While Soviet Russia was increasing pressure on the revolutionaries in Prague, Bulgaria, "Russia's most faithful Balkan ally" as all the papers put it, was increasing tension on the Yugoslav border. There'd been talk of an earlier call up which had rattled the Fourth year and during an exam dictation I'd had to stop for the noise of what sounded like a squadron of planes, flying low, south, towards Macedonia. It was Bulgaria who had occupied Macedonia and a slice of Kosmet in the Second World War and reached Prizren in the First. Flour, sugar and sunflower oil had already become very scarce. Matches and butter had long since disappeared. When I'd 'popped in' as Ilija had taught the students to say, to see Nezir and Mehmet in Prizren, Nezir, son of a blacksmith and shoeing a pony, said his father had already bought in two sacks of flour.
"'Laugh!' he told me, 'Laugh! You younger generation know nothing!'" He said they were eating grass in Prizren in 1915 when the Bulgarians came."
"Heavy industry and armaments are in Bosnia not so much because Bosnia is poor but because Bosnia is the Republic in the middle, farthest from our frontiers" an ex-Partisan had told me years ago. Every one of Yugoslavia's neighbors had laid claim to some part of her territory. And it was Yugoslavia who was continually confronting Soviet Russia by her mere existence outside the Communist bloc. 'Titoism' had been angering the Soviets for years. But one thing was clear, whatever happened in Czechoslovakia it was no longer the Yugoslav Brioni Plenum of 1966 which was setting the pace for the Socialist Democracies but the Prague Spring of 1968.
When the invasion of Czechoslovakia did come troops and tanks were stationed round the windy field that was our airport. President Tito declared that all Czech tourists in Yugoslavia were invited to stay as guests of the Yugoslav people till they could decide what they should do. With liberalization, Czechs had been allowed to travel and had poured into Yugoslavia and down to the Adriatic, the nearest warm sea. Even down in Ulcinj, the southernmost Yugoslav town on the Albanian border, half the cars coming into the camp grounds had Czech number plates and over the fences

were the mild, fair faces, the bright orange tents, collapsible chairs and milk saucepans and the Slav language which sounded to my ears after Serbian, so wan and plaintive.

I hadn't seen one Volkswagen or Citroen with big pink daisies on the side chugging down Marshal Tito Street or land-rovers stenciled with kangaroos disappearing in a cloud of dust towards Macedonia. Bulgaria "redrawing the map again," as *Rilindja* put it, had scared off our Western tourists, even the *hipis* who could be seen on the terrace at Bozur from time to time, on their way to Istanbul, allowing an impoverished student to buy them a coffee and a cognac. In fact, if you were a student in 1968, "The Year of Revolution," it was far more exciting not to think of going anywhere at all, but to stay at home and revolt.

By September Belgrade television was showing the Czechs leaving Yugoslavia; at frontier crossing points in their cars, at railway stations being seen off by Yugoslavs, their arms full of flowers. There were the gladioli, always borne along railway platforms for greetings and farewells. The Yugoslavs and Czechs were crying and hugging each other, the arms and hands parting through the train windows, drawing away as the Czechs were borne back faster and faster away from their Prague Spring and Yugoslav summer.

Albania had denounced the Soviet invasion of Czechoslovakia. Radio Tirana also rapped Bulgaria over the knuckles regarding claims to Macedonia. Floating down into Kosmet over the mountains like the call of the muezzin over the rooftops in Prizren, came the supremely confident invective.

After twenty years Albania and Yugoslavia remained the only two of the Socialist bloc to have defied the Soviet Union and got away with it. The only two to have defeated their occupying forces in the autumn of 1944 with their own National Liberation Armies. Neutral Yugoslavia now had one of the largest individual armed forces in Europe. Even so, President Tito decreed the creation of a new line of defense. Suleiman said the teachers had been summoned back before the start of September exams. Individual cells of local militia were to be created. "We were all given our instructions at the Faculty, and where to go. No! I certainly can't tell you!"

Tito had declared that each organization, each center like a Faculty or a factory, must prepare for its own defense: "Because" said the old guerilla fighter, "in future war will be urban. It will be street to street and house to house."

But like the Albanians and Montenegrins in Ulcinj, the Macedonians on the bus to Skopje and the mix of people from every Republic up in Belgrade Suleiman declared "Ha! The Russians would never try anything with *us!*"

It was good to hear that unequivocal pronoun for once: us, us Yugoslavs.

Twenty-One

The Day of the Flag

November 1968

The student hostel seemed much noisier that September. Martial songs, usually Albanian, started up after dark and then would come the retaliatory Serbian and Montenegrin and about ten a crescendo of thumps and bangs on walls and window sills. That was the warning the warden had started his nightly rounds to check how many students were in each bed. Students were so desperate for accommodation they were sleeping head to toe, two to a bed.

"There isn't the organization or pride of last year." Nezir was already elegiac. "These new students are different."

The pace of change in Kosovo was so fast. The hostel, brand new last September, was battered and scarred. Nezir and Mehmet, both teaching, had dropped in to see me after visiting a student friend.

"It's not good." Nezir said grimly. "There are too many guns there."

Bashkim was Fourth year now, living in the hostel. I would meet him on the dusty farm track leading down to the Faculty. Out in the open, his voice dwindling away over the maize, Bashkim was even more emphatically Albanian than in class.

Kosmet had a new name; Kosovo! This was a great victory because Kosovo or rather Kosova was the Albanian name.

"And it is shorter for when we become... Republic!"

"What about the 'Republic of Bosnia and Hercegovina' then?"

But Bashkim let me get away with that. Wasn't this the beginning of my *third* year in Kosmet — Kosovo — *Kosova* and didn't I live on a local salary like an Albanian and hadn't I got on so well with the Albanian Fourth last year? Bashkim could talk about a Republic in front of me.

Ever since I'd arrived in Kosovo I'd heard the magic number: 70%. Once the population of the province became 70% Albanian, so the Albanian argument went, there would be a democratic obligation to designate

Kosovo a Republic. And with the Albanian birth-rate the highest in Europe that was only a matter of time. "Albanians practice biological warfare!" as the students said. But the whole subject of a Republic of Kosovo was taboo. Kosmet sacred to the Serbs, Kosmet cradle of the Serbian nation, was hardly the candidate for Republican status under Albanians of all people. So when Bashkim told me Kosovo was going to get its own flag, the Albanian flag, the double-headed eagle of Skenderbeu, I dismissed it as Bashkim being Bashkim.

"Why? the Hungarians have theirs in Vojvodina," Suleiman said. "It was Rankovic who made the flag taboo."

But even in America, surely, you only had one flag.

Suleiman was amused. "It seems, after all, you are illiberal and an unprogressive!"

Sometimes I felt I was the only one left in Yugoslavia, especially in the educational system. Sometimes I felt I might as well be somewhere like California. The Faculty had just accepted a student demand for two sets of examinations that autumn like the students in Belgrade. But we'd not had demonstrations last June. In the 1968 Year of Revolution, we'd had exams. Everyone was proud of that. Ilija was saying it could have been worse. Many of the students were demanding the right to take their exams whenever they felt like it, which it often seemed to me, they were doing already.

"No!" he laughed. "Every month!"

Kosmet, Kosovo, *Kosova*, did get the Albanian flag, the red flag with the black, double-headed eagle. All over Kosovo that October it streamed out red and black at the head of wedding processions, fixed to the leading cart or car or rippling over the head of the horsemen as they went to 'fetch the bride.' I saw it from my kitchen window. And throughout Kosovo incidents were reported of the flag being torn down and burned by Serbians.

"It's hard for the peasants to understand," Emina said uncomfortably, "Serbs and Albanians, when they see the same flag as they have in Albania. It's very difficult to explain to the children in school."

The flag had been raised for the first time without fanfare on a Sunday. By chance I'd seen it in the exact historic place in Prizren; on the new flag pole outside the League of Prizren house, cracking in the night wind coming down the gorge of the Bistrica. A group of men and boys were looking up silently as the black eagle, talons spread wide on the plum red ground, stretched and dwindled with the flag against the night sky, like a flame in the wind.

The small lopsided house jutting out its wooden upper storey like the prow of a ship towards the river was one of the most important buildings in the history of Albania. It was where Albanians from all over the Turkish Empire had gathered: Christians, Moslems, Albanians from North and South, Geg and Tosk, tribal chiefs and exiled 'intelligentsia' in 1878. They swore to defend Albanian lands claimed in the north by Slavs and in the south by Greeks. It was the first concerted action by Albanians since Skenderbeu's League of Albanian Princes and is considered the real birth of Albanian nationalism. The building itself had been restored and opened in July as a museum. Inside were the copies of the letters sent to the Great Powers at the Congress of Berlin, to Bismark and the rest; the telegrams and documents, the quill pen and ink stand.

Nezir and Mehmet admitted after the flag raising in Prizren there had been some singing and a bit of a march and some of their pupils had landed up cooling their heels in prison for twenty-four hours. From then on, like other teachers, they were liable for duty, patrolling Prizren, responsible for the behavior of their pupils. Nezir and Mehmet were not only teachers now but members of the League of Communists so they had a double duty to set an example. They'd shown me their Party cards and Nezir had exclaimed triumphantly,

"I knew you'd make a joke about it! I had a bet with Mehmet!"

Poor Mehmet, who'd just lost all his first month's salary playing poker, was losing money right and left.

Albania's Day of the Flag, celebrating the proclamation of Albania's independence in 1912, fell on November 28th, the day before Yugoslavia's Day of the Republic. In 1968 the largest group of foreign journalists ever to assemble in Yugoslavia were gathering in Bosnia with Tito and all the top surviving Partisans to commemorate the first quarter century of the new Socialist Yugoslavia, which was proclaimed on November 29, 1943. It was while they were all assembled there waiting for the celebrations to begin, that our students in Pristina, on November 27th, the day before The Day of the Flag, finally made the headlines in the 1968 Year of Revolution. They gathered in front of the Faculty of Philosophy in a demonstration which turned into what the international press classified as a 'riot' in which ten policemen and several students were badly injured and one boy killed.

I was cutting across the front of the Faculty heading home, having just booked a sleeper on the midnight train to Belgrade. Nada had a baby son, and I was going to see her for the holiday. There was a group at the Faculty steps in the November afternoon gloom. Suddenly I heard shouts and shots as the group started to move, forming a column as it came down towards the road and in a flash there was the red and black of the Albanian flag at the head. As the column swung round, heading for the center of Pristina, boys seemed to spring out of the ground, and so did banners. I saw in Serbian:

"DOWN WITH COLONIALISM IN KOSOVO!' and in Albanian: "DUARM REPUBLIK!" — "We want a Republic!"

They had begun to chant rhythmically: "Du — ARM Re-pu BLIK!"

Suddenly I was the only person in sight along the road watching them go by, standing stock still with a string bag full of shopping and a ticket for Belgrade. As they disappeared into the November grey, there came a rat tat tat like machine gun fire from Mrs Petrovic's block of flats.

Left behind at the bottom of the steps was a group of Faculty members, all except one, Albanian. Suleiman was there and one of my favorite Albanians at the *Fil Fak*, a lecturer from the geography department in big, horn-rim glasses. Fehmi was talking, a sociologist. A fair man, his face was bright red.

"One of them hit me!" he was saying. "My students! When I tried to stop them they said 'If you are not for us you are against us!' and then they hit me and they started marching."

"They had guns," Suleiman told me in English, bemused. "They started firing."

We could still hear the shots, the chanting and ragged singing.

"We were called here to try and stop them," Suleiman said.

Classes were still going on behind us, lights being switched on in the twilight.

"And where were the security organs?" asked someone.

My geographer in his comforting horn-rims was the only one capable of making a joke. "That's Kosovo for you!" he laughed. "The *Voice of America* from Thessalonika forecast this apparently three days ago! It seems our security organs would do better to listen to *The Voice of America!*"

The security organs had started to appear, hurrying down the dusty track beside the Faculty, from our new flats. The first of the police, in their long, grey winter coats, buckling on their gun belts. One of my neighbors was a policeman. He'd just brought me a parcel of British Council text books from the post office.

"Very clever!" the geographer is saying as we watch the police. "The students know they're expecting trouble on the Day of the Flag, especially after the piece in *Zeri i Popullit*, so they do everything a day early!"

Zeri I Popullit was Albania's party newspaper, 'Voice of the People.' It had demanded to know why Kosovo was not a Republic, Suleiman told me, like Macedonia now was. Before the war Macedonia had just been part of 'Southern Serbia' too.

The group finally turned to go inside, pushing through the glass doors at the top of the steps and climbing slowly up the stairs in silence to the council chamber or the Dean's office. But there was no Branka at this time of day to make coffee and bring brandy. Perhaps she was ironing down in Room 47.

"— Where's *Murad?*" everyone suddenly asked. Murad — the Dean now. He was probably up in the biology department, totally oblivious, with his rats.

I was alone in the corridor, not wanting to go home, not knowing what to do except get rid of my string bag. I went up to the top floor, to leave it in the library. The only person up there was Ali, our cleaner. Through the windows along the corridor I could see more police, some half running now down the cart track, fumbling with buckles, belts and guns.

Ali merely grinned, refusing to be drawn. He must have been about twenty-four, perhaps younger, but an old hand, like all the gypsies. I'd thought Ali was Albanian but the Fourth had said, "No! What? Ali? A gypsy of course!"

And I'd been saying "Good morning!" and "How are you?" for a year in Albanian as I came along the corridor, and feeling very graciously democratic while I did it.

"Oh, gypsies use whatever language suits them best," Nezir had said. It was Nezir who'd told me the standard deliberate shocker:

"What is the one good thing Hitler did? — He tried to exterminate all the gypsies!"

Nezir, dark, son of a blacksmith, a traditional gypsy trade, who had been called a gypsy, probably, himself.

I went back to Pristina along the farm-track, then the unpaved road parallel to Marshal Tito Street. By the horse trough was a policeman with a sub machine gun. Then police in twos, even up here, guns at the ready. I turned down the short cobbled street — not cobbles in fact, an American tourist had told me, but granite fishtail blocks — and came out beside the car park at Bozur.

Shouting, chanting and gunfire came from the theatre and beyond, where the government building was, in Brotherhood and Unity Square. Two fire engines were unwinding hoses outside *Texas*. *Milicija* jeeps had arrived, their deep blue lights blinking. All three flags hung over 'Texas': the Yugoslav tricolor, the tricolor of the Serbian republic and the Albanian eagle. Further along was the scarlet of the Red Flag. The Serbians had lost their Royal double headed eagle. The Montenegrins had lost their whole kingdom after the First World War. It was not only Albanians who had been 'pacified.'

Ambulances were starting to drive away towards the hospital. Right in front of me was a man in police uniform with some extras that gradually came into focus; black leather boots, a little black whip or very thin, tapering leather truncheon he was swishing between his hands as he shouted orders over our heads. And he didn't wear standard grey woollen gloves but black leather ones.

There was nothing to do but go back. As I turned I bumped into Fehmi. The Faculty meeting must have ended and Fehmi had been drawn back, like me, to the center because, in fact, he lived the other way. His face was still a fiery red. I found I'd taken hold of his arm tight and was clinging on for dear life though I didn't know him well at all. We pushed our way back through the people piling up against the police barriers, through all the people who didn't know. Fehmi wouldn't have registered it if I'd gone through his pockets.

"These are my students," he was murmuring. "We've been camping together! They wouldn't listen! They said 'If you are not *for* us you are *against* us!' Just like that. And they had guns."

Ambulances and jeeps were still going by in the dusk. "Yes, times *were* difficult," Fehmi was murmuring again. He murmured on ordinary days. When we talked in the corridor while students were passing, I often couldn't hear him at all. Bashful and quiet like most of the Albanian faculty, Fehmi was the antithesis of all the stereotypes of the primitive, wild Albanian.

"But now we have so much! And *now* they are throwing it all away! Everything we've been working for! 'Republic' is not important. It is just a word!" He heaved such a deep sigh that my arm went up and down with his.

"Now, NOW when we have almost everything, NOW they have thrown it all away!"

Agim and Emina had just moved into their first real flat in one of the new blocks on the hill. The whole complex was called Ulpijana, the Illyrian name. I was going there for dinner that night, before leaving. Emina said as I was going to Belgrade she'd have the holiday meal a day early. She had cooked my favorite meal, Elbasan *tava*, one of the few dishes that was really Albanian; pieces of mutton baked in an egg and yogurt mix. She'd roasted a chicken and made a wonderful paprika salad. But she couldn't eat. Suleiman and Ilija told her Agim would be alright.

"If he's not alright in the headquarters of the League of Communists, then where will he be OK?" Suleiman joked.

Ilija had already written off the holiday; for all Party members it would be Faculty meetings from now on. He didn't know what would happen to Murad.

The students had called for Murad when they came back to the Faculty, surging round the steps in the dark some with bloodstained faces. No police in sight. Two older students had disappeared into the building and come out with pictures of Tito which they must have taken down from over the blackboards. They held them up high and the boys chanted:

"TI TO! Teeee TO!" but it soon changed to "MU RAD! Muuu RAD!" and after a few moments Murad had appeared at the top of the steps, the student leaders protecting him from the jostling and pushing, their arms round him, Murad looking even slighter than usual, white-faced and blank as though he were being helped out of a crowd because he was ill. Dean of the Faculty of Philosophy.

"It was started by Law and Economics," one of the students near me had said. But it left and came back to the front steps of the *Fil. Fak.*

I was standing in the crowd too, looking up at Murad. Some of the boys had neatly bandaged heads and hands, as though they'd already been to the hospital and back. A lot of really young boys, too. One of the reasons for the demonstration everyone said after was the refusal to rule the Day of the Flag a holiday, with the closing of schools.

"So. What do you think, Comrade Miss Meri?"

Bashkim had appeared at my elbow, grinning like the Cheshire cat.

Agim didn't come home till half past nine, pale and very angry. He'd been in the Party headquarters with the other staff unable to get out. He said the demonstrators had gone back to the center of Pristina, "breaking everything."

When they came back to the *Fil. Fak.* for the meeting, singing and smashing all the windows with the sticks from their banners and the wooden staves from the fencing along the flower borders in Marshal Tito Street, they'd bashed in all the glass at *The Three Hats* and the windows of two cars which had slowed down and then the coach from Prizren smashing the windows all round, the passengers sitting there, glass in their hair and on their shoulders.

One student was dead, Agim said. Police and demonstrators had fought outside the police station. Several police and students had been badly injured.

"The 'intelligentsia' of Kosmet!" Agim had muttered bitterly.

I had to leave for my train. It was nearly midnight and Suleiman said he'd come too.

"No!" Emina cried. "Mary must go alone! It is dangerous to be a teacher now on the street!"

When I had walked back to the Faculty arm in arm with Fehmi he had suddenly stopped and wrenched his arm out of mine. The students were coming back. "I cannot be seen here!"

Serbians always said it was the Albanian teachers who made trouble. Nezir who must have been a senior at school in the last years of Rankovic had related how he and other bright Albanian pupils had been asked, when they said they wanted to go to the Faculty; "Wouldn't you rather go in the army?"

The plain-clothes policeman who processed my first application for a visa back in 1966 just after the Brioni Plenum had said to Suleiman who'd come down with me, "Ah! I know *you!*" with a wealth of heavy emphasis. And Suleiman had explained after in his dry, low key way, "Oh, he means when I was questioned at the police station."

You could get an education, Suleiman said, if you were Albanian, but you had been discouraged from returning to teach in Kosmet. That was one of the reasons Kosovo had so far to catch up.

In spite of Emina's protests, Suleiman took me to the bus station. Pristina was always silent and deserted well before nine every night, after the last stragglers from *korzo* had drifted home, apart from the pool of noise and activity in the center of Marshal Tito Street, with Hotel Bozur on one side and '*Texas*' on the other. On any average night there would be a *Milicija* jeep or van parked outside *Texas*. This night the windows were broken there like everywhere else, from the outside this time.

Suleiman and I were crunching over glass all through Pristina. The few private cars were overturned, their windows smashed. Those up side streets were tipped over too. Men were sitting in shop windows, behind the jagged glass, on the tiny three legged stools which were the closest Albanians traditionally got to chairs, hunched over oil stoves and with storm lanterns at their feet, guarding their stocks. But the police were everywhere in pairs, with two way radios, revolvers, machine guns, rifles. Suleiman and I were the only people crunching along with our audience of security organs.

Below the theatre steps were banners and staves on the ground and an Albanian flag. Involuntarily I went to pick it up and dust it down, and Suleiman hissed loud enough to make a policeman swing towards us with his rifle, "Leave it alone!"

Abdylla from Radio Pristina was on the bus. They'd just finished the emergency broadcast made by the two leading Albanian politicians who'd flown back to Kosovo from Bosnia where they'd been celebrating with Tito and the others.

"We'll get them back from Bosnia!" one of the Albanian schoolboys had told me exultantly in front of the Faculty. The boys had begun to chant their names but ironically, putting the Serbian 'ic' 'son of' on the end. Most Bosnian Moslem names ended like that and Albanian Moslem names from Montenegro. It had been common in Kosovo before the Second World War for documents and business, when Albanians, in the traditional Moslem way, had no surnames. But the way the students chanted the names they were obviously calling the top two Albanian leaders in Kosovo Albanian Uncle Toms.

Abdylla confirmed that one boy had been killed and ten police were still in hospital. And demonstrations had been held in other towns in Kosovo, places that in a more developed part of the world would be called villages. And Macedonia had reported disturbances too, in her towns along the Albanian border.

The bus trundled back through Pristina over the broken glass, past the police, the *milicija* with their guns and long winter coats, the shop owners sitting over their lanterns in the shop windows. Outside Peony four Montenegrin students got on, swaying and singing, two with bottles in their hands. Standing in the crowded bus they bent low to see out of the windows, the buckled cars, wheels in the air, the battered kiosks lying on their sides. Drunk as lords, they shook their heads and drew their breath in with gusty hisses. Suleiman and Abdylla, looking smaller and more withdrawn as the Montenegrin students swayed above them, sat silently staring ahead no longer at Kosovo after Brioni but Kosovo after the demonstration.

Arriving in Belgrade at six thirty in the morning was always a little grim.

"Albanians have been attacking Serbs!" The woman helping Nada's mother in the kitchen was glad to see me safe and sound. "They've destroyed all the Serbian shops in Pristina!"

No they hadn't. Or rather, yes, they had but they'd done the same to Albanian, I told her. The greengrocer opposite the Faculty, not just *The Three Hats* but the watchmaker, the little booth with fresh bread and *cufta* — the Albanian hamburger. I'd watched them do it. They were Albanian shopkeepers. I went there every day.

Nada had come into the kitchen. "You shouldn't talk about these things when you don't know the facts," she said.

They hadn't been attacking ordinary Serbs, ordinary anyone. I'd been right by them as they came back waving their staves. They'd just been grinning, exultant, like they'd taken a dare and done it. Nada shook her head slowly at me.

One of Nada's neighbors came in for coffee. The Belgrade hospital near them was full of Serbian and Montenegrin policemen he told us. They had sent them up from Kosmet because the hospitals down there were full.

But there were far more Albanian police in the police force in Kosovo now.

"Yes! THAT'S why they had to get the army from Nis! It's so dangerous there now! All the police are Siptars!"

By now there was a frontier post set up on the Macedonian Republic border at the Kacanik gorge, where Muhammed came from, that perfect First year who'd just learnt his English out of a book he'd bought. It had been an awful book, too, with print like a smudged bible. And though I didn't know it there were tanks in the streets of Pristina from Nis, to the north, the 'real' Serbia.

"You know, Mary, you are very naive," Nada observed, when the neighbor had gone. She was holding her new baby tight.

"But I was *there*, Nada!"

" Mary! Please! You shouldn't talk on things you know nothing about. You don't understand. You don't *understand!*"

Part II

Albanization

1969–1971

1969

Twenty-two

The Eastern Question or
On Not Being In The Great Tradition

The British Council was going to recognize Pristina. They were giving me seven-tenths of a lector's subsidy ("We've no money for anymore, this year"), a reward, perhaps, for my three eccentric years in the field. And there was talk of the Americans getting a foothold at the Faculty with a Junior Fulbright lector in English. The Russians had sent a lector for the Russian department at the start of my second year, when I'd still been in Room 47. "Oh, *he's* just a spy!" Murad and the others in Biology and Chemistry had said, grinning. "The Russians were jealous because *you* were here."

I didn't know what living in Room 47 had qualified me as, more lunatic than spy. For the first year there hadn't even been a lock on the door; whenever I heard someone outside I would freeze and half the time either leap into bed or out of it. Though one could say I'd been living exactly like a local, traditional Albanian from the hook on the back of the door that was a wardrobe to the slow electric grill that represented a kitchen; all the women had when they weren't sending a meal to the baker's to cook, squatting on their haunches like nomads round a camp fire. I, too, had no hot water and life in Room 47 had obeyed the most basic principle of all. The lavatory was as far away from the living quarters as possible, not across the yard but down at the end of the Russian department corridor.

I had certainly been in Kosovo for some historic moments. First, The Fall of Rankovic, 'The Second Liberation,' then *Rilindja*, the Albanian Renaissance and, in my third year, the November Demonstration and Demand for a Republic, the kitchen light trembling overhead as the tanks rumbled in again ready for New Year's Eve. Everyone in Belgrade saying bitterly "You and your Albanians!"

It was important Suleiman said that I stay for this fourth year in order to establish the Council connection. "And it will look very good for you when you leave to say you have been 'British Council.'"

Suleiman was very pleased that I was becoming a British Council lector at last because when I left British Council would send a real one, someone to talk to about Advanced English Intonation.

And Pristina was to become a University, the youngest and the first bi-lingual University in multi-national Yugoslavia. It seemed the students like Bashkim had read the times more accurately than their elders. Even though many were still in prison the demonstrations last November had not ended but, if anything, speeded up liberalization. And liberalization in Kosovo since the Brioni Plenum meant Albanization. The English department was going to hold all classes in Albanian now, as well as Serbian. We had three new young Albanian colleagues and were expecting the largest intake of students ever, especially Albanians from Montenegro and Macedonia. That would raise our standards, Suleiman announced, because Albanians from Montenegro spoke Serbian very well and Albanians from Macedonia were much more *cultured* than we in Kosovo.

When I was in Ulcinj, on the Montenegrin coast, I met two students from our *Fil. Fak.* at a concert given by musicians from Djakovica. The audience of well dressed quiet couples listened intently. Gradually they began to stand for the Albanian songs banned before Brioni. By the end they were all standing but still quiet. No burning handkerchiefs, no whirling coats, not even a whistle or a yell. I noticed when the students started talking in Albanian with the two men sitting in front they answered first in Serbian, then hesitatingly, in Albanian. They had shaken hands quietly and made their way out carefully along the row of light metal chairs.

"Here in Montenegro they have no political confidence!" one of the students had explained. "They are not so *Albanian* as we in Kosovo but see they are much more *civilized!*"

No-one had a good word for Kosovo. The elderly Albanian woman I'd met in London who'd attended a girls' boarding school in Tirana before the war had called the girls from Kosmet primitive. "They came from rich families," she'd reminisced "and they slept in their Turkish trousers."

Over the summer I had found a lot of romantic holiday reading in the English public libraries: *Illyrian Venture, Sons of the Eagle, Twenty Years of Balkan Tangle, Through Savage Europe.* From the literature on the Balkans it was clear that it wasn't only the Serbs who'd always considered Kosovo the *Vild Vest.* If the reader was not happy with the province described as 'primitive' or 'backward' there was only the other pair: 'stagnant' and 'savage.'

The Albanians, suspicious of political interference by the Great Powers, had just shot dead the first Russian consul who came to Kosmet in the early years of the century. They shot dead the first Serbian consul in Pristina. Kosmet was the most lawless pocket in the Kingdom of the Serbs, Croats and Slovenes after the First World War and after 1929, in the new Kingdom of Yugoslavia, when the army took on the Albanian 'brigands.' Mrs. Petrovic's father had come to Kosmet then as an officer in the Royal Yugoslav Army.

Before the First World War Kosovo was not even part of the international struggle over who was going to inherit 'Turkish Macedonia.' That had been The Macedonian Question, the first great nationality question of the twentieth century. The Great Powers had launched their international commissions, inspectors and plans for reform. The Serbs, Bulgarians, Greeks, Vlachs, Albanians and Turks had launched massacres, assassinations, terrorist attacks, hostage taking, gun-running and border raids. But Kosovo, Turkey's wild northwestern frontier, remained "...outside the area proposed in the European reforms."

Travelers like Edith Durham, the English woman who'd championed Albanians, were routinely refused permits to travel into Kosmet both by the Turks and their own governments. Their safety could not be guaranteed. Edith Durham tried for years. "My map ceased at the Montenegrin frontier" she wrote, "and beyond was a blank."

As fears grew in the years leading up to 1914 that a future European war would inevitably start in the Balkans, the 'Cockpit of Europe,' more must have been written about Albanians and all the other Balkan peoples than ever before or since. Adventurous Victorian and Edwardian gentlemen of leisure and adequate means, earnest investigators and professional journalists were all continually hiring ponies and Albanian guides and cantering off into the Balkans, the Near East.

I had found *The Burden of the Balkans* by Edith Mary Durham in a second-hand book shop in England in the summer. It was an original copy published in 1905 "...with illustrations by the author."

The writing was sharp and crisp, funny and tough. Gangrene and small pox, ambush and deceit, starvation and intrigue; Edith Durham dealt with everything. Still not able to enter Kosovo, she was circling round it; traveling in the Turkish provinces of present day Yugoslav Macedonia and Albania. Having observed all the mix of the Sultan's subject peoples she had come to admire the Albanians the most. She became their great champion. No wonder Nik and all the other Albanians had mentioned her first to me. But no amount of letters to *The Times* or persuasive accounts in

Balkan best sellers could help the Albanian *Muslimani*, identified so closely
with their 'Turkish masters.' At the tail end of the Turkish Empire it was
hard to find any sympathy for Moslems in the Balkans.

The League of Prizren had not been able to save the Albanians of
Ulcinj. The Albanians of Rugovo had originally been awarded to Montenegro
in 1878 but they had "resisted incorporation" so Ulcinj had been chosen
instead. The people of Ulcinj had resisted too but Gladstone, that tireless
champion of Christians, had sent a gun boat into the Adriatic and Sultan
Hamid had capitulated. By the end of the First World War Kosovo, Yugoslav
Western Macedonia and parts of Montenegro, the northern tribal areas, all
predominantly Albanian, had been awarded to the young Christian state
that had suffered so much: "Poor little Serbia." And now, just over fifty
years later, the new University of Pristina built close by the old battlefield of
Kosovo would be the center for the Albanians from those territories.

On the frontispiece of *The Burden of the Balkans* was a self-portrait of
the author sketched in 1904. Hair short as a boy's, Edith Durham had a
strong, handsome profile like Rupert Brooke. The sketches and watercolors
of Albanians, rifles slung over shoulders, peasant women weighted down
under elaborate costumes, Moslem cemeteries and mountain passes, illus-
trated her direct descent from the Jane Austen world of drawing room ac-
complishments for young ladies. A world that had changed so little by the
end of Victoria's reign that the only sure way for a female to break out was
not to the colonies, where the British had long since taken their gentility
but to the Balkans, where in Kosmet, even at the height of the British Empire, there was not even a British Consul.

In 1969 the scavenger crow was still outside my window, the sturdy
Balkan pony, water buffalo and ox cart. There were the same lopsided, mud-
plastered walls of brick and straw sketched by Edith Durham, still just off
Pristina's main streets and as they petered on to the outskirts the traditional
thorny branches appeared on top. I knew the homes inside these walls were
still just one room, like the home on North Africa Road. The poverty was
still there in Kosovo, the lean Northern Albanian still in white and black
and the blood feud, the suspicions, the Balkan Tangle.

Edith Durham had summed up exactly the 'un-peasant-like quality' of
the Albanian costume crowned by its 'white Florentine cap,' the Renaissance
outline of tight waistcoat over the full bloused linen sleeve of the shirt, the
tight trouser leg. Though she ignores the baggy seat. Maybe that was to ac-
commodate sitting cross-legged. Suleiman said that he always warned Agim
when he went back to his village: "Wear your oldest trousers!" Sitting cross-
legged, Suleiman remarked, had wrought havoc with his suits.

The 'white Florentine cap' immediately conjured up Prizren; the lattice windows of the jutting upper storeys, those mysterious upper rooms where girls were sometimes glimpsed. The winding alleys between the blind town walls cut with black and white shadows where at night silent figures slipped in or out of the high wooden courtyard gates, past the gushing fountains. The moonlight always seemed brighter in Prizren; the full moon hanging high and round in the sky like the Albanian white Florentine cap. Something Nezir said had conjured up that Romeo and Juliet world too:

"Before the war in Prizren the citizens always had daggers for quarrels. The rifle was only for the peasant."

Very little had changed about the blood feud since Edith Durham's day but at least the tradition of head hunting had died. In *Twenty Years of Balkan Tangle* there's a sketch of a headhunting Northern Albanian, his head shaved, one lock of hair left like a pigtail. Edith Durham explains briskly that the pigtail is there for the enemy to carry the head away if the Albanian be killed, so he will not suffer the indignity of an enemy's finger in his mouth. An Albanian she writes, killed to attain manhood. As for Montenegrins, it was only the switch from hefty *yataghans* to lighter knives in the Balkan wars that stopped them taking heads; they took noses instead. She had seen the corpses, she reports, and interviewed noseless survivors.

Margaret Hasluck in *The Unwritten Law of Albania* disputes the headhunter-pigtail theory, noting that pigtailed Albanians are found further south where no tradition of headhunting existed and, on the other hand, a good number of Northern Albanians who did hunt heads did not sport pigtails. It was Margaret Hasluck who briefed the British officers parachuted into occupied Albania during the last war each with a pistol and a belt heavy with gold sovereigns. Edith Durham had witnessed the start of the Young Turks Revolution and the preparations for war on the eve of the Balkan wars in 1912.

It was two women who had written the classic *Travels in the Slavonic Provinces of Turkey-in-Europe* published in 1867 with an introduction by Gladstone who refers to the Albanians in Kosmet as "renegade Christians and brigands" and *Black Lamb and Grey Falcon*, considered the modern classic on Yugoslavia, was written by a woman, Rebecca West. And then there was *An English Woman Sergeant in the Serbian Army* by Flora Sandes, who took part in the 1915 retreat through Albania.

Well, my job was to teach English and maintain standards. It was in the exam room that I was the stern English woman, eccentric perhaps, but indomitable: my moral outrage at open cheating only matched by that of the student in question asked to leave the room.

There were four days left before the September exams. The sun was baking hot. Out on the terrace even heavy towels dried in half an hour; no worry any drips would offend my neighbor below. Far from being the intrepid Balkan traveler I had managed to get myself embroiled in a neurotic little feud with the single Bosnian woman in the flat under mine. This was not supposed to be how the neighborhood policy of flat distribution was to work. We were all mixed up on purpose. In our block of flats there were Albanians above me, Serbians opposite, Montenegrins on the ground floor and the Bosnian below. It had worked with Emina. Emina would always say, "You know, Mary, I don't really feel comfortable with Serbians," but whenever she wasn't at home I would find her in the flat next door, having coffee with Olga.

"Well, *she's* Serbian" I would say, and Emina would always answer, "But she is my neighbor."

The early September sun flooded over the horizon at dawn, straight in the windows. Still nothing but the student hostel between our block of flats and the distant eastern hills. But there was always something to watch because of the dustbins right in front, twelve of them. As the land got more and more parched with summer they took on the role of an oasis. Any animal not harnessed to a cart made for them and humans too. The cows first pushed them over with their big noses; then came sheep, goats, the crows in the morning and the dogs. I'd got to know the regulars. There was the old man who fed his cows slowly by hand, picking out the choicest tid bits; two children with a cluster of sheep and goats, the old woman who limped very badly, stick in hand, sack over her shoulder and the two gypsy girls who went briskly and sulkily for old bread and newspapers. It was a paradise for anyone brought up to feel a pang at throwing anything away.

One old man didn't waste time on dustbins. He came up the stairs thumping on doors and yelling "Come on!" and something unintelligible that was obviously "I know you're in there!" When I gave him some coins he nodded, touched his forehead and blessed me rapidly in what sounded like Arabic. I'd given him some warm old British woollies at the start of the cold weather last year and he'd looked me up and down: "What do I want with your old clothes?"

The peasants hardly registered the new flats even though their aluminum sides flashed like signals in the sun. The old Albanian who regularly stopped to pee when he reached the brow of the hill turned not towards the open country, slipping in among the dusty clattering maize fronds but towards us, to the flats with the small, tight balconies flapping with washing above the pot plants.

I hadn't really gone for a walk since that time with Nezir and Mehmet on the first day of Oral Exercises. An old man had shouted something at us and Nezir had said, "You see the problem for walking here. He is saying, 'Be careful! Her father will be after you with his gun!'"

Women were allowed to walk to the market and back. If a woman were weighted down with two large string bags full of vegetables she could probably walk all the way to Macedonia by herself without arousing comment. I had really turned into a 'Kosovo woman' just like one of the English department visiting professors had predicted, three years before. Fresh from Belgrade with a big leather brief case and a cosy woollen scarf he'd given me a solemn warning.

"If you stay, Kosmet will change you. Don't think you can change it."

I wouldn't even dream of going to the cinema any more without Ilija. Ilija was no good for walks. He'd say "What a good idea!" and "What *fun!*" and have a coffee and a drink to get himself in the mood and then you'd find yourself only ten minutes away from the door and sitting down at a cafe while Ilija ordered a little pick me up.

Four days would have been long enough for any one of those brisk Edwardian travelers to have hired a horse and a faithful Albanian armed to the teeth and hacked through Macedonia and back like John Foster Fraser in *Pictures from the Balkans* 1906 with its jaunty chapter headings:

"Hotbed of Intrigue — A Thirsty Ride — A Dangerous Path — A Cheerless Night."

The stalwart pony trotting along dry river beds, Fraser making shift with Albanian shepherds, cross-legged in the moonlight round the camp fire, sizing up the whole Macedonian "Kettle of Fish" as he calls Chapter One. By Chapter 24 we have: "Albanian Ferocity and Chivalry — A High Sense of Honor — Language — Religion — Customs — Lack of Unity — Outrages — A Nation of Dandies" and off he trotted.

Margaret Hasluck would have been away investigating the pigtail-headhunting theory further. Edith Durham would be riding off into the hills, 'up country' as she called it, with her sketching block and medicine chest, not round at Ilija's watching *The Benny Hill Show* on Belgrade TV.

Students invited me to their villages all the time but, of course, I couldn't accept. Not as long as they were taking our exams. But one of the older Albanian students an 'irregular' had invited me again. He'd just come back from working in England and his English was good. Nezir and Mehmet were back from England too, fresh from that revenge on the Albanian male student, holiday work in the catering industry. They'd only stuck to it for three weeks. Nezir was obviously homesick for his beloved Prizren but he said it was because Mehmet had got into trouble with the police. It was a typical Mehmet story. If anyone were going to be accused of stealing a bath-full of dirty clothes in North London, it would be Mehmet. Nezir could hardly tell us for laughing. Mehmet, dark and indignant, sat there angry all over again. It had been Mehmet, last December, in the grim aftermath of the demonstration who had insisted on being arrested. He had pestered a traffic policeman in Prizren till he'd been taken into custody just to shut him up. Mehmet had lost his father during the Rankovic years, one of those Albanian teachers who had 'died in custody.'

Idriz and Ramazan had worked in England nearly a year. They'd ended up full time barmen in Bournemouth, great friends with the Colonel. Now whenever they saw me it was "I say, time for a quick one?"

All four of them were amused because when they told the English they were from Yugoslavia, everyone exclaimed, " Oh, that's nice!"

They'd obviously enjoyed saying they were Albanian too and non-plussing the English; even more relishing the fact, like I had, that since those burning days of The Eastern Question when everyone took sides, for the average man in the street now anywhere west of Trieste, Albanians, Serbians, Macedonians, Montenegrins and all the others were all the same.

But we were all back in Kosovo, back with the Balkan Tangle. The Bosnian woman below had banged her terrace rail and then banged up the stairs and banged my door the evening we'd all got together.

"Those are *Siptarski* songs!" she'd hissed.

"Noise is noise, Comrade neighbor" I'd countered philosophically, "whether it's Serbian or Albanian!" But then I'd spoiled it by leaning over the stair rail and hissing back: "*Chauvinist!*"

The normally restrained Agim had suggested that I should pee over the terrace rail on her pot plants but calling her a chauvinist was much worse. Even in the bitter infighting surrounding academic promotions it was used sparingly. Rather have a reputation for drinking or chasing women; if you were accused of 'nationalistic tendencies' in Tito's Yugoslavia your career would be over.

So now I had a festering, angry Bosnian woman below. I told Nezir and the others I was going to get away till exams began. Maybe I'd go to the village where the student had invited me.

"No!" they'd all said.

"As your friends," Nezir announced "we are just telling you he is a bottom-licker. It would be very unwise to go and would lower your reputation."

I'd introduced the word 'bottom-licker' to the old Fourth year in an unguarded moment and it had been seized on with delight. I'd tried to sub-stitute 'boot' for bottom but this had been rejected with a Turkish speaker's appreciation for the pungency of the original.

"No," Nezir had said firmly, "It is the *bottom* they lick."

It looked like being an interestingly mixed Fourth year. In addition to the newly identified bottom-licker would be Shemsidin. Far from being a bottom-licker Shemsidin had just announced that he was going to kill the head of the department. That is, if he failed the September exam again. Well, we were saying cheerfully to Milovan in the staff room, Shemsidin had always been a little odd. With his fierce blue eyes and explosive temperament Shemsidin, from a mountain village near Pec, struck me as headhunting material in the classic Albanian tradition, pigtail or no pigtail. But when it came to exam results and final grades, now it seemed all the students were headhunters, even the girls. They were all after us.

Twenty-Three

Hungarian Waitresses and the Macedonian Post Office

The *Kosovari*, those Albanians on the North-West frontier, the leading rebels against the Young Turks, were not the most famous fighters after all. "*Tetovo! Gostivar! Dibra!*" Mehmet had murmured reverently "That's where our *real* fighters come from!"

Tetova, Gostivar and Dibra were the three Yugoslav Macedonian towns on the Albanian border to the south of us. Another frontier. They were not on the tourist route south to Greece and they were not far. Determined to go 'up country' in some fashion at least for the last weekend before exams and get away from the Bosnian woman downstairs, I decided to go to see that Albanian part of Macedonia. Riding a sturdy *Kosovotrans* bus down through the Kacanik pass into Macedonia, I took a fresh change of buses in Skopje. By three o clock on Friday afternoon, the battered old single decker trusty *Transkop*, had roared out of the capital of Macedonia and was charging, head down, towards the great mountain range of the *Sar Pindus*.

The bus was packed with Albanians. There was the white cap, the heavy brown shawls on the women and the green or fawn poplin macs. The women sat pale and silent, baking quietly behind the glass, not even allowing themselves the public display of perspiration. The men conversed with great gusto and tremendous style. Watching these men climb unhurriedly up into the bus, their white shirts buttoned up under their chins but no ties, it was hard to see them as stern patriarchs. In public Albanian women never smiled but so many of the men, weatherbeaten peasants, young or old, had such dazzling smiles. Like Suleiman and Emina's father, Nezir's father had a dazzling smile too. All the more dazzling because it was so infrequent. At Nezir's we all stood up when he came in, quite an effect when everyone was sitting on the floor. Nezir, about twenty-one now, had only just started to smoke in front of his father. Just after the Diploma exam they were talking one day, he said and his father had offered him a cigarette.

Emina told me her father had been a very hard man when he was young. He had married off his oldest daughter at sixteen in the traditional way; "And was always sorry afterwards because he said she had been the cleverest of all of us."

I had remembered Rebecca West's description of the Albanian smile as a "watermelon grin" thinking how well that summed up attitudes to Albanians but found when I'd checked, that she'd written of its "water melon freshness." And there it was, all round the old *Transkop* bus, between the high-backed bus seats like pews with pictures of Yugoslav beauty spots, faded and flyblown above the ashtrays on the back.

Rebecca West talks of the "... social grace peculiar to Albanians" and their "fatal charm." Those friends in Belgrade who didn't see me as fatally eccentric for staying in Kosovo saw me as victim of Albanian fatal charm. "Well," they'd say, wiggling their eyebrows, "you know what we say: Every woman needs a chauffeur or an Albanian." Though before I'd gone to Kosovo the version I'd always heard was "Every woman needs a chauffeur or a Bosnian."

What I'd always found irresistible was the fatal charm of Albanian conversation, not only the movements of the hands and the language itself but its glorious mood of amazement. Albanians peppered their conversation with cries of wonder and dismay; one language in fact that shouldn't have needed them because Albanian had a special verbal mood, the exclamatory. But that was obviously never enough. Here in the bus grave old Albanians were crying aloud, "*Olelele!*" borrowing from the Macedonian ("Alas,' said the dictionary). I heard the Greek "*Opopopopo!*" or maybe the Albanian "*Opopopopo!*" which the Greeks had borrowed and, of course, someone was always giving the Turkish/ Moslem/Arabic cries: "*Allah!*" "*Vallahi!*" "*Aman!*" and "*Marshallah!*"

For smells Albanians favored one which the English would have recognized: "*Py!*" (Pooh!) "*Oof*" and "*Poof*" also came into this category. Scalds and burns and metaphorical scalding, as with a piece of news too hot to handle, brought forth, "*Ooofoofoofoof!*" Though I'd noticed that Nezir and

Mehmet when listening to gossip tended to favor *"Ahvavavava!"* the word drawn out indefinitely, in response to the intensity of the news. That was used for sheer incredulity too, as was the lighter *"Ahfafafafa!"* which hinted the situation was not so bad, the scandal not so great. In this group came my favorite *"Ububububu!"*

Albanians who were a little short of time or preferred something briefer took every vowel and turned it into a cry and then made a whole new set by adding on an explosive 'h': *"Ah!" "Eh!" "Ih!" "Oh!" "Uh!"*

Then they brought the 'h' round to the front and started again: *"Ha!" "He!" "Hi!" "Ho!" "Hu!"*

And finally, frustrated at their inability to express themselves properly, they created a whole series of wondering diphthongs:

"Aaaeeeee!" "Ooooowaa!" "Uuuuuoooooofff!" and *"Aaaaooooh!"* as the hand was raised, and sank back astounded.

Then really struck dumb, they abandoned speech altogether drawing their breath in between their lips, more of a reverse whistle, or out through the teeth, more of a long sighing hiss, clicked their teeth slowly like the ticking of a venerable clock and blew the air out in an almost *"Ooooooo!"*

Tetovo bus station gave me a strange feeling; it was as though I'd arrived in Albania. Everywhere were official, printed signs in Albanian as well as Macedonian. We had Albanian words in Pristina of course, painted by hand on wooden boards, but I'd never seen "Queue here" or "Bay 1" in Albanian before. No doubt because the bus stations in Kosovo were just potholed spaces. There was nowhere to hang a sign that said "Bay 1." Everyone knew where their bus should draw up and just milled about, getting ready for the battle to get on. If it didn't make the right spot they ran after it till it came to rest, banging on the sides and uttering sharp cries of wonder and dismay.

Last November there had been student demonstrations in Tetovo and the other heavily Albanian towns along the border with Albania. Sentences on demonstrators in Macedonia had been noticeably harsher than in Kosovo. That was another reason why we were expecting a higher registration of Macedonian Albanian students this September. It was not a good time to be an Albanian student in Macedonia.

Tetovo's houses climbed up into the wooded slopes of the Sar mountain, along steep cobbled streets stepped every few feet and, like Prizren, there was the ceaseless sound of running water from the mountain streams. Courtyards were being washed cool for Friday evening. The smell of warm wet concrete under the fig and quince trees was as heady as the scent of flowers.

"Be careful, girl!"

An old woman was standing at her gate in the dusk, not in Turkish trousers but an old faded skirt, her feet bare, cooling them off as she washed her courtyard. A Macedonian.

Behind her, planted in old cans, were geraniums and marigolds.

"You don't know what kind of people are here!" she called urgently from her gateway. "Be careful!"

Be careful of the Albanians.

On a drizzly Saturday morning the most interesting thing in Gostivar was the shifting of a bread kiosk from the side of the road onto a truck. The book shops were full of school books for the new school year. The *self-servis* had a new line of saucepans stacked up in the window. Just like Pristina. They always put saucepans in the windows. In fact, Gostivar was just like Pristina. For a moment I saw Pristina as an outsider, and the enormity of my eccentricity in staying there for more than a morning. It had started to rain. I felt for the first time like Nada and Milena must have felt until finally giving up on me. Even if the rain hadn't been coming on harder there seemed nothing to do in Gostivar but sit in an ice cream shop till it was time for my bus.

Sitting in a tiny ice-cream shop in the Balkans though had its international flavor. The two small boys in charge, barefoot and golden brown from the long, hot summer, were conducting business in Macedonian, Albanian, Turkish, Serbian (for me) and 'Rom' for the gypsies.

On the wall was the inevitable gaudy emerald and scarlet picture that looked like a day-glow version of the Bay of Naples, standard ice-cream shop equipment. I'd been stunned to discover it was supposed to be Lake Bohinj — the delicate northern Slovene lake. Behind the counter were framed diplomas. Albanian confectioners from Macedonia were found all over Yugoslavia. Suleiman said he'd survived in Rijeka on the Adriatic for a month waiting for his first pay as a teacher, by going from one ice-cream shop to another greeting the proprietor in Albanian.

These Albanians from the mountain borders here, renowned now for their ice-cream and rice pudding, had been the fiercest fighters in the Ottoman Empire. They came riding down from the hills armed to the teeth in Edith Durham's day. The Albanian tribesmen of Dibra were compared to the Kurds on the eastern frontiers of the old empire; harrying the Christian Slavs here as the Kurds did the Christian Armenians.

One of Julian Amery's tasks he recounts in *Sons of the Eagle*, when he was dropped into Albania with his pistol and gold sovereigns in the Second World War, was to calculate the sympathies of the Dibran clans and the chances of rousing them against the Occupation. Churchillian rhetoric had little effect. They were poor, calculating border people he wrote with an admirable grasp of power politics. Subsidized and armed by the Great Powers they'd been making a living out of the Eastern Question for a hundred years. In 1906 Edith Durham, writing of the "Albanian tigers of Dibra" noted, "Austria is reported to be trying to tame their ferocity with gold."

We had an Albanian student in the English department from Dibra. Hassan was a very quiet, proper young man who always wore a three piece suit.

Dibra had been badly damaged in a powerful earthquake two years before. It had rattled the windows and my bed in Room 47 and sent everyone down 14 flights of the new flats in their night clothes. Apparently damage was far greater over the border in Albanian Dibra but statistics were not available. There were still derelict buildings and gaps in the main street and no hotel, only a room over the central *kafana* which the waitress showed me, with a double row of beds over bare boards and one guest: a moody young man sitting on one of the beds, loosening his tie.

No, I thought not.

"There's Debar Spa up the mountain," she offered, doubtfully. She didn't know if they'd have a bed. She didn't even think there would be a bus. It was nearly five on Saturday afternoon.

At the bus station a fair, stolid policeman took me in hand. "This is not a good place for a girl alone... It's the people here..."

I knew he was Macedonian: the fair, broad face and such a mild, straightforward manner, almost Anglo-Saxon, in dealing with a stray female. He took me across the road to the post office. His friend, the manager, would let me telephone the spa and in the shadow of a municipal building I could come to no harm. Nor, indeed, in the shadow of the post-office manager, another straightforward, fair, low key Macedonian.

"Be careful, please!" he said. "As an English girl you don't know what life is like here and what are the people!"

I asked him how many Albanians there were in Debar, calling it by its Macedonian name, and he sighed heavily, seeming to accept as the inhabitants of Macedonia had done since long before the Balkan wars that any traveler had come purposely to estimate population, language of origin, truth of allegations.

"To tell you the truth," he said slowly, "there can't be more than half a dozen Orthodox (*pravnislavni*) families in the whole of Debar."

Sharp-eyed, slim young men looked me up and down as they passed. Dark, thin-faced, like Nezir and Mehmet. I wondered if Hassan were around, the Second year from Debar in the three piece suit. I hadn't said I was a teacher, let alone British Council yet. Inevitably I was not behaving respectably. Maybe I should have carried two string bags of vegetables along, even a dead chicken.

No bus, the policeman came over to report. I mentioned I knew a student, a Hassan Azemi. He might know of a room somewhere, get the Albanian network going, like Suleiman with his ice-cream men in Rijeka.

"Hassan Azemi!" exclaimed the post-office manager. "A very nice boy. A good family. We will find someone to go and fetch him."

Korzo was beginning in the twilight past the gaps and crumbled buildings like Skopje after their earthquake in 1963.

"She knows a family here — family Azemi."

"That's a good family," the policeman announced with the weight of the police force behind his statement. "A very nice boy. You would do well to go there."

But Hassan should have been back in Pristina, getting ready for exams on Monday. For another stab at 'Travel Broadens the Mind' or 'How I spent my Summer Holidays.' The post-office manager suddenly produced a plan that would tidy me off the streets; no problem to family Azemi, the post office or the local police force. His friend, a post-office engineer, was going up to Debar springs to deliver some cable. That's why he was waiting around on the steps. His friend could give me a lift.

The engineer and his colleague were more easy going Macedonians; no fierce appraisal, no speculative silence. We ground up the dusty track in the dark to Debar Spa. They got me a bed with a great deal of laughter and cajoling that ended up with me signing the hospital register while people in grey and blue striped pyjamas drifted by, wordless and big eyed.

In the deserted dining room the engineer wheedled a meal for me through the hatch and let me buy him and his colleague a coffee and a drink, something no Albanian would have permitted.

"If you are down by the post office tomorrow at nine," suggested the engineer, "we can give you a lift to Ohrid. The bus doesn't come through till ten."

A gypsy band was thumping away at breakfast among the patients in their thin hospital gowns drinking big cups of rich milk and eating chunks of bread and jam. They had a clay pipe, skin covered earthenware pots like bongos and a big old double bass. Three glum, sallow men with hooded eyes. Maybe the music was a prescribed part of the treatment. It was only the prospect of a lift, if I got down the mountain early enough, that could drag me away. Outside a mist covered the mountain. I could only see as far as a wooden bridge over the hot sulphur springs, the rocks below a livid green from the steaming water.

Walking down the hillside through the mist between the early September hedgerows, I was startled by two men who suddenly were there, black outlines in the mist in front of me. They were both in homespun shirts and trousers, wearing white caps. One of them stopped and waited. He told me to follow the stream down:

"It goes the quickest way down, as water does and there is a path beside it all the way."

He came down with me, reversing his route, to show me. His white cap was flat on top, more like a Turkish fez than the round skull cap of Kosovo. Like the Macedonians yesterday at the post office, like many Albanians, he was fair with grey eyes. Because of the cap I asked him if he were Albanian.

"To tell you the truth," he said bashfully, "we all wear it round here. You know, it just means we come from round here." He nodded, the nod like a slight bow and turned to make his way up the path where his companion was waiting, disappearing into the mist.

How strange not to be told, not to know nationality straight off, not to have it thrust at you. I couldn't remember that anyone, in my three years in Yugoslavia, certainly in Kosovo, had ever just spoken for a region like that. From "round here." But then I'd never been deep into the country on my own. I remembered what Mr. Petrovic had said when I first arrived and there was all the talk about "calling *Siptars* Albanians." He had laughed. "The peasants didn't even call themselves *Siptars* until the teachers came along! They went out to the villages and made trouble."

The two men, Albanian or Macedonian, had disappeared into the mist. That patch of mountainside for a moment seemed like the lost Garden of Eden before the apple of knowledge, the snake of nationality. "From round here. …You follow the water down, the straightest way." I nagged at it, worrying the facts. He would have to be Albanian. No Macedonian would want to be thought Albanian. In fact, one highly educated Macedonian girl had told me there weren't any *Siptars* in Macedonia at all. Well, she'd conceded reluctantly, there were some people… "But" she said firmly, "we call them gypsies."

And yet surely no Albanian, especially in the fierce frontier areas, where everyone was so conscious of what they were and what they were not would be bashful about saying they were Albanian. Albanians were never bashful about being Albanian. "From round here." Mist swirled round me. All I could see were my feet and the path, and hear the sound of water.

Following the water down, the straightest way, I reached Debar, Dibra, well in time for the post-office van. The town was melancholy even in the sun; a ruined school, two damaged mosques. I wondered whether Hassan would come back and teach, whether he'd want to, like Nezir and Mehmet with their passion for Prizren: Idriz and Ramadan with their automatic loyalty to Pec; the Macedonian students, Albanian and Slav from the lakes of Ohrid and Prespa, which for us, in the middle of the Balkans, was like coming from the Adriatic. Everyone was so proud of their town. Only my town, Pristina, got no praise.

Next door to the post office was a tiny *kafana*, the size of a coffee stall, with most of its chairs and tables out in the sun. Its coffee was excellent, with a head of *kajmak*, a cream of coffee bubbles on top, two lumps of sugar in the saucer and the water real mineral water. But the waiter would not go away.

"Where are you from?"

The little burnished coffee pot and round tray shone in the sun. The bubbles in the mineral water slid swiftly to the surface again and again.

"Pristina!" I'd answered this set of questions so often that I could snap them out now like a po-faced local girl. It had been years since I'd had to stray back into the Reading-on-the-River-Thames bit. And yet I took it for granted because Albanians sounded so fluent in everyday Serbian, as I could now, that there was really no linguistic problem for them at all and that their insistence on something like the reading of the minutes of a meeting all over again in Albanian was an affectation, basically unnecessary if not actually a tactic of Albanian militants, since the demonstration.

"Are you working?" The waiter wasn't talking his own language either. He was Macedonian.

"There's work here, you know!"

I knew what he was going to say next. They needed a waitress.

"We need a waitress."

The waiter thought I was a Hungarian waitress. Worse, he thought I was an *unemployed* Hungarian waitress. Albanians wouldn't let their womenfolk into a *kafana* to have a coffee let alone serve one and Serbians wouldn't wait on Albanians so Kosovo imported Hungarian waitresses from our sister province over the Danube, from Vojvodina.

After a pause the waiter, or maybe manager, went back inside his tiny *kafana* and looked at me out of the window for a while. There were no other customers. Silent Sunday morning. A little later he sent out the waitress in her black sateen overall and white apron and cap.

"You're Magyar, aren't you?" she said sharply.

I admired waitresses in Kosovo, in the Balkans. I found it hard enough to be a teacher, a female, let alone a waitress. In fact, being a woman in Kosovo was a lot like being a waitress, a waitress in a tough bar.

If I wasn't Magyar — Hungarian — and I wasn't a waitress then pray, if I did have a job then, pause, what was it?

She meant what was I doing showing my knees and drinking coffee and smoking in a *kafana* all by myself on a Sunday morning. There was nowhere to go and no way to get rid of her so I told her, adding a little more to the bad image of Kosovo: "— So! What's the difference between a female teacher in Kosovo and unemployed Hungarian waitress? — Nothing at all!"

" — And then she was picked up by four men in a post-office van and one of them didn't even have a shirt on."

The shirtless postal worker, a plump, dark man, lay back among the coils of cable behind the cab in the Sunday morning sun, singing. There was a festive air about the whole trip, maybe because they were all being paid overtime for nothing at all. The driver, the young engineer from the night before, said they'd been on a big job and were going back to Bitolja via Ohrid. There were three of us jammed into the cab and the one singing behind. We were following the valley of the Black Drim parallel with the Albanian border and just round the new Mavrovo dam, there, out of my window on the west, was Albania. Not away over implacable mountains, but just there. Albanian grass, Albanian hills, a few houses and a block house for Albanian border guards.

Everyone in the cab laughed at my interest. "There you are! *Siptar*-land!"

I was surprised there wasn't a permanent line of Albanians like Bashkim, just queueing up to have a look. The Albanian frontier was near Prizren too. The road to Albania from Prizren had been the road to Scutari, capital of Northern Albania, one of the classic routes for travellers in Turkish times, along the valley of the White Drim. On the edge of Prizren, it was the one major road still dusty and unpaved, flanked by big old mulberry trees as though it were a drive to a great house. On either side were maize and cornfields where little irrigation channels divided the fields and ran along under the trees. Albanians had been renowned as irrigators. They had traveled through the Ottoman empire, working with water.

A perfect place for a walk, I'd suggested to Nezir and Mehmet one afternoon in Prizren. Because it led to Albania it was like a road to nowhere, the only traffic pack ponies — we could go along and look at the frontier. They had said it didn't seem much of a walk to them, and anyway, as teachers, they weren't going to go and stand about at frontiers.

"What do you say when the policeman comes up and asks you what you are doing?"

"Having a look."

"Ah-*vavavavavava!*"

"— A lot of them are coming over now," commented one of the postal workers. "We can't patrol all the mountain areas."

"That's what's sending the numbers up here!"

Apart from the incredible Albanian birth rate, the other fact that worried the Macedonians said Nezir, was that Macedonians, famous emigrants, tended to leave for places like Australia and stay. Albanians earned money and came back. Built a house.

All the postal workers knew about me by then and where I was working. ("*Olelelele!*" cried the fat one in the vest) but I resolved not to argue.

"What's a nice girl like you doing, doing something like that?" they asked. "Teaching *Siptars!*"

"Well, I suppose they need teachers like anyone else," the driver commented reasonably.

"Ha! They had schools years ago! When the Turks were here! But they never went!"

I remembered Suleiman saying so bitterly, "Everyone had their schools at the finish. Only the Albanians had none. The Turks wanted us only as fighters."

I resolved not to argue.

"Students!" one of the mellow Macedonians spat out. "Animals! Animals!"

The demonstration, like the earthquake, had rattled everyone. And now everything was dated not from before Brioni or after, but "Before the demonstration" or "After" as in "I had so many Albanian friends before the demonstration."

I did get into an argument with the postal workers, of course. The fair young driver looked at me sideways.

"You got a *Siptar* boyfriend?" he asked.

But how nice they were being as we rattled along. How Western European they seemed. Even the dark fat man singing at the back, with the sad, black moustache, so cosy somehow. Yet when I got back to Kosovo I would be home. And whenever I slipped off my shoes and sank down onto the carpet under a low wooden ceiling, I'd feel at home. Every time I went from one world to the other I had the feeling of being in a more familiar place, of returning home.

When the road reached the shore of Lake Ohrid the postal workers piled out of the van and went swimming. I played ducks and drakes and ate blackberries. It was on the edge of Ohrid's sister lake, Strugar, back in 1959 playing ducks and drakes that Nada and I had found so many cartridge cases all marked 1916. Ohrid was still a clear and innocent blue that Sunday morning like a bible illustration of Lake Galilee, perfect as an accomplished Victorian water color. The surface, rapt and still, looking limitless, though it reached Albania before it touched shore. A third of the Lake belonged to Albania.

Postal business was completed in just five minutes in Ohrid and half that time was spent pinching wood from the post-office yard with which we later roasted the maize we pinched from a field on the way that morning.

" Meri, Meri, Why don't you come and work in Macedonia?" all the postal workers asked, lying round the fire we'd lit down by the river.

Macedonia was certainly kinder to women. How many beautiful faces I'd seen in just three days just on local buses, honey-skinned, open and assured. Edith Durham had been the one who'd noted that years ago; how much kinder Macedonian men were to their womenfolk than either Serb or Albanian.

"Oh, Meri! Meri! Meri!" sighed the fat man, saying goodbye at Bitolj. "*Olelele!*" He was genuinely upset to let me go back into Kosovo. Even though I'd been so truculent about the Eastern Question, or the Albanian Question, all the postal workers wanted to look after me.

Sometimes it seemed I was the only one in Yugoslavia allowed to coast along like I did with the postal workers. Only I was allowed limitless goodwill in my no-man's land between Albanian and Slav, between teacher and student, between Christian and Moslem, and, with Albanians, between men and women.

TWENTY-FOUR

■

"She thinks peasants have weekends!"

As the exams ended I got a message from Nezir. An Albanian student came to the door very early in the morning: a trip to a village was possible. Nezir had suggested we might be able to go with one of his father's 'customers,' one of the peasants who had their ponies shod at the stables. "Nezir says if you wish it," the student added.

Shoes, socks, band aids, fruit drops, camera, thick British woolly; on the high ridges of Sar, Nezir said you could find ice all the year round. Down I raced through the cool sunlit September morning to get the six-thirty bus to Prizren. And straight to the 'shop,' the blacksmiths, past the mosque, the fountain and the bakers. There were the stables and the high private wall of the family's house next door, the air so fresh and full of promise.

Nezir was at school, teaching. His mother looked worried. Should she send someone for him? It was about eight on Friday morning.

I'd come round later. Go and see Emina's parents. Nezir's mother said to leave the bag. She hung it up carefully, dusty and bulging, on a hook in the hall.

Nezir was appalled. The student had been late with the message, a whole week late. The peasant he'd been planning on us traveling with, had come and gone. Last weekend. But I must stay for lunch. Nezir's mother had made *Prizrenski tava* because I had come and it was almost ready at the bakers. To say *Prizrenski tava* was a mutton casserole was like saying the Taj Mahal was a building. The secret, Nezir had explained, was to have the meat fatty enough to 'melt' the vegetables. And to have a Turkish baker's oven round the corner from which the *tava* would emerge with its thick, black caramel crust.

Nezir's father was sitting outside the stables on his low, three-legged stool, smoking. His usual look of wry amusement on seeing me was even more pronounced. He'd heard I wanted to go to a village. There were some pack ponies in the yard, a collection of sacks and bundles in the passageway and a man talking to Nezir's father as he loaded up his ponies. The customers, as Nezir called them, came every day whether they needed their horses shod or not. Many peasants on reaching the outskirts of Prizren would leave their donkey or pony to make its own way to the stables. Blacksmiths were parking places, Nezir said, centers for the peasants. That was why his father, who had never learned to read, always knew the news from all over Kosmet and Macedonia before he did. With Nezir in Prizren you would always hear the Albanian greeting:

"Oh! Ne-zir! Long life to you!" as a man passed, white-capped, leading his ponies up to the fort and mountain path with the effortless Albanian stride or coming down into Prizen with panniers of charcoal and lengths of wood. Nezir said when he was a boy he used to go to the villages with his father; they were always being invited. Once in the winter his pony lost its way coming home from a wedding and he was taken in by a mountain family.

"You never forget those nights! The way they talk, these old peasants and tell stories! They are such men!"

Many of their customers were Serbs too. "My father is greatly respected by everyone." Nezir had told me. "He was so strong and feared no-one."

Customers 'in blood,' entangled in a blood feud, would often seek protection at the stables because no man dared violate his father's threshold.

Only recently Nezir said, a man had rushed into their courtyard in fear of his life. "My father just picked up whatever was near, a spade or something like that — and just stood and the other man who was following went away."

Even Nezir, a teacher and one of the self-described 'intelligentsia' of Kosovo, seemed to take it for granted that there should be violent confrontations over what seemed like trivial incidents. Recently, driving home from their piece of land in the valley, they'd cut across a corner belonging to another family and the father had taken out a knife. "Luckily my brother-in-law was on our cart and he had a shovel," Nezir said conversationally, adding, "My father is getting old!" meaning he was reaching the time of life when sadly he had to rely on a son-in-law brandishing a shovel to defend the family honor.

I'd heard Nezir's father talking slyly of "Passing the coffee under the knee" and looking at me to see if I understood. It was the traditional Albanian way of expressing contempt for a man who'd refused to 'take the right,' to seek blood for any slight to his honor.

The blood feud had always been a fertile source of travelers' tales and comments on the Albanian character. John Foster Fraser, the perky Edwardian, had summed it up neatly: "Albanians occasionally die from ordinary disease but most of them die from differences of opinion."

It was accepted to be certain death to strike an Albanian and extremely risky to insult one. The Turks knew this but the German officers called in by Sultan Hamid to re-organize the Ottoman Army ignored such oriental hyperbole and several had been shot by their Albanian soldiers for insulting them on the parade ground. There had been such interest in Albanians then, the Albanians of the Empire, the soldiers and civil servants in Istanbul and the provinces and the rebellious, anarchic northern Albanians, the key to the strength of "Turkey in Europe," one of the most crucial factors in the forthcoming confrontation between the failing Ottoman Empire and the young Christian Balkan states.

Talking of the fighting discipline of the Albanians, Edith Durham described an alarm in Prizren which had the whole male population turned out under arms in ten minutes. As soon as the alarm ended every man immediately returned to his daily routine. In the revolt against the Young Turks it was the discipline of the Albanians who liberated Kosovo which was noted. I had asked one of the Albanian historians at the Faculty why, in spite of this, the Serbians and Montenegrins had been able to take Kosovo in the Balkan Wars. He had given the same answer that was always given about why the Serbs had lost the Battle of Kosovo: "Disunity. The Albanians were not united."

Nezir said his father remembered when the Serbs entered Prizren in the First Balkan War. "He says the Serbs bought the Begs with gold. That's why no-one fought. The Begs lied to the people."

My bag had been put in the upstairs room. I'd been invited to stay. Perhaps if a customer came on Saturday whom Nezir liked and who was willing, maybe I would get to go to a village after all. "But" Nezir warned, "there will be *nothing* to do."

Everyone would be sleeping in the only downstairs room, below, seven altogether. Upstairs under the low wooden ceiling there was only the traditional narrow couch like a window seat running round the paneled walls where concealed cupboards held bed linen and Nezir's books. I liked Nezir's house better than any other I'd seen in Kosovo probably because the austere nature of his father had prevented the two rooms from silting up with the standard puffy red and white velvet cushions, the lacy runners and plastic flowers and printed cloths on the walls of the dancing girl before the Sultan or a row of camels approaching an oasis. Downstairs there were nothing but periwinkle blue-washed walls, a radio on the window sill and a dresser with an alarm clock ticking away on its middle shelf. Overhead the dark wooden beams sagged away from the ceiling and left gaps which were used as shelves. A big wicker basket hung from the central beam with the table-cloth folded on top over the day's supply of bread. The first action before lunch was to reach up for the basket.

When Nezir's youngest sister came back from school we ate. Nezir's mother spread the gingham cloth over the carpet and placed the big earthenware dish of *Prizrenski tava* in the middle, sticky black on top from the baker's oven. And we had fresh bread, two round floury loaves hot on a board born home from the bakers too on the head of one of Nezir's other sisters.

Nezir's father didn't eat with us. He sat cross-legged in the corner by the window where the big radio lodged on the elbow high sill, the blue washed walls at least three feet thick. He had a glass of mastika, a saucer of sugar and an ash tray. I could hear the mice scuttling to and fro overhead. They got in the radio too. For all its size it only got Radio Pristina and Radio Kukes, the Albanian station just over the border.

"Listen! How clear we can hear it!" Nezir had declared fervently back in his student days. "They have Chinese generators in Albania now!"

And his father had snorted, "Ha! A radius of twenty kilometres!" Kukes was very close to Prizren. "Chinese! Chinese this! Chinese that! Iron foundries in your back yard! Why didn't Albania go with JAPAN! Then they might get somewhere!"

There was the sound of hooves scraping the cobbles and thuds and clatter in the passageway and a face appeared briefly beyond the radio in the window.

"Oh! Ne-ZIR!"

"Ah! Maybe that's our man!" Nezir exclaimed, uncurling himself from sitting cross-legged in one quick movement. A long conversation in Albanian began in the yard. I could hear Nezir's sisters laughing in the hall. His father grinned and shook his head at me. Overhead the mice scuttled and the clock went on ticking. Nezir came in briskly, ducking under the lintel.

"We have an invitation to go to a village. The peasant who just came must stay in Prizren tonight and we can start back with him tomorrow but it won't be anything special."

Nezir said the main thing was this peasant was a nice person and had recently invited him and his father anyway, so his father would be pleased. It was an Albanian mountain village. The journey would take six hours and we'd be going with two ponies. Nezir's mother was shaking her head slowly, helpless before the absurdity of it all. The children, Nezir's younger sisters who'd been slipping in and now knelt behind their mother like a tidy line on a crusader's tomb, were grinning broadly. Even with their father there, I heard a muffled giggle.

There was the clack of the latch and clunk of wood on wood as someone came into the courtyard. It was Mehmet. He'd heard I'd arrived in Prizren but also he was full of the latest Prizren story. "Sorry, I will tell it in Turkish first because it MUST be told in Turkish and then Nezir will tell you."

An Albanian student had taken a wager to run stark naked through *korzo*. The starting point Hotel Theranda, the time seven-thirty in the evening, the height of *korzo*. The route across the bridge, sharp right past the drapers, the butchers, Sinan Pasha's mosque and the fountain, up the steep bit past the Orthodox church and nearly up to the Catholic one on the brow of the hill and then, no doubt breathing hard and looking out for broken glass, all the way downhill to Theranda and the student holding his clothes.

The wager had been won last night. There had been three policemen running after the student at the finish, but they couldn't catch him. "They were laughing too much."

Nezir's father took this opportunity to make some pertinent comments on the younger generation and Nezir, who'd already heard the story at school, said in English, "It's exactly the kind of thing he'd have wanted to do himself when he was young. He had a reputation then! Ah-va-va-va!"

That older generation was much worse, he said. "Under the Turks it was all jokes and mucking about. They had nothing serious to do with their lives."

They used to do things like betting a neighbor he wouldn't spend the

night in a haunted graveyard and then the rest of the gang would hide behind tombstones, draped in sheets. Not that there was much to hide behind
with a Moslem tombstone. Only recently Nezir said, his father had spent
the night before the feast of Bajram getting his friend the baker so drunk
that all the lambs brought in to be roasted had been charred.

"It doesn't sound very funny to me."

Nezir's father grinned and then said something in Turkish. Nezir translated: "She mustn't expect them to kill a sheep for her. It's a very poor
household you're going to."

Mehmet dismissed the idea of a village. We could go down to the
new motel by the Bistrica, where a new batch of Hungarian waitresses had
arrived. One of his friends had a car; we could make a trip, play poker.

I'd bought a pack of cards for us to take up to the village. It had
seemed the sort of thing you could unobtrusively leave behind, the sort of
small present that wouldn't patronize or offend. Everyone liked playing cards
and being a weekend they would probably have time to play a game or two.

Nezir's father looked blank and then snorted: "Weekend?...Weekend?
Ha! So she thinks peasants have weekends!"

TWENTY-FIVE

■

Six Hours from Prizren

Avni, the customer who'd agreed to take us to his village, was loading up
his two ponies when we came out after lunch. He looked about the
same age as Nezir, in his early twenties, a little shorter, dressed in old grey
trousers and maroon sports shirt made out of the kind of flock nylon used for
night-gowns, and a flat navy cap. Grinning bashfully, he shook hands.

Nezir said we were ready to go. Avni opened his mouth, looked down
at the bag I was carrying, and swallowed. Nezir and his father were enjoying
the joke.

"Well you said we could come!" Nezir said, speaking Serbian for my
benefit.

"Yes, of course you can come!" Avni cried, eyes down, addressing my
bag in a distraught manner "— but I didn't think you were serious!"

Nezir would have stood there the whole afternoon enjoying the joke.

It was his father who said "You'd better get going."

We started up a side street through the dust, past a trio of school girls I hoped weren't Nezir's pupils, swinging by with books under their arms, eyes ahead but taking it all in. Nezir, me, Avni leading the ponies, one laden with sacks on both sides, the other with a deep wood and cloth paddled saddle to which Avni had tied my bag. Behind us, Nezir's father turned back into the stables, still grinning, shaking his head.

Instead of winding up the shady lanes through the vineyards and woods towards the fort above Prizren, we were soon clopping along the sizzling main road while Saturday afternoon traffic tore past. Here came the Pristina-Prizren bus, packed to the roof, all the window seats looking down at us. How high the sides were. Avni had began to relax. He was used to this. The road lined with apple trees cut across the valley, the plain of Metohija to our left, the fields on the right running towards the thickly forested slopes of the Sar mountains. Avni nodded up toward Sar; that was where we were going.

I was limping already, struck down with blisters. It was the first time I'd worn shoes not sandals, since May. We passed a group of traveling gypsies, mending tepsijas and copper cauldrons round a fire; Avni, Nezir, the two ponies and after a while, me.

The ponies only seemed to clop along in a desultory way but they covered ground. Every two minutes I had to jog trot to catch up but I immediately fell behind and yet they never seemed to hurry. Nezir said Avni was very proud of them because they were such good animals. He and Avni covered ground too, without hurrying. I was having the chance to appreciate at first hand what was so aptly described as 'the tireless gait of the Albanian."

"Come on! It was you who wanted to come!" Nezir was turning round, grinning. It was the start of his second year as a teacher; a long time since he'd been my student.

"It's her feet!" I heard him say to Avni as I caught up, doing my jog trot like a child out with grown ups. "She has feet like a duck."

My feet were discussed a lot in Kosovo partly because they were so often seen, as we were always taking off our shoes. Idriz, facing military service when he came back from Bournemouth, had gazed at them longingly. With feet like those, he said, you'd never be accepted in the army; they were wasted on a girl. Mehmet had pointed out that if you were turned down by the army doctors, parents were reluctant to let you marry their daughters; they wondered what was wrong with you. But Idriz said if you had feet like mine it would be obvious.

Avni shook his head over my feet too; drawing in his breath in that

Albanian hiss which expressed not only surprise and horror but when accompanied by a decisive movement of the head from side to side, somber agreement.

"You see, bad feet are her burden," Nezir declared in a pontificating way which was creeping up on him as a teacher in a small town. "She walks to the village — six hours! To CONQUER those feet!"

"Bravo!" cried Avni fervently and they drew ahead again.

Clop went the horses and buzz went the flies. Nezir and Avni were deep in Albanian ahead. I wasn't even pretending to take part in the conversation any more. "We can't wait for you," Nezir had said, "We have a long way to go."

I could see why Nezir had been ready to come with Avni. He was easy to be with, with a gentle, open face. Nezir said he was very intelligent and should have had more education. I certainly took it for granted he should understand our jokes.

"He understands even yours!" Nezir said. Avni was obviously Faculty material.

The road ahead vibrated in the heat. Solitary horsemen passed us, heading toward Prizren. After nearly two hours, just when I'd decided we were going to clop all the way back to Pristina, Avni turned the ponies off the crippling tarmac and the mountains were facing us, their dark green slopes in shadow. We were following a wide track between tall fields of maize, the landscape broad and sunny with fruit trees and clusters of houses. After we'd crossed a dried river bed Avni said we could ride. And though the pony twitched its shoulder blades in irritation and stumbled and lurched into every deep rut it came across, it didn't matter. The saddle was so high in front and behind and so comfortable and I was going to a village, riding where horses were the normal and proper transport. I could have been so many times to Serbian villages with people like the Montenegrin headmistress but I hadn't wanted to go for the afternoon in a car. Nezir had said if a peasant had come from a Serbian village, instead of Avni then we would have gone with him. "My father is respected and welcome everywhere."

The sun was getting lower. All of us were just talking now; me off the horse, Avni on, then Nezir. Avni was apologizing Nezir told me in English, because he had to ride too. "He gets very tired and has a pain in his chest. Last month he was in the hospital with pneumonia and didn't stay and now he has a pain."

A small charge had recently been introduced to help cover costs for every day a patient was in hospital. As peasants were not employed in the "Social Sector" they had no coverage. Peasants should always have infectious diseases a Serbian doctor had told me dryly; then the State will get them well.

Avni was letting the ponies stop and graze, slapping their flanks affectionately as they turned away. He and Nezir went off to choose a water melon growing by the maize and find the man to pay for it. We ate it all, dripping, rose red slices with shiny black pips to spit into the grass. There were no melons in the village, Avni said, it was too high. He and Nezir were laughing a lot. Nezir, I knew, was glad after all that we'd come.

As the sun dropped lower we started to climb, between boulders, over stretches of slate, into clefts that widened into stony, dried stream beds, then dwindled again. Up into patches of copse, the ponies' heads down picking their paths in between, branches whipping their flanks. Nezir and I were letting Avni ride all the time; he looked so tired and drawn.

We forded a stream, made a steep turn and were climbing up into a dark wood, the sky paling above into the deep blue of early evening. It was as though we'd turned the corner from Kosovo into England; the copses, the hedgerows, the cool evening air. Avni and Nezir were laughing about the stream. The last time a group of villagers had come down, Avni said, they'd raced each other to the steep turn and two had tipped off into the water.

"They always used to come down in bands," Nezir said. "It was protection in winter against wolves and it was company — a whole gang of villagers singing, joking, riding down into Prizren. It doesn't happen now."

The ponies climbed tirelessly, sliding on the slate, hooves almost on top of each other in the narrowing ruts. Avni was looking very pale. He made the trip twice a week, usually in one day. Starting at dawn, six hours down to Prizren, carrying wood, their only cash crop; then in the afternoon six hours back All through the winter too. The ponies were sliding now, just on the slate.

"Of course men are killed, riding down!" Nezir said impatiently.

Suddenly we were no longer climbing. Our wooded lane opened out onto a windy ridge, trees rising up on our right, an orchard on the left which just disappeared after five rows, down the side of the mountain. In the distance I could see lights far below. "I think we are here," Nezir murmured. He'd never been to this village either.

There was a fence, a barn with a steep roof, piles of wood visible in the light from an open doorway full of people. Crowding down on the house in the dark were heavy black trees. It was women in the doorway. "These are the women" Nezir said and walked off immediately, turning his head from the doorway.

There were five. They didn't move or smile. Nezir was talking to the men by the house wall. It was going to be like a wedding; I was going to have to stay with the women. I could hear the wind in the trees behind the house. Avni was unhooking my bag from the saddle and one of the women came forward to take it. But it had Nezir's things too — and the cigarettes we'd brought. The woman looked enquiringly at Avni.

"She doesn't speak Serbian," he said bashfully.

Out came Nezir's things in the light from the doorway. In silence the cigarettes. I would be with the women the whole weekend. The men came up and shook hands with me, smiling. Nezir called from the other doorway, "You will sit with the men and sleep with the women."

The house was divided in the traditional way into the room for the men and guests, the *selamlik* and the room for the women which was the kitchen. The men's room was cosy and familiar; the low wooden ceiling, the red and black peasant rug laid over blankets, the three legged black stove against the back wall. Nezir was already pacing over the blankets in his socks. By the door was a chest with an earthenware pot on it and on the wall a little oil lamp.

Nezir told me to sit down; the men were waiting. They wanted me to sit in the corner where the rug was, up near the stove but I knew the corner was reserved for the eldest. It was for the eldest to initiate the conversation so I suggested Nezir, the teacher now. They were all pleased I knew the custom and Nezir sank down cross-legged in the corner with a *Marshallah!* hand on heart. He would be sleeping there he said, and I would be upstairs, with one of the wives.

"You will be with mine!" one of the brothers said. Behind his big black moustache he was really quite young. "— And I will be here with Nezir!" He poked Nezir's foot affectionately with his own toe. "Oh! Ne-ZIR! You will be my bride!"

His name was Issa. In a smart, tight fair-isle pullover and full sleeved white shirt he was the youngest brother, then came Avni. It was his turn to enjoy the joke as Nezir attempted to explain me. Issa kept slapping his thigh and crying "Oh Nezir! *AmAN!*" One of the brothers was away, so there were only four. The other two were older, Ibrahim wearing the white cap and Islam, the eldest, quiet and withdrawn.

Sitting cross-legged on the blankets in front of us, the brothers peppered Nezir with questions. They seemed very fond of him and his father, anxious to know how he was and why he hadn't come.

"Mary came instead," Nezir replied and as we all knew Nezir's father we all laughed.

Islam wanted to know what the doctor had said. Nezir said it wasn't good but his father wouldn't give up mastika and cigarettes because of doctors. The brothers all shook their heads slowly.

"They knew my father when he was younger. They can't imagine him not strong anymore."

Avni had lit the stove. We were sitting on what must have been bracken, springy and tough under the blankets. We'd passed bracken on the way up. The brothers were pleased I liked the wooden ceiling. They were going to carve a center for it, in the traditional way. They had built the house two years before. They talked about that, about teaching at the Faculty, education in the villages, the Second World War and the role of the allies. Only a few minutes had been spent on me at the start; the old questions, how could I be Nezir's teacher, when did I celebrate Christmas and so on.

"It is not that they are not interested," Nezir explained. "But they see you are not interested in what you must always say here in Kosovo. You see how polite they are and quick to understand."

Islam the eldest, stopped Nezir when he tried to open a packet of cigarettes. Avni collected all the packets we'd brought and put them in the little cupboard behind the stove.

"Maybe if we smoke all theirs they will allow us to offer ours," Nezir said.

Islam tossed cigarettes over to Nezir and me, and then to the other brothers, two at a time, but they always landed together on the blanket by our hands.

It was always noted in the old travelers' tales, that one of the many un-peasant-like characteristics of Albanians was that they ate very late. It was nine before Suleiman went to fetch the kettle and bowl and pour water over our hands, the towel on his shoulder. Avni spread a cloth over the rug and Suleiman rolled in the low table, the *sofra*, and brought in the food. The *tepsija* was filled with sweet peppers fried in oil and pieces of soft white cheese. Suleiman gave each of us a chunk of bread and a glass of milk and we all ate briskly, in silence.

No-one had mentioned the wives at all. And in the absence of the women the men did all the tidying up. The food had been placed outside on the step. I thought I saw a face look in through one of the barred windows, but then it was gone.

Avni was putting the kettle on. He was 'tea man.' It was a real job. Avni sat cross-legged by the stove, with the small tea glasses lined up on a tray in front of him. First he ladled in sugar, up to a third of the glass, then that was covered with mild amber tea from the small teapot and topped up with hot water from the kettle. Avni must have done it up to twenty times that evening; tongue between his teeth, first the sugar with a flourish all the way along, then the tea. Never a grain or drop spilt — all of us watching. Then holding the small spoons to one side with a forefinger so the handles wouldn't get up our noses we sussed and slurped the tea up and Avni would turn to Nezir and me and ask in Albanian:

"Are you bored?"

And each time Nezir, hand on heart would reply, "Yo! *Mazallah!*" "No! Heaven forbid!"

And Avni would exclaim, "Thank-you!" take back our glasses yet again and line them up. Part of the skill lay in remembering which glass was which. I asked Avni whether the women were having tea.

"Tea?" He looked blank and then laughed. "What would they want tea for?"

In *The Unwritten Law* Margaret Hasluck wrote that the coffee set never left the mens' room in case the women got into bad habits and began to drink coffee themselves.

The door opened and two figures ducked in. There were the white caps, the black and white costume, black cummerbund round the waist, jacket sleeves cut short in mourning for Skenderbeu, the flap at the back like a sailor's collar. Kicking off their shoes in the doorway they stepped on to the blankets, placed one foot across the other and sank cross-legged, forearms already resting on their knees. There were those brilliant Albanian smiles, wide and fresh as water melon slices.

"They are our brothers' nearest neighbors," Nezir said in English. "I think the brothers are lucky."

The two neighbors were much older than our brothers but far more lively. The younger one who looked about fifty said he was the farmer, his brother the shepherd. Avni took back our glasses and added two more. The neighbors were being told about me, how I'd come back yet again, to Kosovo to teach. Smiling, they said what did I think of Albanians and the way they lived?

I said to Nezir I wanted to say a whole string of complimentary things but as a woman —

"Don't talk about women, please" Nezir said sharply. "They don't like to discuss their women *at all*. You will offend them."

Islam tossed everyone two cigarettes again which landed side by side exactly by our hands and Avni lit another splinter of kindling for us to light them with. The farmer had a transistor radio which he kept putting up to his ear under his white cap. He'd been apologizing with his big smile: "I just got it and now I'm like a teenager. I take it everywhere, even in the fields."

He turned it up louder and put it in the middle of the blankets for the ten o'clock news from Radio Pristina. That was the news in Serbian, from Belgrade. Avni filled the kettle again from the water pot by the door, throwing the room into shadow as he passed in front of the little lantern. The water pot had a maize cob stopper. The blanket sprung up immediately behind him, smoothing out his foot prints. It had to be bracken under there. By the end of the news the two sets of brothers were talking in Albanian. Nezir said they were discussing a blood feud. The shepherd, the oldest man in the room, with the impressive white walrus moustache, had been asked to act as an emissary between two families in blood.

"I am afraid they will not speak in Serbian now," Nezir said. "You would find their Albanian very hard anyway because they speak it as peasants, with local forms and not correctly."

I was content to watch. One of the new Serbian assistants who had started coming down from Belgrade, had exclaimed during a First year oral with Albanian students this September:

"Look at their hands! They're using them like Italians! Serbians only use their hands like that when they're angry."

The children, dancing at weddings, their fingers fluent and grave as ballet dancers; the old women with their sunburnt hands raised to a cheek, over the mouth, or, palm facing outward, in amazement or resignation and above all the Albanian man in the white cap telling a tale. The white cap could be as important as the hand. Worn a certain way, the cap could start a blood feud. Squatting against a wall waiting for a train or bus or in a hospital corridor, the owner of the hand would let it hang negligently over the knee, wrist slack but when he started to speak the hand would rise. The cap would be tipped forward, then to one side with a single finger, then cocked over an ear with the palm of a hand and then, after a while, the hand would return from its story telling parabolas, the forefinger or open palm tipping the cap back. The story over, the hand would return to the knee.

"I love to listen when they speak proverbs" Nezir was saying. "And the way they say something. With peasants it is very clear but never obvious. They hate to be obvious."

"Neighbour," the shepherd suddenly said to Avni. "Can you see well enough to pour the tea?"

Avni, with an exclamation, stood up in the unravelling, crosslegged movement and turned up the wick. "You see?" said Nezir. "It's not a great example but see he will never say 'Can we have more light?'"

Nezir asked Islam when the village would be getting electricity and Islam said they'd been promised next year.

There were two more visitors that night even though it was so late. It was nearly eleven when two young men arrived, sitting down heavily side by side, backs against the wall. One fair, one dark. Nezir started to take part in the conversation, rapid and low in Albanian. The new arrivals talked little and were so curt and abrupt I was surprised the older men were not offended.

Nezir said the two brothers had quarrelled and were dividing their communal household.

"It's a terrible mess. There are twenty-nine people to be provided for."

The fair brother who'd fallen silent and just stared at the wall, had been shot and wounded in a confrontation with a forester. It happened a lot Nezir said, over rights to wood in the mountain forests. The dark, younger one had sworn they must avenge the insult to the family. But his brother had been willing to listen to the judgement of the local elders and it had been their decision that in this case it was honourable to accept blood money. His brother, accusing him of dishonouring the family, refused to live any longer under the same roof. Now, as everything had been held in common according to the Unwritten Law, all would be divided according to the Law. The only things exempt, Margaret Hasluck said, were the symbols of family life; certain things which must be left in the kitchen and the tea or coffee set which symbolized friendship and hospitality. And if neither brother moved, the house itself would be partitioned. All the food, the livestock, every pot and tree would be assessed and divided. The Law said:"The eldest divides, the youngest chooses."

"It will ruin them," Nezir said. "Look,this brother tried to be progressive and change things, not to drag his family into a feud and now it is worse than if they had started one."

I asked him whether they might eventually reunite.

"No. Pride divided them and pride will keep them apart. Albanian pride. Bloody Albanian pride! Look at them! All saying 'Very bad!' 'Very bad!' Talking about the blood feud and with terrible stories of it, what it has done to families." Nezir was muttering savagely, watching the three sets of brothers in the lamp light.

"And you know ALL of them have their own feud! Our brothers? Of course!"

Avni had just poured out tea again and the eight of them, crosslegged on the blankets, were all holding their slender, tulip shaped glasses with the little metal spoons, all shaking their heads and drawing in their breath with the hiss of disapproval.

"Yes, they are saying 'Very bad' for the two young brothers but see the two old neighbors? See the old shepherd who is going to try and make peace between two other families and hear what he says when someone mentions his feud! — 'Neighbor! I will leave this house if you say another word!'"

"Can you imagine this is nineteen hundred and seventy now? You see nothing changes with us Albanians! Five hundred years and nothing has changed!"

TWENTY-SIX

Playing Cards

When I opened my eyes I saw the back half of a camel. One of the cloth pictures was tacked up behind the bed. The bed was very comfortable, a big box built against the wall and the sheets were handwoven in a delicate ribbed fine cotton. Issa's wife got up at a quarter to five. She was sleeping on the outside and moved very quietly but I was awake. A cock had been crowing loudly under the window and then the sheep bells began to ring as the sheep were collected for pasture and then came a clonk, clonk down below as someone began to chop wood. It was Sunday morning.

I lay in bed till six but as soon as I swung my legs over the edge of the bed, Issa's wife opened the door with a big smile, stationing herself with her back to the window, to watch me get up. She was stolid and plump with a slight double chin, probably still puppy fat and like so many Albanian girls she looked totally English, so ordinary with her mousy hair, grey eyes, pale skin, looking even paler against her healthy red cheeks. Her breathing was very heavy and asthmatic. It gave her presence an irritating, labored quality as though she'd been running hard to keep track of me. She'd put my dusty battered bag up on top of her table, on the plastic cloth. Beside the table was the bride's chest. Living in the traditional way, each brother and wife had their own room over the two communal rooms below. Issa's bride offered me a small metal mirror. That and a photograph of Issa in soldier's uniform were the only other things in the room.

I couldn't think of anything to say. Issa's bride looked on the brink of helpless laughter as if anything I might say would send her over the edge. For some reason it seemed terribly important that she shouldn't laugh at me. It wasn't when I was with the men that I felt I had no place in Kosovo but when I was with the women.

Yes, I'd slept well, I said in Albanian. A bursting grin was just checked and Issa's bride composed her face again. I will not talk about the weather I resolved though, in fact, I could have given a perfect weather report. My Albanian was front page *Rilindja*: "Meeting to address the socio-economic problems arising from the blood feud" and Radio Pristina Albanian. I could have announced "And now, dear listeners, the outlook for tomorrow," just like Violeta.

It was impossible to see out of the window because Issa's bride was in the way but I'd had a look at half past five when the sheep went off. The ground sloped away past a steep-roofed barn and stable, across the orchard and disappeared on the other side of a very English-looking hedge. Beyond that was only a haze. Down below, would be the plain of Metohija.

With toothbrush, soap and towel and accompanied by Issa's bride, breathing heavily, I went down the open stairs into the kitchen. There was a fire already burning in the fireplace, with a chain above it. A three legged stool stood near the fire and under the stairs was a small wooden cradle. There was no kind of oven or stove. The only two windows on either side of the door were too high to look out of and were barred. On one was a tin mug. Beside the open door was a flour chest raised off the ground and a young woman was dolling out flour onto a board. There was no floor of any kind; I tripped over a rock as I went out. This was where the five wives lived. There was nowhere to sit except the stool and on the stairs.

I thought of what Mehmet always said; the bachelor grumbling about the demands of Prizren girls. "We say 'Marry a peasant girl.' She will be always happy because life is so hard in the village."

The wife kneading the dough smiled up at me as I reached the door. She was very pretty with a warm, sunburnt look, her hair hanging down in a thick plait over one shoulder, from under her scarf. Her trousers were flowered cotton and she wore an old cherry red jumper and, like the other women, the red woven woolen mat across the front like an apron. Another wife appeared, putting her hand to her mouth as she smiled. She looked about eight months pregnant and had no teeth at all; her cheeks were sunken in. With slightly hooded eyes and fine skin she looked typically Albanian. Just as I wondered whose wife she would be, another wife arrived pushing past Issa's bride and the pregnant wife. She was pretty too, with a sharp, tight frown.

"Good morning! Are you well? Did you sleep well?"

She said everything in Albanian and then again, briskly in Serbian. Nezir said later she only spoke Serbian because she came from a mixed village but she was so sharp and alert. It was as though she'd learned Serbian as part of an effort to get on or get out, like someone going to night school.

"Girl! What is it like with you? Do you have such a kitchen?" And she gave a brief, sharp smile.

Outside the kitchen door was the saw horse and chopping block and a six foot high pile of short, thick planks criss-crossed. Two small children were standing in the sawdust and shavings looking at me and four more a little further away. None of them looked more than about four and they were all in little Turkish trousers made out of the same checked cotton. With the women watching from the doorway I didn't try any Radio Pristina Albanian on them but just walked through them with my toothbrush, soap and towel, looking for the water tap. It was a little mountain stream caught in a pipe jutting from the bank a few yards from the house, stopped with a maize cob. Just as I was balancing on the stepping stones in the muddy pool under the pipe, Issa's bride came down the slope, ostensibly to do some washing. Grinning broadly, she obviously wanted to carry on watching my preparations for the day but Nezir appeared too, coming out of the mens' room so she retreated.

It was cool and fresh, the sky clear; still only six thirty. Up by the kitchen the high hedge was already spread with washing. Nezir, washing his hands, wanted to know what the women were like. He was pleased when I said I thought the prettiest and sunniest one making bread would be Avni's wife. It was the way she smiled at me as though Avni had been talking about our journey yesterday. She would be the right age too. Suddenly two girls peered curiously over the hedge from the lane, hearing a strange language, but did not stop.

Down the lane where the two girls had come from were the roofs of two grey stone houses but Nezir said they belonged to an entirely different village. The brothers' village was a scattering of houses that spread for several miles. Their house, with the wood crowding in behind and a small field of corn half cut on one side, looked like a house built in open, bleak country in the north of England. The walls were of grey stone, all shapes and sizes laid in mud, the window frames the shiny yellow wood like the ones sold in the Pristina market. There were four small high windows along the bottom, with the two doorways, and above a row of narrow windows, the bedrooms for the five brothers and their wives.

We had scrambled eggs for breakfast, the soft white cheese and more fresh, fried paprika. "Well, you said you liked it," Nezir reminded me.

After that, Ibrahim brought in a heavy pancake. Only the three of us were eating. Ibrahim apologized because there would be no meat while we were there. "Cutting the cow" as Nezir called it, would come later before the winter and killing a sheep, if it came at all, would be for the festival of Bajram. Chickens, I'd read, were not considered worthy enough for guests. Ibrahim sat holding the loaf of bread like a wheel in his lap, cutting out big, steamy wedges. It was baked in a metal tray, covered with a lid which was heaped with hot ash from the fire. Nezir said that was the way the women in Prizren used to bake their bread before they started sending it out to the bakers. According to "*Nomads in the Balkans*" published in 1913, that was the way the Vlachs baked. The pretty young wife in the cherry red jumper had brought the food up to the halfway point exactly where the wall of the kitchen ended and the wall of the mens' room, the *selamlik*, began.

"We saw you last night" the Serbian-speaking wife had said, by the kitchen door this morning. "How difficult it was for you without *dimi* — trousers — to sit comfortably and we were sorry."

So they had looked in the window.

We were supposed to be having a rest because of our long walk yesterday. Ibrahim and Nezir stayed in the *selamlik* and Avni and Issa joined them. I went down to the orchard where the two ponies put their ears back when they saw me. I looked in the doorway of the *selamlik*, and Nezir said we'd go for a walk after lunch. I went to the kitchen and hung about in the doorway like one of the toddlers. The wives grinned at me. I still didn't know what to say, not even in Serbian. We had nothing in common not even the great sisterhood-of-women things like marriage and childbirth. Nor, if I thought of my endless omelettes and packets of biscuits, even cooking. And to the wife who spoke Serbian I felt like speaking least of all. What good would it do. *Shall I send you some books? Do you want to run away?* Maybe she was married to the brother who was away.

The children came up silently behind me in a cluster, like chickens. Their hair was uncut, their skins delicate, eyes big and round birthday card eyes. Each one had tiny blue beads round its wrists and in its hair. The boys' hair would be cut in a ceremony when they were about seven. There was a temptation to leave it as long as possible because once the hair was cut and another male officially joined the household then that boy would become part of any blood feud.

I picked up one of the toddlers in an effort to show some traditional female reflexes and he or she stank so much I had to go and uncork the stream and wash my arm. The Serbian-speaking wife watched me from the doorway with her sharp little smile.

Avni was apologizing because the brothers had to work. It was still Sunday morning but as Nezir's father said, peasants didn't have weekends. Islam, the eldest, was away cutting wood, Avni was loading the newly cut wood on to one of the ponies. Ibrahim was still talking to Nezir and politely switched to Serbian when I joined them. He was talking about a sugar factory he'd worked in near Belgrade after the war when he'd been discharged from the army. They went in coaches to other factories; they played football and learned hygiene and attended lectures. Ibrahim had worked there for fifteen years. Everyone was 'Comrade' he said, all together, Serbs, Bosnians, Slovaks, the directors.

Nezir told me in English that Ibrahim had been away too long; he had no special skills back here, living in the communal way with the brothers. He'd come back because Islam, the eldest, kept sending him letters telling him how his loyalty should be to his brothers, how they needed him, how he should take a bride and have children. His son now played round his feet as he trimmed the wood. Ibrahim looked in his early forties, dark and quiet, like Avni but much broader with big stubby fingers and a worried, burdened look. Nezir said that like all the brothers he had good reason to look burdened.

The eldest son of Islam, the eldest brother and head of the household, was an idiot child.

He'd lain in the *selamlik* last night, in the corner, waving his legs in the air and giggling. Islam had smiled at him and looked slyly at me as though I should admire his child. He was certainly the oldest, at least ten but he couldn't be sent off with the sheep, or given any basic task. Worse, he was deliberately vicious. He'd already attacked one of the other children; now they were all having to be watched.

"That's why I keep my son with me now when I work." Ibrahim said.

When I'd gone to the lavatory Islam's son had thrown stones at the door and sniggered. He would have been a burden to any family, let alone a poor one and especially as the eldest son of the eldest son. According to the Unwritten Law the head of the house should be, if not the eldest, then the most able. But the slow and wary Islam was probably the least suited of all the brothers. Nezir asked what his wife was like. She must have been the one to come in last, standing behind even Issa's wife, peering round at me, picking her nose and giggling. Nezir said that explained everything — the dirty children, the lack of organization. The head of the household is supposed to choose the best wife to organize the women, not necessarily his own wife. But thinking of Islam's closed and wary face, I found it hard to see him choosing another wife, let alone the quick, sharp, Serbian-speaking one.

"Are you bored?" cried Avni in Albanian, appearing in the doorway.

"Yo! *Marzallah!*" No! Heaven forbid!

"Thank-you very much!" Avni exclaimed with a grin, bowing, hand on heart.

The pretty wife with the sunny smile was cooking, preparing lunch as she'd prepared breakfast. It must have been her week for cooking. The Law says the mistress of the household allots the tasks to the wives and they are rotated on a weekly basis. She smiled her sunny smile. The other wives were nowhere in sight. I had come to get the cards. After a few bashful sentences in Albanian I retreated; she was busy cooking.

Ibrahim was smoothing the rug; Avni cross-legged, rubbing his hands in anticipation. With Islam and Nezir there were five of us so Avni and Islam played against Ibrahim and Nezir or me till lunch, an easy game called *Pishpelik*. Islam couldn't count up his score, not even to ten. Avni his partner added it up, Islam looking intently out of narrowed eyes, watching the counting.

After lunch, sweet paprika fried in egg and hot fresh bread, apples and plums, Avni rubbed his hands again and got out the cards. But I kept pestering him and Nezir until we did go for our walk up past the house, through the pine trees and suddenly we came out into an open, grassy stretch, another tough looking stone house by itself, a low stone wall, bracken and heather and blackberries. And away behind us the land went bounding down in vast waves of grass-green forested slopes, down and down. And down there, down below, were peaks.

I was walking backwards looking at the view and eating blackberries. Avni scolded me for eating things out of the hedge: I'd become ill. So much for the natural wisdom of the peasants, I thought. "Vitamin C! Vitamin C!" I cried but Avni was adamant. Soon we were back in the woods, the track worn so deep over the years it closed in on either side waist high. A herd of sheep being driven down, flooded round us, their hooves pattering through the tree trunks round our heads. The shepherd in black homespun, holding a crook, greeted Nezir and Avni. Before and behind the sheep walked a Sar mountain dog in the spiked iron collar, defense against being bitten in the neck by a wolf. Bigger than Alsatians, one was cream colored with a tail like a chow, one grey. Both had snub, bear like noses. Nezir said proudly they were the only dogs who could fight and kill wolves and would, alone, attack a bear. Sar dogs never herded the sheep. They were only for protection. The dogs passed us, aloof, watchful. "Don't go near them!" Nezir warned.

As we came out of the little wood, suddenly ahead of us were ranges of forested peaks rising up and a narrow blackberry lined lane leading stolidly towards it all. The sun was getting low.

"You can come tomorrow with Issa,' Avni said, "and go further."

But tomorrow was Monday and Nezir had classes.

"Oh! Nezir will stay!" Avni exclaimed.

I was sorry Avni wouldn't be free on Monday. Perhaps it was just because we'd all made the trip together, but I felt most at home with Avni and he had the best sense of humor. I asked Nezir in English whether he didn't agree.

"That's all you think about," he said " whether Albanians have a sense of humor."

He picked up a hefty stick and twirled it round his head. "I'm taking this home to keep for my wife like a true Albanian!"

It caught on a low branch and disintegrated, showering him with rotten flakes of wood. He was left holding about three inches. Soon Avni and I had to sit down we were laughing so much. Nezir started to head for home.

"Oh Ne-ZIR!" Avni called after him from the grass, "Why are you not laughing?"

After our supper of eggs, fried paprika, milk and cheese, Avni got out the tea things and Issa the cards and the four of us played, taking it in turns, someone counting for Islam. Issa and Avni slapped their thighs and rubbed their hands, flinging their cards down with an *Allah!* when they were good, an 'Oof!' or a 'Poof!' when they were poor. And the two brothers came again, the farmer and the shepherd. They played cards too and Nezir and I watched. We had the ten o clock news from Belgrade, via Radio Pristina, on the transistor. Avni was tea man again and again we declared we were not '*merzite*' — bored — No! *Marzallah!* Heaven forbid!

Ibrahim was upset on Monday morning because his son missed having his picture taken. I'd photographed the children all in a row, gazing at the camera but Ibrahim's son had been with him and when he'd appeared all the film had been used up. There had been the sunny bride, peeling potatoes by the kitchen door, the wives in a row too, Issa and his bride in all her finery. I'd spent half the morning waiting for Issa's bride to appear. She'd gone upstairs to get ready for her photograph and was gone for one and a half hours. When she finally appeared she was in her wedding finery; lilac flowered nylon trousers, a white wedding blouse and gold necklace. The other wives smiled tolerantly. She'd only been married six months, they'd told me. By the time she emerged Issa had disappeared. He finally arrived in a jacket, big moustache bristling and they both took a deep breath and held it and came out looking as though they'd been lined up against the house wall to be shot. Nezir asked Avni to take a picture of us on the ponies and Avni did, clicking the little nob twice to be sure and heaving a big sigh of relief to have got it right.

Nezir had decided he could stay another day. He only had two classes on Monday and when he didn't turn up, Mehmet would take them. So in the morning we took the rug out into the orchard under one of the plum trees and Issa brought the cards. There were four of us; Issa, Ibrahim, Nezir and I. Avni had left for Prizren, the two ponies loaded with the wood, the wood that had to pay for everything, Nezir said; the tea, sugar and the cigarettes, the salt.

"What about everything else?"

"When you're a peasant there can't be anything else."

The wood was sold to be made into the wooden pattens, those high soled mules everyone wore, dragging them to and fro across the courtyards. Avni got 1500 dinars each trip, so 3000 a week and shoeing cost 500 a hoof; so that was 2000 right there. Three thousand dinars was about a pound.

Issa had been gathering plums and came and poured them on to the rug, the small, oval, purple Yugoslav plums. There was a soft thud from near the hedge under the pear tree. I said to Issa we could each have a piece of pear too.

"No, excuse me, no we can't. That's Ahmet's pear."

Ibrahim explained that last summer when they had needed money the brothers had sold the pear tree to Ahmet, one of their fellow villagers. Now the pears, whether on or off the tree belonged to Ahmet.

"Yes, It's a good tree," Ibrahim said. "Ahmet would not have bought it if it wasn't."

The brothers had asked me about English food and I had said one big difference was that Yugoslavs could never imagine a meal without bread and traditionally, the English could never imagine their main meal without potatoes. So Monday morning the sunny bride had been peeling potatoes by the kitchen door and at lunch time we all had to wade through fried and then mashed potatoes, eaten with bread.

"You must be careful what you say," Nezir told me. "You are a guest and as far as they can the brothers will do everything they think you wish."

After our English lunch Issa said he was ready to take us for our real walk, high enough to see both Kosovo and Metohija far below. A group of boys were playing a kind of cricket or baseball on the first grassy stretch up beyond the wood, the bowler using a piece of stick for a ball, the batter a shepherd's staff, the others standing in a classic semi-circle as fielders in front. Issa borrowed a staff as we passed and joined in, giving the stick an almighty crack not forward but high up, everyone waiting to catch it when it fell and Issa trying to swipe it up again before it hit the ground or was caught. Issa was out first ball.

Issa led us at a fast pace. We soon passed the boundary between our village and the next: a cross set in a cairn of stones on a grassy ridge. There were the remains of an old police post too, from the time of old Serbia, Avni had told us yesterday, that is from between the wars. We came to another marker.

"This the Italians did," Issa said.

That must have been in 1941. The Italians were only here, occupying Kosovo, for three years at the most. And up they came straight away from their headquarters in Prizren, toiling up here and left their mark. It wasn't far from the others. Like a dog peeing where the others did.

"And this one is from the Turks," said Issa.

Boundary stones were sacred for Albanians, Margaret Hasluck wrote. Albanians swore by stones. A blood feud never changed boundaries. *The Unwritten Law* stated that though a hundred men die the stone remains. A man's house was sacred too. If it were empty for a hundred years, it was always known whose house it was and no-one had the right to take it.

Brushing out of a copse into a lane, we found ourselves on the edge of a mountain. At our feet were treetops covering slopes and gorges away through the sunlight. Issa turned us round and pointed ahead, to a higher forested peak. There — there were the limits of their wood-gathering rights. It all looked impenetrable, bear-infested furry green. — "See! The next village boundary began ... there!" Nezir saw. Issa lined me up behind his pointing finger as though I were firing a rifle but I still couldn't see. It all looked virgin forest to me. But every inch of forest, every tree, all that looked so remote and majestic was delineated, demarcated, spoken for like Ahmet's pear tree, even the windfalls, the fallen branches.

Avni had told us yesterday how hard it had been a few years ago; men climbing up here on winter nights to steal wood. How they'd not dared show a light because of the foresters, how they'd risked their lives for fuel. I'd asked Nezir whether Avni had been talking about the years before the Brioni Plenum. Had the Plenum affected them much, up here?

"Of course!" Nezir had been amazed at such a stupid question.

We were climbing up through the trees, higher than the villagers' rights of wood gathering and came on the first summer pasture, a broad meadow with beech woods on either side. The grass, close cropped by sheep, made it seem all the more like an immense cricket pitch or stately lawn. It was about four o' clock and we were walking slower, sweating in the sun. Issa started telling us about the latest blood feud on the verge of breaking out.

A man had betrothed his daughter to a young suitor for two million dinars. That was two years' wages for me, as a lector at the faculty. He'd taken the money and then sold his daughter again, to another young man from another village. Now the first man had neither bride nor money and what's more had been made a fool of. Issa said he couldn't imagine why the father hadn't already been shot. I couldn't imagine how any Albanian could think he could get away with it. With an Albanian it was bad enough to make sarcastic remarks. "If you were a man," Nezir had remarked when we were discussing teaching methods, "with your ironical remarks and sarcasm to make us work, then you would certainly have been at least hit by now."

Yes, Issa was saying, buying and selling of brides is wrong but who will stop it? If I were Issa I probably wouldn't want to stop it till I'd sold my daughters too. Issa would have worked at least two years for his bride and it would be hard to give up the idea of some unearned income when his daughters got older. The payment for the wife is payment for a worker and a good investment. "Our mountain women are incredibly strong, stronger than the men," Nezir had said.

"There is much competition for brides. Issa tells me at the moment there are not enough to go round. You can stay and find a husband! Too many boys are born."

That was what gave Kosovo its incredible vitality; all those families of six or seven boys, still on the land, still in Kosovo.

But what about Issa's bride — her heavy, labored breathing. If the most important thing was to be strong? Would that have made her cheaper?

Nezir laughed. "Ask Issa if you're so interested!"

One of those questions which seemed so straight-forward when reading *Nomads of the Balkans* until you come face to face with the person. "So, how much did you pay for your wife?"

Though Issa might not have minded the question. He'd already asked me proudly what I thought of his bride. He couldn't ask Nezir or any other man. Nezir said Issa had mentioned that there were no children coming yet and he'd been married for six months. That would have been why his wife had been chosen for me to sleep with as there were no children to disturb me. She was as quiet as a mouse, even her breathing beside me soft and unobtrusive. She had waited up late Saturday and Sunday till nearly midnight. And I'd not really talked to her. A sweet smile and she just wished me goodnight. Very soft in Albanian, the adjective coming after the noun: *Naten e mire*, Night good; *gjuehen e embel*, Dreams sweet.

Issa was merciless. We had to keep climbing, to the higher ridge, sweat stinging our eyes, and though there were deep shady woods on either side he drove us on. Finally with a break in the trees he led us to the very edge of the grass and there, there over the tops of trees, woods, forests, valleys, gorges, everything there in the distance —

"See!"

Yes, I saw this time. There was the whole of Kosovo to the horizon.

"And now!" Issa herded us in the still boiling sun across our football pitch of green, our double cricket pitch of grass. "See! METOHIJAAH!"

The plain of Metohija. If it had been dark, Issa said, we could have seen the lights of Prizren and Djakovica. We were on the great dividing ridge between Kosovo and Metohija. Nezir said our village was the furthest away of any of their customers. More than six hours travel and the peasants would go down to Kosovo. We were on Sar, snow-covered for four months of the year and when you climbed up high enough you found woods and hedges, herds of sheep and forests. The authors of *Nomads of the Balkans* related how they made the Vlach children laugh when they all set off climbing up into the beech woods, up to the summer pasture, because they said in England big trees came on the flat. Everyone knew, the children told them, that you only got forests up mountains.

Down below was the sizzling plain, Kosovo: the Pristina bus charging along, its dusty sides too hot to the touch and if we swivelled round and crossed the grass and waited an hour it would appear, grinding along the melting tarmac to Prizren in Metohija. Far down below were the grapes and water melons, the mosques and gypsy musicians, the piles of rubbish in the back lanes, the police stations and tiny crumbling forts raised a fraction over the citizenry. Down below were the occupations. All they did up here was leave their mark and retreat. The whole geography of resistance became clear and up here resistance seemed Anglo-Saxon; reserves of sturdy English apples, plums and pears, cornfields, boys playing cricket, forming their characters, hedges full of black berries, bracken to sleep on and beech woods to explore, fresh mountain water, cool air, the temperate zone.

"The village where we have come is one respected by all Albanians," Nezir said as we stood looking down at the old Turkish plain. "In Albania it is known too. It has a great tradition of bravery. One of the great leaders against the Turks before the Balkan wars, came from here. The Turkish troops burned the village down. And under Rankovic once the whole village was turned out one night into the snow to stand in the winter, to confess where one Albanian was and no-one, not even one woman or child would give in."

Three boys joined us, all with hefty staffs and we trooped into the shade of a beech wood, the boys calling to each through the trees, the sunlight coming in shafts between the trunks. Perhaps there used to be *hajduks* up here; Balkan Christians taking to the forest in spring to harry the Turks and slipping back home when the bad weather came. We drank from a mountain stream deep in the wood, all lining up, waiting our turn. The water made my hands ache it was so cold. The boys led the charge out into the sun again slinging their shepherds' staffs away across the turf and then collecting them as they walked along. Ahead almost on the skyline was a large herd of sheep, their bells ringing. Nezir was asking the boys what they were going to be. One said a *hodja* a Moslem priest.

Would he go to a *medrese*? A religious school?

"Yes!" he shouted, slinging his staff away across the springy turf.

We reached the herd. The shepherd, his heavy black hooded coat on the grass behind him, was up there for the whole summer. He knew Issa and the boys. His big Sar dog studied us. Issa had a surprise for him. He sat down cross-legged on the turf, clearing a patch in front of him free of sheep droppings and rubbed his hands. Issa, said Nezir, had asked him to bring the cards. The boys and the shepherd were enchanted. The shepherd sat up, cross-legged, the boys gathered round. Issa, Nezir, the shepherd and me; four for *Pishpelik*.

The cards, brand new two days ago, were dog-eared and limp. They'd been flung down in triumph so often since then, seized with relish, clutched in despair. The Sar mountain dog, looking even bigger now we were sitting down, patrolled the sheep first one way, then the other. He lay down heavily, still looking at us. The sheep bells, roughly beaten out of metal, dinged as the sheep wrenched and ripped the turf. I gave up my place at cards to one of the boys, Nezir did to another and we went away over the turf to look one more time at Kosovo on one side and Metohija on the other. We could hear the sheep bells on the breeze and the voice of Issa, above the others as he dealt the cards.

"I'll never play *Pishpelik* again as long as I live" Nezir said.

When we'd been talking about the case of the bride who'd been sold twice ("Sounds like Earl Stanley Gardner" Nezir said) he had explained that no Albanian ever marries a girl from his village. Like the all the other customs it was part of the Unwritten Law, a safeguard against inbreeding but also to ensure friends and alliances in time of trouble.

"So your wife's family will come to your aid even if no-one else does."

Each household's strength was considered, like Montenegrins, in terms of 'guns;' the number of 'men' from the age of twelve. Rich men kept young relatives living with them if they were good shots, a permanent bodyguard. And sons and daughters like medieval princes and princesses were betrothed when children, to further friendships and confirm alliances. The farmer, whom we'd met with his brother the shepherd, had already betrothed his son of seven. We saw him that evening when we were all invited to go for supper, lying on a sheepskin, near the stove, a handsome boy.

The brothers lived only two fields away. We walked there in the moonlight. The mens' room was on the first floor, spacious, able to sit fifty men but warm and cosy because underneath us and on the walls were sheepskins, black, white and dark brown, each one representing a 'kurban bajram' a sacrificial *bajram*. We had seen no sign of the women and the brothers, tall and lean in their black and white costume, seemed like two bachelors, self-sufficient and content; the shepherd with his weatherbeaten face like an old sailor.

Nezir asked the farmer whether he would betroth his daughter as he had his son. He said he would see when she got older, about school and marriage. "I would not like to do anything against her will."

When it was time for us to eat the shepherd came forward with the bowl and kettle for us to wash our hands. His brother followed with the towel. One after the other we held our hands for the water, the brothers bending low, feet deep in the sheepskins. They looked so perceptive, with their shrewd glances, their deft movements. I knew it was because of them Nezir was missing classes. It was when Avni said we'd been invited to the brothers' that Nezir said he'd stay. Nezir suddenly whispered; "Look!"

The shepherd, the older brother, was holding the bowl and kettle now for his brother. "Did you hear?" Nezir said softly. "The younger brother has just said 'No, brother, you are older. It is not fitting you pour the water first for me.' I can't tell you how wonderful it sounds in Albanian!"

The farmer, the younger brother, took the kettle and bowl and poured the water first over his brother's hands.

"These are real Albanians!" Nezir said. "This is what being an Albanian means! If they go on like this they will make me *cry*!"

After supper, the shepherd, joking about how undomestic he was, got out the tea things and put on the kettle.

"Now you will have a real mountain evening!" Nezir declared. "Now with two such men you see real Albanian life as it was lived. They will talk about the history of the village and the Turkish campaigns. And when they speak they use such proverbs and sayings! I swear you can have two faculties and not be so quick as them."

Issa had sat up too, rubbing his hands. He smoothed the strands of sheepskin in front of his crossed knees. He'd brought the cards over because tomorrow we'd be leaving and taking them away. Ibrahim, Avni and Issa sat up. Avni turned to Nezir and me near the stove and asked us if we wanted to play. "NO!" I said.

The shepherd, waiting for the kettle to boil, looked up at me from under his eyebrows. He understood. But after all, the brothers were their guests too.

Nezir muttered savagely in English, "We'll take them away tomorrow! I'll take them away just for spite!"

At ten we listened to the news on the transistor and said goodnight. The farmer came with us to the end of his field and shook hands. His brother was coming all the way and going up to the pasture. "I'm going to sleep with my sheep!" he said laughing. "I never sleep under a roof at this time of year!"

We said goodbye in the lane near Ahmet's pear tree. The shepherd loped off, through the moonlight and shadows in his black and white.

We were going back a shorter way that would only take four hours, striking the road at Suva Reka, the first small town on the way from Prizren to Pristina. That was where the village went to the doctor. From there we could catch one of the Pristina buses back to Prizren. Islam had left early in the morning because Tuesday was market day in Suva Reka. Saying goodbye to Ibrahim and Avni, we started about eleven with Issa coming to show us the way. The wives flocked down to the field gate to shake hands with me and say goodbye so Nezir turned away immediately, walking on ahead with Issa. They looked an attractive group in the sun, colorful in their red mat aprons, Avni's wife the prettiest, her gold earrings shining, skin a beautiful sun-kissed color like a Macedonian girl. They were all wearing gold bracelets. Behind them the children stood in a row, big eyed. Ibrahim was there holding his son and Avni, by himself to one side, grinning fiercely because he was so sorry not to be free to come down with us.

The wives had come up to me that morning, a deputation, when no men were about. The one who spoke Serbian their leader, with her authoritative "Girl!" She had asked me if it were easy to use shampoo on the hair. How was it done? Did I have some with me to show them? No, but I could get some in Prizren; give it to Nezir to leave in the stables for Avni to pick up.

The Serbian-speaking wife looked doubtful. There was no reason to think I'd do anything for them. It had been the men who'd said on Sunday morning, "The women are working in the field, cutting corn. You can go and talk to them" and I didn't go.

I'd been enjoying hospitality in the time-honored, traditional way of female travelers in the Balkans; special, honorary, temporary status with the men and yet unlimited access to the female world. The double status that no male traveler could match. But I didn't feel like a traveler anymore. I'd been in Kosovo too long.

I had become a Kosovo woman; the new kind, frightened of being dragged back into the world of the old kind. Like the Albanian girl who cried at her new husband, "I've been to Teachers' Training College! You can't ask me to clean the bath!" The fear of Emina, still not legally married to Agim, even though Agim was the perfect husband. Agim, helping Emina so much, fearful one day Emina might become like so many of the women in his village, gaunt and worn out. Like one of the Third year who in an oral exam had been asked about his family. "My mother died and my father married again and now I help my new mother because I don't want her to become so tired and die too." Emina's mother, fluttery and timid, broken not only by her eldest son's exile. Emina had said "Father was a hard man when he was young. But then such was the custom."

Issa led the way down the lane, past Ahmet's pear-tree and down through a cluster of grey stone houses; the path worn so deep that the courtyard doors started at waist high level, their front door steps made of boulders. Perched on rocky outcrops in the sea of cornfields they made me think of Adriatic stone houses. There didn't seem to be a mosque anywhere.

"Oh, we have one," Issa nodded vaguely over fields and woods. Nezir asked if he went and Issa laughed. "Oh, *Bajram* to *Bajram*" which is like saying "Christmas and Easter."

He swung down beside us, face shiny in the midday sun, still wearing his fair-isle pullover, the white cap perched on the back of his head. The lane wound on down between fields and hawthorn and blackberry hedges, under plum and greengage trees. Boulders still reared out of the ground underfoot and in the middle of the meadows, among the flowers. Butterflies, '*flutur*' in Albanian, fluttered by.

My bag was crammed with plums, hard boiled eggs, cheese, bread, apples, everything except Ahmet's pears. Issa was swinging it so hard I was afraid it would all sail out. Nezir told Issa to turn back; he'd been walking down with us for half an hour. I joked at least we could take it in turns to carry the bag.

"No!" cried Issa, swinging it away out of reach, " I am 'Porter Number One!'"

He'd been a porter on Skopje station, that summer, he said. I stopped dead, stunned.

Issa, whom I saw as so young and naive hadn't mentioned Skopje, hadn't shown off. Skopje was, after all, a capital city with many tourists going down to Greece. Issa had taken Skopje in his stride, the tireless Albanian stride.

"Porter Number One!" squawked Issa again at the hedgerows imitating a bourgeois Macedonian lady with too much luggage and on we went.

If I had seen Avni and Issa without the white cap I'd probably have thought they were Serbian, swinging along, not too tall, upright and jaunty like they do in central Serbia, trilby hats low and straight across their foreheads, coats slung across one shoulder, looking like amateur bullfighters setting off not so much to fight the bull as maybe have a drink with it.

"Go back, Issa!" Nezir half commanded. Forty minutes had gone by and still Issa came down. We couldn't get lost; we only had to follow the path.

"It's no good telling me when to leave you," Issa said cheerfully, "Islam has told me when."

That is, Issa was escorting us out of their territory. If anything happened to us within those limits, it would be the brothers' responsibility. It was an hour before Issa left us, at a point where the path plunged steeply, forded a stream and looped up the other side of a gully, round the walls of another of the Adriatic clusters of grey stone houses. Here Issa said goodbye. He said something to Nezir in Albanian, laughed and turned back up the path.

"Issa says he is sorry to see us go — 'even though Mary has been keeping me from my wife for three nights.'"

The path forked on the other side for the first time, and we hesitated. Then we heard "OH NE-ZIR!"

Issa, cupping his hands was calling across to us; we should take the upper path. He waved and turned away, youngest brother and Porter Number One.

When we reached Suva Reka three hours later, carts and horsemen were still leaving the market and we met Islam, starting the long ride back. He leant down from his horse, which was bigger than Avni's ponies, his narrow, cautious expression now looking haughty and horseman-like. We shook hands again by the side of the road and thanked him for his hospitality and he rode on very upright, taking the route we'd followed coming down. Back up through all those layers of scenery, through the red earth and Spanish oak scrub, the wide sweep like moorland, then onto the slate, the country lanes and hedges between the meadows and cornfields. He would get back at dusk like we had, riding into the yard as night fell and the lights of Prizren and Suva Reka started to sparkle below in the distance. And maybe the two brothers would come round, the farmer and the shepherd, and talk over our visit and Issa would bring out the battered cards.

1970

TWENTY-SEVEN

▬

Montenegrin Easter

Suleiman had come back from a year in California with a new respect for Emina and me. "You are both really quite fashionable. American girls don't bother how they look either."

He could make coffee now. I thought I heard him say once to Emina, "Sit down, I'll get it" but I might have been mistaken.

The English department had certainly changed; brimming with students now, most of them having learned some English at school. Suleiman, Ilija and I had wanted to divide the students according to their ability but the new Albanian assistants said there would be too many Serbians in any advanced group. It would look bad for Albanians. So the students were divided by nationality. This was much harder on many Albanians, those from Montenegro whose first language was Serbian, or those like Nezir and Mehmet. "All the text books, everything we did in grammar was in Serbian" Nezir grumbled.

"We have to face it," Suleiman announced. "From now on it's all politics."

The Third and Fourth were still mixed but when the students heard I would be leaving the Faculty and came round to say goodbye, the groups were either all Albanian or Serbian.

Nezir had already given me an incredible present. It was the ramskin from his first *Kurban Bajram*, Sacrificial Bajram, when he'd bought a ram for the family for the first time, with his teachers' salary. Nezir said the ram had never been shorn and as he stood in the courtyard his coat was so long you could not see his legs at all.

"What a nest for fleas!" Faruk, the actor exclaimed. "They'll be coming up from Macedonia!" "Wrap yourself in that when you are sick" Agim told me "and it will take all the aches away."

The skin was golden. It lay on the floor like a rippling corn field, a great lion's mane. It stopped everyone in their tracks.

"For an Albanian" said Mehmet, "your room is like a dream."

For a Serbian it was a shock: it was too *a la turka*.

Milenka, leading the charge of the Serbian Third year down my hall with a bottle of Three Star Export Brandy and an early farewell card, had given an abrupt "Oh!" on reaching the doorway. In my room you had to take off your shoes.

It was Milenka and Olga who'd invited me to Pec for the Easter weekend. Pec, the historic center of the Serbian church, would be the perfect place on Easter morning to hear the Orthodox cry "Christ is Risen!" Nada and Milena would be pleased. I would be doing something Serbian in Kosovo for a change.

The weather was beautiful, another Kosovo spring, my fourth. And my last. I wasn't sure what I would do next but I knew I should leave. Dig myself out of Kosovo. "You're one of us now, Mary!" everyone was saying. That was the problem. Just as no-one in Pristina had believed I would ever stay now no-one thought I would ever leave. I was starting to think that myself. The longest spell of regular employment in my entire life had been in the Balkans.

The girls picked me up on Good Friday morning, down the hill. There was still livestock grazing round the Faculty. It was such a bright April day I was afraid my big boxes of chocolates would melt in the back window of the car before we got to Pec. One of Milenka's neighbors was taking us, a quiet, middle-aged man. The girls were learning to drive. Milenka said that's why she hadn't been to classes lately. "I take my test next week!" Olga was taking her test soon too.

"Mother says, 'Either pass your driving test or your English exam. One or the other!'"

So much for the English Department.

Milenka and Olga shared a room in Pristina, they were both giving English lessons. I'd be staying with Olga's family in Pec. "But to me for Easter dinner, Sunday!" Milenka commanded, tossing back her red hair.

Our driver turned round and grinned. Didn't I know Milenka used to be the champion runner of Pec? Of course. That long auburn hair streaming in the wind, the energy, the gusto, those sturdy calves.

I admired Milenka. She didn't let Kosovo cramp her style. Noisy, witty and irreverent, when Milenka came into a classroom, the class began. She had a generous bust and full lips and could put down any boy, Serb or Albanian and in good English. But she remained nice, a nice girl. I didn't know how she did it.

Olga was wearing mascara and green eyeshadow. She had big black eyes, black hair combed straight back, like a ballet dancer, flat and shining. She was in black trousers and top with a trendy, sleeveless, emerald green, string bag cardy thing on top. I didn't even know the words any more for those things.

The car sped through Pristina and up the hill past the hospital in a rush of talk of landlords, cars, clothes and parties. With all the eyeshadow, noise and laughter, I felt I was on holiday with tourists, suddenly, passing through.

The girls wanted to know about Radmila, one of our visiting teachers from Belgrade. Middle-aged, single, deep in research, speaking perfect English with dry wit, taste and sensibility, Radmila had been terribly ill and missed classes for several months.

"It's true, isn't it, Mary," they asked, "Radmila had a bay-bee?"

I gave up. If they said that about RADMILA what on earth must they have said about me?

"Is Milovan really leaving?" Milenka asked as we turned onto the Prizren road. "— Ha! Then I'll pass Diploma now!"

Serbian students as well as Albanian had always blamed Milovan when they failed. Milovan who in oral exams would sombrely command the mute, paralyzed student in front of us who had forgotten all his English, even 'yes' and 'no' — "Well, then. Tell us a joke." I wondered whom the students would blame now. All Serbian heads of department would be leaving now. Murad had become the first Rector of the new University of Pristina: Doctor of Biology, the Albanian blacksmith's son whose family had fled from Scutari because they were 'in blood.'

Suleiman had forecast trouble in the heady days of celebration about Albanian language rights. "'Mother tongue!' 'Mother tongue!' That's all we hear like some magic formula! You'll see! Albanian students will think they *must* pass now. They think simply because they speak Albanian they don't have to work anymore!"

Olga used to be an excellent student, like Milenka, but she wasn't coming to classes any more. She didn't say why.

We were stopped for a road-worthy check. Larks were singing over the newly ploughed fields. The traffic was getting heavier. Maybe they were all Orthodox Christian families, Serbians, going home for Easter, heading across Kosovo to the lusher plain of Metohija. The landscape here was like a simple Turkish interior. Perfect proportions, exact relation of poplar trees to road and horizon; the hills and distant mountains edging the plain of Kosovo all round like the scallops round a Turkish dish.

The mountains rose up as we approached Prizren: more buildings now climbing up into the furry folds and creases above the town. We drove straight through, swinging round to the Pec road, past the little cafe *London* and the sign post opposite: "Albanian frontier 17 KM" pointing down the mulberry lined road.

"Have you ever been to Prizren, Mary?" asked the girls.

Milenka said *she* hadn't. I couldn't believe it. PRIZren in Serbian, PrizREN in Albanian.

The stress was always on the last syllable in Albanian names, the 'e' silent: Kosovë, Gjakovë, Prishtinë. In Serbian it was the opposite, of course, at the beginning.

We sped past LANDOVICA, LANDOVICË and the memorial to the two young revolutionaries and friends, Ramiz Sadik the Albanian and Boris Vukmanovic, the Serb, who were executed there together in 1943. They were our symbols in Kosovo of Brotherhood and Unity. The wedding buses and cars from Prizren always came out to that spot, the gypsy banging the tambourine and the wedding guests singing, a little excursion for the women before they headed back into Prizren to 'fetch the bride.' Tito's torch was starting from there that year, to arrive in Belgrade for his birthday. The torch had been made by two silver-smiths in Prizren. The first runner was a student called Bashkim, (Unity), from a little place I'd never heard of, *Liri*: Freedom.

On the outskirts of Djakovica Olga suddenly exploded: "Look! They've got to have their name first! Every time!"

There was the name, written twice as they were everywhere now, even if the difference between the Serbian and Albanian was only one letter or the mute Albanian e:

GJAKOVË
DJAKOVICA

Every notice in the department had to be in both Serbian and Albanian. Ilija, as secretary, was always trying to catch one of the new Albanian assistants to duplicate his Serbian notices. If only the Serbian went up it would usually be torn down. Suleiman's answer had always been: do everything in English like they do in the English school in Istanbul. Write everything in English. That will shut them ALL up. The new Albanian assistants didn't care much for Suleiman. They told the students he was a 'Turk.' I didn't think some of them cared much for me, either. Well, even Nezir and Mehmet said I was very hard on Albanians, that I should realize their standards would be lower.

Just past Djakovica and on the road to Pec or Pejë or Ipek for the

Turks among us, we ran into another road block. The mountains were marching with us, beyond the fields and orchards, in majestic navy blue shadow on their western slopes, the beautiful Albanian frontier. A young policeman in the light grey uniform was approaching slowly, with the professional policeman's plod. Our driver wound down the window. The handsome policeman leant his elbow on the top and said, "*Mire dita!*"

And in the same measured way, with the same deliberate emphasis on the three syllables, our driver replied, "*Dobar dan!*"

Good day in Albanian versus Good day in Serbian. Each syllable in Serbian canceled out the syllable of Albanian that went before.

Our driver explained in Serbian we'd been checked. The car was roadworthy.

In Serbian: "Where is the first aid box?"

At home in Pec. "I do have one," the driver said mildly.

"No first aid box in the car," the handsome young policeman intoned, po faced, "That will be five thousand dinars, Comrade. You know the law."

Olga was blazing, neat nostrils twitching. Milenka was silent, heavily ironic. In silence our driver paid and in silence we drove off.

"*Siptar!*" Olga exploded.

I wondered if it would have made any difference if the driver had spoken Albanian. Like most Montenegrins from Pec he said he knew it. Albanians were so delighted when I spoke Albanian. They didn't always know I was English or thought I was a roaming Hungarian waitress. I'd never heard a Serb voluntarily speak Albanian, except Nikola, the Montenegrin student in Nezir's year.

"I KNEW he was *Siptar* as soon as I saw him!" Olga was exclaiming.

"Can you always tell?"

"HA! You can tell them a mile off!"

The first year I taught at the Faculty when it was still a compliment to say of an Albanian, "His Serbian is very good" I'd heard about the Albanian student on a visit to Belgrade who'd gone to a dance and danced with Serbian girls. "— And they never even knew!"

"Knew what?" I'd asked the first time.

On our left was the long avenue of tall chestnut trees leading to Decani — Decane, one of the greatest medieval Serbian monasteries. Fran, the Albanian country Catholic from Nezir's year, was teaching there. He had come up to my flat when Robert Kennedy was killed. He'd been crying. And I had thought the whole thing about being Albanian Catholic was just of historic interest. Along the road were the '*kule*,' the stone houses of

Metohija built by the Albanians. Squat, grey towers with slit windows, about as cosy as a Norman keep. No Albanian, it was said, ever sat at an open window. The cryptic explanation was: "It's not good for your health."

Sometimes it still wasn't. A common enough headline in *Rilindja* ran: "Victim shot through window." And there was still the traditional re-action, if spoken a little more ironically nowadays: — Well, if you're going to do something like that, i.e. sit by an open window, well, what do you expect?

When the Young Turks conducted their campaigns against the re-bellious Albanians in Kosovo before the Balkan wars, one of their decrees was the widening of windows.

"What's that over there?" I asked.

"Pec brewery!" Milenka cried, "The best beer in Kosmet!"

Olga lived not far from the Patriarchate at the mouth of the Rugovo gorge. A mountain stream rippled down outside the gate with ducks swinging round in it, tails wagging in the cold afternoon air. Her brother was in the kitchen. Dark too, very handsome and direct. Elbows on the kitchen table, he talked football. All the best players in Kosmet, he announced, are from Pec. "It's the air."

Nezir said it was the money. He said the best were from Prizren but they couldn't pay them so much and Pec lured them away.

Olga's mother, dark and lively, was coloring eggs for Easter. Other women kept dropping in, dressed all in black too. The kitchen was full of noise and laughter. I felt homesick for Belgrade suddenly. Nada was still teaching, her young son almost four; everyone still living together in the same old flat. Milena had married again and she had a little girl. Even with her mother there she put in such long days. Up at five, out to work by six, fourteen hours later, nodding off. ("Mary! Wake me up when the news comes on!") Everyone in Belgrade would be glad to hear I'd spent Easter in Pec.

Olga brought me *slatko* to the kitchen table, the syrupy fruit preserve always offered guests in Serbian households. She stood waiting to take my glass of water and spoon like an Albanian daughter of the house, as Serbians always did when *slatko* was offered. Another neighbor joined me for brandy and cake in a flurry of jokes and laughter. Tall and handsome, the sleeves of her black sweater pushed up, she leant strong brown arms on the table. Compared to the Albanian women who would come across from the court-yard next door it was like sitting opposite a man. She was wearing a black head-scarf too. Milovan Djilas, said Montenegrin women always wore black because they were in mourning for their place in society.

Olga was a "real" Montenegrin. Her family name was listed by Edith Durham as belonging to one of the original Montenegrin tribes. Over the Easter eggs she was pleading with her mother and brother to be allowed to buy material to make another pair of trousers.

As dusk fell Olga grew impatient to take me on *korzo*. Out in the dark, the tiny mountain stream gurgling past the gate, she took my arm, breaking into Serbian. We crossed the water by miniature bridges, frogs croaking and gulping round our feet. Very high up on the mountain side lights shone through the frosty air making the crooked white walls on either side of us seem no more than wainscot high as they meandered down to *korzo*.

"HOW can you live alone?" Olga burst out in Serbian as we turned our first corner and started to meander down too. She repeated the question in English. It was as though she had been waiting three and a half years to ask me.

"Mary!" she cried passionately, "We all wonder how you can do this!"

I wondered how people could live without a room, without even a drawer sometimes it seemed, that was really their own. Olga had her own room, that alone put her in the privileged class in Yugoslavia. There were posters on the wall, bright cushions in jewel colors and a small shelf with a big English language dictionary. Olga had been an outstanding student in her first year. I remembered Milovan commending her in the oral. Dark, intense, bright-eyed, eyeliner then. Such thoughtful, precise answers in English to thoughtful, precise questions. Olga had loved grammar and Milovan had blossomed and lost his austerity for a while. There had been so many good students in that year. We'd been jubilant. At last something to build on. What on earth had happened to all that First year?

Down the lane past Sefi's shop. Sefi was a First year Albanian student who had taken his perfect English accent and grasp of verbal phrases off into the radio repair business. Kosovo was a graveyard of English department talent. I'd bumped into Muhammed a month ago in the doorway of a bus going to Skopje. The student who had just taught himself English out of a book; the First year who had got me through my first year.

"Muhammed! Whatever happened to you?"

The Kosovo shrug and the Albanian smile. "Teaching, Comrade Miss Meri."

In a village school, probably. At least his English was good. Probably betrothed like Fran, the Catholic, long before he ever came to the Faculty, and now married, like Sami, who'd shown up in the Third year with three children, well, not *with* them.

Another corner and we were on *korzo* but *korzo* was absolutely deserted. Whatever happened to *korzo?*

"Yaaoow!" Olga smacked her forehead. "I forgot! It's TV *Kviz* — Golden Hits! The semi final! Everyone wants to see who will win. The prize is a German Ford!"

We caught the end of *Kviz* and then after supper watched a Marx brothers comedy from Belgrade. That evening, I suddenly remembered, was the Orthodox Good Friday in Pec "Home of the Serbian church."

We were sitting round the kitchen table on our upright chairs under the bare light bulb. It would have been much more comfortable on the floor, *a la Turka.* But there was the luxury of an inside, western bathroom. No stumbling down in the pitch black to the outside privy in wooden pattens, trying to adjust to water instead of paper. Albanians called Serbians 'rusty bottoms' because they used paper.

The best room had a little verandah and I went out to look at Pec once more, under a brilliant Easter moon. It was shining over the roof from behind the house, throwing black shadows violently away from everything below. In the cold, frogs were still croaking. The air, as Milenka said, great for *sportists*, making my lungs creak.

Olga's mother cornered me on Saturday morning over coffee. She did hope Olga would pass her Third year exam. Of course, I, as a Faculty person, a teacher, knew that Olga would lose a whole year if she failed. "What about the driving test, then?" I wanted to ask. She said Olga had not been well lately. Olga, whom I could pass for being honest, told me last night going down to *korzo,*

"I can't come to classes, Mary... I don't know why."

Idriz lost half his third year. He played football and 'caught cold.' In Kosovo people still fell prey to vague, eighteenth century maladies. I was told of a healthy young man who ate something that disagreed with him and died next day. People were suspicious of ice cream; cold things hurt their throats. Just as I decided it was hypochondria or they hadn't worked for their exams somebody died.

Idriz disappeared in his fourth year too. The others had told me he'd broken his collar bone speaking Serbian at a dance. In fact, he'd got into a fight because of Mirko.

Mirko had joined the Fourth halfway through the winter term. A broken-nosed, gravel-voiced Montenegrin who'd done his military service, done everything, he used to wander into Oral Exercises in the afternoon, quietly drunk. Apparently one evening Idriz had bought him a beer at some student dance just after he'd riled up a bunch of Albanians so when the

Albanians came after Mirko Idriz fought alongside him till he was felled by a chair.

Why hadn't Idriz said something in Albanian? The Fourth year Albanians had been shocked. It was a question of *besa*, honor. Idriz had bought Mirko a beer. Mirko therefore was Idriz' guest. When Idriz finally reappeared one afternoon, Mirko had come out of his row with a great rattling of chairs, put his arm round him and growled, "This is my blood brother!"

Milenka arrived and we went for a morning stroll up towards the Patriarchate and the mouth of the Rugovo gorge. The tiny church buildings below us looked like the ecclesiastical version of the *kule* with their defensive, narrow windows, like a collection of pill boxes holding the pass. Last year Idriz and Ramazan had shown me round the churches. Idriz, patting the venerable old mulberrry tree outside, said Pec used to be full of mulberry trees. It was a center for silk making. *Ipek* was the Turkish word for silk. But he hadn't known that the tree was supposed to be the one beneath which the decision was made to leave Kosmet in 1690, that historic exodus of Serbian families north from Turkish held territory.

Olga said the Albanian tribesmen of Rugovo had given their word to guard the holy Christian places of the Patriarchate and Decani through the Turkish occupation. "Our Albanians here are the finest! Everyone knows that!"

It was said that the re-establishment of the Patriarchate in Pec in 1590 marked the resurrection of the Serb nation. And in Prizren, beside the Bistrica, there was the League of Prizren house, the birthplace of Albanian national consciousness. Kosovo housed them both. Like the Battle of Kosovo the honors remained even: Tsar Lazar died that day; Sultan Murad died that day.

As we turned to go back we saw a bowler hat just off the road, hung up in some brambles above the river. It was brand new with a pale leather band all round inside. Bowler hats were called 'half cylinders' in Serbian. A 'cylinder' was a top hat. We poked at it with twigs but it was just too far away. A young man was clopping up, leading a pony. That kind of splay-footed, open-mouthed amble I recognized as Albanian a mile away. The kind of Albanian who shambled by just as you were talking about the lithe, upright tribesman.

"He'll say it's his!" Milenka sniffed. "You'll see! The Siptar *biznizman* with his bowler!" She called out in slow, sarcastic Serbian, "No doubt this is yours which you just dropped."

"Well, I think it's, perhaps, my friend's!" he said, telling lies excitedly and we left him scrambling down, lithe enough to get a bowler hat out of the brambles.

Though we got up in the dark on Easter Sunday morning by the time we reached the gateway on the river bank dawn was breaking and we'd missed the Orthodox cry of Christ is Risen! The small congregation was already re-entering the church.

There were only about thirty people, mostly old women, but the number grew steadily, the church brightening as the morning wore on not with daylight but candles. As they flickered, the uneven surfaces of the frescoes showed up; eyes, halos, elbows, dark, steadfast faces painted on bumpy plaster. With every candle the average age of the congregation grew younger.

The stone cold floor gradually chilled me through, hour after hour. Olga stood beside me quite still and almost silent from four till nearly nine. Her black eyes shone in the candle-light, lips pressed together a little tensed, frescoes and black and gold icons behind her head. Olga had been one of our two student Party representatives in her first year. It had been Olga who had made the only accusation against a fellow student for reportedly attending the November demonstration in 1968. I'd stood up and announced, Well, I never saw *any* of our students there. And as I was the only person to admit having watched the march leave and come back and actually stayed for the meeting, there the matter ended. I wasn't sure if she'd meant Bashkim or not.

Milenka arrived at nine bursting with energy, having sensibly slept in. She pointed out the important frescoes over the shoulders of the congregation, in a robust whisper. Last year Idriz, Ramazan, Fikrije, the lone Albanian girl in the Fourth, Nezir and Fran had all come to the Patriarchate with me, apologizing for not knowing what the paintings meant.

Outside there was a steady stream of people coming through the gateway by the river. It was not the usual sparse congregation of old women but a great number of men, their dark suits showing up against the rebuilt monastic walls, exchanging greetings and Easter eggs. Above our heads a pony clopped down the mountain road, led by a turbaned, down at heel Albanian, cheeks doll red in the cold air. Nezir had told me how their Serbian customers used to bring them Easter eggs every year.

Perched up on an old section of the garden wall round the main church some men and boys were singing, arms round each others' shoulders, heads back, looking more like conscripts on the eve of military service than a congregation. Another group had started on another wall. Neither group sounded very religious though with the somber Montenegrin songs it was often hard to tell.

Guns were being fired off in celebration and in spite of the family groups and old ladies in black it was basically a very masculine crowd handing out Easter eggs and certainly not just the older generation.

Milenka understood what I meant. "Yes, now people celebrate quite openly. Doctors and teachers too." That is, people who should know better, who should set an example.

There were more 'political weddings' now in Kosovo when the menfolk started to sing songs considered inflammatory and nationalist in nature. Agim said the manager of Hotel Bozur had just been fired because he had let a group sing Serbian nationalist songs. Many more of Emina's pupils had openly fasted for Ramazan she said, and none of the others made fun anymore.

"If you ask them why, they say 'Well, they are doing it. That is the Christians. Celebrating their holy days. So why shouldn't we?'"

And that Easter morning Milenka and Olga told me "Well, they are all doing it for their festivals. Why shouldn't we?"

Someone came towards us through the crowd, Ramazan, Idriz' best friend. He nodded to Olga and Milenka, first years when he was in the fourth, one of the glorious Fourth. Olga said we were just leaving which was true. We'd both had enough of the Patriarch, nearly five hours.

"I just came to say 'Welcome to Pec.'"

Ramazan and I walked back together through the monastery gateway, beside the river, the girls behind. Ramazan must have been the only Albanian there. He'd come to ask me to have lunch at Fikrije's. Fikrije's mother was incredibly young. She must have married when she was about fifteen. We'd visited her last year. She sat on the floor between two new arm chairs. Propping her elbow up on the seat of one, she'd laughed up at us sitting in a row on her brand new sofa.

"We bought them to be modern but I'm sorry! I can't get used to a chair!"

When Emina's mother came to their flat in Pristina she always sat on the floor. "She says chairs are so uncomfortable. They make her bottom ache."

I had been in Kosovo long enough to register the insult of keeping on one's shoes in a Moslem room. In Djakovica one evening a Serbian neighbor had come in and walked straight past our heads as we sat on the floor, to leave something on top of the television. It had been such a shock to see her shoes on the carpet as though she had clambered up onto the dining room table in the middle of the guests and walked up and down among the plates. Nothing had been said, and everyone had just sat quietly not catching anyone else's eye.

But when it came to footwear, most Serbians as well as Albanians automatically left their shoes at the front door in response to the farmyard conditions outside and skidded into the hall already in their socks. Almost all flats, both Serbian and Albanian, had spare slippers for guests. When guests outnumbered slippers, the host or hostess would slip out of theirs and nudge them over with a toe. When slippers got very old they were put outside the front doors to die. But before they did, they were the cause of the loud slapping shuffle down to the dustbins and back, one heard repeatedly, echoing up the well of the stairs, as defying gravity the locals managed to keep those flattened, battered pieces of leather or plastic on their feet, down the stairs and back.

'When slippers were provided for Albanians the decisions began all over again. The shedding of slippers seemed quite instinctive, I never saw the guest look down. Sometimes feet reacted to the threshold of a room. They lifted themselves over the door jamb leaving the slippers on the other side. In my room some carried on just to the edge of my reed mats, others ploughed on, as though registering the fact that these mats were cheap from the market but then flinched on getting close to the tendrils of the rug. Looking back you could see where the decisions had been made. A few feet took the western route, avoiding the ram-skin and decisions altogether, ploughing on right up to the couch from the other side of the coffee table. The slippers were kept on and once or twice even shoes. On one unforgettable occasion they were self-conscious Albanian feet, proving how western they were and progressive.

Like everything else in Kosovo, the shedding of shoes had political meaning. If someone in their doorway announced:

"Here we keep our shoes on!" you knew exactly where they stood.

Ramazan took his leave. The girls swung round, Olga distant, Milenka suddenly prim and buttoned up. It made me think of *korzo* last year in Pec when I'd been with the Albanian Fourth. We'd met Nikola, the Montenegrin who spoke Albanian, and he'd said to me, like Ramazan, "Welcome to Pec."

We'd all walked along for a little. It had been a reunion of sorts but after a minute or two Nikola just left with a slight nod, like Ramazan now. I'd always thought of that Fourth year, my Fourth, as getting on so well together.

I must make an issue of Idriz. I've just had a letter from him in the army and I've promised him I'd go and see his family.

"Of course!" says Olga with great enthusiasm, taking my arm. "We'll go and see them this evening, after *korzo*. I would like to go too. Idriz' family is very nice."

At Milenka's everyone was upset. The meal wasn't cooked. The electricity was off. Milenka's mother, nearly in tears, cried angrily, "They do this every year!" Meaning the Party officials. They didn't want people cooking big Orthodox Easter dinners, celebrating Easter. One of the neighbors wondered quietly if it was less ideology and perhaps more nationality; more Albanians now, with power over the power. Certainly I knew where I stood at Milena's. When I arrived Milena's father said firmly,

"No! Comrade Teacher Meri! Here we keep our shoes on!"

Monday morning. Easter Monday and I had Oral Exercises back in the capital. Olga came with me to the railway station. She was staying behind to make her trousers. Another week of classes lost. I was loaded down with food for the short journey and Easter eggs. Olga's mother was searching high and low this morning for something to give me. I'd brought presents for Olga and Milenka as well as the ostentatiously big boxes of chocolates precisely in order not to be beholden, and Olga's mother searched for something to beholden me.

Olga kissed me and waved goodbye. I wondered if I'd even see her in classes again that year. The little local train chugged off, full of students returning to Pristina too, through the most beautiful green and wooded countryside, a real April landscape.

"I saw you yesterday!" The dark, thickset boy in the corner seat leant forward.

He was a student at Law and Economics and I was the English teacher and he saw me yesterday with "That Olga!"

"The next time you come to Pec come to my house and have real Montenegrin hospitality!"

"I know that Olga! You should get to know the real Montenegrins of Pec! There are many bad people here! You, as an English person, don't know! They are dirty and primitive. It's very hard to live here! Be my guest and you'll be alright!"

With heavy, elemental, weary sarcasm, the sort Milenka employed on the young Albanian eager for the bowler hat, I started to refer his statement to reality. We both knew he was talking about Albanians so let's look at the record. Just the few I'd known for a reasonable period: just Albanians I knew from Pec. I missed out Shemsidin the wild eyed Third year who threatened to kill Milovan. He was too much of a liability in these kinds of confrontations. Maybe I could discover he had a mad Montenegrin grandmother. The student nodded at each name. Fikrije he didn't know. Ramazan was OK. Ali, a real pest. "Now there's a clinical case!" We were agreed on

Ali. Bashkim, was straight like a Montenegrin. You certainly knew where you stood with Bashkim. And what about Idriz?

"Don't tell me about Idriz!" exclaimed the student. "I was at school with Idriz! We were in the same class!"

I wondered what he could find to say about Idriz.

The student from Law and Economics spoke slowly and clearly: "Idriz is one of the best people in Pec! He is a golden man! You don't have to tell ME about Idriz!"

Then he said something which quite a few Serbians and Montenegrins had said. I didn't know if it were true or just a handy excuse to be hostile, not to try anymore.

"You know, I had so many Albanian friends before the demonstration."

But I was more preoccupied with something he had said at the start, something about "That Olga."

He said he'd seen us both walking along yesterday and he'd been driving a car but he wouldn't stop because he wouldn't dirty it with "That Olga."

"Her brother is one of my best friends," he said bitterly, " but I would do this to Olga!" and he twisted his hands together in his lap as though he were wringing the neck of a chicken.

"I am going to have to tell her brother — someone must — she goes with Albanians!"

Meaning Albanian boys.

TWENTY-EIGHT

■

Smuggling Tea to Turkey

There were always buses roaring out of Yugoslavia, even from Pristina, to Venice, Vienna, Budapest, Sofia and Istanbul. Whether it was the Day of the Republic, or the First of May or International Women's Day, the buses would take off in all directions. One of the Albanian students had told me that *Putnik* even laid on a special one every year from Kosovo: PRISTINA-MECCA. Certainly quite a few older men in Pristina wore the green fez denoting they were *hadji*, Moslems who had made the pilgrimage to the holy places of Islam.

About the only place free of bus loads of Yugoslavs was Greece where the regime of the right wing Colonels was still in power. I was boycotting Fascist Greece and couldn't go to Albania with my current passport stamped full of visas for Kosovo, even if I'd wanted to. But I had to see Istanbul before I left, that Mecca for Albanians. Every Albanian I knew seemed to have at least one relative or former neighbor there. For them, "Going to the capital" meant not Belgrade, Zagreb, Sarajevo or Thessalonika but Istanbul. Nezir and Suleiman said the journey to the old imperial city was becoming little more than a business run for small traders. It was certainly the place where Kosovari bought their gold, the bracelets for wives and coins for dowries and those big eau de cologne bottles shaped like a camel or Cleopatra's needle. The chenille flock hangings like Issa's bride had up in the village came from Istanbul and the sets of Turkish tea glasses and tumblers with roses on the side and 'Hos geldiz' in gilt lettering: 'Welcome.'

Nezir always said Prizren was the best place in Kosovo for connections to Turkey. There was a coach which left Prizren regularly for Istanbul. In fact, he was going to take his mother when classes ended in July and he offered to get me a ticket.

The evening before the journey I went down to my greengrocer to buy some lemons and fruit for the journey.

"You'll see!" he exclaimed, "The fruit there! Everything there! So cheap! Such quality!"

Behind him were heaps of the last luscious, black Prizren cherries, strawberries, peaches big as Bramley cookers, plums and figs. Later there would be grapes, melons, pears and the big red apples from Pec and Macedonia.

"Aahh! But Istanbul! You'll see!"

Obviously Istanbul was the Mecca of greengrocers too. This young greengrocer, almost opposite the Faculty, had his window smashed in during the demonstration. He was one of the shopkeepers I practiced my Albanian on.

"I *understand* Albanian," he said patiently one morning after I'd worked my way through my Albanian shopping list. "But actually," pause "my mother tongue is Turkish."

That is, I'm not one of your peasant Albanians just off a cart, in from the village, down from the hills. The greengrocer was a little out of date. At the Faculty that was the fashionable kind of Albanian to be since the demonstration. In fact, it had always been an unfailing way to rile most Albanians, like Nezir and Mehmet or Suleiman, to call them Turks not Albanians because their mother tongue was Turkish. Nezir was deeply offended and angry because his new brother-in-law had given his firstborn child, the family's first grandchild, a Turkish name.

"If he puts her down for classes in Turkish at school I will never speak to him again!"

And yet I couldn't imagine Nezir and Mehmet without Turkish; their wealth of Turkish jokes, their Turkish nicknames for everyone. I couldn't imagine playing poker in Prizren in any other language. The old imperial language of administration and public life in the Ottoman Empire had become so intimate and personal in Kosovo, the language now of the courtyard, of mothers, grandparents, childhood and love. Emina always marveled at the accident that Agim, from a village, should have spoken Turkish, that by chance his mother was Turkish-speaking. "Somehow I couldn't have married Agim if he hadn't spoken Turkish."

Nezir had told me to be down at the parking area near the football stadium by nine thirty a.m. There was no shade. By nine-thirty-five rivulets of sweat were chasing each other down my legs like drops down a window pane. At a quarter past eleven an old coach trundled in, raising dust, YILDERIM, 'Thunderbolt' in Turkish, painted in red and yellow on its side. Everyone got out to stretch as the driver jumped down and marched off. There was Nezir and his mother.

She looked different. Very stiff and awkward. I didn't think she'd ever gone to Belgrade, or even Skopje, let alone Istanbul. Something about her was different. She wore a new raincoat, long and black, a black scarf over her forehead like a helmet, those inevitable thick brown stockings even in July, on legs awkward and surprised because the trousers had been hitched up under the coat. But then she opened her raincoat shyly — A skirt! For the first time in her life she was wearing a skirt.

"She's going to the big city," Nezir said, grinning. "Father told her she must be smart to see her brother who's done so well."

They were going to visit one of her brothers who'd left Kosovo before the Second World War, whom she hadn't seen for over thirty years. The family had said she mustn't look the country cousin in front of his wife. No woman wore Turkish trousers anymore in Istanbul.

Mine was the only empty seat left, next to Nezir's mother. We rattled out on to the road but swung back, heading south, for Skopje, the way old Thunderbolt had just come. We needed to go east, towards Bulgaria not south. Back we went, back down to Macedonia in the mid-day heat to park round the back of a windowless garage. The driver swivelled round in his seat and shouted, "Don't get out! Nobody move!" He climbed down out of the bus and disappeared.

Nezir's mother, dressed as though for a chilly autumn evening, was cool and dry, sitting quietly looking at the faded *Putnik* photograph on the back of the seat in front. She had the old parliament building in Belgrade. I had the Gazi Husrev Beg mosque in Sarajevo in front of me. Everyone on the bus, the usual lively mix from Prizren, were sitting quietly in their seats, apparently looking at the old tourist photographs in front of them too. We were at least six hours late and not even facing in the right direction and no-one seemed to have noticed, let alone complained. Nezir behind us, gave the classic Balkan shrug; that almost imperceptible movement that in this instance meant, in addition to everything else "...and please remember everyone knows me on this bus."

It was thirty-five minutes later, well after two in the afternoon, before old Thunderbolt was even facing north again, rattling along towards the Morava valley. The streets of southeastern Serbia looked so blank and deserted after Kosovo and so solidly long-established. The one-storey houses baking away behind their little front gardens, sturdy shutters against white-washed walls. The one-storey trees, those short, lollipop green acacias flanking empty stretches of cobbles. Everyone liked to go to bed in the afternoon in Kosovo too, especially in the summer but there were always people in the streets, always life and vitality. Certainly Kosovo had more inhabitants to the square mile than anywhere else in Yugoslavia; the average was 72.4, in Kosovo 104.

We didn't get to the Bulgarian border till tea time; in front of us a long line of holiday cars. Finally a dashing young Bulgarian in a peaked cap collected our passports. When they came back I discovered on my transit card I'd been put down as a 'Turk.' Inside her Brittanic Majesty's black and gold 'Without let or hindrance...,' in the middle of the big pile of utilitarian red Yugoslav ones with the gold star, there I was: Nationality: Turkish.

Nezir was jubilant. "Doesn't this just *prove* how stupid Bulgarians are!"

Everyone else in old Thunderbolt, all the Prizrenites, enjoyed the joke too. But I couldn't help wondering if it might turn out to be one of those jokes that was hard to explain; for example to a rather more observant Bulgarian official on the way back.

We were so late arriving in Sofia that what was supposed to be an evening stop for a meal turned into a five minute pause at half past nine in front of the Alexander Nevsky cathedral, just long enough for Nezir and some neighbors to take off their watches, have them valued by a group of Bulgarian gypsies and put them on again.

"*Hajde! Hajde!*" Come on! Come on! yelled our driver appearing abruptly out of nowhere as he'd been doing all day and herding us back inside. He was a dark, tough-looking man with an emphatic black moustache he chewed savagely as he drove. It took him longer to settle himself in his seat and rearrange his cushions than he'd allowed us outside on the pavements of Sofia. Finally he gave a grunt and we roared off into the Bulgarian dark. But not for long. An hour later Thunderbolt slowed down and stopped. It was pitch black outside. The driver strode down the gangway as though he were going to attack someone at the back — perhaps smother them — he was holding his cushions. No, he was clearing everyone off the back seat. Then he stretched out flat with his cushions and closed his eyes.

On both sides of the road were inoffensive stretches of Bulgarian hedge. We were absolutely nowhere. One of the young children started to cry. No-one else made a sound. That was what had been odd all day. No-one had complained; the crazy detours, the meaningless, stifling stops, the ordering of us about. Nezir muttered something about the driver having to sleep.

What about us? Sitting bolt upright in the middle of the night in the middle of nowhere?

And then, reluctantly, it all came out. Everyone aboard battered old Thunderbolt was smuggling. Smuggling tea, Nezir said.

But surely tea was Turkey's national drink; surely "Smuggling tea to Turkey" was some kind of Balkan saying like "Carrying coals to Newcastle."

"Tea is very expensive in Turkey," Nezir whispered. "Double what it is in Yugoslavia."

And everyone on the bus was in on it. "— Your MOTHER?"

"Well...They asked for money to help pay the driver and the others..... so we had to know..."

"Why didn't anyone tell ME?"

I'd waited too. I'd fried in the Kosovo and Macedonian suns and hung about on the Bulgarian border. I also sat propped up in the middle of a chilly Balkan night on a Bulgarian secondary road and all I would get out of it would be a stiff neck.

"Go to sleep!" hissed some smuggler from behind.

"I hope you get caught!" I hissed back. I couldn't remember ever having been so angry in my whole life. Nezir's mother was looking at me in alarm.

In the end I had to get out of the bus and walk up and down the road while some fatuous young Albanian grinned down at me through the window with that fatuous Albanian grin. Nothing but Bulgarian hedge. Nezir had joined me, looking worried. My teeth were chattering. Four years. — Four years in the Balkans and suddenly everything seemed as inscrutable, private, po-faced, baffling, alien and devious as though I'd only just arrived.

Here I was counting myself a veteran and I might just as well be a pink faced tourist trying to side step my first hungry gypsy child. And what was worse, I had another year to go. I couldn't believe it. I'd said I would stay *another* year in Pristina, after all, my fifth in the Balkans.

Suleiman had told me it was an eminently sensible thing to do. "Especially as you have no plans made. As usual." This coming September Pristina was to become a real British Council post with a full subsidy in pounds sterling. Teaching in Kosovo was finally money in the bank. And with the flood of new students I would be needed. But *this* September, Suleiman instructed me, Think ahead. Post graduate studies. Well, *Albanian Uprisings in Kosovo: 1908-1912;* one would certainly be hard-pressed to find anything more fascinating than that. Plan for Success — Suleiman had a book he'd bought in California he would lend me. Though it seemed I would have been better off financially just filling my suitcases with tea.

Nezir was explaining in the cold Bulgarian night air, "You see, there are men who've built houses in Prizren from the tea trade to Turkey."

"It's really the border guards," he said. "...We've been waiting for the border guards to change. And when we get to the Turkish frontier," he paused warily, as my teeth chattered away in the dark, "well, um, actually ...we'll have to wait for the guards to change again..."

Dawn found us beached by the side of the road again, by a new section of Bulgarian hedge. Across the road was a little cafe locked and deserted, its metal tables and chairs wet with the dew. We were waiting for 'our' guards to come on duty at the Turkish frontier. But I no longer cared. Bulgaria in the early dawn was enchanting even through Thunderbolt's dusty windows. As we started up again, everything was looking so neat, like Slovenia, and like Slovenia there were window boxes everywhere crammed with flowers and in the dawn all the roofs were rose pink.

Thunderbolt rattled gently along, dawdling towards its tryst with 'our' border guards, down long, poplar-lined roads, golden corn waving over the hedges and donkey carts clopping by, driven by plump sunburnt women in straw hats. It was like a Renoir painting — a chocolate box Renoir — Or, perhaps as I kept nodding asleep, perhaps it had only been one cart, one donkey, one straw hat. Then I'd heard the clopping, and along came another one.

The Turkish border was like a huge car park. Officials were prodding tires, feeling suitcase lids. Couples had their luggage open all over the bonnets of their cars. There was someone beside a big Mercedes with their shoes off. Perhaps American observers were on hand. A big operation was underway to clamp down on opium production in Turkey.

"Now we'll see!" I said triumphantly to Nezir, thinking of all that tea. I was surprised at how vindictive I felt.

"You've got very hard since you've been over there" my family and friends were telling me back in England.

I'd got older for a start. And life for those of us who didn't get houses by smuggling tea to Turkey was hard enough and I was glad to see that those of us who did were about to discover the same thing. I could see no less than four officials, sweating in the sun, walking over to old Thunderbolt. Then there was the one telling us to get out. Five. All serious, even stern, solid family men.

We had to line up alongside the bus, luggage open at our feet. The driver was up on the roof behind us, chewing on his moustache, getting down the bundles. The five Turkish officials were bending low over the first cases, arms hanging loose like gardeners about to start planting. They began to go through everything, very thoroughly. No cries of triumph or despair yet. Nezir was next. Fingers efficiently slid through shirts, picked up socks, by-passed brown paper packets.

"*Cok Isla*!" deadpan — "Very good!"

On to me. "*Cok Isla*!" Indeed! All five of them. All around me, swift, knowing fingers bypassing brown paper packets. I should have known. The Balkans: Bulgarians, Albanians, Serbians, Turks — They'd not been together for five hundred years for nothing. It was like the Commonwealth. The club. All went to the same school. The Balkan club. Men, women and children shut their cases, zipped up their bags piously, no-one catching anyone else's eye, and climbed soberly back into Thunderbolt. It was Sunday morning and we were in Turkey.

Suddenly everything was Turkish wherever you looked. Nezir was excited. Everything had to be evaluated, assessed. I felt the same. There was the first Turkish tree, Turkish horse. Turkish crops. Everyone studied the Turkish crops. And then the first big Turkish town, Edirne, where we stopped. And there was the first big Turkish mosque. Nezir went back to the coach to get his mother. Half asleep as we all were, she raised the palm of her hand slowly to her cheek:

"Allah!"

Not one but four minarets, one at each corner and the courtyard was like some great college rectangle in Oxford. Even the big mosque in Sarajevo was like a parish church compared to the cathedral of a mosque in front of us. There must have been places at the central fountain and along the walls for at least fifty men, maybe more, all to wash at the same time, each their own tap; the green streaks made by the water repeated along the walls, the seats smooth blocks of stone, maybe marble. An army could worship here — the army of Islam marching west.

We should have been overawed. The mosque was built by Sinan Pasha, the greatest Islamic architect, at the height of Ottoman power. There was another famous Sinan Pasha, an Albanian, who was five times Grand Vezir of the Ottoman Empire. Governor of Egypt in 1568 and conqueror of the Yemen, he became Supreme Commander of the successful Tunisian campaign in 1574 and six years later conqueror of Georgia. This Sinan Pasha was the son of Balkan Christians from Dibar, where I'd been picked up by the Macedonian postal workers. He had been taken in the blood tribute, that famous irony of Turkish rule; the claiming of young Christian children from the subject peoples to be trained as dedicated Moslem servants of the state. The Grand Vezir who had allowed the Serbian Patriarchate to be re-established at Pec and who appointed his brother to be first Patriarch, had been another Christian child, taken as a young boy from Bosnia.

Moslem Albanians like Moslem Bosnians had been crucial to the administration of the Ottoman Empire for centuries. *Thirty* Grand Vezirs of the Ottoman Empire were Albanian! Bashkim had declared one afternoon. Whatever the subject of Essays or Oral Exercises, whether 'Autumn in the Countryside' or 'My Favorite Animal,' Bashkim always had a knack of introducing these nuggets of information as though they were not only important but totally relevant.

The Kopruilus, I had read, who reorganized the Empire and staved off its decline for two centuries were Albanian as were so many dedicated civil servants, exiled in far corners of the vast and ramshackle empire. Mehmet Ali, the founder of modern Egypt, was Albanian and it was the Albanian Governor of Tripoli, Ismael Kemal, who declared Albania's independence in 1912. Nezir said there was an Albanian minister in the present Turkish government but as the names so often were the same, like Ibrahim or Mustafa, it was hard to register them. And I added a name too, thinking of our criminal trip, the busload of smugglers: Eljesa Bazna. Born in Pristina, 1904, father a *hozha* who abandoned Kosovo when the Serbs took it in the Balkan wars. He ended up as valet in the grand old tradition of quick-witted Albanian guides and interpreters for visiting Westerners, to Sir Hugh Knatchbull-Hugessen, British Ambassador to Turkey during the Second World War. Eljesa Bazna was better known as Cicero; The Greatest Spy of World War Two.

Two of Nezir's uncles met the coach in. These two had only left Prizren the year before. Together with a third brother and their three families they were living on one floor of an old wooden house in the old part of Istanbul.

It was Hussein who led the way home, swinging suitcases, walking fast. Across the wide street and into narrow ones, up through dusty lanes like Prizren, round corners, past water taps and children playing, past heaps of gravel outside new houses, flattening into single file as an old Cadillac or Chevrolet bumped past, one of the famous Istanbul taxis. The sun was still beating down. It was still Sunday. I wondered if I would ever find my way out. Up past triangles of gravel and dust, tiny squares with their water taps, cats and toddlers. Into an alley, up and round, through more toddlers and cats and Hussein disappeared into a dark doorway, still swinging the suitcases, up the stairs out across the landing and through the door and there was everyone together, *a la turka*, a la Prizren — and over their heads through the windows were roofs, a tiny Byzantine dome, a minaret, boats and the Golden Horn.

The brothers' three wives were there, a teenage daughter kneeling on the floor cutting out a dress, some children we'd swept in with us from outside, an older couple sitting against one wall and in the middle of the floor lying on a mattress a very old woman with hooded eyes and yellow, shrunken face. She was the person we were introduced to first. As she raised one limp hand Nezir's mother and then Nezir pressed it to their lips and forehead. It was the old woman who led the questioning and was in charge of the conversation for as long as she wanted.

"Hullo! Hullo! You've forgotten me!" The old man opposite was talking to me in Serbian. "I'm from Prizren too!"

It was the neighbor; the man always sitting in the stable with Nezir's father in the afternoon. Yes, he was visiting too. There were many, many people from Prizren he said, in Istanbul.

I said it would be a wonder if there was even half a pound of tea left in Kosovo. Nezir said, "Don't start that again!"

But it was too good a story. The young wives were all laughing. The one going out to make coffee was killing herself laughing in the kitchen. Even with Hussein and the brothers and the old neighbor from Prizren, the wives were so relaxed and open. And Nezir's mother had started laughing too. She really had a loud laugh. She was sounding almost like a Serbian. I'd never seen older Albanian men and women together, joking and laughing. Perhaps it was just that the old neighbor had such a light-hearted manner, the brothers too. Perhaps it was the influence of the capital, Istanbul.

There were half a dozen toddlers and young children among us on the floor, going from lap to lap in that child-high world. But Nezir's mother was finding it impossible to sit comfortably. Everyone was joking about that, too. I wondered if Nezir had noticed the difference it had made to his mother, so angular and awkward in her new skirt. The tulip shape of the trousers, the graceful column so mysterious and feminine, so cosy and comfortable, gone. Loose and easy for work or sitting anyhow, free as a man; somewhere for the children to bury their heads in or clamber into. It was as though her whole way of life had disappeared with a few yards of material.

Hussein, the tall, dynamic brother was impatient to show us Istanbul. It was already late afternoon. I must stay with them! As long as I wished! Nezir and his mother were going to stay that night too, getting a good night's sleep before meeting the long-lost brother on the other side of the family and his unknown wife. Hussein led Nezir and me down the dark wooden stairs, shooing off the oldest children who wanted to come too, cats flying out into the sun ahead of us.

Skirting planks, sand and cement mixers, Hussein apologized for the old house. They would eventually buy the whole house they were living in, and either renovate it or sell it and buy a new one! But life is expensive in Istanbul, and things must go slowly, slowly! he cried, leading us down the lanes at a near jog trot. Hussein was taking us to his shop first, which he had to open anyway, for the afternoon trade.

Hussein had been one of the ice-cream-and-lemonade Albanians in Prizren. His two brothers were tailors and the plan had been to build up the tailoring business in Istanbul. We'd been shown the work room; a gloomy place with no windows, the treadle sewing machine in the middle of the floor. But what had begun as the sideline and was now the mainstay of the family, was Hussein's shop.

That was why Hussein was so full of life and energy, Nezir said. The odd one out, the brother who was not much of a tailor, was suddenly the success of the family. Nezir was pleased because Hussein was his favorite uncle.

Hussein's shop was tucked into one of the narrow streets down near the Golden Horn. It was so familiar from Yugoslavia with its marble topped tables, the big old fan overhead, the gaudy pictures on the walls and the huge old white fridge vibrating in the corner, yellowing away like an old tooth. Hussein brought us ice cream and lemonade. He was selling all the old favorites; the Turkish sweetmeats, the *halva* and *tulumba*, little sausage shaped doughnuts soaked in syrup, *boza*, the fermented maize drink which was something really Albanian. And in the morning, Hussein said, they were rushed off their feet with the breakfast trade; *burek*, Turkish savory pastry, bread, milk and yoghurt.

The *kalfer* arrived, the young apprentice. Another Turkish word still current in Kosovo, in the rest of Serbia too. Hussein handed over to him as the late afternoon trade began to drift in; children for ice cream, fathers for lemonade and rice pudding and the man who had the shop opposite, a radio and television repair business. He had last seen Nezir he said, when Nezir was a little boy, playing around the stables. It was Suleiman and Emina's older brother, the one who originally had the room by the courtyard gate in Prizren, with the big old radio and the *Life* magazines under the bed.

But Hussein had to drag us away; we had to see his city. He was speaking Turkish so fast to Nezir I couldn't hear whether he was getting an Istanbul accent yet. We were suddenly out by the water, Hussein steering us through the barrels and baskets and shouting men on the quay. It was a market. He couldn't stop to think of the Serbian words for it all, the vegetables, the fish; "Look! Look! *Bak! Bak!* — the gleaming blue-black piles of *patlizan* — aubergines — But I knew the Turkish words for all this too, for cherries, tomatoes —

"Look! Look! *Bak! Bak!*"

Yes, even the cucumbers looked brighter, more glossy in the sharp salt air.

"*Bak! Bak!*" Nezir had started too. "*Marshallah!* They have everything!"

And all that bustle on a Sunday evening. How sleepy and slow Nezir and I were. It wasn't just the result of having been up all night smuggling tea. How slow the movements of my Albanian greengrocer back in Pristina, how unnecessarily thorough as he twisted *Rilindja* into a cone for my three lemons. And think of the women selling tickets at *Kosovotrans*, of most of *Administracija*. Those girls at our *Self Servis* crouched vindictively over their tills.

"Well," as we told our visitors, "we were five hundred years under the Turks, you know."

Pigeons were underfoot, the Galata bridge ahead and a great sooty Manchester mosque rose up by the quay where the steamers were coming in, deep chunky steamers like great tugs, all that polished rail and brass work. The mosque was smoke-blackened like the inside of a Byzantine church where candles had burned for centuries. Trafalgar Square pigeons jumped and toddled along its steps and a Trafalgar Square photographer crouched on the spattered paving.

The steamers seemed to be arriving and leaving all the time. Everything was on such a vast scale. The wonderful choppy fresh water under the steamers surging in across the Bosphorus, bucking at the quay. The seagulls shouting "OW!" overhead. I vowed I'd find a room somewhere near the water tomorrow first thing. First thing after we've changed some money,

Nezir said: "Hussein knows an Albanian…"

Hussein was leading us over the bridge. We had arrived at the perfect moment when the sky was turning pink. Men in rowing boats rocked below us, frying pieces of fish and sliding them into hunks of bread like our boys did in Kosovo with the *cufta*, the little Balkan hamburgers. The sprinkle of salt, the spring onions and they handed them up, knees bending to take the movement of the boat. Hussein had to buy us each one, though we were full of his ice cream and lemonade.

"Eat! Eat! *Ekmek! Ekmek!* Such good value!"

Yes, the hot fish, fresh bread, the salt on the fish, the salt on the air and the sheer size of everything. The water, the dusk falling over the great Manchester mosque rising up behind us like a Victorian railway station and the minaret-laden skyline piercing the sunset over the water just like it did on the Turkish calendar in Suleiman's old room near the courtyard gate in Prizren — and the sound of Istanbul Turkish all around.

Twenty-Nine

Capitalism

Nezir's cousin, Ibrahim, wanted to meet me. He invited Nezir, his mother and me to have a drink by the Bosphorus one evening. On the terrace a waiter in a white dinner jacket wove through the tables and palms towards us, startling Nezir's mother as he whipped out a pad and pencil above her head. She was perched on the edge of her chair in her new raincoat and skirt looking blindly at the lights across the water.

Nezir had confessed that he found staying with Ibrahim's parents, his long-lost uncle and aunt, a strain.

"What can you expect! After thirty years in Istanbul they are not like us at all."

Ibrahim was in his late twenties, still unmarried, very polite and rather shy. He had light brown hair and a dark grey suit and worked for Goodyear Tires. I wondered whether he'd marry a Turkish girl. Suleiman had said Turks didn't like their daughters marrying Albanians. All the family pictures I'd been shown in Kosovo of relatives married in Istanbul showed brides in traditional Western white tea cosy wedding dresses with bouquets and little Western smiles. None of the rigid Madonna-borne-through-the-streets-in gold-and-white iconography of the Kosovo brides. Emina had one of those traditional weddings, "You must sit five days without moving."

The young bride stayed in the inner room. A sister or older woman fanned her, brushing off the occasional fly as she stared ahead, motionless, silver flowers stencilled on her cheeks, golden strands like Christmas tree tinsel cascading down on each side of her face, a little coronet of white and gold flowers on her head. Always the big puffy sleeves, gold brocade bolero, the voluminous Turkish trousers in white satin, the golden slippers. And every morning at dawn the new bride had to get up and sweep the courtyard to show her new mother-in-law how industrious she would be. I'd read that the highest incidence of suicide in Turkish society was among young wives. Certainly in Kosovo I never envied young women, however beautiful they might be. It was the old women who looked so serene and assured, sitting smoking cigarettes and gossiping at weddings, waited on by the young.

Ibrahim would have made a suitably bashful groom dancing over the cobbles in the mens' courtyard before finally ducking into the bride's chamber, being pelted with rice as he ran the gauntlet between the women. They would clap him through with saucy grins and ribald comments, mewing and giving those high calls like native Americans on the war path while the weatherbeaten gypsy woman, hoarse with singing, banged and slapped the big tambourine.

Ibrahim invited Nezir and me to take the classic boat trip up the Bosphorus to the Russian border. There were the guards and barbed wire marking the edge of the Soviet Empire. Earlier that year there had been serious student riots in Istanbul.

"You need more equality here," Nezir told Ibrahim, "like we have."

"You're very proud of being a Yugoslav when it suits you" I observed.

"I AM Yugoslav and of course I am proud of Yugoslavia! And even if I *weren't* Yugoslav I'd *still* think our system is best!"

I wanted to ask Ibrahim about travelling in Turkey. After Istanbul I wanted to go further east.

"No woman should go east of Ankara alone!" Ibrahim warned.

Well, four years in the Balkans had certainly wiped the smile off my face. And anyway, Istanbul was bad enough.

"That's one thing Yugoslavs don't do," I told Ibrahim, "even in Kosovo. They don't pinch bottoms."

"And it's not just a question of the bottoms!" Nezir exclaimed. "Do you see boys and girls here walking together? They are *fanatik* still, the Turks."

I wanted to go as far east as possible to the Syrian and Iranian borders and then north to the Black Sea the region closest to the "crazy mix" of Kosovo, as Murad had called it, where Slav and Turk met. The Romans had called part of the southern Caucasus 'Albania.' Certainly the Rugovo dance was danced there too. I'd seen the Georgian State Dance Company perform it in Belgrade, the costume identical except not black and white but black and red, the colors of the Albanian flag. There was the line of warriors and the great drum, the drum beat call to arms.

"You should not go there" Ibrahim told me. "The Black Sea people are very faithful and loyal but they carry guns and have the blood feud. Every household has a gun."

"I'll feel right at home." I said.

I wondered if Nezir still considered Ibrahim Albanian. When I'd asked, he'd just shrugged, reluctant to admit there might be one less Albanian in the world. But Ibrahim didn't speak Albanian. Did not speak it AT ALL Nezir had said and that must have been something Nezir found hard to forgive his uncle. The whole great movement in Kosovo for Albanian rights since the Brioni Plenum, since my first year, had centered on language. That was why up in the language wing of the Faculty, above the Albanians in the Albanian department and the Slavs, the Montenegrins and Serbians, in the Russian department, the Serbians, Montenegrins, Albanians and Turks in the English department, the real Kosovo mix, were going through such a turbulent time.

It sounded like Ibrahim would be another 'lost' Albanian like our two students from Montenegro near the Albanian border. Ramiz and Ali spoke only Serbian and called themselves Montenegrin.

"Oh, there are many Albanians lost from there!" Bashkim had told me.

Ramiz and Ali were half lost. They still retained their distinctive non-Slav names. One more generation the Turkish names would be gone and their descendants would be 'lost.' But Bashkim told me a success story. A young lecturer at the *Fil. Fak.*, brought up as a Serbian speaker in Montenegro, had decided to learn Albanian. Now he was teaching at the Faculty in *Albanian*. He had recovered his true identity.

"If he can do it," Bashkim concluded, "so can others!"

Mustafa, a student in Bashkim's year, had once, in Oral Exercises with Bashkim present, unwisely shared his dream of going to live in Istanbul and marrying a Turkish girl. Istanbul, he'd announced, while Bashkim groaned, was the only real capital between Rome and Jerusalem.

Bashkim had addressed the class. "I've been begging Mustafa for six months every day just to say just ONCE that he is *Albanian*; not 'Turk,' not 'Yugoslav' but *Albanian*. I told him I will go on my *knees*."

And Mustafa had burst out "I'm SICK of all this! I don't want to be ANYTHING. I'm just a human being!"

And Bashkim had retorted with only a hint of self-parody: "NO you're not! You are Albanian first and *then* a human being!"

It had always been said of Albanians that they might become Moslem but they never became Turks. H. R. Brailsford in 1905 wrote that Albanians would never wear Turkish uniforms and "the name by which Albanians decry their Turkish officers is quite unprintable."

Edith Durham had noted that the western traveler in Constantinople was almost always dealing with Albanians: the civil servant, the 'faithful and honest guide' and the soldiers marching by: 'the magnificent Turk.'

"When you meet someone who cries up the splendid physique of the Turkish army, you always find he has seen the Albanian regiment."

And now some Albanians in Kosovo were calling themselves 'Turk' and sending their children to Turkish-speaking classes, now when both religion and Empire had waned. Certainly Serbians were much more comfortable with Turkish speakers, the town Albanians, and in the language of politics this was translating into a feeling of alliance between the Serbians and many town Albanians; two embattled minorities moving closer in the engulfing tide of Albanians.

I discovered that what Bashkim had said about Turkish films was true. They were dubbed. "Because Turks are so stupid!" Bashkim had told Mustafa, "They can't read!"

Nezir and I had sat through a cowboy film in which Steve Macqueen talked Turkish in a deep rumbling bass. Nezir was marking time till he could leave the city, playing truant from his Uncles' flat. He didn't seem happy in Istanbul.

"When I speak Turkish people pretend not to understand!" he burst out one morning. "I won't speak Turkish in this bloody place any more! I'll speak only English!"

I wasn't getting on much better than Nezir. When I said a few words in Turkish and explained why I knew them — teaching in Kosovo — expecting at the very least a certain benign interest, I was told with a sharp, disapproving air, Albanians were "*Cok pis!*" Very dirty!

And most times when buying fruit or asking prices I was addressed in Serbian straight off. I couldn't work it out. I wasn't in Yugoslav clothes or those strange, prison grey summer sandals that Yugoslav factories still turned out like a grim reminder of the Socialist People's paradise. But when I said I was English, with a hint of the grand declaration too, I was given disbelieving, sometimes mocking smiles. I was nothing more than one stray from the bus-loads of Yugoslavs, some provincial English teacher, perhaps, flooding over the border to buy up stuff cheap. And perhaps I had slipped into Serbian, even as I was saying I was English, because hearing Turkish my reflex now was to speak Serbian as though I were in Kosovo.

I'd bought a bus ticket to Antakija, Antioch, down on the Syrian border. The day before I left I went round to Hussein's ice-cream shop to say goodbye. Hussein, wiping down the table top, exclaimed, "Why didn't you take a ticket on OUR bus? I told you we had a bus!"

Hussein had indeed said he and his brothers had bought a bus, a red one, with money from the ice-cream and sweets and I'd said Oh, Really? And made a mental note that if I went around hearing grown-ups telling me in Serbian that they had bought red buses with their ice-cream money then I obviously needed to work much harder on my Serbian.

"With the money we make on the ice-cream shop we bought a bus" Hussein explains again as he brings me my ice-cream and lemonade, "and it goes to Samsun on the Black Sea twice a week."

What a perfect match Hussein and Istanbul were. Istanbul was full of private bus companies, maybe just three brothers and a bus with a blackboard on a street corner, covered in routes and competitive prices. I'd chosen Antakija, Antioch, on the Syrian border, because it had looked the furthest away from Istanbul, a diagonal right across Turkey so if I changed my mind or Ibrahim were right about not going east of Ankara, then I'd be bound to see a lot of Turkey, just scuttling back.

Nezir disapproved. He was already longing for Prizren, anyway.

"If you must see something else in Turkey then you should go to Konya or Bursa. Everyone in Kosovo would be interested to hear about those places."

Bursa, an old capital of Turkey, was said to be the grander version of Prizren. 'The old people in Prizren talk of Bursa. Many Albanians when they left Kosovo went there."

Bursa was the place where the body of Sultan Murad was taken from the battlefield of Kosovo.

The other place, Nezir said was Konja, "...because of the dervishes."

There were still dervishes in Kosovo and ceremonies every year. The world center of the Bektashi sect had been in Albania before the Second World War. The Bektashi were said to be a cheerful, tolerant, unorthodox and un-fanatical lot. They had flourished in Albania and Macedonia but not in Kosovo where after 1878 the towns had become swollen with thousands of Moslem refugees from Austrian-occupied Bosnia and the newly-lost regions of southern Serbia and Montenegro.

One of Emina's cousins was related to the new Sheikh of the Dervishes in Prizren. Nezir had told me on Thunderbolt how his brother-in-law had scandalised Nezir's mother by making fun of the way the dervishes had mourned the old Sheik's death.

"When the time comes he'll be back," Agim had said of the young Sheikh. "He will conduct the ceremonies, walking on hot coals, that kind of thing."

But till then the new Sheik was working like an Albanian Catholic, in a silver filigree jewelry shop on the Adriatic. Agim said he had a nice car.

I walked along the endless queue of buses and lorries lined up for the ferry to the Asian side looking for my bus. I could have been sitting up near the driver on Hussein's bus, having an eye kept on me all the way to the Black Sea. But I was lucky. There was a girl in the seat next to mine and she even spoke some English. The sky was turning pink behind the Manchester mosque as we bumped on to the ferry. The young conductor came down the gangway sprinkling our hands with eau de cologne. There were plastic wastepaper baskets placed alongside the seats and plastic flowers wreathing the dashboard. The young girl next to me whose father was sitting in the seat in front was going to a town near Ankara.

"I want to improve my English," she said and "go away!"

"I will never marry Turkish boy!" she muttered fiercely as the bus bumped off the ferry, gathering speed as we disappeared into the dark on the Asian side. "They are fanatic!"

Mehmet's favorite song was one from Tirana. He only knew the first line and would chant it endlessly when he was playing poker:"See the girls and boys arm in arm! The old fanaticism forgotten!"

Big signs: BANKASI CREDIT ISTANBUL; snow on the peaks of the Taurus mountains, pine forests, whole carcases of sheep and cows hung up by the roads for sale. Car crashes, a bus on its roof, wheels in air. The sound of cicadas growing louder and Radio Cyprus, down towards the Mediterranean, past crusader castles and strings of camels led by donkeys. The Turks brought camels to Vojvodina when they reached the northern Banks of the Danube on their drive to Vienna. In Sombor musuem, near the Hungarian border, among the Avar and Goths and Hun barbarian remains, there are camel shoes. One of the lines I always remembered from Andric's *The Bridge on the Drina,* talking of the Ottoman retreat from Europe: "Many Bosnians died in Hungary defending their estates."

At last along a bare, hot winding mountain road in the treeless midday heat up to the Syrian border and Antakija, Antioch, which turned out to be a hotter, barer, uglier, rougher Prizren. How the Turks from the parched Anatolian plain must have loved the Balkans; the forests and fast mountain rivers, the running water of Moslem Paradise.

Suleiman said Prizren had always been called one of the coolest spots in the Turkish Empire.

"The old people say you will find no more beautiful place than Prizren in the whole of the Turkish Empire" Nezir had said, "so why must you give yourself problems by going to look?"

THIRTY

■

Bloody Albanians!

The car had taken over Kosovo. Emina was upset because I joked now it was really time for me to go. Agim was going to buy one, she said — "Now we can make trips!" Suleiman was already planning where Agim would drive on their holidays. There were still no private cars in Albania. Kosovo was more and more West Germany to Albania's East. Nik agreed. How clever Tito was being. Our students sounded pretty naive now to idolize Albania. Nezir said he'd been shocked to the core to hear his own pupils say; "Who wants to go to *Albania*? They don't even have cars!"

"The younger generation! We would have *died* before we said something like that!"

Now it was nothing for students to pile into a car for a concert or football match and roar off to Prizren in an hour across the flat and round those blind, newly paved corners in the Crno Levo pass between Kosovo and Metohija, car tapes going full blast. Though it was not until the end of the year that Mehmet, in the ongoing rivalry between Prizren and Pristina, announced triumphantly: "We've got *semafor!* First in Kosovo!"

Traffic lights. Of course. On market days police were on duty at strategic points. The rest of the time it had always been just carts, bicycles, trucks and everyone for himself. But everyone wanted a car now.

Only Nezir remained untouched. "I work in Prizren. I live in Prizren. I like Prizren best. Why do I need a car?"

Albanian families could often afford a car more easily than Serbian because they still all lived together even in the towns. Idriz and his brother, both married now, still lived in the same family compound in Pec. And with *kredit* almost anyone could afford a *Fica*, a small Fiat made in Serbia. Weddings now, both Albanian and Serbian, were assessed by the number of cars cruising through the streets to 'fetch the bride,' horns blaring. One Sunday morning in Prizren I counted thirty-five cars, the gypsy in one of the leading *Ficas* a little cramped as she threw up her tambourine, one of those big gypsy tambourines the size of a dustbin lid.

But Yugoslavia had become the worst place in Europe for road accidents and Kosovo was the worst in Yugoslavia. It used to be said when an Albanian died the question was never "What of?" but "Who did it?" Now when Ilija asked, "You know the young lecturer in the Russian department?" "You remember the manager at Stadium cafe?" You knew it was something to do with a car and something bad. Branka was in brand new black from head to toe."Don't ask!" she cried. Ilija said her brother-in-law had just been killed leaving her younger sister with four small children.

Certain spots on the road to Belgrade were becoming lined with big bottle green wreaths, like those round Partisan memorials. In Kosovo it was the vehicles themselves left along the roads, twisted and scarred, that marked the deaths. Agim said there was no machinery in Kosovo to remove wrecks. A wreath hung on the branches of a small tree where the poplar lined road to Prizren joined the Pristina-Skopje road. In the early hours one morning two young teachers from Pec had missed the turn and their *Fica* had careened across the road to smack into the only tree for miles on that main stretch. The car had caught fire. After a few days they both died. The small burned out car stayed smack up against the tree. On the way to Prizren that weekend we all looked out of the bus windows and the murmur had come, "The two young teachers from Pec."

Coming back on Sunday we saw from the bus a wreath hung in the tree. From then on every time a bus or car swung round to take the road to Prizren where the withered wreath on the tree was becoming as brown as the metal beneath, you knew everyone was thinking, "The two young teachers from Pec." No-one ever said they were Albanian or Serbian; just the two young teachers from Pec.

With the car had come a whole new dimension to the blood feud. One road accident was already legend. An Albanian boy had been killed on a deserted country road and the young Albanian driver had put the body in the car and gone to find the father. The Unwritten Law did not recognize motive. Blood demanded blood. After an accident a driver would always take refuge in the nearest police station before the avenging family could track him down. This young Albanian placed his life in the hands of the father; it was for the father to kill or forgive. And the father of the dead boy, his first born and only son, responded to his courage, the supreme virtue for Albanians:

"He was a man too," the narrator said, using the word '*burra*' (warrior — a real man). "He embraced him and became as a father to him."

That October British Council asked me to translate in a court case for a young Englishman. He was on his way to Greece when his van had killed a young Albanian boy dashing across the road after school. The driver was being held in Bozur, confined by the police for his own protection, while the other passengers were sent for their safety right out of Kosovo to Macedonia. The young Englishman and the young Albanian father, both fair and handsome, could have been brothers. Across the court room the Albanian family, an instant formidable group of young men and older, sitting all ram rod straight, stared ahead. Their lawyer, an Albanian, commenting comfortingly to the British Vice-consul, pointed out how progressive this young peasant was; sitting quietly in a court of law, waiting for justice to be done.

The Albanian lawyer had been talking to the Serbian lawyer representing the British boy before the trial began, to work out the amount of blood money, that is the insurance, to be awarded to his client.

"He's not been found *guilty* yet!" exclaimed the Vice-consul, "and if he is it's a matter for the insurance company to decide on compensation!"

The Albanian lawyer's voice was low and urgent. This death was not only the death of a first born but had ruined the family. The father had been working away from home, leaving his twelve year old son as head of the house, protecting his mother and younger sister. Now he had to come back to his cottage on the little blind bend in the road, where there was no job, nothing at all, just a few goats and a cow on the slope above. And here was the lawyer persuading him to stay vengeance, to be progressive, to accept compensation, insurance. If there were no blood money and the driver and his passengers were let go, then the wrath and anguish of the family would fall on the lawyer.

What about the witnesses asked the Vice-consul — What about the receipt from the North London garage saying the brakes had been checked?"

The three of us looked at the Vice-consul. The Serbian lawyer said gently, "There will be no witnesses. Not for your side."

"It is for the *court* to find him innocent or guilty! It is for the *insurance company* to decide any award!"

The Vice-consul seemed to me totally devoid of reason, in a mad little world of his own. The urbane Serbian lawyer told me patiently not to worry, not to worry and he was right. The driver was found guilty. I congratulated him. The Vice-consul looked at me.

Now there would be blood money, the Albanian lawyer was safe and the family would get some help. The Vice-consul looked at me again. He put his hand on the young driver's shoulder and moved him off towards the door.

I still felt he was in a strange little world of his own. A receipt from a North London garage! "Of course!" said Murad when I'd been talking to him about how hard it was to leave, "You're a *Kosovar* now!"

But Kosovo was changing, even the blood feud. That year, 1970, in the summer, Albanian tribal leaders and elders in Montenegro had held a great *Kuvend*, a tribal meeting, and given their sacred word, *besa*, against the feud. Nezir, in great excitement, had read out the article on the *Kuvend* from *Rilindja* in old *Thunderbolt* on the way to Turkey.

"For the first time ever the whole prestige and honor of the tribal leaders has been thrown against the feud!" The *Kuvend* had finally decided it was impossible to outlaw the blood feud immediately by decree but the first step was taken; a declaration that vengeance must be confined to the murderer. "...No honor can be attached to killing any but the killer only dishonor."

This would help end what *Rilindja* prosaically called "Loss of manpower" when none of the men in the communal household could venture out, the boys, at seven, not able to start school. Ramazan from Pec had disappeared from Diploma Literature classes for nearly a year. All I'd got for a long time when I enquired was the Balkan shrug until one morning after class a Serbian girl had just announced "So! He's not able to *leave his house!*" Apparently soon after Ramazan had come back from being a barman in Bournemouth his cousin had killed a man. "We had to be inside for six months," Ramazan explained, "till it was decided by the elders."

Even the sluggish or inarticulate Albanian student could always be counted upon to wake up in Oral Exercises if the subject of the blood feud were raised. Nezir and later Bashkim would always argue passionately for the death penalty. The only crime that carried the death penalty in postwar Yugoslavia they said was treason. "But the blood feud is treason against Albanian society!"

In November *Rilindja* reported a second tribal gathering. There on the front page were the turbaned elders and tribal leaders of the thirteen villages of Rugovo, the famed '*Rugovari*', one with a big walrus moustache like the shepherd brother up in the village. Beside them were the 'intellectuals,' the 'progressives,' together with school children and students reading aloud telegrams and greetings in the sharp mountain air. The tribesmen of Rugovo, with all their authority and prestige, were pledging their *besa*, against the blood feud.

Rilindja, always the chronicler of blood feud deaths, was now documenting the crusade to end them. It was a sign of how much autonomy had come to Kosovo. There were Marxist analyses by sociologists and lawyers, pleas by teachers and victim's relatives and photographs of 'peacemakers,' hollow-cheeked old men, turbaned or in the white cap. Some pictures captured the moment when men from opposing families 'fell on each others' necks' in the embrace that traditionally ended a feud.

When we'd been up at the village Nezir had described the traditional way of asking to make peace with the family of a murdered man.

"A group of elders goes from the family of the killer to the house of the killed man. They take a baby of a few months in the cradle. Then they turn the face of the baby towards the pillow and wait. The eldest man of the family has to make the decision. There are three choices. The man takes the baby in his arms, showing he accepts to make the peace. The man doesn't turn the baby over but one of the other men, the most sensitive one does, that means he accepts the revenge to be taken on him rather than let the baby die. The third is very rare; that neither the eldest man nor another one touches the baby and the baby suffocates and dies."

Agim said the law governing firearms was being tightened. Permits were only being issued in three categories; "Some leaders, men dealing with money and hunters but the hunters must have good characters and belong to some hunting organization."

Emina's principal had complained to me; "It's very hard to get a gun now — They even wanted to refuse *me!*"

But why did he, principal of an elementary school, need a gun?

He grinned. "I need it for hunting!" Pause. "I need it because I'm *Albanian* of course! For us to sleep in the house without a gun is like sleeping with the door open."

He told me of a raid on a country wedding he'd just attended. Police visited weddings he said because that's the traditional time to let off guns. They'd come in, two Albanian officers, one Serbian. They'd prodded the mattresses, and looked under the rugs. They'd tipped up the pots. Searching Albanian houses couldn't take long; there were so few things to be gone through.

"Did they find any?"

The principal looked pained that I could even suggest such a thing. "Of course not!" Pause. "— We'd buried them all beforehand!"

Agim said Italy was the place where most of the guns came from; *Berettas* were very easy to get there and very cheap. Prizren had been famous throughout the Balkans and the Ottoman Empire as a center for armaments. The silver smiths in the old days were not turning out filigree brooches and bracelets but firearms of inlaid silver.

The gun was not only the prized possession of an Albanian; according to the Unwritten Law in the communal household it was his only private possession.

Nezir said he'd heard Bashkim back in their student days advising a fourth year student who was celebrating his first salary as a teacher.

"What shall I buy?" mused the student, "— a record player or a gun?"

"Are you Albanian or not?" cried Bashkim, "a *gun*, of course!"

When I'd first started teaching, from time to time I'd run across some soldier in the English department corridor, shaved head, big boots, looking bashful and out of place until he was greeted with roars of welcome as the doors opened after class and Ilija or Suleiman and assorted students poured out and saw him. They were our students doing their military service and it wasn't the uniform that made them look older. Most of them were. If a student could pass his third year exam and become 'absolven' not only could he cut his time but he could deter military service till 26. Now, after four years, I was the one greeting my old students, the shaven-headed, booted brigade in their great coats, the red star on their caps.

This year it was Nezir's turn. Like all the other conscripts from Kosovo, Nezir was hoping against hope to be posted to Zagreb or somewhere in Slovenia, somewhere entirely different. What Yugoslav students feared most about military service was not war but boredom. Strangely enough, when it came to the military experience Balkan Yugoslavia had more in common with Sweden than any other country in Europe. Their armies were the biggest, the best equipped but politically neutral. No NATO, no Warsaw pact. That meant no maneuvers in Poland or West Germany; no weekends in Dresden or Budapest.

As a leader of the non-aligned, third world, Yugoslavia was prominent in the UN. The plum jobs for English graduates had always been the UN jobs, like the ones Nada and Milena's friends in Belgrade managed to get; translating with the UN peacekeepers in the Gaza strip. None of our students from Kosovo, the third world itself, would ever have got a chance at something like that.

For the peasant from a village or small town in Kosovo, though, to see the thick Hapsburg walls and smart little shops of Slovenia would be like going abroad or just to be stationed in any little town with smooth paving and girls swinging along by themselves.

Kosovo, on the other hand, was the worst posting in Yugoslavia. The young soldiers walking out on Sunday afternoons always looked glum and kept their eyes down. Following the mixing principle they were no doubt the boys from Slovenia and Croatia, from Vojvodina, even the Adriatic. Though Nada said the Adriatic boys mostly went in the navy. For all of them trudging through the mud or dust in their shiny boots, we were definitely another country where they'd been instructed not to look at the womenfolk because the Serbians in Kosovo were not real Serbians anymore, they'd been living next to Albanians and the Albanians were primitive and had the blood feud and if you looked at their women they would kill you.

Suddenly in the corridor there was Nezir: the shaved head, the big boots, the rough winter coat, the red star. And he was disgusted. Not only was he not getting a choice posting to Croatia or Vojvodina he was being sent to a tiny town in Bosnia — and what's more a Moslem one.

But Nezir wasn't really worried about the army. Albanians from Kosovo having such a reputation, he said could be useful. Apart from driving the officers mad: "Comrade officer! He only speaks Albanian! He is from the village!" a conscript known to be from Kosovo could scare the other soldiers. "They have heard such terrible things about us. So you frown and mutter something in Albanian and they say '— Leave him alone! Don't you know he may *kill* you? He's a bloody *Albanian!*'"

1971

THIRTY-ONE

Sharra

It was spring again, my last spring in Kosovo. The treacherous icy slope down to the Faculty turned once more to mud and sinfully small lambs were being sold in the butchers. Back home in my English suburb Moslem girls were walking to school past the forsythia and peach blossom, trousers under their skirts, like girls in Kosovo. Their Pakistani grandfathers and turbanned Sikh uncles strolled slowly along between the front gardens and parked cars, keen eyed and full of authority like old Albanians. It seemed almost quaint and old fashioned to go abroad to find an exotic mix any more. The mix had come to us, even in the suburbs.

There'd been a whole new crop of Albanian students at the start of the year back in September, and so many of them girls. A group of them had surrounded me in Marshal Tito street, so glad I was staying after all. Exuberant, open-faced, as lively as Milenka, the fastest runner from Pec, their faces shining with newfound liberty.

As we'd talked two old ladies had wandered by, white permed hair, skirts and cardigans in familiar pastel shades, those wistful dreams of summer; useful plastic handbags held firm. I'd never seen anything like it in Kosovo. It was like watching two Rugovo tribesmen lope down Oxford Street. Pristina's 'touristic organs' must have waylayed some unsuspecting coach load on their way to Greece. There was that Stan Laurel indestructibility about them, that innocent imperviousness.

"Ah! *English!*" one of the Albanian girls breathed, enraptured. "One day *we* will have old women like that!"

Milenka and Olga from Pec had turned up intermittently in the Fourth year. It was their friend Radmila, the student who had asked for money to buy a poor Serbian student shoes, who became the most regular. She attended every class, tense, conscientious, a fine-boned beautiful blonde. Her boyfriend, a dark and handsome rather sulky Serb, waited for her in the corridor every day after class. As she left, he would lever himself off the radiator silently, and they would walk off silently, side by side. He appeared faithfully and stonily all school year and then suddenly one April afternoon caught my eye and gave me a big smile.

Radmila, holding his hand, wanted to talk. Could I please come with her to Sar for the First of May holiday, to help translate for the First International Student Ski Championships to be held in Kosovo? We would have free board and lodging, even be paid something and the Student Sports Committee car, a Mercedes, would take us to the foot of the mountain on Friday morning.

This would be my last chance to see Sar and Ilija said spring was best, when the air was heady with narcissus and hyacinth covering the spring meadows and higher up, blossoming right out of the melting snow. The Sar range was called 'Sharra' in Albanian, 'the saw' and Sharra was indeed like a row of teeth, the classic mountain outline; one peak after another rising up in a magical way on the horizon at dusk, suddenly visible, tinged with pink as the sun went down.

I knew snow was still up there. We could see it from down below so I clumped along to *Bozur* on a hot Friday morning at the end of April in boots, scarf, coat and gloves, not an inch of me showing, like an Albanian country girl. There was no Mercedes, of course. Radmila's boy friend turned up, skis on his shoulder.

"We will bring him in secretly with us!" Radmila was uncharacteristically cheerful all of a sudden. "This is the first time I am allowed to go away with him but I say my teacher is going too and so it's alright!"

So I'd been asked along mainly as a chaperone or probably just to look like a chaperone. They were holding hands already and it was only half past nine. Radmila announced we must go to her flat for coffee. Obviously her mother had to see that this teacher existed. When I saw her mother, things started to make sense. Radmila's mother looked like Joan Crawford.

Back outside Bozur Radmila worried we'd missed the Mercedes. Waiters were putting tables and chairs out on the terrace and laying out tablecloths for the first time that year. I wanted to take off my coat and boots and lean my elbows on a clean cloth, clean as it was the start of the season, and watch Pristina go by. Ilija, the person to do that with, was back in Vojvodina for the holiday. In fact, when you were with Ilija the world didn't go by it came up and said Hallo.

I bought *Rilindja* off the gypsy boy outside *Bozur*. First official results of the 1971 census: nearly 30% increase in the population of Kosovo since the last census in 1961. And that was despite reduction in all other nationalities except Albanian. Serbians were down and so were Montenegrins from 23.5 to 18.4. When I asked Emina whether it was true many Serbians were leaving Kosovo she said, "That's what everyone says but everyone I know is still here."

A lot of Serbians had told me they would leave if they could.

The Albanian percentage of population: up from 67.1 to 73.8! Well over the magic 70% quoted when arguments about Republican status came up. The figure for University of Pristina entrance quotas: for every thirty Serbians, seventy Albanians. And then came the quota jokes: What is the best thing to be to get into a Yugoslav University now? An Albanian peasant girl. Pause. It also helps if you can read.

Still no Mercedes but Radmila's boy friend persuaded one of his friends to drive us out to the starting point for the climb to the ski center, Brezovica, where the air was heavy with the scent of dying narcissus. They lay scattered on the ground pulled in hand-fulls from the meadows and now dying round the car wheels and abandoned on the terrace.

There was no landrover, no jeep. It was after eleven and really hot. We had one more coffee on the terrace above the dying flowers. We were going to have to walk up the mountain. "It's only three hours," said Radmila.

First we forded the mountain stream that separated the cars from the land-rovers and jeeps. I was suspiciously wobbly doing even that. Ahead was a meadow of brilliant green grass dazzling with spring flowers. I recognised the narcissi and cowslips and near the water marsh marigolds.

"Come on!" called Radmila's boyfriend, making for the trees. We were climbing up through the most beautiful beech wood. Streams crossed our path pouring down over boulders and through the trees below. After twenty minutes we sat in a row on a tree trunk by the path, breathing hard. The sun was finding its way down the mountain in a beautifully haphazard way, from leaf to leaf, then skipping a tree and landing on one further down. All around was the sound of roaring mountain water but close by were only tiny streams just trickling through cracks in mossy rocks. Radmila's boyfriend stood up.

This time after only ten minutes I was looking for another tree trunk. Radmila liked sitting on tree trunks too. She held hands with her boy friend and they gazed down through the tree tops together. I started off first, to totter ahead and gain some ground.

"*Dobar dan!* — Good day!"

A man had drawn level on one of the curves. With my eyes down the first thing I noticed were his tennis shoes. There was that springy, tireless walk, the bull neck and broad shoulders, the closest Albanians got to corpulence but this man was so jaunty, so artlessly friendly to a solitary female, so un-Albanian and YMCA, I was getting alarmed. It was partly those tennis shoes. No-one wore tennis shoes in Kosovo. Especially not grown men. He wrested my bag from me and bounded along. Suddenly he was talking about unfair judges. "It's the judges! The judges! The system!" He must have been put away somewhere; those are institutional tennis shoes and he's escaped and Radmila and her boy friend were curves behind, down below on their tree trunk.

"I'm a judge! " the man was saying in Serbian. "A judge! A judge!"

He smiled a beautiful Albanian smile which given his tennis shoes and conversation, appeared alarmingly witless.

"I've come all the way from Kosovski Mitrovica to be a judge!"

Of *course!* He was going to be one of the judges at the skiing championships. He was an Albanian physical education teacher bursting with health and goodwill. He must have been about forty, hair cropped very short. That's what gave the institutional look. Yes, he was promised transport too, he said, but he wouldn't be so daft as to believe *that.* Anyway, it was much healthier to walk! Yes, I agreed, tottering after him. He was carrying my bag, doing all the work but even so, fording a small, innocuous stream I sat down in the middle. My legs just folded up. The Albanian teacher didn't laugh. He put out a hand and heaved me up and somehow with him there I find I've sat down in the water and not got wet.

A string of pack ponies passed us clopping down to the valley, the leading one with a high, padded saddle. And then with the arrival of rocks and bare patches between the trees the Albanian judge took my hand and started to cut across the curving track and we scrambled up the last rocky bit as though we really were climbing. Far below I could see Radmila and her boyfriend had started to totter a bit too. The trees had gone and suddenly above us there was nothing beyond a stretch of scrubby grass but the steep roof of a small building, sky and the beginning of snow. Snow. Stretching out of sight, between scattered pine trees, dazzling in the sun. The ski-lift was ahead, its pylons disappearing over the skyline. There were three or four steep-roofed alpine houses here, a mixture of bitten grass and snow and inside *Yugo-cokta* on sale, Yugoslavia's answer to Coca Cola and a group of teenagers hanging around in a desultory fashion just like they did at sea level.

The Albanian skiing judge made off across the snow in his tennis shoes, to cries of recognition. It was like a county show; a man with a clip board, someone in a massive polo neck, two young doctors I recognized from the hospital and then suddenly hissing down between the pine trees young people on skis, in day-glow scarlet and pink anoraks. Some of the foreign skiers must already have arrived.

The official opening was on Saturday afternoon. Our main task for the rest of Friday turned out to be smuggling Radmila's boyfriend into our dormitory which was for female *administracija* — two waitresses, a secretary, kitchen assistants and us — and drying out our socks and boots.

Saturday morning and the Austrians and Italians arrived with contingents from other Yugoslav Republics, grinding up in jeeps and land-rovers and throwing the office into a panic. Lists hadn't been typed, the course not marked out and worst of all, the sun was so warm that the snow looked suspiciously soft and messy. Around the ski-lift and the administrative buildings was a real Kosovo tide mark.

Radmila and I played truant from the office and went up to the top of the ski-lift. She came up behind me with her boyfriend so I was on my own for a few minutes at the top. Albanian students from the Physical Education school in Pristina were marking out the course. Most Albanian students looked as though they had something to do with physical education; when they really did the effect could be overwhelming. Vivid in dark blue track suits against the snow, their arms full of poles, the students talked about Kosovo's prospects. We won't win, not enough experience, they said, but the important thing was that foreign competitors had actually come. And from other Yugoslav Republics too. But there were no students from Macedonia, the Republic which was so close. The students shrugged. Perhaps the Macedonians were piqued that it was our side of Sharra that had been chosen and not theirs, the better known ski center above Tetovo.

"They've come!" repeated one of the students, glowing as much with pride as physical fitness. "From Italy! From Austria! From Roumania!"

Radmila and her boy friend arrived. He registered the students and swished off without a word on his skis. Radmila stood politely in the snow, hands in her pockets, a little way off, waiting for me to finish talking. The Albanian students nodded to me and swooped off with their poles, disappearing over the dazzling white rim of the snow down between the pine trees. Radmila came closer when they were gone.

Why didn't we just hold a Kosovo championship on Sar? No need to go outside the Republic. Serbians taking on Albanians. What an international *that* would make.

We all gathered that afternoon for the opening ceremony. The teams lined up in front of a microphone planted in the Kosovo tidemark of muddy snow. There was to be an opening address and speech of welcome by the President of the Kosovo Regional Executive Council. An Albanian, he would give his speech in Serbian and I would come straight after with the translation into English. I stood in the snow behind the microphone, leafing through the speech of welcome. The English was terrible. I wondered which of our present or former students was responsible for it, or worse, which member of staff. The President ended and looked round. He waited till I came up and handed over the microphone with a shy, melancholy smile. I'd always liked the look of the President of the Kosovo Regional Executive Council.

My standard English started to drift away over the snow, slowly and clearly in little puffs of phrases, at the speed perfected from so many dictations; long, involved sentences with no verbs on the theme of Brotherhood and Unity, Youth and the Future towards the student teams lined up behind their countries' names.

ITALY BOSNIA SLOVENIA AUSTRIA ROUMANIA SERBIA KOSOVO

Afterwards the group of team leaders who'd been chosen to be judges got together. I couldn't see my Albanian judge round the table, the one I walked up the mountain with. There was no Albanian there at all. The Kosovo representative was Branko, a fussy Serbian, very tense. He made me sit next to him, telling me to translate every word. I was to be a symbol of the new international status of Sharra. Climb to the top of an unspoilt mountain in a far away corner of Serbia and there to greet you is standard BBC English, a Native Speaker. The only problem was I didn't know the procedure, I didn't know technical terms. I didn't know one end of a ski from the other.

Around the table were the team leaders, one from Roumania, two from Italy, three Slovenes, Branko, a Bosnian and an Austrian. Rising up from the middle was the overpowering scent of mountain hyacinths, stuck in a *Yugo-cokta* bottle and in the corner by a table of drinks a barman whom Radmila knew, a young Albanian who was the spitting image of Steve Mcqueen.

Branko kept prodding me in the ribs as the discussion got under way. He wanted Kosovo's own BBC English to dominate the proceedings but inevitably it was the three Slovenes who took over, in spite of their modesty and good manners. Not only did they know what they were talking about they could say it in German, Serbian, Italian, English and enough French to cope with the Roumanian, a fat, red-faced man in a Roumanian thick knit. Like elegant, foreign visitors who happened to speak Serbian, the Slovenes sorted everything out: a cheerful, older man in the massive polo neck sweater, a pretty, dark-haired, very intelligent looking girl and a handsome young blond man, Toni. Sitting on my left, Toni had already told me he was something in Import-Export Lbuljana and his *hobi* was "experimenting with sex."

It was the Italians who seemed the most foreign: very dark, with fierce blue-black five o clock shadow already and an extremely aggressive attitude to rules and procedure. The Austrian team leader was an elegant and beautiful woman with silver hair. She was sitting next to the Slovene in the polo neck. It looked like they were old friends. Steve Mcqueen was dishing out brandy, beer and mineral water, deft, detached. Ignoring Branko's prodding I watched them all round the table, round the hyacinth, the *zumbul* — a Turkish word. I'd never seen a group of sportsmen before at close quarters. How perfect they were: humorous, polyglot, polite — except the Italians — diplomatic and so healthy. And above all the Slovenes who were holding everything together, sliding smoothly from Italian to German to Serbian and English and knowing all the rules.

Branko was in despair on Sunday morning. Forty percent in the first heats had been disqualified; taken the wrong course, got in a muddle, tripped over their skis — "What have we done wrong?" he moaned.

And Toni, the young Slovene who experimented with sex in his spare time, and the older one in his chunky cosy sweater, said cheerfully,

"Oh, we have up to *ninety* percent disqualifications in Slovenia! Don't worry! Everything is perfect!"

Outside, one of the young Slovene skiers was squatting by the mountain stream that ran between the buildings constructing tiny, complicated water wheels out of tins and bits of wood. He was making the paddles from match boxes. As we came and went we watched the project nearing completion. After an hour and a half he had three wheels turning, all connected, all moving at different speeds. Everyone was stepping over them very carefully. How strange to remember after nearly five years in Kosovo that people like those were also Yugoslavs.

We all went up to the course for the first events. The two young doctors were there and the Steve Mcqueen barman. I hadn't seen Radmila at all. The Committee was angry with her. By contrast I appeared intensely hardworking and was made a committee member ushered into an even more private room where there was Albanian brandy on the table and Albanians as well as Serbians sitting around in dark suits smoking too much. I would get more money now, Branko said. Well, I couldn't chaperone Radmila during the day, she could be anywhere. At night she slept on the bunk opposite mine and her boyfriend on the one below; that seemed supervision enough.

The Albanian Physical Education students were spread out in their midnight blue track suits over the slopes, ready to replant knocked over poles. We all congregated at the Finish where there was springy heather to sit on and the smell of hyacinths in the sun. Behind us was a blackboard propped up against the heather and a megaphone, mouth down on a bush. The Slovenes were there and the Austrians all in beautiful but sensible thick sweaters, so everything would be alright.

Steve McQueen, who Radmila said was a tailor in real life, presented me with a bunch of hyacinth and spring flowers and Branko handed me the megaphone. I had to announce each contestant for each heat. No-one was listening but Branko was adamant.

"At the start is..... At the finish is....."

R.P., Received Pronunciation had come to those pure, untouched spaces. On Mount Sharra were lynx, brown bear and chamois, it said in the booklet on Kosovo we'd all been given. Experts considered the ski runs on Sharra among the best in Europe. Sharra was the only mountain in Europe left where lynx could be found. I was wondering whether ski runs were the same as summer pastures.

"There *is* a god, everyone knows that," Mehmet used to declare, deadpan. "He only speaks Albanian and he lives on Sharra!"

That evening after supper the chairs and tables were cleared away, the empty chairs lining the walls immediately creating that air of desolation and foreboding which meant we were about to hold a dance. It had to be on the Sunday night because Monday, May Day, was Finals Day and the end of the championships. I was expecting a gypsy band to come in, stamping the snow off their shoes or some students with violins and accordians but a massive rectangle of electronic equipment had been placed at the back. A fair lanky Albanian with a shock of long hair he tossed back every few minutes in a very up to date way, seated himself behind and after twiddling some knobs sent forth a blast of noise that rattled the chairs. We had our own disco.

No-one was dancing. The group of Physical Education students had swivelled their chairs sideways and were shouting at each other through the noise. Radmila and her boyfriend were nowhere to be seen. Two young conscripts stood disconsolately in a corner, holding *Yugo-coktas*. The usual bane of Kosovo social evenings, incredible in the rest of Europe, was in evidence; too many young men. A tall middle-aged man came over to me holding a drink. He leant forward and shouted in my ear. MAY HE SIT DOWN?

He brings me greetings from Milenka in Pec. — HE BRINGS ME GREETINGS FROM MILENKA IN PEC!

He was her physical education teacher when she was a runner. He shook his head nostalgically. We shouted at each other through the music.

"MILENKA'S GETTING MARRIED IN THE SUMMER!" he bawled "— LEAVING PEC!"

The music stopped for a minute. The lanky Albanian tossed his hair out of his eyes and fiddled with the knobs.

Yes, Pec was the best place in Kosovo for sport because of the mountain air but it was a difficult place to live in — like all Kosovo. Because of the people — THE PEOPLE!

Here came the noise again. "THE PEOPLE! — KNOW WHAT I MEAN?"

"LET ME GET YOU A DRINK!"

It struck me that Milenka's old Physical Education teacher had been drinking quite a bit already.

The clutch of Physical Education students from Pristina, the Albanians, collectively caught my eye and grinned. What a waste for them just to be sitting round the walls especially as they were not drinking. The middle of the floor remained empty. I wanted to go over and ask them please to dance *Shota*, the Albanian wedding dance, one being the suitor, one the young bride, turning his wrists and dipping his head; "Spread your wings and fly, little duck!"

With the fierce beat thumping out of the machinery they would be better off doing the Rugovo warriors' dance. But anyway, it didn't really matter. It was only us Kosovari sitting glumly round the walls. Real village hall level.

Milenka's ex-teacher was approaching, two glasses held carefully. He was very tall. He would be Montenegrin. Any tall Yugoslav who drank a lot I labeled Montenegrin. Well, Pec was the place for Montenegrins.

Yes, he said, looking glumly over at the gorgeous Physical Education students, Kosovo was a difficult place to live in because of THE PEOPLE.

That was very true. "THAT'S VERY TRUE!" I wanted to shout. At him. AT HIM.

Perhaps there weren't any foreign students there. All away doing sophisticated Western European things by themselves. The two tanned Austrian girls with the long golden hair and big busts hadn't even come to supper. The Physical Education students were starting to look wretched. Our instant inferiority complex. Kosovo! What did you expect! WHAT DID YOU EXPECT?

The door burst open and three girls surged in; jeans, long hair, one without a bra. They didn't look at any of us sitting with our knees together round the walls. They stood for a moment with their heads on one side like the warriors in the Rugovo dance, listening for the beat of the drum, the fundamental throb under all that noise and then they started. They were strung out in a line as they danced, like the *kolo*, so, like *kolo*, anyone could join in. The Albanians from the Physical Education Teachers' Training College stood up as one man.

"THEY'RE THE SERBS!" Milenka's teacher shouted, "FROM BELGRADE!"

So they were the Serbian girls, the team from Belgrade University who had led the Albanians onto the floor, who had saved the Championships. Now the golden haired Austrians appeared, the Italians too, even the quiet Bosnians. The sophisticated, well-brought up, middle-class Serbian girls from the capital, dancing like crazy Rugovo tribesmen, with the Albanians.

In the Finals on Monday, it was the quiet, serious Roumanian team who won most but one of the Serbian girls took the individual girl's cup. It was all over by lunch time. The awards were to be handed out in *Bozur*, Hotel Peony at the farewell dinner that evening, the holiday in fact, the First of May.

After lunch the skiers set off happily walking down the mountains in big family groups. They liked it with no transport. The Albanians and Serbians were all promising them desperately, next time, NEXT time there would be a proper road.

"Oh, I do hope not!" exclaimed the elegant silver-haired Austrian.

Branko had left me in charge of luggage. There it sat, piles of expensive stuff placed outside, on what was almost mud. It started to rain.

I had to see the luggage off, scrounge a lift in the jeep, tipping out waitresses and brand new Albanians who had appeared out of nowhere in dark suits and satin ties. I had to be down at the bottom to join the skiers and take them on a guided tour in the coach — an English-speaking tour. They had to be delivered back to Hotel Peony in time to get ready for the dinner at seven thirty and I had to be ready at seven thirty too. Ready to translate the main speech by the President of the Regional Executive Council. I'd only slept about two and a half hours the night before. I had got talking to the Albanian working the disco and his brother. A lot about equality for women. Albanian young men were certainly fascinated by the subject of the modern Albanian woman. It was a whole new world.

The skiers were all mixed up with the locals on the hotel terrace at the bottom of the mountain and when I shepherded them into the brand new coach provided for our conducted tour I had to winkle out all the Kosovari sliding in for a free lift. This was a tour strictly for the foreign teams and guests from other Republics and the driver, frightened of letting his brand new coach anywhere near us locals, wouldn't budge till the last Kosovari was out.

We passed family cars filled to the brim for the First of May, an excursion bus. The rain had stopped, the sun was out and everything was a fresh, apple green. The microphone wasn't working so I talked about Kosovo past and present to the first two rows, the Slovenes and Bosnians who listened politely while behind them the Italians, Austrians, Serbians, Roumanians and the rest talked and looked out of the windows by themselves. Someone was pointing out a water buffalo. We were on the Skopje-Pristina road finally, no time for Gracanica, one of the gems of medieval Serbian architecture. On the brow of the hill I roared, "Pristina!" for everyone to hear. There it was spread out down below, all glass and aluminum shining in the sun, a real Brasilia rising up from the mud. There was my block, beyond the hospital.

"That's where I live!" I heard myself saying.

Down the hill and left, making for the battlefield. The sun was getting low, shining through the smoke surging up from the chimneys of Obilic.

"Tell them it's the biggest power station in Europe!" piped up a short, dark man in Serbian, from the third row.

He should not have been on the bus, for a start. He was not foreign and he was certainly no athlete. Obilic did look huge. Pollution was becoming a big problem now. The students were saying the rivers were no good for fishing anymore.

Well, this was the battlefield, Kosovo. The great Balkan battle between the cross and the crescent. The Turkish occupation: 1389 to 1912. The Slovenes shook their heads slowly in that familiar Yugoslav gesture of wonder. Well, Slovenia was under the Austrians for a thousand years, till the end of the First World War, and she survived.

We were making for the tower, the planted land here bright with young spring shoots, the earth a rich, royal purple. This was the granary and also the treasure chest of the heart of the Balkans, the disputed heart. The loss of the plain of Kosovo, the granary, to Serbia, was the biggest blow to the new state of Albania which was seventy per cent mountainous. I couldn't remember where I'd read that. Must have been a pro-Albanian. This central pale green pool on the relief maps between the sandy colored highlands and mountains, this countryside uncluttered as a Turkish interior, this Chaucerian freshness was a little time pocket in Europe. So look out of the windows now. Here was the future black country of Yugoslavia: here was 64% of the coal reserves, 67% pf the lead and zinc, great reserves of nickel and bauxite and uranium. No wonder there was such unease about any problems in Kosovo.

There was no time to stop at the tomb of Sultan Murad and see the china door knobs, just time for the windswept, short, but oddly gaunt and menacing tower by itself, the memorial to the battle.

"Ten minutes!" I bawled in the coach doorway. It was so fresh after the rain. The skiers were moving slower, rather stiffly. It had been At the Start for them and At the Finish; the disco last night and the walk down the mountain through the wood today. Inside the doorway at the foot of the stairs below the curved daggers on the wall, were two old Albanians talking in the gloom, their white turbans showing whiter. All the visitors took a long look because of the turbans and because one of the old men was sitting cross-legged on the bench. Up we went past the verses on each stair and out onto the windswept little flat top overlooking the future black country of Yugoslavia. "No record of such another rich area in Europe being left under-developed for so long."

The skiers stood about in the breeze and wondered what they should be looking at. Just the sacred ground. I couldn't talk anymore. One of the Slovenes who'd been studying the bronze map on the parapet suddenly began to point, talking to the skiers round him. The other Slovenes started and all at once there were serious groups of skiers at the four corners of the tower, each with a Slovene student, listening in German, French, Italian and English to the story of the battle. Of course the Slovenes knew about the battle. They were Yugoslav. And all those fresh, serious, sad faces, hearing about the battle for the first time, the great, dark central scar. How untouched and innocent they looked, above the throwaway Western European grace of their clothes, their lives.

The big *kafana* in *Bozur*, our old Hotel Peony, with a top table and two long branches was completely taken over by the skiing championships. Waiters were finishing laying the tables when I arrived at seven fifteen, breathing hard.

"Have a drink!" Branko called from the dining room.

"Don't drink!" I was telling myself. On two and a half hours sleep — Keep off the drink!

At half past seven having heard everyone assembling we pushed through the doors. Steve Mcqueen and friends grinned at me from the bottom of the bottom table but I had to plough on up to the top, near the band stand. That was where I did my first bit of English language teaching in

Kosovo; writing down the words of 'Heathrow Check' — *Hit the Road, Jack,* for the Albanian-Turkish band. That was the first time I'd been lectured by Albanians about drinking and smoking and wandering about on my own, that pre-Brionale October of my first visit, pre-teaching, pre-demonstration, pre-everything. And it was only last week I'd been introduced to the Albanian wife of the head of the Kosovo League of Communists, coming back from the market, a tiny dynamic woman. "Why are you leaving? You are so much at home with us now. ...No, you should do *exactly* what you want..... Because you are a *woman?* Rubbish! Do *exactly* what you want!" Why hadn't I met her before?

The dark singer who'd sung with the band that Saturday night, in English, had come to try the First year exams once or twice, and he'd got through to the Oral. He'd sat in front of us, the exam *Komisija,* shy, polite.

I'd asked him, to help him out with material for conversation, "Didn't I hear you sing when I first came here? In the hotel?"

And he'd replied, twisting his hands on the desk, "Yes." Well brought up, not telling everyone about me wandering into Hotel Bozur, scruffy and alone. And I'd asked, to enlarge on that 'yes,' "Do you prefer singing folk songs or modern songs?"

After a pause he'd said, "I am singer of folk songs."

And afterwards Ilija had said, "Oh dear! Why did you ask him that? That year he was sent to prison for singing Albanian songs!"

He had failed the Oral and then failed the written exam, again. I saw him sometimes on Sunday afternoons strolling with his young son near Emina's flat and he always smiled shyly and politely and I thought each time, "Why didn't I try and help him pass?" I would now.

Time for speeches and I'd only had half a glass of wine. Someone moved so I could get to the microphone beside the Secretary of the Regional Executive Council. Toni, the young Slovene, was grinning at me from his end of the top table. The other Slovenes, the leaders and the team, looked serious. They would hear if I made mistakes but I knew they were on my side, they wouldn't tell. So civilized, so nice, so fair and concerned. So civilized. I kept bleating this word to myself.

"...Our first on Sar," the President of the Regional Executive Council was saying in Serbian "...in our beautiful touristic place of Sar... Brotherhood and Unity, Youth...and an omen for the future." Pause.

There were the Bosnians across the table cloth, so nice and civilized too — They had been so fair and understated, like Slovenes. Albanians always seemed to have a soft spot for Bosnians — everyone did. There were so many jokes about them being thick headed, but nothing really malicious.

I wondered how long the tiny Slovene water wheels would last, turning in the mountain stream on the peak of Sharra, up there in the dark. Maybe in the rush to leave with all the luggage, they'd got trodden on. There was the brick-faced Roumanian, so civilized — out it came again — such a sad bon viveur's face, such a sensitive fat man. His team, dark and aloof, hadn't sat with anyone else or danced. One boy played the guitar and they'd stayed clustered round him. How Western European the careless Serbians and Albanians seemed beside the Roumanians. Radmila told me later she'd seen the Roumanian team coming out of the Yugoslav Peoples' Army cinema in a row, all looking red. They'd been to see some Danish sex film, she said. But it wasn't so bad. She'd been with her boyfriend.

After each long sentence in Serbian I said it all again in English and sometimes my sentences were suspiciously short and there was a pause while the President looked at me enquiringly and then off he went again. Down near the swing doors that led into the kitchen some of the locals round Steve Mcqueen's area were getting restive and starting to talk.

"Just a little longer, Comrades, please!" I said in Serbian and then again in Albanian and there was a sudden crash of pleased laughter. From everyone.

The President of the Regional Executive Council gave me a smile. I'd liked all the top people I'd met in Kosovo. Perhaps I came at the right time — after the Plenum and perhaps I was going at the right time too.

Murad, Head of Biology, agreed. "You came at the best time. These five years have been the best."

It was the Roumanian, the fat man with the brick red face, who came forward on behalf of the visiting teams to propose a toast. He did know English after all, delicate, hesitant English with a delightful French accent. He told us all slowly, how he and all the visitors would never forget the warmth and naturalness and charm of Kosovo and its people. He sounded so genuine, so almost surprised that it should be so, and the Slovenes nodded and then he paused and said slowly searching for the right words,

"Really, how can four days in a strange place produce this feeling ...of much affection...and to feel so at home?"

Albanians would have said because there was an affinity between Albanians and Roumanians but the others were nodding in agreement too. Well, hadn't I said it was my nicest evening, hadn't I felt at home when I first came too.

Someone was leaning towards me and saying in Serbian "Well done, Mary!"

A strange man was leaning across the front of a very smartly dressed woman. Branko, congratulating me on the other side, told me who he was — someone high up in something. The waiters were beginning to clear the tables and I garnered in some wine before it all went. The Slovene team leaders came over and the Austrian woman, the Roumanian and we talked among the empty glasses.

The man who'd said Well done! was joking about being married to a Serbian. He was Albanian. The very smartly dressed woman was his wife. She was warm and friendly. No naive provincial airs. He was an Albanian and she was a Serbian. Just like that. And they were married. I shook my head from side to side in the Yugoslav gesture of wonder. She was saying he'd drunk enough; time to go home.

"Excuse me," I said doggedly, "You're married — To each other?"

They smiled. The Slovenes had started smiling too. They thought I was drunk. I was groping a little in Serbian, like the Roumanian in English, for the right word.

"And it works...? I mean, you know. Serb... Albanian... Just like that?"

The Serbian-Albanian couple were laughing. The Slovenes translated this into German and Italian and suddenly everyone was laughing and shaking their heads at me. They all thought I was drunk. All the civilized people at the top table.

Part III

Consolidation

1974–1976

1974-1976

THIRTY-TWO

'Hepi End'

Back in England my beautiful ramskin rug began to shed. I taught for a while; English as a Foreign Language in an immigrant center and in the D stream of a local school. A Ph.D. student contacted me to translate everything in Albanian newspapers, starting in 1946, concerning Albanian support for the Communists in the Greek Civil War and could afford to pay handsomely. After all those front pages of *Rilindja* and Radio Pristina news reports, Communist Party comments on foreign policy were my kind of Albanian. I went to some Balkan conferences and felt important in a limited but very specific way. Maybe, as Suleiman had suggested, I should try to start a Ph.D. "At *your age* you should get serious!"

I did finally begin a Ph.D. at the London School of Slavonic and East European Studies: '*Albanian Uprisings in Kosovo: 1908-1912*.' "A fascinating but little known period!" as I explained to anyone who was interested and the vast majority who weren't. It was hoped that I would tackle the fascinating but little known period in Kosovo between 1966 and 1971. I was the only non native who'd been there! Precisely. And anyone could know who my unnamed sources would be. I certainly had had no problems with politics in Tito's Yugoslavia and I wanted to keep it that way for all my friends there too.

So back to 1908-1912: The British Museum, the Foreign Office blue books, the Edwardian editorials in *The Times*; Origins of the First World War. Living off my British Council money like a grant, I was back to the student days when I'd squirreled myself away in the library, amassing fascinating quotes and sharp definitions until I came to "A voracious appetite for unrelated scraps of information is one of the signs of a pathological killer."

Emina wrote that the young new British Council lector was learning Albanian so well! And the new Fulbright had made a party and Agim had taken them all to his village for a wedding. Agim had never taken me to his village.

One day there was a message for me. I was invited to apply to the BBC Overseas Service as a translator in Serbian and Albanian. My adviser at School said Apply! There probably won't be a job for you even if you DO get a Ph.D. So I did and to my surprise passed the tests.

From then on, I spent most of my time listening to Radio Moscow's midnight broadcasts in Serbian to the Socialist Peoples of Yugoslavia: from one Party to another. My finest moment came when, chosen to partake in monitoring Tito's opening speech to the Central Committee of the League of Communists, I sharpened the pencils, lined up the papers, handmaid to the head of the Serbian team, so preoccupied with doing everything right I forgot to turn the set on. We lost the first five minutes of Tito at a critical moment in the twilight of his political life.

It was while I was working at the BBC, getting older and no wiser, that Suleiman called, in the fall of 1974.

"What would be best is for you to work here as another lector while pursuing your Doctorate. You know people in the Albanological department. The archives are opening up in Istanbul and we have an Oriental department now. So much material!"

I had connections — *veze* — and Suleiman always had liked 'native speakers' for his department.

Emina had written too. "It would be wonderful if you came back. It would be much easier for you. There are so many lectors here now." Two young married couples, Fulbright for language from the States and a British Council lector and his wife in my old flat and also a young American 'Dr. Martin' teaching literature. He had come to Pristina, just as I had, because by chance he had made Serbian friends from Belgrade but there had been no post available in the capital. A University had opened in Nis and most of our Serbian faculty had switched there, so Pristina had no head of literature.

"You would like him" Emina wrote. 'He likes plants and doesn't mind anything. He wants to know recipes and how the mats are made."

Agim had gone to meet 'Dr. Martin' at Kosovo Polje off the train, Emina told me, and he thought that Kosovo Polje was Pristina and he didn't seem to mind!

It sounded like "my" Pristina had been over-run. It sounded like Dr. Martin might well have brought along a guitar and was singing *Puff the Magic Dragon* with the First Year.

Going back to Kosovo would mean giving up excellent benefits and a pension with the BBC. Bad choice at my time of life. It was not a sensible thing to do. The BBC Personnel Manager had already ruined a beautiful summer day by telling me that I was fifteen years behind with my pension contributions. But, looked at another way, that released me. It was obviously too late to be sensible.

Pristina was so bright at night; so many street lights everywhere and concrete underfoot even up above the Faculty where the maize used to be. Blocks of fourteen storey flats Bam Bam Bam where the old farm track curved down towards the hospital. Strange new University library; it looked like a Byzantine space craft had landed. BANKOS, KOSOVOINVEST, AGROKOS. There were Albanian birthday and New Year cards and plastic bags with *Rilindja* printed on them. Cars parked everywhere, like Belgrade, nosing everyone off the pavement so *korzo* went surging along in the middle of the road. Most impressive of all, so many Albanian girl students, as noisy and bright as their Serbian sisters, even walking hand in hand with boys. I'd only been away three years, from 1971 to 1974. But suddenly there were jeans everywhere, long, straight hair on both boys and girl students and I even saw on a T shirt: 'I AM PROUD TO BE ALBANIAN.'

Ironically, as Albanians and Serbians grew more similar they were becoming more and more separate. Our Albanian students trouped into one room; Serbians into another. There was no need even to know each others' names anymore. Everywhere there was the sound of Albanian. Often Albanian was the first language proffered in shops. And when I instigated an old style social evening just before Christmas, I was not aware of any but Albanian students till I asked for a Montenegrin *kolo* and a Serbian song and a few students flashed shy, surprised smiles.

Murad was Dean again. And 'Dr. Martin' who came from Miami didn't sing *Puff the Magic Dragon*. He didn't sing at all. But he did become Senior Fulbright Lecturer in Literature and he had a really good skill for the Balkans: he could catch flies with his bare hands.

I had met 'Dr. Martin' first in Suleiman's little office. I was getting ready to go to Murad and sign my contract and 'Dr. Martin' breezed in, black leather coat, beard, dark hair — "Let's all go to lunch!"

No thank you. I was already wary of him and the others. Students were calling out Hi! Martin! in the corridor. It seemed all much too slack. But I was lucky. So many old students, old colleagues and such warmth, telling the newcomers: This was *our* teacher! She was the first!

I was staying with Emina and Agim in their new flat up the hill, till I could find a room. Suleiman, not married yet, still came for meals. Head of the department, head of the biggest collection of native speakers of any English department in Yugoslavia!

Pristina had a big new store with an elevator. Emina and I rode up and down it a few times with the children and the gypsies just to get the feel. And Emina, her face a little red, treated me to a glass of tea sitting in the new cafe where Texas used to be, at a little round table out in the middle of the floor.

I hunted up Murad, still happiest up in the Biology department. Talking about old times, he said, "Oh, that was a very neurotic period!" Meaning all the Serb-Albanian tensions. He knew I knew I'd got my old job through *veze* — *lidhe* in Albanian — connections — like a real old Balkan hand. By the time I'd signed my contract it was already December. All the 'native speakers' listened to carols on the Voice of America and the Fulbright couple and 'Dr. Martin' made plans for New Year. Greece: Athens and Delphi. Take the night train down through Macedonia to Athens for New Year then Delphi. Other Fulbright lecturers were going, from Sarajevo and Montenegro. I had found a room and was going to try and get on with some research and, besides, I was older than the others with this quaint BBC accent and odd habit of tucking my paper handkerchiefs up my sleeves.

'Dr. Martin' asked me to come. I was surprised. When he'd first got a good look at me he was obviously saying to himself: I travel all the way down to the middle of the Balkans and the first thing I find is a neurotic English woman.

"Take it from me, as someone who's done a Ph.D." he said, standing outside Emina's block of flats, dark and dashing against the snow. "You can always work on a Ph.D. but you can't always go to Greece for New Year."

We went to Delphi where the attendants made Martin and the others park their handmade laurel wreaths in the cloakroom. We drank too much and I showed off, dancing Balkan style round the restaurant tables on New Year's Eve in Athens. On the stairs outside a girl was sobbing. Her brother had been killed fighting the Turks on Cyprus.

In the early spring break, January and February, 'Dr Martin' and I went to Spain and down to North Africa, to Morocco where I was amazed at how open and saucy the Arab women were on the local buses after Kosovo. We came back to Pristina pretty much a pair.

Though with 'Dr Martin' right from the start nothing had followed the rules. He had said let's go to dinner and taken my hand all the way down Marshal Tito street, reciting poetry loudly and the first film we went to see was *Last Tango in Paris*. "You can't do that in a small place like this?" I said. But we did.

And the very best thing apart from everything else; there was someone to go for walks with. We checked out the wild flowers in the spring, we saw the orchids growing up on the snow line on Sar. There were lambs and kids and calves wobbling around the April landscapes. We went to Prizren and visited Nezir and Mehmet and walked up the gorge of the Bistrica, and up to the fort and beyond. For the first time, without a string bag, dead chickens or vegetables but with the one indispensable accessory — a man.

Suleiman watched events unfold with a confident benevolence. Now, Martin is Capricorn, he told me so you can't hurry him. He's basically a worrier; that means he won't ask you to marry him right away.

Well actually, he did. But he was very drunk at the time and said he wished he hadn't the next morning.

"Well, there you are," Suleiman said. "You must be patient. After all, you've waited this long."

That was true. And he was younger than me. Not that he looked it which was the important thing. Everyone approved. We stayed in Pristina for another year, so everyone all had a chance to check 'Dr. Martin' out and make comments. Mrs. Petrovic and Murad, Ilija, Branka, Nezir, Mehmet and Idriz, Milena and Nada in Belgrade and above all Nada's parents who'd been worried about my eternal single status more or less since they first met me as a school-leaver. Ilija reported that I'd broken all the hearts of the Fourth year female literature students.

And the strange thing was I was finally doing something I'd always said I would. "Why don't you marry one of us, Mary?" every Yugoslav used to ask me. Though they'd always added the proviso: "Well, marry a Slovene. They're the only ones who do any work." And my stock response would always be, in my everlastingly slipshod Serbian or meager Albanian, "Well, I need my own language. If I ever get married it will be to an American: my language but Yugoslav energy."

"I knew it" Martin joked. "It was all a plot. You lay in wait for an innocent young American."

And apparently it really had been a plot. "Well, I thought Dr. Martin was just right for you," Emina confessed much later. "I thought you and Dr. Martin would get on. So Suleiman worked things out."

Part IV

Disintegration

1988–1999

1988

THIRTY-THREE

The Question of Kosovo, Yugoslavia's Problem Child

It's Milena who meets me at Belgrade airport because she has a friend who drives a taxi. Her hair is a glossy auburn and she's wearing jade earrings. She's looking fabulous. "Well" she says, "I just got divorced!"

Back at Nada's, where I'm staying first as always, Nada wonders wryly if divorce would help our appearance too. Probably not. We were all born in the same year, a year we've conveniently begun to forget, but we don't have Milena's cheek bones for a start. Milena's second husband was a big, burly hard-drinking Serb. She has two children, a boy and a girl. All three of us do. I still find it hard to believe that I actually got married and had children just like everyone else. And now even with a son of twelve and a daughter of eight at home we can afford for me to go back for the first time to Yugoslavia since I was there with 'Dr. Martin.' Things are not so good in Belgrade in 1988.

"We are spending all of our money for food." Nada says.

The ramshackle Yugoslav economy, having barely survived for years according to the experts, is finally on the verge of collapse. Even when I was teaching in Kosovo the idiosyncratic Self-Management system had already become a joke: "What do the Vietnam War and Yugoslav Workers' Councils have in common? They both cost a million dollars a day!"

Now unemployment is ominously high especially in Serbia. There are strikes and demonstrations by hungry workers and inflation is running at 250%.

My first morning in Belgrade I hand over a sheaf of crisp, new notes for eight airmail stamps at the post office and I'm told, "More! More! Come on!" I'm parting with what, twelve years ago, would have been a third of my monthly salary as lector at the Faculty, for eight miserable stamps just for postcards and as I hesitate the people in the queue behind me are saying impatiently, "Come on! Come on! *That's* not enough!"

Belgrade itself under bright blue skies is looking good. Buildings are newly painted. Prewar intricacies, all those plaster twiddles and garlands up around the windows and balconies, are picked out in cream and white, revealing as though for the first time how much escaped the bombing. Down below here and there are solid stone archways: a touch of Zagreb, capital of Croatia. Croats are always so dismissive of Belgrade. They make it sound like Pristina. I remember how bitter Nada was in Zagreb when we went first in 1956. It was the first time she'd talked about the war. Yes, she said, Zagreb had no damage. The Croats had welcomed the Germans in 1941 and Zagreb remained an elegant city. Belgrade, already having the distinction of being destroyed more times than any other European capital, defied Hitler and was pulverized, to be dismissed in the post war travel books as "having nothing to offer the tourist."

But this fall there are pedestrian precincts in the center complete with concrete tubs of geraniums. The young women are even more elegant with an eye for color that continues to elude the Anglo-Saxons. There's a boy playing classical guitar, hat on the pavement in front of him and gleaming expresso coffee machines in smart cafe windows. At the start of October 1988 Belgrade seems finally to have caught up, a European capital.

Milena works mainly from home. She has a computer and fax. In Nada's flat MTV is on non-stop. Nada's son, a student at Belgrade University, is into heavy metal. Milena's daughter sits carefully sewing round the edges of holes she's just made in the legs of her jeans while we watch 'Allo! 'Allo! on Belgrade TV, the BBC comedy based on laughable characters from the German occupation of France. There's a funny Serbian TV play too set in the opening hours of the war. Dim Serbian peasants run around with ox carts and large fortifying bottles of plum brandy exhuming old First World War rifles while in the background Belgrade burns.

But there are no newspapers or magazines anymore in Belgrade in the Latin alphabet, the 'Western' alphabet. Even Nada's text books on English are in Cyrillic and the only folklore music on sale is of the national epics, the hard, stony songs about fighting the Turks, the *Muslimani*. And everywhere in the book shops beside the *Guiness Book of Records* and Dr Spock's baby book I see the word 'Kosovo': *The Truth About Kosovo*, *The Battle of Kosovo*, *Serbia in Kosovo*, vols. I and II, and *The Question of Kosovo*.

Tito had called Kosovo "Yugoslavia's Problem Child." 'Dr. Martin' and I had stood by the side of the road with everyone else welcoming him when he came to Kosovo for the last time, setting forth his 1974 Constitutional Amendments, his formula for preserving Yugoslavia, for the survival of the country after his death, getting a little chewy with his words like the aging Churchill. The classic question always asked about Yugoslavia was: "What will happen when Tito dies?" And the gloomy answer I'd always heard had been surprisingly consistent over the years: Yugoslavia would disintegrate and the only real uncertainty was whether the disintegration would be violent or non-violent. So much for my little America.

Emina had worried when Tito came because the teachers handed out little paper flags for the children to wave, the Albanian, the Serbian Republic, the red flag, the Yugoslav and the newest, the Turkish. "And the children all wanted the Albanian ones and threw down the others."

It was the year after Tito died, in 1981, that violence broke out in Yugoslavia, in Kosovo. As in 1968, it had all started with the students protesting living conditions and the continuing poverty of Kosovo, but this time had exploded into what *The Economist* called a "nationalist insurrection" with demands once again for a republic. The army had been called in. Officially only twelve people died. Kosovo was put under martial law.

It was at that time Emina got very ill and suffered from agrophobia. For nearly two years she refused to go out. When I heard, I'd thought of her reaction on the night of the 1968 demonstration when Suleiman had insisted on taking me to the bus station; the self-effacing, quiet Emina near hysteria: "Mary must go alone! You must NOT go out! No teacher must be seen on the streets!"

Sitting next to me on the flight to Belgrade was a young Croat, beautiful, smart and very articulate. You could always rely on Croats to tell you how badly Serbia was treating the Albanians of Kosovo. Political conditions were still incredibly harsh now she said, in 1988. "They get fifteen years down there for what would just be some comment made in the newspaper in Croatia."

The current headlines in the summer and fall of 1988 had nothing about persecution of Albanians. SERBS RALLY AGAINST GENOCIDE IN KOSOVO, they shouted: MASSIVE CROWDS DENOUNCE ALBANIAN TERROR.

Throughout that summer street demonstrations called *mitings* had been held all over Serbia demanding the return of the two autonomous provinces, Vojvodina, with its large minority of Hungarians in the north and Kosovo in the south, to total Serbian control. But the Albanians were ninety percent of the population by now, a figure that would have made

Bashkim and his friends delirious. The Serbs are saying it's the result of persecution; they are being driven out. In the *mitings* Serbs and Montenegrins from outside Kosovo are being called upon to mount a crusade to rescue their brothers from Albanian oppression.

The *mitings* are growing larger and more explosive. The last one in Nis, capital of southern Serbia, topped 100,000. According to the commentators there is one very clever politician behind them, a new "Balkan strong man" who has ridden into prominence on the Kosovo Question, using it to gain control of the Serbian League of Communists. He is on *TV Beograd* Tuesday night addressing a demonstration of angry workers in front of the old parliament building: Comrade Slobodan Milosevic.

I'd been window shopping near the parliament building just an hour before Milosevic spoke to the workers. There had been no sign, not even extra police, or I would have stayed.

" If you saw something you liked why didn't you *buy* it?" Nada cried in exasperation. "— It will all be more expensive tomorrow morning!"

Milosevic had been called out to speak to the workers from a shoe factory. The TV camera is on the crowd. They're chanting "How much are you paid?" and "People are hungry!" Milosevic begins to speak and, somehow, in one sentence he has headed them off and suddenly they are shouting "DOWN WITH ALBANIAN GENOCIDE IN KOSOVO!"

The other republics have been resisting Milosevic's push to regain control of Kosovo and Vojvodina, for Serbia to beome the dominant republic, to upset Tito's checks and balances. But Milosevic is breaking all the Yugoslav rules. He's inciting nationalist fervor, encouraging "nationalist manifestations." Commentators are foreseeing Yugoslavia falling apart over Kosovo, "Yugoslavia's Problem Child."

And the question being asked now as the *mitings* grow larger, the rhetoric more violent, Serbia more alienated from the other Republics: "What will happen if Yugoslavia dies?"

Next item on Belgrade TV news after Milosevic: a damn has broken near Pristina. The question is not How did it happen? but Who did it? That's Kosovo: like the world of American lawyers, nothing is ever an accident. 'They' were responsible. Someone must pay.

" — You see now what's been happening," both Milena and Nada are saying to me angrily, "in YOUR Kosovo!"

Nada is full of angry facts about Albanians; facts, that when you examine them are ridiculous. Fadil Hoxha, one of the leading Albanian Party Members, an ex-Partisan, "— doesn't even have a Yugoslav passport!"

"All the top Albanians in Kosovo came over the border from Albania!"

Another *miting*: Raska in the Ibar gorge, the station for Studenica, the monastery. I remember one fall evening, on that long trip round Yugoslavia when I'd met the band, talking to the young Serbian boy up at Studenica who was getting in the monks' washing outside by the beehives. He was going to study to be a priest but not there in the mountains. "Here? There's no cinema — There's not nothing to do nowhere!"

"Those in the western areas" Nada is saying, "do nothing." She must mean Croatia and Slovenia. "They can not imagine the things that are happening here!"

The news is reporting the unveiling of a new statue somewhere, a Serbian soldier from the Balkan wars. Kosovo is mentioned again.

I have to call Kosovo. I have to tell Emina I'm here. We can't get through.

"They've cut the line," Nada says. "Something is going to happen."

We keep trying. "They're tapping the line" Nada says. We try Maria, Nada's cousin who's living in Pristina too. No answer. We try Sava, Nada's Montenegrin friend there. The line is out of order.

"You see?" Nada tells me. "Something is going to happen."

The television is on all the time. "Give us GUNS!" ... "DEATH to Albanians!" Now in Novi Sad, the capital of Vojvodina, the biggest, most important *miting* so far. Party functionaries talking, talking as always in Yugoslavia. Nada's son dressed in black, long black hair, arrives and departs, looking for a tape, scrounging some dinars, calling his friends. He glances at the screen and rolls his eyes. I am so grateful that at least one male in Serbia of fighting age is not inflamed about Albanians.

I've always been on the defensive with Serbs about 'my' Albanians and 'my' Pristina. And because I'm always thought to be so pro-Albanian I'm trying to evaluate, not pre-judge. There has to be some truth to all the allegations. I've been brought up to believe what I'm told, too. Yes, I've seen militant Albanians up close. I know Emina and Suleiman have been told by some Albanians, like they'd been by Serbs, "If you want to speak Turkish — then go to Turkey!" I'd been around long enough to see a new generation of uppity career Albanians at University level, only out for Number One as my Mother would say.

But most of the things being written, the rumors being spread were shop worn long before Queen Victoria died. Moslem Albanians digging up the bones of Christian children and feeding them to the dogs! Raping nuns! The sort of credulous tale that had been dealt with by Edith Durham in a crisp letter to *The Times* in 1903. But Milena, of all people, is repeating this stuff too.

"Mary! I never could believe it! In our country!" And, "No, I couldn't believe it either! But they had a report on television!"

Milosevic, I've read, has taken over the media in Serbia. The young Croat woman on the plane had warned me, "You'll find it's impossible to talk to Serbs any more. I can't talk to my Serbian friends at all." But still, I have to keep an open mind. Something Milena has said worries me: "Why are the Serbian peasants leaving the land in Kosovo? Peasants never leave their land. They are not political."

I'm going to have to ask peasants when I get down to Kosovo. I settle down to sleep on Nada's couch, still with the ornate gilt clock in the middle of the shelf above, flanked by *Fowler's Modern English Usage* and *RAT I MIR*, 'War and Peace,' the folk art and brilliant ceramics. My head is throbbing. I see myself trudging round Kosovo, looking for peasants. That's no problem. Kosovo is full of peasants. Kosovo's problem is that it is full of peasants. There is such pressure on land. The Albanian birthrate remains the highest in Europe, one of the highest in the world.

"You and your Albanians!" Nada keeps bursting out. "NOW you see what your Albanians have been up too!"

But Serbs have always found the very existence of Albanians ('Siptars!') offensive. That's always been the biggest problem. My head aches. This is why there are journalists. They fly in, show their credentials, talk to some top people, some dissidents, sum up the scene and fly out. I don't even know what I should really think, even about Yugoslavia, half the time, till I've read something in the newspaper. The international correspondents are hovering now, waiting for Kosovo to explode, for a big Serbian *miting* to be held in Kosovo itself, in the middle of the overwhelmingly Albanian population.

All the journalists who visit Pristina hate it. Drab, dirty, ostentatious now, money allocated to the poorest province squandered on overblown buildings overshadowing the same old flyblown cafes, the mud, the shifty, glum populace. My home for seven years altogether. One of that shifty, glum populace myself.

"*Mary! Peasants never leave their land!*" But so many of these peasants have no immemorial claim to their land anyway. There's been so much upheaval. Agim has said many of the Serbians leaving are not "Kosovari" at all. They were settled in Kosovo after the First World War, after the first great exodus of *Muslimani* Albanians following the downfall of the Turkish Empire. And the same thing happened again after the Second World War.

Some of these people, in their head-scarves and ox carts, have moved around like Americans. And peasants are shrewd too. This is happening in

South Florida. Anglo householders and farmers, the rich peasants there, are selling their houses or land that their families homesteaded in living memory and moving north, like the Serbs in Kosovo: selling dear and buying cheap further north in 'real' Florida where they won't have Hispanic neighbors and have to speak Spanish. A lot of them say they feel driven out.

I left a Kosovo rigid with ethnic tensions and went straight to South Florida with 'Dr. Martin,' to another trilingual area, not Turkish, Serbian and Albanian but English, Spanish and Haitian Creole. People don't smile much in South Florida either but I say like I said in Kosovo, I like living here because of the mix. Murad would have called us the Caucasus of North America; the 'crazy mix' that makes anywhere else seem dull.

The television is on till one or two in the morning. Wednesday night, now 500,000 in Novi Sad, capital of our sister province, Vojvodina. Nada, like me, stays up too late. She brings out *pita* and homemade *vinjak* with herbs in it, at one in the morning. "Good for the stomach!" she says sternly, like her father used to. He is dead now, Milena's father is dead and mine too. Nada who never drank and was as slender as the folk song said, like a young peach tree, has got plump and she cooks. She feeds her dog under the table and croons to the cats.

"Wine — Let's try this Dalmatian black — I mean *red*. Come on, Charlie! Correct my bloody English!" Nada, still teaching, is deep into menopause too. "Yes, I eat. I cook. And it's better. No pills!" Nada's new flat is still too small, crammed with peasant art and paintings, photo albums and newspapers; like my house, full of stuff.

And Milena, who always wore her hair very short and looked good without ever trying, not Belgrade style at all, met me at the airport in those dangly earrings and a new shade of auburn and has made me write down a whole lot of exercises for firming the facial muscles. And me, the everlasting bachelor, the one Nada's father always sent up a private prayer for on New Year's Eve, except it wasn't so silent, either — "Let's hope the New Year brings Mary... happiness!" Not only married to Dr. Martin but first child at thirty-nine, second a bouncing girl at forty-four. My biological clock had not been so much ticking as striking midnight.

And Emina, resigned to being the barren wife: "My mother says Agim should divorce me," she'd confided back when I first met her, "because I can't have children." She has a son. He's nine. Vlaznim already speaks English well in that perfect Albanian English accent:

"Hello, Aunty Meri!" he bellows down the phone as though his voice must carry all the way to South Florida. "We are quite well! HOW are you?"

Thursday morning 8.am. Novi Sad still on television. The *miting* has not dispersed. The special police have been called in. This is what the Marxists always talked about, the power of the masses, the working class or here, more likely, the unemployed. Almost no women in the crowd. Low voices are picked up by the microphones on the podium, scared officials. Everything is getting out of hand. Thousands of men are chanting "Tomorrow we go to Ko-so-VO!"

I still can't reach Emina. But I talk to Maria, Nada's cousin. She'll meet the bus in and I'll stay the first night with her. There are no *mitings* yet in Kosovo. Squads of Kosovo Serbs and Montenegrins are being bused north to the *mitings*. There are thousands of unemployed to pick and choose from. Unemployment in Kosovo is running as much as fifty percent, though most of that manpower would be Albanian. I've promised Nada and Milena to stay only the weekend in Kosovo but I'll see. No-one knows what is going to happen.

When I come back to Belgrade I'll stay with Milena. As usual no-one has a spare bed. No-one has room for their own families let alone visitors but it doesn't matter. That's something in Yugoslavia that hasn't changed. I sleep on the same old couch round the corner from the front door. The postman comes up the stairs with the pension for Nada's mother and sits and talks to her. "Good morning!" I say as I trail past to the bathroom.

I've done one good thing before leaving: I was in the *self-servis* and saw everyone filling their baskets with cooking oil. I got some too! Five bottles! Because of super-inflation everyone is buying as much as they can and hoarding. With rumors of deliveries, queues appear outside the supermarkets as though Belgrade is Moscow. Nada's mother shakes her head. "It's like a war."

Everyone is at the bus stop in Pristina after all. Maria told the others so Sava, Nada's Montenegrin friend, and Emina, Agim and Vlaznim are all there beaming under the street light. And the whole business with the phones: I had the wrong number for Emina, Maria had just been out, and Sava says, yes, they did cut the phone off but it's because she didn't pay. "My kids were calling Belgrade all the time and I couldn't afford the bill!" Things are not so bad. We are just all too paranoid.

I go home with Maria, Nada's cousin, for one night, give her the family news. I'd first met Maria in Belgrade back in 1956, a shy young teenager on holiday from Slovenia peering round the door at the English girl sleeping on the couch. I'd been puzzled because Nada called her "my sister." "That's what we say in my language" Nada had told me. And I'd thought how close and warm and perfect personal life in Yugoslavia was. Here in Kosovo it's still quiet, Maria tells me. In Novi Sad, capital of Vojvodina, things are out of control. But of course, everyone is more worried about the wild Albanians of Kosovo than the low key Hungarian minority in the civilized Vojvodina over the Danube.

Standing by my bed, hugging a pillow, Maria says "I'm scared. All the names they call us. I wish we had just a little house. If things got bad we could just leave — leave it all." Maria's husband is an Albanian surgeon. They've been in the States and she speaks English now, fluently. Her children are away at University. Right now she's all alone in the house. It's the biggest house I've ever been in, in Kosovo. There's a big dining-room table, eight tall chairs, a broad staircase. After the usual cramped flats it seems almost baronial.

Maria says goodnight. I'm sleeping in a real bed in a cold bedroom. It's that cold week or two before the heating comes on in October, up here on the plateau of Kosovo. Everything is very quiet. Around the house are new blocks of flats climbing up the hill. Only a few lights still on. "I think we will die because of this house," Maria had said flatly, standing in the doorway. "We will die because we are rich, because we have so many things and won't leave them."

Walking down to the Faculty Emina holds on happily to my arm. "I want to smile so much because you are here again but if I am seen to smile I will be called 'Serbophile' because things are going badly for us Albanians now and they will say 'How can she look happy?'"

It's still the same old scruffy Faculty, the chewed down grass in front. Students all in jeans and lots of black. Many Greek students. Poorer ones who can't afford to study in Greece, Emina says. And they come to Pristina because the Greek government doesn't recognize the Republic of Macedonia so they don't go to Skopje, much closer to them further south. No, no students from Albania. Familiar faces from the English department in the buffet: two, teachers now, were my students. One of my old colleagues, an Albanian, says "So! How many *bodies* did you see in the road this morning in our TERRIBLE Kosovo?" but none of us really laugh.

Emina has to go to the office and I have coffee with another old colleague, a Serbian woman. An Albanian faculty member asks if the seats opposite us are taken. But then his companion sees a table that's free. Bending over his coffee cup the Albanian apologizes profusely for leaving us. He is sure we'd prefer to be alone — Not that he means we wouldn't like to share our table — but — but — As he retreats he nearly touches another Serbian Faculty member, a female, and the flurry begins again.

Serbians always called Kosovo their *Vild Vest* but of course it's Serbia's deep South. With the liberal era under Tito long since gone and in the aftermath of the 1981 uprising, here it is: the deep South again, before civil rights where a black male must not brush up against a white woman. An Albanian has only to touch a female, a Serbian, by mistake now, and she can cry Rape.

Friday. Eight hundred Serbian school children from Pec arrive in Belgrade for protests against Albanian harassment in Kosovo. There are two Albanians among them. Agim, home for lunch, sniffs.

"Yes, the Serbs say it is dangerous to go to their classes because of Albanian intimidation; they are 'scared of Albanians' but they're all in the discos together every night!"

The Serbians are boycotting all classes at schools and the University. The boycott sounds like a student's dream: high drama, no work, and the way things were going, no way of making up lost classes. The Serbian teachers from Belgrade are traveling down to Pristina just to pick up their salaries, raise their eyebrows in despair, and go back again which according to some members of the Albanian faculty is more or less all they'd ever really done, anyway.

Strange that our whole elaborate world of political correctness in the *Fil. Fak.* and everywhere else has been smashed apart. We teachers took such care against 'nationalist manifestations' and 'chauvinistic tendencies.' Coming straight from Kosovo to the U.S., as an English citizen, had been such a natural transition. Not just a new linguistic tug of war between Spanish and English but the jumpy separation of Church and State. Discovering, when the children began school, that the most sacred day of the Christian calendar, Good Friday, could only be an American school holiday under the guise of 'Teachers' Work Day' had seemed, after Tito's Yugoslavia, the most natural thing in the world.

Suleiman arrives and we have lunch together in the kitchen, leaving the television on in the other room. Package soup, paprika cabbage and potatoes. There's no meat, no hard cheese, no fruit juices but I have brought coffee and tea. Emina apologizes for not having 'black' bread on the table, the coarse, cheaper bread I'd always preferred.

"The poor are getting up at dawn to queue for it. They cannot afford the white. So I mustn't buy it anymore or someone will go hungry because of me."

I ask if it's true that there has been harassment of Serbian peasants in Kosovo. Agim and Suleiman pause and say yes, and nothing else.

Albanians come in from outside the province, Emina says, and make pressure. Albanians from Southern Serbia, Montenegro and Macedonia.

"Look at Mehmet," a colleague in the department. "I say why? Why be against Serbs?" and he says, 'My grandparents had a miserable time with Serbs in Macedonia.' I wish they would all leave!" Emina cries vehemently, "And let us live like we did before!"

"These are the people who worry now," Agim said, "the extremists."

"We are O.K.," Suleiman said, "We are moderates."

The announcer on the television in the other room is saying that the Albanian engineer in charge of the damn that broke will be put on trial.

Emina and I go walking down by the stadium where there's a new covered mini mall. We get talking to two young women in the crystal and china shop. Hooded eyes, pale, pale skin: Albanian-Turkish faces.

Thursday will be the big demonstration, the *miting* in Pristina, they say. They are going to Prizren with their children. Yes, they will probably lose their jobs but "It's better than being killed."

Suleiman says as the *mitings* are Serbian and most of the police are Albanian now, people are really worried. Agim says as most of the police are Albanian they will bring in the military. Milosevic already has 1,000 paramilitary police in Kosovo, sent down in September. As always in Kosovo however much the statistics change the balance of fear and distrust remains constant.

Ten thousand are rallying in Titograd, Montenegro: "KOSOVO IS OURS! WE HAVE SUFFERED ENOUGH!" but the police are breaking them up. Also *mitings* in Arandjelovac, Sabac, Urosevac. Late that night I lie in bed listening to the World Service BBC in Vlaznim's room, with the pop stars on the wall and a 1988 calendar from Istanbul. First item: 100,00 in Latvia, a nationalist demonstration. The Soviet Empire is starting to break up. Second: Demonstration in Moscow, demand for democratic rights and then, "Ethnic struggle is going on now in Montenegro. More big rallies held in Serbian towns."

Thursday comes. No big *miting* in Pristina: it was another rumor. Vlaznim reports the two Albanian students who went to Belgrade with the Serbians from Pec have been beaten up by Albanians. Emina's neighbor comes in on Saturday morning to have coffee. She's an Albanian doctor, very sharp and aggressive. Still, most professional Albanian women always were sharp and wary, like Violeta at Radio Pristina. I ask her about the Serbian stories of rape. Rape exists everywhere, she says, but the fewest cases come from Kosovo. And if there is talk of Serbians and not Albanians that is because of course

Albanian girls would never admit it, not in traditional Moslem households. 'Rape' here is economic pressure, she says fiercely, it is ignorance.

She's in a pink sweat suit and looking very tired. She has been up till three in the morning preparing eighteen kilos of peppers for the winter. So that's one reason she's being so sharp. And she says she's very scared.

"My daughter is having nightmares, dreaming of war. And what can I do? Only sit with my arms folded and wait."

"What did you think of her?" Emina asked when the doctor left. "She is one of them that is why she is scared." An Albanian extremist. "She won't speak to her Serbian colleagues. She is full of hate. My friends say how can you be with her? But she is my neighbor and her husband is mean. She is another one, you see, not from here, from Ulcinj, Montenegro. She is scared. She is on the list. The Serbians have been very clever. Good politicians. They've written everything down. That is why people like her are frightened."

The doctor had nodded out of the window at the block opposite and down below at the garbage strewn entrance, the children playing near the overflowing dumpsters.

"I have only two small kitchen knives for when they come. What will happen when they come to the entrances with guns?"

Sunday morning and I'm going to Pec, then on to Prizren. I'll try to see Idriz and Nezir and Mehmet. I tell Emina I'll be careful. She's worried because Agim can't take me in the car. He must be on call. He works for the regional government, the Kosovo League of Communists, which is locked in the fight for its life right now with Milosevic's Serbian Communist Party.

The new bus station is just down from the new blocks of flats. Lots of space but the same pungent smell from the lavatories, the same row of gypsy shoe shine men, the Albanian girls and women in their long pale macs, pale faces, thick scarves and woollen stockings and two old women in the Serbian town dress of Kosovo: a kind of Turkish trousers, a red mat in front like an apron.

I ask for a seat near the window and the ticket seller asks me if I'm Greek. The bus driver has *MARSHALLA!* over the dash board and a Rambo sticker. We pull out of Pristina Nat King Cole crooning *Mona Lisa* on the radio. For all the building, Pristina still is scruffy, with an air of poverty. I can see what the journalists mean. The younger men and boys are all in jeans now; the older Albanians still wear the white cap. They still have the piercing eyes and air of authority as they walk slowly along the bus but opposite me is a tubby little Albanian man, under a white cap, folding and re-folding a check handkerchief, making the edges sharp into a smaller and smaller square.

Big, black-grey crows. They hop and walk: three hops and then a walk. A row of beehives, peppers, flowers, squash, marrows, cabbage in the gardens, and small haystacks. The last of the roses, apples and plums. Little *NON-STOP* grocery. A boy is fetching water. Another boy with four little piglets. Poplar trees line the road, beyond them, silver birches, water buffalo and in the distance, the mountains.

Building is everywhere, individual homes, brick by Kosovo brick. Elvis Presley on cassette now. A little Moslem graveyard. Brick walls around the houses and yards. A cat. Is that a Serbian or Albanian cat? In the distance, rising behind rose red roofs, mountains wreathed in clouds. Albanian songs now. It's still dry. On the Sunday morning farming program they'd been saying crops were scant this year, 1988 a dry summer, yield low. Cows are grazing along the scrubby parched grass verges. You can see the red clay behind their muzzles.

In Metohija some new houses along the road are four stories high with defensive narrow windows at the top, the modern version of the traditional building housing the extended Albanian family. Brothers still bring their brides home to live in the compound together in the time honored way. I'd forgotten how Adriatic bare the mountain slopes are; only the tops are a deep fuzzy green. Sheep and goats are grazing. People up ladders are picking the lovely red Pec apples.

HOTEL DARDANIA. An Illyrian word. Every name makes a statement. Illyrian names make the Albanian statement: we were here first.

PEC. Ahead over the roofs, forested green mountains rear up in some places just beyond the kitchen gardens. That's Pec. I stand for a moment, thinking where Idriz' house would be and a truck bounces by over the uneven paving, four young men standing in the back, engulfed in the billowing flags they're holding. Four Yugoslav tricolors and the International red flag. Some crowded private cars rattle along in the same direction. I suddenly realize — It's a *miting*.

There are two young men sitting on the cobblestone kerb.

"Is there going to be a *miting?*"

They look up at me, squinting a little, trying to place me. They haven't answered yet.

"And you're not going?" I ask dryly. To me, an old Kosovar, they're obviously Albanian.

They go on looking up at me. "No! But we'll take you then come back."

The two young men stand up. More cars race by behind us. They have poker faces, no reaction.

"What about the truth?" I ask, almost to myself, "What about the *pritisak* — the pressure, against Kosovo Serbians?"

One of them says softly in Serbian, "We are not all bad."

As we're at the bus station there are one or two taxis parked nearby and they call over one of their friends. "Take her to the *miting!*" and we rattle off in a flurry of Albanian thanks and goodbyes.

The taxi heads down a country road past front gardens and verandahs where people are having Sunday lunch. More roses, vegetable gardens. My taxi driver shrugs when I ask him about Serbian accusations. I don't care about being polite, about looking eccentric. I'm finally realizing I've always been eccentric. But there's no time to lose. It's imperative to get the truth, to bring it back to Belgrade.

The taxi driver shrugs again, a little bland maybe. "We all get on fine in Pec...Maybe in the villages..."

I'm speaking Serbian because it's easier for me, but some Albanian too, to let him know I'm on his side. I want to be on Kosovo's side, Serb and Albanian, the Kosovari. Tito called us that when he came down to our new University of Pristina. Murad the first Rector standing there with a big grin, as always looking as though his tie was under one ear. Our Serbian landlord, grumbling about some Albanian boys who had smashed his geranium pots, had talked about Serbians leaving Kosovo. That was twelve years ago. "You know, they go up to Kraljevo and Kragujevac and people call them, 'Half Blacks' and '*Siptars*' because they come from Kosovo. They say they are dirty, call them *Muslimani*. A lot of them come back. They don't feel at home there. They are Kosovari."

We can't miss the *miting*. There are cars parked everywhere on the country road and clusters of people walking round the side of a village school. My taxi driver says very dryly. "I think you can find your own way now."

It's a beautiful sun-filled afternoon. Everyone seems in a good mood, like a picnic. There are lots of high school children and older women in cosy black coats with fur collars. Behind the school is a bald football pitch and a platform up at the far end in front of flag-draped goal-posts. Right behind the goal posts is an orchard, rows of little apple trees laden with the wonderful apples of Pec leading away towards the mountains.

The pitch is slowly filling up, people strolling in all the time, talking quietly, greeting each other. There are a few women in the traditional black scarf and long skirt, some hennaed matrons. Many of the older men have watch chains across their fronts. Someone is already speaking up between the goal posts, flanked by portraits of Njiegos, the legendary nineteenth century Montenegrin poet-priest-king, and Vuk Karadzic, the great Serbian scholar, and Tito. The speaker is condemning "Albanian Fascism' and 'Albanian hatred.' He's demanding the resignation of some local Albanians and two Serbs. There's a murmur of approval and scattered applause. Policemen in long winter coats are standing about on the edge of the pitch, in twos and threes, arms behind their backs, very low key, talking among themselves.

The speakers are using the old name for Kosovo — Kosmet — the name used when I first came. With what triumph Albanians like Bashkim had welcomed the changing of the name. — Now we would become a Republic! They had such almost mystical faith in the unstoppable process. Bashkim has been in prison, Emina told me. For two years. A young English teacher, representing his Albanian students in their demands, in the 'insurrection' of 1981. He has a little shop now, a *butik*, up a cobbled side street in Pristina. I went to see him. He goes to Istanbul and buys stuff, he says.

"I make a hell of a lot more money now than teaching!" His English is very good. He stood in the doorway of his little shop looking down the road. "But where is Martin?... You were sooo lucky!" Meaning I was so lucky to 'catch' 'Dr. Martin.' Bashkim grins. He always was a straight talker.

Bashkim had closed up the shop and we'd gone off for coffee. "Mary, prison was terrible," he'd said suddenly. "What men will do to men."

There's another Serbian speaker now, waxing lyrical about Pec and Metohija between the goal posts. "Every drop of our rivers... Every breath of our mountain air!" Be hard to wax lyrical over Pristina.

I'm still studying faces even though I know they must all be Serbian and Montenegrin just to be here. Still the observer, really the observer now. I'm a female over fifty and as a face on the street, for men I no longer exist and the women don't care. After the first shock it's liberating. In Yugoslavia and especially Kosovo where attention was so overwhelming and endless I feel like a ghost. I can move around and do what I want and no-one registers me at all. Never again the everlasting, "Where is your husband?" and "Why do you know our language?" Let alone "— What are you doing tonight?" Even Milena, who still looks so good, remarked drolly, "Have you noticed how young men nowadays never want to know the time?"

Some of the older men are sporting great warrior moustaches, RAF handlebars, old Montenegrin veterans. One young girl is wearing the grey army Serbian cap, others in the pillbox Montenegrin cap. Many of the younger men in heavy knit sweaters and beards look like they've come out for a Sunday stroll after reading the liberal Sunday papers. Beards are something new. Taboo, except for Orthodox priests ever since the war, they'd been the badge of the Cetniks, the Serbian Royalist nationalists. Making a chopping sign across your chest, signifying a beard, meant you were talking about a nationalist.

An Albanian has begun to speak and the mood of the *miting* changes. He's pleading for the youth of Kosovo to grow up without hatred and live together. Booing starts and chanting begins to drown him out. The older people are saying mildly, Let him speak. I make my way up to the goal posts wanting to see if there are ringleaders; if people have been bussed in to this village football pitch. There's a microphone and a video camera but all I see is a gang of self-conscious high school kids who feel they should make some noise. I wonder if this Albanian is being very brave, or very political, an opportunist, thinking of the way the wind is blowing. Another Albanian speaks briefly too: he calls Albanians 'Siptars'; that should help him with his listeners and either stammers or is so caught up in the tension that he says "Ko Ko Ko KOSmet" every time. But he pleads for unity and there is some applause.

Suddenly there's an outburst of clapping and all the Serbian matrons, the mothers and grandmothers, are beaming and soon wiping away tears as a young girl's voice rings out. She's one of the schoolchildren from Pec who went to Belgrade, now reporting on the solidarity shown by the Serbs in the capital.

Every Serbian speaker has talked about the suffering of Serbs in Kosovo for forty years, since the end of the war, as though Rankovic, the Serbian head of the secret police, must have been an Albanian. Every speech finishes with the obligatory and perfunctory, "Long Live Brotherhood and Unity! Long Live Tito and the Communist Party! Long Live Yugoslavia! I start clapping whenever Brotherhood and Unity is mentioned. I keep clapping stubbornly, willing more to join in. Usually they do. Interesting, the chemistry of groups. Maybe some think I've been sent down from Party headquarters.

None of the speakers has mentioned the central catastrophe of Yugoslav life now: the astronomical inflation. Emina says like Nada, "Now all our money goes on food. We hunt from shop to shop like gypsies."

In spite of the inflammatory rhetoric the mood as the *miting* ends is mellow. Everyone is satisfied. Everything has been said. All the things that couldn't be said all those years, just muttered in the corners. A historic moment; the Serbs retaking Kosovo with words. But now Kosovo is 90% Albanian. How can that be reversed?

The slogans and placards have all been turned away from us, facing the video camera. We, the participants in the *miting*, I realize, haven't even seen what we've been gathered round. For all we know the slogans might read 'UP WITH ALBANIANS!' or 'SERBS ARE STUPID!' Even here, we're being orchestrated for the camera.

LONG LIVE BROTHERHOOD AND UNITY! LONG LIVE TITO AND THE COMMUNIST PARTY! LONG LIVE YUGOSLAVIA! and the *miting* is over. The school children start a raggedy kolo, dragging the flags around with them, and the loudspeaker sends forth *The Drina March*, the dismal classic from the First World War.

We start walking back round the side of the school and onto the narrow road which turns us into a procession, strolling along under the placards and flags, the banners protesting Albanian rape and genocide on Sunday afternoon. Neighbors in the procession are greeting neighbors leaning on their garden gates. All smiling. Two Albanians, thin, older men in white caps, I see gliding off through the trees, disappearing. Another old Albanian, trying to cross the road, pushes through our column to sit down on the dusty verge, looking baffled and uncomprehending. He sits there, holding his cane between his knees looking at us as though we're all apparitions.

We are a long way from Pec. I'm just wondering how long when we turn into another little school yard and there beyond the parked cars is our picnic indeed: crates of green or red Pec apples and free beer and fruit juice. The juice is in the silver packets which are so expensive now. There's a real packaged lunch; pita bread, sausage and creamy cheese. Behind the crates someone has propped up a picture of Njegos on the classroom window sill.

Having eaten, people are starting to drive off and I make myself barge up and ask for a lift before I'm left with the empty beer bottles and crates of apples. A middle-aged man, his wife and a young daughter, a Montenegrin family who are so amazed I'm an Englishwoman I can't get in one question about rape or genocide. The man offers to take me to my friends I'd come to see.

Well, it's an Albanian family," I say truculently.

"What's the name?"

When I mention Idriz the Montenegrin slaps the steering wheel: "Idriz! A wonderful family! A golden man! You know, he and my brother are like blood brothers, really. It's a long story..."

Idriz is home. He steps through the high wooden courtyard gate and shakes hands with the Montenegrins. They ask about families and friends, decline to come in and leave. Idriz is just the same except he's got three teenage sons in jeans and tee shirts, lining up shyly to be introduced. Idriz should be sent on tour to major Serbian cities. This is an Albanian.

His wife, Fatma, is putting henna on her hair, ready for work on Monday, and they have a couple visiting. Ibrahim and Nexhat are Exhibit

A for me: a modern Albanian couple, reminding me how fast things are changing in Kosovo. I have brought a half bottle of Teachers Scotch, and Nexhat drinks too. She is as sharp and funny as her husband, commenting on politics but she's just a housewife, she says. I tell them all I've been to a *miting*.

"Did they pay you?" asks Idriz, smiling.

"No, but I got a free lunch."

We toast Brotherhood and Unity in Serbian and Albanian. We toast the fact that we are *internationalistas*. We toast Tito and the peoples of the world. There are fresh dahlias on the coffee table and the last summer roses on top of the television. The mountain slopes with their pale mosques still rise as they always have done beyond the quince trees in the back garden. We get through that half bottle of Scotch and then a *Kosovo Kabernet Rezerv, 1985* as we watch the television news, the reports of the *mitings*. Fatma brings out *meze* to go with the drink but no more sausage and hard cheese, crackers, peanuts or even pretzels. A little soft white cheese, grated carrot, a few olives.

Idriz, Ibrahim and their wives seem genuinely surprised things are so tense in Pristina. Maybe in the villages things are bad, Idriz says. "In Pec we are OK."

Why do people, Serbians, leave Kosovo?

People are always moving, Ibrahim says but everything here is put on to the Serb-Albanian problem: everything here is called *pritisak,* pressure. And as for all the stuff about joining with Albania, "I went to Albania for ten days with my Aunt — She wanted to look up some relatives. My God! No Yugoslav Albanian wants to live in Albania. They have nothing!"

The news is reporting there is a big *miting* in Titovo Mitrovice, right on the edge of Kosovo: 30,000 even though it was forbidden by the authorities. Titovo Mitrovice used to be called Kosovski Mitrovice, where the Trepca lead and zinc mines are. The police are beating demonstrators in Montenegro again. The party men in Montenegro are still resisting Milosevic and his *mitings*. This is still the old Yugoslav world of the Six Republics. Croatia and Slovenia have been protesting not against Albanians but Serbia's treatment of Albanians in Kosovo. The Kosovo Question, say many observers, will destroy Yugoslavia. The Bosnians are not allowing the Serbs to hold rabid anti-Albanian *mitings* in Bosnia. Good old Bosnia.

It's almost evening. Too late to go to Prizren. Idriz invites me to stay the night and we go out for an evening promenade down by the Bistrica. Macaroni and cheese for supper. How hard for Fatma in these tough times with three teenage boys to feed. I've bought another bottle of wine to replace the one we'd drunk but we get so tense watching the news we drink that one too. My *miting* is mentioned on the evening news: it ended 'without incident.' Before going to bed we watch the end of *The Big Country*, Gregory Peck, grizzled and stubborn, under the last red and yellow roses on top of the television set.

The sheep are down from the mountains. We can see them from the bus, in pens near the road. There are gypsies in tents by the side of the road too, and carcasses of cars. Beyond them, irrigation ditches, corn, and a sudden glimpse of a girl washing clothes in a stream and a boy cantering off on a pony, hunting rifle under his arm, pointing down.

Idriz says firmly the blood feud is a thing of the past. That would be a lasting legacy of Albanian control of Kosovo, whatever happens now. Under Serbia, from the old pre-war kingdom to the days of Rankovic, it was understood the more Albanians that killed each other off, the better. Can it really be true? If Idriz says so it is. There are eight truths in Yugoslavia now, Agim told me, like Milena. "Every time you cross a Republic border or autonomous region the truth changes."

Nezir is another Albanian whose judgement I've always trusted. It's a Monday morning so easy to find him in Prizren: he's teaching. Solid family man now and head of the English department. Idriz works for the government. "He works too hard" Fatma had said. "If everyone were like Idriz, the country wouldn't be in this mess." Stunned to find me in the staff room Nezir waylays colleagues to take his classes for him so we can talk.

In Prizren the Serb boycott of classes only lasted a day or two, Nezir says. The Serbs who are Moslem "stayed with the Albanians." That's what Idriz' son said in Pec, about his school; the Moslem Serbs called Bosniaks "stayed with the Albanians." Outside the sun is streaming down, the wonderful Kosovo Indian summer.

Yes, Dr. Martin is fine. Yes, the children are fine. And Nezir's are too. — What about Kosovo? Nezir sighs. The coffee and mineral water arrive on the little brass tray just as always, except the Turkish coffee is much thinner everywhere now. Nezir brings a bottle of brandy out of the cupboard.

What about the Serbs leaving Kosovo?

"The biggest problem here is there is so much pressure on land and there is so much money. All the sons coming back from Germany and Switzerland and those places and all want to buy land and build a house. There is SO much money in Kosovo!"

I remember when 'Dr. Martin' and I left for the States, wanting to change our money. Kosovo must have been the cheapest place in Europe to buy Deutsche Marks. All those sons and brothers, the average family in

Kosovo is 6.7, no longer hanging around on Belgrade street corners but guest workers in Germany, Switzerland, Belgium.

"They don't drink like the Serbians. They save their money and come back. So any Serbian can sell his land here for lots of hard currency, go north, buy a house with half and put the other half in the bank."

"That's the other thing," adds Nezir. "You know, yes. You've lived here — It is very, very hard for Serbs to accept that we Albanians can be equal to them. Can be doctors and lawyers or live in good houses. So when they see us doing well, living well — They need to find another reason for it."

Soon after I'd left Kosovo the first time, I'd met a young Afro-American who, after we'd talked for a while, had asked me, baffled "How come you know what it's like to be black?"

A white woman with a BBC accent. Because for five years I'd been on the defensive every day always tensing for a fight; anything from an angry argument to a veiled remark. I could sense when people were waiting for me to go away so they could say what they really thought. I'd developed a thin skin and a truculent attitude. Everything had to be assessed from minute to minute; how a shop assistant reacted, the look on a face. And I'd seen my students, the best ones, like blacks in a white world, have to wrestle with divided loyalties. When Serbian was their best language, to abandon that and struggle with Albanian in order to be a good Albanian, when gradually their harshest critics became no longer Serbs, but other Albanians who accused them of being Uncle Toms if they didn't have an attitude.

All the bright, sharp, sophisticated Albanians I know, and all the stupid, provincial, crass Serbs but I'm still feeling there must be something to what the Serbs say... And if just one Albanian steals, is stupid or eats with his mouth open — You see? Meri! Meri! ...Weren't we right?

Two more of my ex-students come in to the staff room. Hassan from Bashkim's year, and Nikola! One of the old Fourth year, the Montenegrin who spoke Albanian. Looking so much older and burned out. I ask about Mehmet. He drinks too much, Nezir says. We're getting through the whole bottle of brandy here. These Albanians who never drank. Maybe because they're older, maybe the tension this year, the political situation. We start to reminisce, tell jokes, holed up in the dusty, gloomy staff room, the sun shining outside, the sound of the children at break. Nezir a little cautious now we're not alone. I remember him describing the Rankovic years. The careless word, the private joke and if you were reported, the police station.

And the demonstrations — the *mitings*? They have to stop, says Nezir. They can't go on getting bigger without something happening.

Coming in on the Pec bus to Prizren I'd been talking to the Albanian next to me and he'd walked with me towards Nezir's school stopping by the gate under the trees. A young, self-described *bizniz-man* impatient with questions, he had not seemed particularly sensitive or aware but as we said goodbye and shook hands, he hesitated, not letting my hand go.

"If you are a journalist" he said, "please write the truth." He looked at the ground, looked around. There was the battered gate, the school yard.

"Albanians are not scared of death," he said slowly. "They're not scared of war. If it's coming let it come but…" He was gazing across the road, into the little park, watching a trickle of young boys come through the trees and squeeze through a gap in the wall.

"But civil war is terrible. It will be …women and children…I just want you to know whatever you are… — Just tell the truth about us. The truth." Embarrassed, he dropped my hand and walked away.

At Milena's I'm sleeping in her son's room. I share it with Dusan's bike and the ironing board. We're in the center of Belgrade. I pop across the road to a little grocers for some of the lovely Yugoslav fruit juices. When I open the fridge a little later they're all gone. Dusan, twelve and Zorana 16, have siphoned them up. Their mother can't afford to buy them.

No-one goes out anymore, Milena says. There's not the money. But we take the bus across the Sava to Zemun on Sunday morning. The only sound is an outboard motor across the tranquil water as we walk along the promenade and have a wonderful lunch at a fish restaurant, sturgeon. Milena pays. When I protest Milena says, "— Hey! *Platimo plastik*! All of Yugoslavia is living on credit cards now!"

We visit an artist friend of hers, walk the old winding streets, but get back across the bridge and home as sunset falls over the rivers. There's a curfew now. Clear the streets by 10:00 PM. "Safety cannot be guaranteed." A young man has been knifed down by the Danube. "But it may not be related to anything."

Milena's daughter had reported that all army officers' children had been told to keep off the streets for their own safety.

"Ha!" Milena had snorted "What about all the other kids?"

More police everywhere. Crises in parliament. Party members talking, talking, while the *mitings* grow larger. My Secretary of Education, the Albanian who'd made it possible for me to go down to Kosovo, is out, resigned. The top Albanian in Belgrade, Milena says. Constitutional crisis continues in Kosovo. Talking, talking. Supported by the other Republics, the Kosovo Albanians are still holding out against Milosevic.

At Nada's one of her father's old friends is visiting. He was at the court of King Alexander before the war, now an embassy chauffeur. People are being turned away from hospitals in Kosovo he says. He heard it at the embassy. They are taking only emergency cases. They are ready for violence.

Nada and I have already nearly come to blows over the Question of Kosovo. It's those "documentaries" again. Albanians flooding over the border! I've now seen the one of the old Albanian, his face hidden as though he's a criminal, talking about how he came over the border in 1948 and — wait for it! *Never became a citizen!* That was the year of Tito's break with Stalin when Yugoslavia would have welcomed Albanian refugees as anti-Stalinists. This old man could be Agim's father.

Nada is angry with Albanians, she's angry with Montenegro resisting Serbian demands for official support. She's angry with the Slovenes demanding fairer treatment for Albanians. For the first time I hear her angry with Tito. She's seeing plots from the very start: the Communist Party, the other Republics —

"Oh yes! They have been weakening Serbia ever since the war!"

And Nada, who is half Slovene, half Croat like Tito was, whose husband, Stefan, has a Czech father has just declared, "Well! If Suleiman is Turkish-Albanian — Why does he live in Yugoslavia at all!"

And I yell, "So if your children are half Czech, half Yugoslav then maybe they'll be allowed to live in Yugoslavia for......HALF the year?"

Silence. The only argument I've won. The cats have fled under the couch, the dog is crouching under the table.

Walking down by the Danube Milena had said "Somehow when I got your letter that you were coming, it made me feel young again."

Milena has said firmly, "No more politics."

We are all three in Nada's flat for the last time. Tomorrow, as no-one can afford to go out, Milena will 'make a party' and then the next night will be my last. Nada says, "Yes, when Mary said she was coming back, I felt so happy."

Nada gets out a box from among all the other piles, full of letters and photographs. Under all the slick, colored ones there they are — The three of us in black and white, in long dirndle skirts feeding pigeons in Trafalgar Square. Nada and Milena on the beach at the Isle of Wight. Long before college, long before children. Back all the way to 1955 when we were all still at school and Nada, who had started off a pen friend, came to stay. ("I have a cat called Mouse and like painting and Frank Sinatra and have seen *Gypsy Colt* twice because he is so wise and nice horse.") Milena had been staying, by chance, a few streets away, having landed up with a family of Jehovah's Witnesses. She had begged us to take her in so we'd pushed the twin beds together in the back room and the three of us took turns sleeping over the join in the middle.

Nada's son and his friends drift in. Tight black jeans, black tops, long hair, dreamy expressions. They look like pages to Renaissance princes. We have found Nada's old hoard of signed photos of the stars. There they are! Lana Turner, Gina Lollabrigida, Gregory Peck.

"Oh, yes!" Milena exclaims "Mary! You were SO crazy about Gregory Peck!"

Audie Murphy — Simone Signoret — We peer at the signatures. Did they really all actually sign them? I wet my finger and try one, rubbing the faded ink. Nada gives a mock howl of outrage and holds them close. Her son and his friends back away. "Mama? MAMA! *Ciaou!*"

"Hey!" Milena calls after them "The curfew! Don't be out late! Remember the curfew!'"

I need to go shopping. I have a husband and children now to take back things to and I have thousands of dinars to spend. I've helped Nada and Milena out by changing dollars for dinars and now I'm knee deep in dinars. I'm not a big spender and Nada and Milena refuse adamantly to take any dinars back. So I go round Belgrade buying a few cautious things for the family like nice leather belts and then stock up on things to leave behind: wine, toilet paper, jams and juices, coffee and soap. Bystanders are looking through the restaurant windows at a wedding still staggering on in daylight, women dancing with their arms up high, palms turning, like Emina dances, a brandy bottle with a rose stuck on the side. The bride in white still up at the top table. How much this must have cost.

There's a great story from the First World War about the Serbs firing on the Austrians from the Turkish fort, from Kalamegdan, across the river. They run out of ammunition. But the order goes out: "Fire anyway!" Serbia has run out of money, out of credit, out of luck but Spend anyway! When I get back Nada presents me with a wonderful wooden chess set for my son, a beautiful peasant woven dress for myself. She has been off to the most expensive Yugo-Export shop.

"We pay with plastic!" she says breezily "Come on!" Nada was so pleased to hear my son was good at chess. Yugoslavia ranks about third in the world for chess. Everywhere you see people playing chess or you did. And Milena gives me presents too including a beautiful new Yugoslav cook book. There are the burnished turkish pots and platters. The book is full of the most beautiful photography; still lifes of solid earthenware, peppers, stuffed vine leaves and rich homemade stews, the crumbly pastries, the black cherries in brandy — the simple spoon set across the glass of fresh water beside the sweet preserve on crisp, handwoven embroidered linen. The traditional greeting that comes from the Turks, the East. Everything gathered from the six Republics and two provinces by a Slovene cook and published elegantly in Ljubljana, Slovenia.

It's the night before I go. I'm taking Milena and Nada out. Just the three of us. We will go wherever we want and spend whatever we want. For the first time in my life I feel like a man. Just shove your hand in your pocket, call for the food and drink, slap down the money among the plates and leave. Nada and Milena can't argue because they know that all my dinars will soon be worth nothing anyway. We go to Skardalija, one of the best known restaurants in Belgrade. We walk there, in a row across the pavement, like teenagers. Skardalija is almost empty. There's a gypsy band all in red, a brass band, no sad, stringy violinist. No 'Merry Widow.'

— And what will we have?

We will have everything. What brandy? The best. What wine? The most expensive.

The *meze*, the Turkish word for appetizers; the cheeses and ham and olives and *ajvar* — the paprika preserve — the meats, the fresh bread and creamy *kajmak*. All the salads, the crunchy cucumber, cabbage and tomato, the roasted peppers, those wonderful sweet peppers in their Christmas greens and reds, tipped over by the cart-ful in the markets, spilling out in bonfire heaps. All the meats, the pork and beef, grilled and roasted, the crusty real bread. Like every wonderful Yugoslav meal I've ever had, since the first evening Nada's father took us out, when I first came, and we had the grilled meats at a little open air cafe, the sound of horses clopping in the background over the cobbles, the group at the next table singing *It's a Long Way to Tipperary* when they heard English. And I don't care how much it costs. For the first time in my life I'm really acting and feeling like a Yugoslav. Well, not a Slovene but definitely a Serb. For my dinars there is no tomorrow. And we will have music. We can own the band. They love us and we love them. By this time we love everyone. I will be careful not to ask for songs from Kosmet, Kosovo but there are the wonderful songs from southern Serbia and Macedonia, the *sevdalinka*, Turkish love songs from Bosnia, the gypsy song *Sweet Tea*.

The brass instruments catch the light. The tallest member of the band is bent over some kind of tiny flute.

"Why is it, "Nada cries over the music with a wicked grin, "that the biggest man always has the smallest instrument?"

There are wonderful jokes circulating in Belgrade about what's going on, about life in Yugoslavia on the eve of who knows what, in 1988. Mostly *crni humor*, black humor and mostly jokes that need the neatness of their mother tongue. But one is pretty clear.

"What's the difference between an optimist and a pessimist?" Milena yells through the gypsy brass band.

"The pessimist says things in Yugoslavia can't get any worse! The optimist says, 'Oh, they can! They can!'"

1994

■

Balkan Winter

A little bottle of scotch and a can of ginger ale. A nice little packet of nuts. Settling down as the flight takes off, Miami: London. Watching the BBC news, British Air. This evening we have Martin Luther King's birthday and the Los Angeles 'Quake of 94.' It's Monday, January 17, 1994. The earthquake was on the morning news as I finished packing. Aspirin, cheddar cheese, vitamin pills, garlic sausage, ballpoint pens. Tennis shoes. If they don't fit they can be sold. Socks. Agim had asked for socks. When I called I had asked what should I bring. From Emina, just a silence. Nada too. They need everything.

The BBC news has nothing new on Yugoslavia, *ex*-Yugoslavia, the *former* Yugoslavia. Diplomats are still trying to get a permanent cease fire in Bosnia; in Geneva now. "We are at the end of the diplomatic road."

War hadn't broken out first in Kosovo after all. The war had started in Slovenia, of all places. Slovenia and Croatia had declared their independence from the Yugoslav Federation in June, 1991. In Slovenia there were some skirmishes, burned out cars and tanks at border crossings, interviews with older conscripts from the Yugoslav Federal Army and the Slovene militia who spoke English well enough for prime time American news. They would be the '*staris*,' the students who'd put off their military service as long as possible and now maybe considering that hadn't been such a good idea after all. But Slovenia had done surprisingly well, had captured hundreds of soldiers, boys really. There they were on CNN, flashing big grins and V signs through the bus windows. Slovenia, with no great tangle of Serbs, Croats or Moslems, just full of Slovenians, the Yugoslavs with the pens in their shirt pockets and their strange fascination for work, just packed up its trade fairs and went home. But then came the war in Croatia and the following March, in the spring of 1992, Bosnia. Tanks crushing through golden corn fields, blood under a bright blue sky, it was as though Yugoslavia was producing a colorized version of the Second World War for Nineties TV, the cameras training our eyes on those blocks of flats in Sarajevo every night, hunting out the blackened hole or the curtains still hanging behind the broken glass, blood on the walls. And all I could think was what a waste — what a waste of precious housing. That family waited so long for that tight little flat.

The man next to me is not eating his peanuts. He only ordered a juice. He could have got rum, scotch — anything. Nada says for two weeks now they've had no wine. They can't afford meat anymore. I can't imagine Yugoslavia, Serbia, without meat or wine and strong drink. I ask the man next to me for his peanuts. "I'm going to Yugoslavia," I explain.

I want to go up and down the aisles asking for the unopened cookies, the chocolates, the little bottles, the small squares of cheese — I can take it all to my friends in Yugoslavia, actually to Serbia. But maybe I shouldn't say Serbia and Belgrade. Maybe the passengers won't give it to me for Serbia. Serbs are the enemy.

I could say I want the peanuts and cheese and nice little packets of crackers for Moslems. My Moslem friends. No, not in Bosnia, in Kosovo. That's Serbia, too. No, they're not fighting there. Yet. Yugoslavia always has been too complicated to explain to most people.

I suppose I'm breaking the embargo against Serbia. Bringing comfort to the enemy. Nada and Milena. This is history, happening right now. The Serbian nation is entering the history books again. No longer "Poor little Serbia" of the First World War; the gallant Serbia who rose up against the pact with Hitler in 1941: "The Yugoslav nation has found its soul" — Churchill. I was always so eager to tell everyone about Yugoslavia and especially Serbia. So frustrated when no-one even seemed to know where it was. Everyone thinks they know Serbs now: Serbs the beetle-browed, drunken thugs of the cartoons and of the war.

In the British Air bathroom I'm tempted to take the toilet rolls. Serbia is in the throes of hyper-inflation. Nothing like it has been seen in Europe since the last days of pre-Hitler Germany. The last time I talked to Nada on the phone she said her teacher's salary would buy four rolls of toilet paper — today. But only three tomorrow. And that's *Yugoslav* toilet paper. At the rate of inflation by the time I reach Belgrade those rolls will be worth at least three months of Nada's teaching. I want to scavenge everything. Having grown up in the war, which will now no longer be 'the last war,' I click easily, too easily, my family say, into the Somalia mode. I find it hard to throw away even a used envelope because when you turn it over there's a whole new side to write on. The Somalis created a whole economy, a culture, out of the UN presence, from what the US troops threw away.

I ask the man next to me, if he doesn't want a liqueur, would he still order one, please? — Now what do I say? For the Moslems of Kosovo? He does, but he's looking at me in a funny way. Any moment now he's going to ask the flight attendant if he can sit somewhere else.

Combat troops in camouflage stand at the ready, spaced neatly on the runway at Budapest airport. And plain clothes men in bullet-proof vests are moving very quickly through the crowds inside. But they were at Heathrow. There's a hint of snow in corners and crevices and the sky is grim. The only joke we've had on the phone is how this is true friendship indeed, worthy of a Serb or Albanian, to leave a place like Miami in January for Belgrade. Nada, Milena and Emina all sound so tired on the phone, so bone tired. Because of the international embargo against Serbia, Belgrade airport is closed so Nada said everyone flies to Budapest and takes a minibus, a van 'whatever there is' down to Belgrade. The arrival area is full of smart young Serbians drumming up customers, in perfect English, for the Belgrade trip. I hand over my precious dollars but then have to wait two hours. I won't reach Belgrade until late.

Our mini-van holds a Belgrade University teacher in a fur coat and hat, a girl with a violin, a housewife and another girl. No-one talks much. There's one man who sits up by the driver in total silence, looking exactly like Harvey Keitel. We all have lots of luggage. I'm worried about the border. I went wild on the socks for Agim, thinking of Vlaznim too who is big now, and Suleiman. They'll think I want to sell socks in Belgrade on the black market. And pens. And tights. I may lose it all.

Hungarians say *SZUPERMARKET*. Because I know this is Hungary I feel how bleak and strange everything is; the traces of snow, the bare landscape. If this were Vojvodina I'd feel at home. I was always so full of the Yugoslav-ness of Yugoslavia. Serbia was 'given' Austro-Hungarian Vojvodina after the First World War, full of Hungarians, and given Kosovo, full of Albanians, from the Ottoman Empire. Slices of territory crammed with people like raisins in a cake. Just handed over. Serbia's mini-Empire. And yet Nada and Suleiman and Austro-Roumanian Ilija grew up together as 'Yugoslavs'; bright students of English, with their Serbo-Croat English grammars. 'Austro-Roumanian': how clumsy that sounds. Ilija was not Austro-Roumanian. Ilija was Yugoslav.

The Serbian girl with the violin is grumbling about the embargo.

"— Yes, we are all at fault — but why just blame us? Why punish us?" The Serbs. On the radio talk, endless talk. Talk about the Geneva talks on the war in Bosnia. I thought it was just under Communism that there was endless talk. A commentator quoting *The Daily Telegraph*: British foreign policy and the importance of rich, Moslem nations.

Just before the border we stop at a little village general store. Opposite is a kiosk where we change money in the dark, and then barge into the shop, grab a metal basket and Go! I'm trying to figure out how many Forints to a dollar; how much everything is. The bus driver is saying "Hurry!" The Hungarian assistants are looking fed up at yet another invasion of desperate Serbian women. Cheese! Bread! Milk! Sausage! I'm trying to figure out what's most important. They're grabbing everything. Fresh fruit — yes! Tangerines, Riesling. I'm going to need some wine after all this. But I've miscalculated my Forints and the sulky girl cashier dumps out my precious tangerines and Riesling, leaving in macaroni and soup powder.

Snaking away in the dark is a long, long line of red tail-lights: the crossing point. Our driver asks for a few Deutsche Marks from each of us — "Dollars will do" he tells me graciously so we can be granted 'diplomatic immunity.' He collects our passports, drives right up to the guards and there's a friendly word, a clap on the back and we're through.

To get a visa I needed an invitation letter and Nada had faxed over a page. "You got your visa very quickly," said the nice Serb over the phone, from the Yugoslav Embassy in Washington, "because the letter from your friend was so nice, telling of your long friendship." I hoped he wouldn't get into trouble if someone found out I'd gone down to Kosovo.

The streets are deserted in Serbia. But it's after ten. Just one *MILICIJA* car. Then the lights finally of Novi Beograd. They've certainly still got electricity. And then across the river and into Belgrade. We leave the young violinist in a gloomy doorway just over the bridge. She must have been worried when the Pentagon talked about bombing the bridges, the Serbian supply lines to the war in Bosnia. And the Belgrade ones to teach the Serbs a lesson. That was the time Milena had called. "Hey!" she'd yelled down the phone. "So! When are you guys going to bomb us?" Nada and Milena live not far from the river bridges. In fact, back in those far off summers the boys used to arrive under Nada's window, barefoot, their oars still dripping on the hot pavement.

The van takes each passenger right to their door. Nada's entrance still has the old World War 11 shrapnel and bullet holes round the sides. Nada's son comes down to help me up with the luggage and Nada is in the doorway.

One of Nada's front teeth is just hanging by a thread. She can't afford to go to the dentist. If you need to go to hospital it's even worse; "You must take your own sheets, soap, aspirin, surgical gloves for the doctor to examine you — he won't have them."

Nada's dog is dead, poisoned, but they have a new puppy who raids the chair by the couch and trots off with my socks and underwear. The two veteran cats prowl along the half empty shelves and close their eyes at him. Most of the peasant art and beautiful ceramics are gone. Aleksa, Nada's daughter, takes the puppy out to Kalamegdan park every day. She's nineteen now, a student at Belgrade University but her Faculty is closed. There's no heating and as no-one can afford to run their cars the buses are so full that she couldn't get there anyway. She kneels by the couch, black eyes bright, wanting me to come out right now, for a walk. There's been a fresh fall of snow.

Aleksa looks stunning against the snow. She's wearing the new Miami Hurricanes jacket I've brought. I landed up bringing two. This one in bright green and gold satin, dazzling enough for a Prizren wedding, I'd got for Vlaznim, Emina's son. It was an 'impulse buy'; something celebratory and defiant for the bleak Balkan winter. And then thinking of Kosovo now, of the Serbian and Montenegrin soldiers, the police and militia and random bully boys, it seemed not the brightest idea to present an Albanian teenager with a provocative trophy jacket. Just another reason for Emina to worry when Vlaznim went out. So Aleksa gets the bright one and Vlaznim's will be the dark green, slightly worn one my son handed over gallantly at the last minute.

The puppy wags its way ahead of us over the frozen footprints, a wispy, bright eyed mongrel Aleksa rescued off the street. "I like my dog because he is a mix," Aleksa states with a sly defiance. I wonder if Aleksa is making a political statement. In the new lunatic world of ethnic cleansing, untidy, accidental mixes are a reminder of what Yugoslavia used to be all about.

Belgrade seems full of dogs. Apart from a beagle and a poodle with a sweater wrapped around its rib cage, they are guard and attack dogs, like the black German shepherd with the spiked collar that watches us go by in *Studentski Park*. That first morning as Aleksa and I took the puppy down Knez Mihailova, the old central street where we always walked on *korzo*, past the old book stores towards Kalamegdan and the park, three young men came striding past shoulder to shoulder. They had close cropped hair and nasty grins. Each held the leash of a dog straining forward; a big husky with ice blue eyes, a Sar Planinac like the dogs the shepherds had up in the mountain village and another big black German shepherd. They were 'Diesel boys' Aleksa said.

Belgrade is full of gangs now, she tells me; 'Diesel Boys,' the

'Montenegrins' and 'Arkan's Boys.' Arkan, born in Pristina, is the most notorious of the Serbian killers in Bosnia.

Milena had asked only for two things: an orchid and a copy of *Vog* — *Vogue*. I take her orchid, *Vog* and some dollars round right away. "You see?" I say proudly — "Not big bills. Everyone said don't bring big bills!"

Milena starts to cry. I'm making everyone cry.

Milena still has her dog and Zorana's cat, but the children are gone. We helped get them to England. Dusan graduated from high school the summer the fighting started between Serbia and Croatia. He'd not been accepted yet at University and was about to be called up.

"If this were something to fight for, you know I would be the first to say 'Go!'" Milena had cried down the phone. "But this is not war! This is madness!"

Milena has taken in a refugee student from Bosnia, a shy girl who walks the old dog when she is away. "I felt guilty, guilty night and day about the war," Milena says, "But now I can't cry any more." On a shelf is the cobblestone from the Belgrade demonstrations in March 1991. "My last weapon in the fight for democracy!" They'd called in the tanks as though it were Kosovo. "That was the last chance. If the military had come over to us then, then maybe, maybe..." By the summer there was full scale war in Croatia.

We were lucky, getting Zorana, Milena's daughter, to England, too. Just before I left Belgrade on my last visit in 1988 I remember a friend reading Milena's coffee cup: "Here it is in the cup. See? You will not live with your children."

Ivan, Nada's son, left too late. "He wants to stay here and see what happens," Nada had said at the start of the fighting. Ivan had a rock band. By the time she'd asked us to help the British authorities had tightened up against the flood of refugees. In spite of the guarantee letters and phone calls Ivan was turned back at Dover.

"We spent so much money on that trip," Nada says wearily. "We sold so many things..."

But Ivan, in his mid-twenties, tall and thin, hair like John the Baptist, ate a rotten can of meat when he went before the draft board, and fainted clean away. He managed to escape the army. Three of his friends have already died, Aleksa told me. Two of them just got out of their truck and stepped on a mine. Aleksa's boy friend served on the Mostar front. "He won't talk about it but now he carries a gun."

I asked Ivan whether there was much student protest about the war.

"At the start of the war when we thought it could make a difference."

It is so quiet outside. Even allowing for the snow, the double windows. No cars, voices low. Inside, Aleksa and Ivan keep MTV on.

Nada takes me along to meet her colleagues. She is organizing a new timetable. "But why should they come?" Their salaries are worthless anyway. The only thing to do is to give private classes where pay is in hard currency. At least everyone wants to learn English now; everyone wants to leave.

Zivko is in the staff room. Zivko, who always had a jolly good time in England, drawls in his Oxford English:

"They are ALL completely mad. SOMEthing will happen. I hope death. OB-viously bloodshed. I am a pacifist" he lowered his voice "but I want the blood of the leaders to run in the streets!" And then he says,

"It began in Kosmet. It must *end* in Kosmet."

Certainly Milosevic began with Kosmet. That was where he found the key to his political power, on the battlefield of Kosovo. The emnity between Slav and Albanian "in the districts both claim," Edith Durham wrote in 1905 is "...the first of the great Balkan hatreds."

If this were really a war of Ancient Balkan Emnities war would be raging in Kosovo rather than Bosnia. In all my years in Serbia I never once heard a bitter comment about Bosnians.

A few weeks after I left Yugoslavia in November 1988, Serbia won the battle to end Kosovo's autonomy. Kosovo would be ruled directly from Belgrade. There had been no massive orchestrated *mitings* in Pristina after all. It was all done with words. Milosevic, the communist, adept at resolutions, amendments, maneuverings. The TV had been on constantly at Emina's, cutting from live reports of *mitings* in Serbia and Montenegro to the permanent sessions of the Kosovo Regional Council, where Agim worked, addressing Comrades' resolutions, concerns, demands from Belgrade, Agim never home, Vlaznim translating it all for me. "Now, write this down!"

When Kosovo finally lost the Albanian miners marched from Mitrovica in the first snows of winter and led a five day vigil in Pristina against their leaders signing away their rights, their loss of autonomy, everything won since the Brioni Plenum, the Second Liberation of 1966.

About a month later, in January 1989 right in the middle of Super Bowl Sunday the streets of Pristina were there on the US network news: water cannon, riot police and tear gas. Nine dead. The journalists called Kosovo's fight to regain its autonomy the Albanian 'Intafada.' There were the pictures of dark young men throwing rocks; heavily armed police roughing up old Albanians. Since then the situation in Kosovo has been described as pure Apartheid; the Albanian majority in Kosovo kept in line by the army, the police and the special security forces.

But the journalists write that while war destroys Bosnia the traditionally hot headed Albanians are holding firm in the face of Serbian provocation: there's nothing but praise for their coolheadedness. The policy now in the traditional *Vild Vest* of Yugoslavia, Kosovo, with its rifles and berettas, is non-violence, passive resistance. The only heavy firepower, everyone knows, is in the Serbian army camps.

"Oh yes, the Albanians are clever," Zivko says, "much smarter than us Serbs."

Kosovo has been luckier than Bosnia. War in Kosovo everyone agrees means international conflict; Albania, Turkey and Greece would join in. So there are American troops stationed now on the border between Serbian Kosovo and the newly independent Macedonia. They must be guarding the pass at Kacanik where the old *Kosovo-trans* buses used to rattle down to Skopje.

Zivko lights his pipe. "Do you mind if I smoke? I have good tobacco and drink that I accumulated earlier so I don't notice now my stomach is empty."

Nada had brought some homemade bread into the staff room, just an end of yesterday's loaf and while we've been talking Zivko has surreptitiously eaten it bit by bit and now he's getting all the crumbs. Maybe that's why Nada brought it in. When she comes back, I screw up the paper to throw it away and she cries "No! I can use that!"

I think of all my accumulated plastic bags I could have brought. They wouldn't have weighed anything. Zivko is saying, "Bachelors are the first to die." With money worthless and the shops almost empty and prices astronomical, if you don't bake your own bread you starve.

When the postman came up the stairs at noon with the monthly pension for Nada's mother, Nada just shoved the stack of newly printed, crisp notes covered in zeroes behind the clock above my couch.

"If we could have got to the bread shop with this by six we could have bought a loaf. Now there is no more bread to buy and tomorrow all this paper will not be enough for a single one."

"There are so many suicides now in Belgrade" Zivko says "and heart attacks." He and the others have just come back from a memorial service for one of their middle-aged colleagues.

The night before I leave for Kosovo, at about two in the morning Nada and I hear a hum from outside. A low hum, like *korzo*. We open the window and there at the end of the street we see a line of people in the snow. Nada says, "They are starting to wait for bread."

Vuk Draskovic, leader of the Serbian Renewal Movement hands out bread "and sometimes a little flour" once or twice a week for the people of Belgrade. The capital is full of refugees, Serbs from Bosnia and Croatia. They qualify for international aid. But the local residents don't. They are not refugees. They are starving in their own homes.

My bus ticket to Pristina costs 34 million dinars. About twenty-three dollars. Nada's husband Stefan came down with me to the bus station. I had to ask at the ticket window then rush off to change money, a quick, shifty transaction in the little cafe next door then rush back to buy it before the price went up. That was Friday. I'm leaving on Monday, SUPER-DINAR day, the promised last, positively last, attempt to stabilize the economic situation in Serbia and stop this chaos.

There's a noisy kolo in the air and a little car parked by the booking hall draped in the double headed eagle, the flag of Serbia, and a black and gold Cetnik flag. Stacks of grey Serbian army caps are on top and religious pictures and a portrait of King Peter propped against the wheels. A man with a bushy beard is trying to drum up some attention.

"Cetniks" Stefan says. "They're trying to rehabilitate Mihailovic."

Mihailovic was the Serbian Cetnik Royalist leader in the Second World War. Tito executed him. "Mihailovic made a mistake" Stefan says. "He was the victim of Communist propaganda."

No-one has a good word to say for Tito anymore. If you do, you lower your voice. "Mary is a Titoist!" I've had that introduction this last week, in a conspiratorial tone. Milena says "They are spitting on Tito which doesn't make him more guilty but makes them feel more clean."

Only Ana, the old woman who comes to help at Nada's, had declared in a loud strong voice as she held out her hand wet from the sink: "Ha! So you are from America and I am from Yugoslavia! Yugoslavia! And I wish we were back in Tito's time!" She didn't come this Monday morning. Nada says all her pension now will not cover her bus fare.

As we pull out of the bus station our driver looks at the car draped with all the Serbian nationalist paraphenalia, the saints in lurid colors, and exclaims scornfully, "Ha! I fought five years!..." Good! I think. He's not falling for all that blood-stained rubbish. And I realize I'm feeling the sort of emotions it was hard to understand when I'd first come to Yugoslavia eleven years after the Second World War when Christianity conjured up visions not of black and gold icons, soaring pillars and uplifted congregations but cold-eyed killers with crosses on their chests.

On *Radio Beograd* the opening of the new Serbian Parliament that's coinciding with Super-Dinar. A minute's silence for the war dead and then an address. There are almost no Albanians on the bus and no sound of Turkish or Albanian though I've seen a girl with a baby get on, hooded eyes down, looking timid, blank-faced, how young Albanian women are traditionally supposed to look in public. Translucent skin shadowed by the headscarf. It would be easy enough to pull Kosovo Moslem women off buses. The voice on *Radio Beograd* is talking about the 'Satanizing' of the Serbian people. I hadn't heard that word in Serbian before. "...What we have given the world..." the voice intones but then jumps from Czar Dusan straight to Nikola Tesla, inventor of the alternating cylinder, with nothing in between. That is the Serbian problem.

We are going down the *auto-put* and it's empty. Snow melting under a bright sun. The bus is warm. All the flats are warm and the shops. I think cheap electricity is keeping Serbia from revolution. Everything is closed and deserted: every cafe, every gas station. No trucks, nothing; no cows in the fields. All I see is a frozen scarecrow and a man sitting watching ten sheep. There's a mindless Serbian kolo on the radio. I'd forgotten how boring Serbian kolos can be because always before there would be the mix: a Serbian kolo and then a Slovenian polka, a soulful love lament from Bosnia, a lyrical song from Macedonia. Now all we get is the relentless round and round, the mindless energy of the Serbian national dance. And outside the bus a Serbia transfixed, grey and deserted, grey as the rumpled homespun army uniform on the young soldiers. What the hunt for the Greater Serbia has brought Serbia to. And then I remember that it's SUPER-DINAR day and all businesses, banks and offices have been closed while the new money is introduced. One new Super-Dinar is the equivalent of a million old ones. They've knocked off all the zeros and started again.

That Milena says is the problem with the Serbs: they always want to wipe out everything that went before and start again. How can they wipe out seven hundred years of the Turks? From Czar Dusan to Nikola Tesla? We always used to laugh at the Greeks for calling Turkish coffee *Greek* coffee, for trying to sweep all their Turkishness and Balkan mix under the genteel classical mat. How offensive to see a little mosque in Thessalonika turned into a scruffy cinema. How much more tolerant and sophisticated the Peoples' Republic of Yugoslavia had seemed about these things even though Tito and the Partisans had swept away God and King. Now they are swept away themselves. Everywhere in parks the eye is registering empty flower borders and places which would have been the focal point, just a mound of bare earth now, like graves and I'm trying to remember: was that a Partisan memorial there or a statue of Tito?

But still the only thing that draws the eye this Monday morning in Serbia is the newly turned soil in the graveyards, many by the road and the big new, funeral wreaths. We pass an army camp, a deserted factory. I wonder if most of these places are closed anyway: no money for parts, no money to pay. It's not just today.

"They want to destroy us, the whole Serbian people! " Nada declares. "Who? — The Vatican, the Germans...Who knows?"

And I want to say, "Why does anyone have to bother? You've done such a good job yourselves."

The kolo doesn't wind down, it just stops as though the band has suddenly lost interest. Now the radio is quoting *The Washington Post*: "The Moslems deserve most blame now for the continuing crisis in Bosnia."

Our bus turns off the motor way and is slowed down for the first time since Belgrade. It's a funeral procession, the priest carrying the cross, men behind in long dark coats holding the big, official wreaths against their stomachs and in the middle a tractor moving slowly along, carrying the coffin. Because of the large, bottlegreen wreaths, and two men in army uniform, I think it's a soldier's funeral. But I've thought the same for all the freshly dug graves along the way.

We stop for lunch at a little place by itself just off the road, with a rooster in front doing its low goose-step over the ruts and a little dog bustling about on short legs. The restaurant is nothing more than a flat roofed cement box with a sign attached to the roof: *TOPLES BAR*. I'm an old hand at these Balkan bus stops: I'm through the restaurant and into the Turkish lav, breathing through my mouth, not looking, while everyone else is still stretching their legs. There are a few young men and soldiers having a beer and on the back wall behind them a mural, lights on either side: Njiegos, the Montenegrin poet-king, and *Sveti Sava*, the greatest Serbian saint with big black crosses all over his robe. Like the Turkish lavatory the mural leaves a lot to be desired.

Out in front by the bus there's a man with three dice, three little cups and a little portable blue baize table. Around him a ring of men and boys and young soldiers who look so young you want to ask them: "Did you finish your homework before you went off to be a soldier?"

The weatherbeaten man with gold teeth and three dice keeps talking and moving his sunburnt hands. He's taking bets. I can't believe it. Men are tossing hard currency — German marks — on the baize. They always lose. The circle laugh, smoking and turning their heads to spit. Behind us on the deserted road, a police car races by. Passengers are getting back in the bus, two women saying, "He lost his wedding ring and he's playing again!"

Radio Pristina is coming in clearly on the bus radio now. White capped mountains appear on the horizon and overhead in a clear blue sky, trailing white, banking and swirling are three fighter jets. A program of Questions and Answers on the new Super Dinar. Pensioners will get the new money first. "What will happen? Will things get better?" The speaker, like everyone else, says he doesn't know.

The bus driver stops for a young conscript who stands behind him, bending over slightly, talking as he rides the few miles down the road. Across the valley I see a mosque with its own row of poplar trees. How brave and solitary it seems shining white in the winter afternoon sun. How could you 'ethnically cleanse' Kosovo? Two million Albanians? Ninety percent of the population? The *Muslimani* Albanians?

"All what's worst has happened," Milena says flatly "in our accursed land. Everything we said was impossible, unthinkable. So — why not?"

Military check point. Uniforms like Belgrade; a blue combat uniform with beret, looking high alert and ready for trouble. A handsome young Serb with a profile made for Milosevic's evening news comes out of the glass booth and swings up into our bus, swinging his gaze round the passengers, his automatic held up across his chest. We all sit quietly and look ahead.

"OK to go?" asks the driver.

New, solid, brick houses, many three stories high; such big family houses are not necessarily Albanian as I'd thought. They're now familiar from the evening news as the camera pans slowly down the Bosnian streets behind an UNPROFOR armored car and they stand gutted, or flicker with flames. Now many Serbian refugees are being resettled in Kosovo, taking over Albanian property. Thousands of Albanians have left, Emina says, the Turkish speakers to Turkey.

Radio Pristina is back to the opening of the parliament in Belgrade and someone is intoning: "We fight for country, cross and golden freedom!"

Carcasses of old cars by the road, magpies, rubbish everywhere, people everywhere. Children straggling home from country school, bright and sharp, chins up checking out the bus, just like I remember. Girls too. My good old Kosovo, teeming with life as ever. Down into Pristina over the ruts, young men and teenage boys everywhere, greengrocers' brimming with fruit, with green and orange and red. Not the drab empty shelves of Belgrade and how oriental still. The journalists always do this bit: the bright plastic harness, Turkish slippers, the kettles and cans and lengths of brocade, the hanks of rope and the watchmakers, the turbans on the old Albanians. I'd been so worried. Kosovo under martial law: beatings and savage interrogations. Police raids. Albanians dying in custody again like Mehmet's father.

When I could get a connection to Pristina, Vlaznim's voice would always come strong down the line:

"Don't worry, Aunty Meri! Everything is fi-i-i-ne!" But the last time he had said, slowly, "I must say, things are not so fine, we can say."

Emina says electricity is often turned off to the Albanian parts of town, and Vlaznim must try and study in the cold by candlelight.

Damn! I'm thinking as we trundle through Pristina, I should have brought candles.

Pristina looks awful from the new end of town. Monstrous blocks of flats rise from a sea of mud and litter, no trees. The row of taxi drivers are all grinning at me and my monster suitcase. How lively they seem. All Albanian, I know. For one thing, they look so Western, just like the Bosnians, and how Irish. Having visited Ireland for the first time after five years in Kosovo my reaction was how Albanian the Irish looked. The Albanians may have been pre-Celtic Illyrians but from the look of things they weren't much concerned with ethnic purity. Idriz' sons in Pec were like a row of Kennedy boys. I'm emphasizing all this in my head, my internal dialogue *za inat* 'for spite' against the Serbian mentality. These Balkan *Muslimani*, Bosnians and Albanians, presented as the barbaric scourge of the Christian Serbs by Milosevic look so much more Western and like us than the average Serb. And, like the Irish, here's another dig at the Serbs, the Albanians have such social grace and ease.

Even so, I don't want to part with many of my precious single dollars to taxi drivers, even if they are Albanian. Single dollars are priceless now. No-one wants to exchange more than they need. If you get dinars back they're worthless. In the end we agree on two dollars.

My taxi driver worked in radio and television and knows Nik and Abdyllah from Radio Pristina. I end up giving him an extra dollar after all because he said his last fare was a *milicija* and they have to take the police and military free.

Overflowing garbage and graffiti greet me at the dark entrance: SEX PISTOLS, SKINS, the peace sign. The stairs smell of cabbage and as always total neglect. It's cold and bleak but January is always bleak. Old shoes outside the door and there is Emina, then Vlaznim and home-made bread in the kitchen. There's a sack of flour on the floor and through the window over the little clothes line and terrace rail, beyond the flats opposite, the hills rise up, close in around the town like the hills round Sarajevo. And up there somewhere from the bus I'd seen a blue painted tank, gun turret facing, innocently enough, away from the town.

Agim has become a gardener. Out on the narrow balcony there's a row of potato plants in pots, withered pepper and tomatoes, some herbs brown in the January cold. Agim has also turned himself back into a farmer. The brother who left the land and went to the town, now at weekends takes the bus back to his village and tills his piece of land there. "Luckily he didn't sell that piece to the other brothers so we have something" Emina says. 'And so we survive."

Even before unpacking everything, the very first morning I had to go down to the open air stands opposite Emina's flat and for five dollars buy dates, oranges and bananas. The fruit had blazed across the road more bright and inviting than anything I'd seen in Belgrade but for Emina it might as well have been in the capital. She had no dollars or Deutsche marks. I come back triumphantly, just like the old days with the badge of office of the female, the bulging string bag and joking like the old days, "Look! Look! Eat Eat!" in the old Turkish influenced Serbian of Kosovo and Emina, her voice trembling, intones as though making a vow:

"If I do not live, my son must live, if only to repay you... I am not religious like my father. He went five times a day to the mosque ..." She can't go on.

Emina has always helped everyone, regardless of nationality. And has always said, "I am like my father...I do not think what nationality they are."

She said when her father died in Prizren many Serbs came to his funeral "Because he had saved so many Serbs, his neighbors, in the war."

There is a charitable organization to help Albanians, the Mother Teresa, named after the world famous Catholic nun who is an Albanian originally from Skopje. Albanians receive bread, rice, shampoo, soap and so on Emina says. Their neighbor, the militant Albanian doctor, gets a lot of stuff there but Emina and Agim don't qualify. Agim, who refused to leave the Communist Party when it became the politically smart thing to do, now has refused to quit his job. He worked for the local administration in Kosovo and he won't stop even though it's all Serbian now. He is a 'loyalist' he says, so must be considered *trathtar*, Albanian for traitor.

Albanians, gradually dismissed from all employment in the province when Kosovo reverted to direct rule from Belgrade, forbidden to conduct business in their own language, have retaliated by shunning the imposed Serbian structure altogether and creating their own. It is a point of honor not to be part of the official Serbian world. Agim, for whatever reason, has refused. So his family gets no Albanian aid and Agim's Serbian salary is worthless now as soon as it is printed. But as Albanians they certainly do not qualify for charitable help from Serbia.

So here I am lavishing care on my Serbian friends, the new pariahs of Europe and now find my closest friends in Kosovo are technically 'traitors' not part of the gallant Albanian struggle at all.

Paprika flavored cabbage, potatoes and homemade bread for lunch. Emina apologizes like Nada in Belgrade, doling out pasta, potatoes, beans, onions and cabbage. And again I insist it's very fashionable, very healthy, very upscale — Hey — homemade bread!

"Food for German soldiers to march on!" Nada had said in disgust. But as always in Yugoslavia it all tastes wonderful. And as always we start with soup. That's why I have brought loads of soup powders and flavorings. They pack so tight too. "Look! Look!" I joke, "Eat! Eat!" and have to stop. I'm making Emina cry again.

We have Turkish coffee made with Cuban coffee and I persuade Emina to eat half an orange. I've brought vitamin pills for Vlaznim too because he's still growing and it's winter.

As the winter dusk came in there was a soft knock on the door and I heard Emina answer not in Turkish or Albanian but Serbian.

"It's the wife of the professor, my neighbor" Emina said when she came back. "She came for a little cooking oil." Would I mind, Emina asked, if we gave her just a little of something from what I'd brought? Her husband was a Serbian professor at the *Fil. Fak.* "Near retirement and the police came and drove him out of his office one day. He came to sit with us. He was so shocked and upset. They said he was an 'Albanian sympathizer.' He spoke Albanian well. That was all. And he didn't mind Albanians. They are old and now they have nothing. And sometimes his wife comes to the door and I try to give her something."

I sit there thinking: hatred defines nationality now. Hatred is the key to survival. The Serbian professor didn't hate Albanians so he has been robbed of his Serbian pension. Agim and Emina don't make distinctions between Serbian and Albanian so Mother Teresa's charity is not for them.

"We are moderate" Suleimen had said, back in the tense days of *mitings* and constitutional manouverings in 1988, "so we are O.K."

But there's no place for moderation any more. Moderation means you're destroyed by both sides.

Emina has to go to the Faculty, to *Administracija*, for something for Suleiman. He is in Istanbul now. As we go down the old familiar street Emina tells me about what happened when she wanted to thank a Serbian colleague who had donated blood when she was very sick a year ago.

"I went to the flat with chocolates and her father was there and afterwards she said 'Oh Emina, why did you come to thank me? My father was so angry. He said how could you give your blood to a *Siptar?*'"

The Faculty of Philosophy is even more run down than in 1988. Only Serbian classes now. There's a policeman on the door and the smell of the Turkish lavatories meets us half way down the corridors. One of the same cleaners is still there. He recognizes me too. He just looks but when we leave shakes my hand and in a low voice tells me things are very bad. He's Albanian so if he works at the Faculty then he should be *trathtar*, traitor too.

At the Faculty I have a unique experience. Two women cringe away from me. As I stand in the doorway of *Administracija* they suddenly draw back in horror behind their desks as though in a silent movie.

Emina had spoken to the man by the window in Albanian. And the two young women closer to us had cringed away.

"They think you are Albanian," Emina explained. "They've just arrived. They're Serbian."

Just arrived from 'real' Serbia, like low grade administrators in a colonial outpost. Not 'like'; they *are* low grade administrators in a colonial outpost. Arrived in darkest Kosovo. Well, a lot of Serbs used to say "Meri! You're in Afreekaaah!" A lot of Albanians, too.

When I had first come to Pristina all those years ago, as a potential Faculty member and the Faculty chauffeur, like the Secretary of Education in Belgrade across the big, conference table had asked "Aren't you scared. Don't you know we have tails?" I'd thought they were joking. Then, as more Albanians said the same, I decided how paranoid not Serbians but Albanians must be to think that kind of mind-set could still exist. That was the Serbian mind-set that Milosevic used, the emotions he orchestrated. The Albanians should have been sent round Yugoslavia to warn.

The mind loves to classify. Everyone I'm registering on the streets as Serbian now are the dark, noisy, coarse-looking, over-made up women and girls, like recent ex-gypsies. What historic irony. The Serbs demonized Albanians for so long and now whatever the Croats or Bosnian Moslems have done in the war it is the word 'Serb' that conjures up the most terrible images in postwar Europe.

With all the building, I ask Emina if many Serbs are coming to Kosovo. "No, they are scared of living here."

But more and more war refugees are being re-settled here.

On the pavement outside the Faculty someone spins round. A middle-aged housewife. Vera! She is from Bashkim's old year. Shy, hardworking, steadfast Serbian Vera when Bashkim was being a bumptious Albanian. Just as I'm classifying Serbians as credulous idiots here is Vera, sweet, earnest, good English. I re-divide the world immediately; there are the Veras and Eminas and there are the rest of us. Vera and Emina are sharing the new burdens of being a housewife; their whole day must revolve around the baking of bread.

And like everyone in Belgrade, they say "Men must be married. If there is no one to bake bread they will starve."

Vera is still teaching. About Albanians I don't know where to start to ask. Though I read of the Sociology professor, Fehmi, the one swept aside by his students before the 1968 demonstration, is the spokesman now for the Albanian shadow government of Kosovo. Fehmi, who had cried, "They've thrown it all away!" Now everything we had built up is swept away. All education in Albanian beyond the primary level has ceased. Everything since the Brioni Plenum, the Albanian *Rilindja* — Renaissance — gone. Albanian education is now conducted privately, in peoples' homes, donated spaces. All the old names, my old colleagues, teaching clandestinely or retired, subsidized by the Albanian fund. Albanians living abroad are tithed. They give money to provide text books and salaries in hard currency. All the observers and journalists agree; Albanians, in the chaos of ex-Yugoslavia and the war, have become incredibly well-organized.

But I wonder if Idriz' three sons are alright in Pec; Nezir's in Prizren. These boys of military age. Idriz has to be alright. All the Serbs and Montenegrins call him a golden man. I wonder how many 'golden men' are dead in Bosnia. And Croatia. Emina says Bashkim is a Minister now in the Albanian shadow government of Kosovo. And another of my Albanian ex-students, the same year as Bashkim and Vera, is head of the Kosovo Information Bureau in London.

The Bureau weekly bulletin is full of incidents of Albanians harassed, robbed, detained, beaten up, tortured and killed by the Serbian authorities. It sounds like the worst days of Rankovic. At the very least Albanians probably should not be seen talking to foreigners, let alone having them as guests.

Emina says it's O.K. They have a Serbian neighbor who works in the police station and she's explained about me before I registered. But still, I'm not staying at the *Grand*. I'm staying with real people.

"Don't worry! You mothers! Whatever it is you always worry!"

Vlaznim is breezy. We walk down into Pristina together through the sharp January wind, his friends tacking on. Vlaznim in his Miami Hurricanes jacket, his new bouncy tennis shoes and new jeans. But his friends are breezy too.

What about being beaten up, attacks on Albanians? What about the new collecting of arms? That chilling reminder of the worst Rankovic days.

"Oh! We have the money!" they all say. "Serbs may have the power but Albanians have the money!" And as Serbians are paid in worthless dinars it's easy to bribe the police with hard currency. "We are *bizniz men!*"

It's true. Pristina is bursting with goods, the shops full. There are new Mercedes Benz crowding the pavements. Refusing to rise to Serbian provocation Albanians have organized their standard of living based on hard currency, trading everything, even drugs and gasoline. They load donkeys up and send them over the border. They're obviously shining up all those old skills left over from the days of the Turks, now bursting out into the post-Communist world.

Alex, one of 'Dr. Martin's' prize Serbian students, a hard-drinking, fast-talking disciple of *Catch 22* and *Rolling Stone* magazine had remarked in 1988 "You know, everyone's on the make in Kosmet. I mean, Slovenes, they don't even know how to steal!"

"Serbs refuse to do business with Albanians now but Albanians do business with *everyone*," Vlaznim is saying. I think it was Edith Durham who observed how after some skirmish or minor campaign Albanians were coming round to the enemy soldiers ready to sell them trinkets and snacks. They'll fight them and then turn around and sell them souvenirs. I had remarked to Vlaznim how all the Albanians in the shops seemed to know some English now in Kosovo.

"Oh, enough to sell you something!"

And why do Albanians have businesses and Serbs not? "Albanians have capital! Always enough to start! Always big families; someone away in Germany or Switzerland." Someone abroad accumulating hard currency.

But the 'taking of arms,' the handing in of guns demanded by the police? The teenagers laugh. 'We sell arms to the Serbs!"

Parked on the pavement in front of the Faculty of Philosophy is a jeep; INTERNATIONAL ASSOCIATION OF THE RED CROSS AND THE RED CRESCENT. The *Milicija* are dressed like they are in Belgrade, in combat gear as though they've just jumped off the back of an army truck ready for trouble. But Pristina on the surface at least is more calm than in 1988. Yes, says Agim, as long as the war continues in Bosnia, "We are O.K."

In Pristina I've heard gunfire only once, less than in Belgrade. "Oh, the barracks are near" Emina had said quickly. Every Albanian balcony seems to flower with a small white satellite dish. They cost 1200 dollars, in Istanbul. "To get the real news — from the world," Vlaznim declares. From Turkey, Italy, Tirana, not the Serbian-controlled media. Each dish a statement.

"Albanians all have them" Vlaznim announces, "to check what you call in America the Serbian bool sheet!"

I'm taking Emina to Prizren for the day. She hasn't been able to afford the bus fare for about two years. Her beloved Prizren. If I don't take her she won't go; she'll keep the money for food. And boots. Emina needs new winter boots. She promises me she'll buy some.

The flats rise up behind us as we slide down to the bus station, over the snowy mud. Pristina, with its big blocks of flats and the hills close all round, is eerily reminiscent of Sarajevo. In the mainly Albanian parts of Pristina now, there's no electricity at all for up to two days at a time; in January no heating and no lights. Even in the good old days, under Tito, we had power cuts. I remember so many nights marking papers by candlelight, putting my precious candles in front of a mirror, to make the light go further.

Private enterprise at the bus station: *BIZMARKET* a private bus to Prizren. But we still mill about in the old Socialist way, vague, not knowing when the bus is arriving. And it's still touch and go if the driver will let us on. Emina speaks Turkish and then it's O.K. "I spoke first in Albanian so he was negative."

Maybe he's a Turkish-speaking Albanian, a town Albanian from Prizren. It could mean he is actually Turkish or even a Serbian from Prizren who knows Turkish and for whom Turkish-speaking town Albanians are allies against the flood of Albanian peasants. The old intricacies. Judging the linguistic situation right will get you on the crowded bus. We pay in New Dinars. The Super Dinar is holding.

Along between the poplar trees and at the first village a policeman stands about in the prewar way, in an ordinary policeman's uniform, looking as cosy as something out of a children's book. And down by the river at Suva Reka we pass a brand new *mosque*.

"Well, the Serbians are building churches now," Emina says, as though that explains everything.

I could never be a journalist. The facts get in the way.

The big, brick houses. So much building. Many of the houses windowless like some reminder of the war but not from bombardment, they just haven't got their window frames in yet.

"Albanians still say you should have big families," Emina says, "Sons. At least one you send abroad, they say, at least one to stay home and at least one to fight."

In Prizren, just one pair of Serbian *Milicija* are walking up from the river, looking like Marines who've just landed, striding along in step. The sound of Albanian is everywhere, no longer Turkish. Rubbish tipped down the sides of the river banks, rubbish everywhere. The biggest upheaval in Kosovo remains the physical one of the third world; the peasants coming to the towns. That is the basic pressure in Kosovo, maybe deeper even than the Serbian Albanian conflict. The small towns of Kosovo swamped, engulfed, by refugees from the mountains, economic refugees from the overpopulated land, just as Belgrade now is engulfed by war refugees.

And everywhere Emina greets sad-faced, weary women whose husbands and sons have left, "All the young have gone."

Bus agencies advertising to Germany, Austria, Switzerland and Sweden where the Albanians are working and now being tithed — sending money back whether they want or not. Also buses to Albania, Turkey and Bulgaria. The Albanian-Serbian frontier is still closed, Emina says — "The buses go through Macedonia."

It's Wednesday, still the market day in Prizren and pulsing with life, even more than in the old days. In 1988 Kosovo was still officially a Marxist economy like the whole of Eastern Europe. It was still East and West. Now everyone is a *biznizman*. There's everything here. Jeans made in Turkey, saucepans, plastic flowers, tennis shoes, spilling along the pavements up and down the side streets. Vegetables, bananas, oranges, dark green spinach dripping with vitamins, meat, nuts, bright pink candies, table mats. We buy food to take back to Pristina. There is so much more than in Belgrade. I want to buy spinach, oranges, meat to take back to Belgrade. I could have just brought my money over, missed out on the enormous suitcases, and got everything I needed in Prizren. Maybe somewhere here, up one of these side streets, there's a green and gold Miami Hurricanes jacket.

Nezir, of course, would not be at school. He will be part of the underground teaching world somewhere in some unheated room, trying to keep the standards up. Pride of course, will help keep standards up and *inat* — spite. The Serbian police raid these makeshift school rooms, beat up teachers. The Serbian police raid the markets, the Albanian shops, the successful *biznizmen*; extorting tribute, like the Turks. Vlaznim and his young friends may enjoy showing off but this is colonial rule. Run, as Alex would say, by those guys who brought you Croatia 1991 and Bosnia 1992, the show that's still running.

Emina said dryly one of her Serbian neighbors told her, "Well, Emina, you will be alright, as long as you remain just an ordinary person and don't try and be anything special."

That is, as an Albanian and Emina, who is starting to come into her own as middle-aged women do in Moslem societies, had answered crisply, "I don't like *that* idea thank you very much!"

Emina wants me to meet the husband of a good friend of hers; an Albanian doctor.

We walk along the Bistrica river to his clinic. I ask Emina about Maria, Nada's cousin, married to an Albanian surgeon too, who'd been so frightened in 1988. They've gone to Klagenfurt, Austria, Emina says. "Just over the border from where she grew up in Slovenia." And the big house?

"They put all the furniture together in one room and someone is looking after it."

And, I hope, eating the quinces and pears from the trees in the garden.

The doctor runs a little clinic down by the river. He was a surgeon, practiced in Europe, returned to Kosovo but resigned from the hospital in Pristina when he saw the way the politics were going. Emina seems to mean both the politics of the Albanians and the Serbians.

Now the once eminent surgeon serves in his tiny clinic, often till 2 a.m. He has a nurse and a little surgery where his patients sit up high one at a time in what looks like an old dentist chair. Emina and I have been ushered in from the row in the waiting room and we sit on the couch behind a coffee table, facing the doctor and his patient. He has the charisma, the calm and the twinkle in the eye; you know he's good. He's dealing with the ordinary and downtrodden, like the washed out Albanians who used to line up at my Health Station Number One. We sip our coffee. In front of us is a little tray of instruments. One woman in the heavy wraps of the Albanian country woman, husband standing close by, has a bad cough.

"Did I get this from vitamins?" she asks anxiously and the doctor smiles over at me.

"No," he says gently, "you got it from smoking."

After the woman is a young Albanian boy, small, bright but hurting. The surgeon sorts him out, wraps him up and holds out his hand, palm up.

"Hey!" he says in Albanian, "you're a *real* Albanian! Give me five!"

And the small boy pulls back his hand and lets fly, wham into the surgeon's palm.

I feel conscious of the fact that the surgeon has to talk to me in Serbian. The language of war now, and the language again in Kosovo of police, interrogation and soldiers. On the wall of the waiting room is a notice in Albanian: "Any documentation in Arabic from the *Hoxha* can be translated into Albanian or *Bosanski*, the Bosnian script."

And I wonder, are these missives from the priest or even spells like the special soap from Bosnia? And note they are not even using the word "Serbian" any more.

That evening I call Alex and he comes round to see us. We can offer him Scotch, some hard cheddar cheese and peanuts! Vlaznim loves listening to Alex. Vlaznim's English is good but Alex, 'Dr. Martin's' star pupil, knew *Catch 22* by heart, had a dog-eared note book full of slang and neat phrases, and even read Thomas Pynchon. It's a shock to see him; an early middle-aged man now with grey in his beard.

Alex says war was inevitable. "I saw this coming fifteen years ago. This is settling historic scores, settling unfinished business from the Second World War."

He agrees with Emina; what was new in Kosovo was the pressure on Kosovo from Albanians in the other Yugoslav Republics. Now the Albanian shadow government of Kosovo is saying with the break up of Yugoslavia and the new world of mini-states, independent Slovenia, Croatia and even Macedonia, their goal is total independence from Serbia and ultimate union with Albania. But it will all be loose, up-to-date, like the European Union. This is the '90s.

Alex with his up to the minute *Rolling Stone* English has been much in demand. He has been translating for the journalists coming to Kosovo "waiting for the other shoe to drop." He doesn't seem to think much of these Western journalists any more.

"Why does the West interfere? Who asked them?"

He tells of translating for "some army guys" armed with clipboards who were counting the number of tanks somewhere in Kosovo. It must have been Kosovo; Alex is making us laugh about the mud. "They were sliding around, up to their knees. And the guy writes down — Let's say '— Forty-five tanks!' And one of his other guys slides round and says, 'Sir! Sir! Actually it's fifty-two!' And they carefully write down — '52'!"

"And I say 45 — 52 — What does it matter? Take them all away! Take them all away from us and we'll kill each other with knives!"

Alex, it seems, is presenting the war as the result of Ancient Balkan Emnities. Code for him, as for the West, for There's nothing anyone can do. Well, what did I encounter day after day all those years in Kosovo? — But I still have this stubborn memory of Yugoslavia from the early sixties, so many people in every Republic vowing, with a breezy disregard for ideology: "You'll see! We are such a mix — We have everything here! We'll be a little America!" Well, what does one encounter every day in America?

Maybe it's only a pose with Alex. I won't have a chance to find out because I don't have a chance to talk to him alone. But it was also Alex who used to come out with the same classic contradiction: You couldn't trust Albanians. I wouldn't let one near my sister — but — "Hey! You don't have to tell ME about Albanians! My best friend is an Albanian!"

Alex is brimming with terrible jokes, black humor. Humor at its blackest about the war. I ask him who's doing the killing.

"You know — the people who are nothing. Butchers. Given a gun to kill and then they have something. Butchers."

One of the most notorious war criminals, Arkan, was born in Pristina, one of ours. A 'Kosovar,' still young, so he must have grown up after the Brioni Plenum. Wanted for criminal activity in Europe. He has a tan, says Alex. Handsome guy. Now his *brother-in-law* was a great guy — one of Alex's students when he taught at the Faculty. "One of those killed at the start." Arkan hangs out in Pristina's Grand Hotel with his 'watch dogs' says Alex.

"He speaks English very well," Alex tells us, "learnt it in European prisons."

The Grand Hotel is the new center of Pristina, taken over now by the Serbs. Where the journalists go. For us it was always little Hotel Bozur with the knights on the front riding out to Kosovo. I have to ask at the imposing desk of the Grand about buses back to Belgrade. And the man behind the desk remembers me — another ex-student. Ilija must have loved the Grand. He's back in Vojvodina. The Albanians didn't want him at the Faculty any more, Emina says. "They took his flat."

The bus leaves in the late afternoon, reaching Belgrade sometime after eleven. Milena will meet me. Emina promises she'll buy winter boots. Agim has got his socks, Vlaznim his Nikes, his everything. Emina needs boots. There's no snow but it's cold. I have homemade bread for the journey but no hard boiled eggs. When we were at the police station registering me, a young Serbian woman had swirled into the office holding something in her hands. A brown egg. She was triumphant. It was worth three electricity bills, she said. I didn't even start to ask her how that worked.

Emina had told me, smiling, about their young Montenegrin postman who comes in to chat sometimes. "He says 'You know, it is very good for us Serbs that you Albanians are here. Because you are so good at buying and selling or it would go badly with us!'"

The New Dinar is holding steady. Agim said prices are starting to go down and I bought my ticket in New Dinars. No problem.

It sounds like the same dull *kolo* on the bus radio, going round and round. *This* is Greater Serbia? Back in the arrogant, international Yugoslav sixties and early seventies we'd have said, What do we have here? Provincial Bulgaria on a wet Sunday? Stodgy, stubborn Balkan peasants just going round and round with the *kolo*.

As night falls a golden moon rises, ranging low over the hills ahead. Last night Emina's neighbor came in with her daughter who's about ten to say goodbye. Ana and Vlaznim had played chess on the floor in front of the television. Rabia, her mother, is a Serbian-speaking Moslem from Montenegro married to a man from the borders of Macedonia and Bulgaria who is half Albanian, half Czech. Rabia had made sugar cookies. Emina is almost out of my American cheese and nuts. She is too generous, bringing out everything for neighbors and guests. I'm leaving behind more nuts and stuff I haven't even told her about. And some coffee for the elderly Serbian professor and his wife. "Say it's from an ex-colleague" I tell Emina, "in memory of better days at the old *Fil Fak*."

The moon is like a big golden harvest moon in January, low over the hills. Black clouds low now, on each side. For the first time ever Emina had asked me what she thought they should do, where could they go. And for the first time ever, I don't feel there's any future for Emina and her family in Kosovo. Suleiman has gone to Istanbul. He said it was just for a term but Vlaznim said he took his favorite books and his little table. But Istanbul may be changing too. Emina says now her brother's eldest son there, the handsome, lively one has become so devout. His wife wouldn't see Vlaznim when he went. She stayed in the inner room and just exclaimed "How deep his voice! He must be a fine young man!" Emina told me sadly. "They are wearing the veil again. Vlaznim calls them 'Mafiaaah!'"

Last night Emina put on some music to cheer us up and started dancing, elbows up at shoulder level, wrists turning, giving little cries like mews, like the women do at Turkish weddings. Then Ana began to dance, grave and provocative and Vlaznim, moving the chess set away, started to turn and dip in the tiny space in front of the television, the young man advancing and retreating, little skipping steps and yearning wrists. And I feel these are the very last days of the Ottoman Empire, the end of Turkey in Europe which was Kosovo. The conflicted world talked about long before Queen Victoria that, in fact, has taken just about the whole of the twentieth century to die. In spite of the wars in Cyprus and Lebanon, I hoped somehow Tito's Yugoslavia, especially Kosovo, could preserve the 'crazy mix' as Murad called it. Now as mosques are built in western Europe and Moslem feast days are noted in English diaries, here it is coming to an end.

Now it will be something only for emigres and exiles to cry into their drink over, listening to the old haunting music. One of Vlaznim's friends plays the shepherd's flute and goes down to Macedonia. He can get up to a thousand DM a night, playing to the Macedonian Albanians back from America and Australia while they cry into their glasses.

Let everyone go, leave for broad, sunny spaces. I'd see them just over the border at Venice, back in the late sixties, the peasant women in black from the Adriatic and Macedonia, with their wooden suitcases and black head-scarves, their mute children, leaving the hard stony places, standing on the end of railway platforms. One lost all her luggage once. I'd been screaming at the Italian porter for her. It was chugging away on the wrong train and she had to go to Genoa to get the boat.

But some of the worst killers of the war are the emigres, men who came back from those sunny spaces and good lives. Milena said just before the war she'd been in a hotel elevator in Zagreb when three men had got in. Milena, half Croat herself, said "The hair stood up on my arms. I looked at their faces. They had come back to Yugoslavia for a reason." As Alex would say, to finish the unfinished business from the last war.

That night, back in Belgrade sleeping in Dusan's old room, I have a dream. I'm cleaning out a shiny aluminum butcher's van, hosing and sluicing it down, at eye level with the gleaming cold bed of the truck. All the joints and ridges where stuff catches. And the water and whatever was there is swirling out past my eyes and hurtling down the drain.

I'm coming down with a filthy cold, and one major pre-occupation is paper handkerchiefs. I'm blowing my nose on Christmas Tree green paper napkins Emina gave me. A treasured possession — "Look! From the days of Tito and Socialism!" she commented wryly, "When we had everything!" Emina said it's her fault I'm sick; the flat was so cold. I said it's the Serbs' fault I was so cold; they're the ones who turned off the heat.

Milena, heroically ignoring my streaming cold, takes me off to an artist's cafe in Zemun across the river on Saturday night and to the cathedral on Sunday morning which is half full.

"All these old women!" Milena comments. "They could have come while Tito was alive if they really believed. You know there was no problem. No-one cared but NOW they are here!" Now Milena says you see people wearing up to three crosses on their fronts; "political conversions." One of the funniest is Mohammed from Radio Pristina. With a name like that, Emina tells me, he has converted to Catholicism. Maybe he wants to work in the Mother Teresa organization. But that's historically consistent for Albanians; never fanatic about religion; adamant it's always said only about being Albanian.

Kalamegdan is under snow still. We take pictures on the walls of the old Turkish fort just like tourists, Milena brooding about Serbia, the Serb character. "Under Turks the Serbs learned only to grumble and make less. It's the Serb nature to avoid trouble. NOT to fight! Always talk of 'The Turks'! If Serbs were such fighters why were they five hundred years under Turks?"

And someone wants to meet me: someone intrigued by the fact that I spent so long in Kosovo. After lunch one of Milena's old friends brings him round: the son of Aleksandar Rankovic, head of the Secret Police under Tito. Tall, urbane, a grave, polite sense of his own importance, the sort of demeanor you get from a good private school. One of the 'golden children,' the sons and daughters of top Party members and Partisans. I wonder what his position is now. We all sit talking about the war, the current war. Rankovic's son reports the private opinion of a European ambassador that America wants to start a war in Kosovo, not prevent it: "In order to destabilize Europe. The EEC is too dominant in the world now."

On Kosovo I'm too eager to show I know a lot: I contradict. I sound like an 'Albanian-lover.' Rankovic's son, handsome, cosmopolitan, switches off. It's as though he's stood up, snapped his mind shut like a briefcase, nodded politely and left. He turns to Milena with a comment on the cat and I've lost him.

That Sunday night we go to a rock concert, a small one, held above a book shop in the center of Belgrade. One of the friends from Saturday night organizes them, a gentle bearded man in a fair-isle sweater. Mark says he is a nuclear engineer but his life is music: he played guitar with Jimi Hendrix and Eric Burden when they came to Yugoslavia. He calls it 'djez' but it's dynamic rhythm and blues though at the packed tables in the gloom none of the young Belgrade students move a muscle. They all have that laid back, drab black, scruffy look. The no money, no hope look, a godsend for wartime: their reality is so fashionable. There are three guitars, harmonica, a drummer. Mark says they were the last band to play in Sarajevo, in 1992; they just got out as the blockade tightened. Now one of the boys on guitar is a refugee from Bosnia, the lead guitar is a Croat; he's a Serb. The music is wonderful, such positive energy. I tell myself no-one who plays like this could be a killer.

And suddenly it's my last morning in Belgrade. Suitcases all but empty, I'll be striding through the airports like Wonder-woman swinging these great rectangles with uncanny ease. There's certainly nothing to buy: empty shops, silent streets. Belgrade has reverted to the city of 1956, the year of my first visit. Apart from a few jammed buses with dirty windows, the occasional military jeep, Belgrade is a capital dominated by voices and footfalls. Any sleek car sliding by belongs to a politician or a war profiteer or both. The world of consumer goods is not there. For food you must get up at dawn and go to the market and, like 1956, only a few *butiks* flourish, little shops where imported objects lie behind the glass isolated by their immense cost: a fur, an Italian *tvinset*, a bracelet. Now only for the Mafia women Aleksa says. We pass them in the street, beautifully coiffured, manicured, pampered young women in furs, the women of the war profiteers, the new rich.

When I had suggested to Aleksa on one of our walks we could go for a coffee just as a reminder of the simple delights of pre-war Belgrade she had politely refused. No-one eats or drinks out. The solid old Belgrade restaurants with their sensible big white tablecloths in the dark, paneled dining rooms are as empty as if they'd been raked by sniper fire. Aleksa says she wouldn't want to be seen inside. Anyone who can afford to go in would look like a war profiteer.

The New Dinar has held a week. Today a wet, rainy Monday, prices in New Dinars are appearing a little timidly on small squares of paper, landing shyly and erratically on the few articles newly displayed in one shop window; on the dark grey skirts but not the fuzzy sweaters.

The book shops have books but no prices: HOROSKOP, Astrological Dictionary, Dr Spock again. *The Fall of the West*, Spengler in four volumes. *Churchill's Yugoslav Mistakes*. That must be the fact that he supported Tito instead of the Royalist Chetniks. In a news kiosk there's a magazine called *Army* with a town plan of Sarajevo and environs. The siege of Sarajevo goes on. How far off and innocent those days seem when the most chilling news from Sarajevo, from Bosnia, was the slow starvation of the abandoned animals in the Sarajevo zoo.

A boy in light blue jeans looking chilly in the winter cold has been stopped by police. He's up against the wall, his hands behind his neck. Behind us the beagle trots by, ears swinging, on his way to the park. Across the road a pink electric sign suspended above empty shelves declares JOLLY TOURS.

I turn for home; nothing to buy. And then suddenly I come upon two trestle tables in front of an empty, dark store front and there is the international currency of teenagers everywhere: Tee shirts. Not only that but Tee shirts that fulfill the teenagers' toughest criteria: totally unobtainable at home and as outrageous as possible. A pile of them announce in the Cyrillic alphabet: I LOVE SERBIA. No-one is supposed to love Serbia now, not even the Serbs. On the other pile the Cyrillic lettering encircles the Royal double-headed eagle of Serbia in red and gold: ONLY WITH GOD'S

HELP AND IN UNITY WILL SERBIA BE SAVED.

The young man behind the tables grins at me encouragingly, rocking from one foot to the other, hands in pockets, collar up, head down. Yes, yes, dollars are O.K. We love dollars he says. He asks me if I'm with Unprofor, the UN protection force. I joke I'm *privatni* Unprofor, private relief, come on a private mission to help my friends.

He wants to know why I speak his language. Testing his reflexes I hit him with my traditional hammer to the Serbian kneecap. I taught in ...Kosovo I say and stand back.

"But I'M from Kosovo!" the young man cries in amazement. "I'm from Pec!"

"No! Not Montenegrin! I'm a real *Serbian* from Kosovo — from old historic Serbia!"

And there beside the Tee shirts are the dark, brooding faces of the saints and apostles on postcards and calendars from the monasteries of Kosovo. Their painted eyes stare up from the trestle table in the street, mimicked by the dark bearded faces seen on newsreels of the war in Bosnia.

To make sure I understand, the young man gets out his ID card. "You see? I'm from near Pec" and is suddenly bashful. Here he is on a main thoroughfare in Belgrade, a *biznizman* showing me that actually he's from a village. Most of our students would never want to say they were from a village, they would always say they were from 'near' a town. Well, I've been telling everyone I'm from near Miami, because I wouldn't get very far saying 'Homestead.' Most people in Serbia have been very worried for me because of the violence they've heard about in Miami.

Yes, my young 'Kosovar' says, he's been a student, too, attending classes at the University of Pristina. It's my last day in Serbia, my last encounter in 1994 with the world of Ancient Balkan Emnities. I can't resist mentioning Idriz, Idriz Gafuri, the 'golden man' of Pec.

"Oh! There are so many Gafuris down there!" the young man exclaims innocently, no anger, no paranoia, no bitter comment on booming Albanian birth rates. As though, wonder of wonders, Albanians, *Muslimani*, are just people after all, as though there isn't the whole weight of the Turkish Occupation and all the wars in his Serbian head. I could lean over the Tee shirts and kiss him.

I hand over my American dollars and shake my young Kosovo Serb by the hand. I feel so proud and pleased with him I could be his mother. With a flourish he throws in four bumper stickers for free. We can cruise round Homestead declaring; 'WITH FAITH AND GOD! FREEDOM OR DEATH! the Slav letters weaving round a skull. The other two have a neat rhyming phrase in Serbian: WITHOUT A KING NOTHING WORKS!"

Some Serbians are saying despairingly, in my favorite Slav accent, "What our people really need is a Kink."

Back at Milena's with just a few hours to go, I hand over my spare ballpoint pen, my half bottle of face cream, the last band-aids. All I'm holding on to are my bright green paper napkins for my cold. It's a great feeling, almost spiritual, relieved of worldly goods. But at lunch time Milena's mother comes up the stairs carrying a tablecloth she's been working on all summer for a table that must seat eight, heavy in handstitched linen. And Milena digs out another hand-crocheted table cloth weighted down with hours of work and a surprise parcel from Nada — a blouse in unbleached, handwoven linen. I stroke these instant heirlooms reverently. I'll wash them always very gently in cold water I vow. No! No! cries Milena's mother, "These are made by our people. They'll last for ever!"

That's true. The blouse following tradition is designed to be beaten against stones in a river. It would hardly notice forty minutes in a GE washing machine. It's the flimsy Tee shirts I should probably wash reverently by hand.

While grumbling that Serbs are 'primitive' ("We must give even when we have nothing,") Milena is trying to persuade me to pack six heavy crystal glasses with weighted bottoms and a faded wooden red hen and yellow butterfly. "I know the children are too old but they must have something!"

Nada had brought round cheese from the market while I was out, homemade paprika relish and two bottles of homemade Serbian plum brandy which, given the current situation, is generous beyond belief. But she's coming later with Stefan, and the minibus isn't picking me up till three thirty in the morning, so we'll eat and drink everything up tonight, I vow.

Milena has made fresh bread. I've saved a last bar of chocolate and a packet of Georgia pecans. I'd brought her a bottle of *Dzoni Valker* Red but we've decided that's *rezerv* for when things get even worse, or, who knows, to celebrate if they get better.

Milovan arrives. Another old friend from years ago. I'd thought he'd left, taken his family and gone like so many of the educated middle-class but he's hanging on, like Milena, Nada and their families, like Zivko, somehow keeping the old Belgrade alive, through the inundation of refugees and poverty. Milena had said "The refugees are angry at us, they have lost everything in Bosnia and Croatia and blame Serbia." Zivko, scavenging the crumbs from Nada's bread had declared, "We have nothing in common with these Serbs from Croatia! We hate them more than Croats! Different dialect, way of living. Primitive. They are lazy and stupid. They know only how to fight and the other Serbs are Bosnians." Aleksa had said bitterly, "Our boys went to the front to fight for the Bosnians and they stayed in Belgrade as refugees."

I have hoarded a little chocolate, soap and dollars for Milovan, too, and apologize for crassly tipping them in his lap, like I really am some aid soldier about to go home, tossing stuff off the back of a truck.

"It's not just that you brought things," Milovan says. "It's because you came." He is embarrassed because he is about to cry.

Milovan has two teenage girls now. "I can buy them nothing. Nothing. And the worst thing is," he gives a wry grin and a sniff. "They don't complain."

Milena has put on the TV Beograd news but we aren't taking any notice even though now there's a war on. That's the big difference between this year and 1988. Milena has said of those days of rabid *mitings* and anti-Albanian propaganda, "Somehow we were told what we wanted to hear. It was lies. I see that now."

Now it's too late. With the Bosnian Moslems more and more intransigent, these are the darkest days of the war. "I don't think our generation will see peace," one of Nada's friends told me.

Down in Kosovo I've been told Milosevic will keep the war going as long as he can because he is the number one war profiteer. He has his own bank on Cyprus, opened it with his own money. But Milovan says the war will go on till "the last Moslem is dead in Bosnia. Because Europe and America don't want a fundamentalist Moslem state in the middle of Europe."

Milena calls out from the kitchen, "Exactly! Turkey wants this new state because in this way she can destroy Serbia!"

No, not you, Milena.

"Mary! It is obvious. You have to agree. Everyone is out to destroy Serbia!"

Not Milena, too. *Sergeant Pepper* is playing. Milena who's been saying how crazy and stupid Serbia's 'primitivism' is, its self-destructive pattern.

"MARY! The pattern is there! Everyone has always wanted to destroy Serbia!"

Someone is coming up the stairs. I see the hat first, a big Dr. Zhivago fur hat. Sasha has just dropped by on his way home from the National Theatre. Sasha is weary too, but droll. He's artistic and rather swishy. He's a lot of fun.

"Mary," he asks firmly, with great seriousness. "WHAT is the price of an egg in America now?" We figure out that eggs are, in fact, cheaper in Serbia.

"Ah! You see?" Sasha exclaims triumphantly, and then, dryly, "Of course, it *does* depend if you have any money..."

Sasha has a great story about what has saved the artistic community at the National Theatre from starvation. A truck of potatoes spilled right outside in the street and all the artists and musicians piled out rejoicing "to bring in the harvest."

Nada has a sack of potatoes just inside her front door. She and Stefan arrive at ten and we start the second bottle of brandy. I've taken the label off so Nada doesn't realize it's hers. Everyone is saying they are waiting for March, "the Ides of March" the anniversary of the demonstrations in Belgrade. Milena was not only there, she was one of the mothers who marched to the Serbian parliament against the war.

Milena says the embargo is worse than useless. "Everything has just become blamed on embargo. So it suits politicians." Milena sees an angry, desperate Serbia filled with angry and desperate refugees as ripe for civil war. "Then the biggest problem would be getting from here — the center of Belgrade — to a frontier" she said matter of factly.

A Moslem friend has just called Milena from Australia. He managed miraculously to get himself and his family from Sarajevo to Adelaide. "He sold everything and bribed everyone," she explained, "Unprofor. The UN people. Of course, whoever was necessary."

He's told her she must keep two small bags packed at all times to be ready to leave — to leave everything and just go. "Choose what you want and put it in the bags."

"How do you choose?" she had asked, looking round her flat. *Sergeant Pepper*, all the records. The cat, the dog, the cobblestone from the demonstration against the war, the handmade lace curtains up at the windows, the books, the little Japanese vase her grandfather had brought back from the Far East when he'd made his way home in 1918 from being a prisoner of war. At least her children are out of the country. I'm leaving in two hours. It's one in the morning.

"Ah, Mary," Sasha says quietly, "You are leaving" he pauses "And we are staying."

There's no self pity in his voice but his eyes fill with tears. I've seen so many grown men here with that same look, I realize, in the last two weeks, on the verge of tears. Emina had called from Pristina when I was out, Milena told me. "She was crying. She said, 'Tell Mary I bought the boots. God will repay her.'" When I'd described how hard things were for Emina in Pristina, Milena's eyes had filled with tears too, "They are destroying all the good people!"

In all those hard years when Milena worked such long hours when the children were small she had managed to scrape together enough extra energy and money to build a small house on one of the Adriatic islands. Even before open war between Serbia and Croatia she had not dared go: "When they see Belgrade number plates they burn the cars." Now any day she may lose her job. Her firm deals with exports and because of the embargo should be closed down.

I have come expecting my friends to be like they've always been; in desperate circumstances now, grateful I came, but resilient, sensible, cheerful, making the correct political judgements, 'making company' as always. And they have. Even while their world is being destroyed. And my gracious contribution has been to resist getting into arguments about who started the war, moral questions about the failure of the Serbian intellectuals. And to ask questions and relish the drama of it all. Well, that was why I always came back to Yugoslavia; it was always so much more vivid and dramatic than the Anglo-Saxon world. But for a long time too it had seemed so much more sensible, in many ways more pragmatic, more real than my Anglo-Saxon world.

And now, as Sasha says, I'm going.

The minibus to Budapest airport arrives promptly, drawing up at the wet, cold curb at three thirty a.m. The driver is an older, gentler, very considerate man; not very Serbian, I think automatically. Milena sees me off. We vow we'll meet soon. Maybe the States — maybe England with Dusan and Zorana. — Hey, maybe back in Belgrade. "Save the *Dzoni Valker!*" I joke.

It's quite bright even at this hour. The center of Belgrade is lit up. Electricity is cheap but there are no workers cleaning the streets. They're waiting to see if the New Dinar means their pay is worth anything. High above the graffiti on the grey plaster walls; MOTLEY CREW, SEX PISTOLS HERE, SID VICIOUS, there's the occasional garlanded or helmeted head that makes me think of the city decor in the first Batman film. My Belgrade: Gotham City waiting for Batman. Needing Batman rather than a Kink. Needing Superman.

The trouble with us Serbs, Zivko said, "is we ask, not 'What can we do?' but 'Who will save us?'"

The minivan, stopping outside apartment buildings, at shadowy doorways, fills up with the same kind of passengers I came with. Middle class, middle-aged housewives going on a shopping expedition and a weedy, thin student sitting next to me. Pulling away from our last stop on a deserted side street in Novi Beograd, we hear a horn behind us and a small white car, a Yugoslav *Zastava* pulls alongside. We pause. It draws level with our driver.

Police, I think. Plain clothes. As we move forward cautiously, it does too. Then it pulls away, cuts in front and stops. The driver's door opens. A pause. Not the police. I think of our gentle, white-haired driver, the thin rather weedy student next to me, all us house-wives sitting like hens on a perch. Belgrade is plagued with armed robberies now. Jelena, one of Nada's friends, was actually robbed on one of the crowded buses with the dirty, broken windows. The biggest import from Italy now; reinforced, bullet proof front doors. Real money, hard currency, is kept at home or, in our case, carried over the frontier to buy things. We see the close cropped hair first, as a big, burly young man shoves himself out of the car. He straightens up, arm on the car roof, blinking at us and scowling. Drunk no doubt; one of the Serbian bully boys. There could be another three squeezed in. We are all silent, waiting. He hesitates, pulling himself up to his full height and then slowly flaps his jacket open towards us, once, then twice, like a rooster about to crow. He hesitates, eyes narrowing. We wait. He shoves his big head and shoulders back into the car. It doesn't move. It doesn't move and then finally it does.

"Don't follow!" one of the women whispers, "Wait! wait!"

We wait till the white car slowly disappears up the street.

I used to like to see the notice on the *kafana* walls announcing the penalty for breaking glasses. I loved Yugoslavia as cowboy country. When I worked in Kosovo, each time I came back, even from Belgrade, I would feel like the school Ma'am climbing down from the train, eyes down, in a poke bonnet, picking my way over the railway lines. I had followed the frontier south, when Belgrade became too 'civilized.'

Now Yugoslavia is cowboy country indeed where gangs of drunken men with bad breath and broken teeth keep riding in. And the nightmare is that it's always the start; it keeps repeating the start; there's no second part, no-one to stop them. No hero, no good man, no saint, no Gregory Peck, no American cavalry, no knights in shining armor rising up from the mists of Kosovo, no Kink.

The Tee shirts were not such a hit in South Florida after all. The children, having grown up with me and my Yugoslavia, were wary of how they put it: "Well... no one really understands about Yugoslavia and everything and it's really hard to explain."

1997

■

THIRTY-FIVE

Waiting

They are still marching in Belgrade, over three months now and Milena hasn't missed a night.

When I asked what should I bring Milena said "Whistles! Ours keep breaking!"

"You should be here, Mary!" she was yelling down the phone. "Our people are not marching for bread though God knows they should but that their vote was ignored!"

Just under a year after the Dayton Accords ended the fighting in Bosnia, the people of Belgrade and then other Serbian towns took to the streets protesting fraud in the 1996 November local elections. As winter set in their numbers grew.

They marched every night and most nights the police, holding those riot shields up that looked much too big for them, stood quietly in slightly wavy lines in front of the cameras, like children in a Christmas pageant. President Milosevic must have been waiting for Kosovar, the reaper, the wind that heralded the Belgrade winter, to sweep into the city across the rivers from the east, beyond the Carpathians. Kosovar would clear the streets. "When Kosovar arrives" Nada had explained to me carefully in a pen friend letter years ago, "you usually hear the glass breaking and things rolling about."

But as the sleet turned to snow everyone went on marching, carrying candles, blowing whistles. Sometimes you couldn't see faces on the TV screen just hear the shouting from under big black umbrellas. Sometimes there was a whole street full, grinning huge grins, touched by falling snowflakes: old people, old dogs, students, with grandmothers cheering from balconies, those nice old balconies in the middle of Belgrade with the plaster sheering off and a few stunned old plants dying off in December. They blew whistles to drown out Milosevic's Belgrade evening news, opening windows into the

bitter cold and banging on saucepans. Girls presented the police with flowers and the students faced them with mock riot shields proclaiming WE
LOVE YOU TOO.

What began as a protest against election fraud had become a democratic movement to unseat Milosevic. Thirty thousand, a hundred thousand; two hundred thousand, half a million. Belgrade was finally experienc-
ing what Eastern Europe had in 1989. Then Serbia was not exulting in
breaking free of Communism but stirring itself up for war.

"Who knows what will happen? What is important is that the people
became *self conscious*." Milena said it with deliberate emphasis; conscious of
themselves, their own worth, the democratic principle: "That they had voted
and their vote was thrown away."

"I march" say the students, "therefore I am."

Belgrade airport is open now. Luggage is x-rayed before I leave the airport.
Checking what's being brought in. Maybe checking for whistles. A warm,
surging, noisy mass of Serbs enveloped in a haze of cigarette smoke accost-
ing me. Which plane is this? Moscow? Amsterdam? It's the middle of March.
After Miami, after *England*, everything is so grey. Like the perpetual cigarette smoke everywhere. Like looking at Serbia through a perpetual haze of
self destructive cigarette smoke.

Yes, Milena says, driving her old car back into Belgrade, Serbia is
dirty. Corruption is everywhere. It's a dirty feeling. The only good thing is
the marches. Oh, there's everything to buy now but so expensive. Will the
opposition make any difference? "They are divided. And they are not sup-
porting the students. The students are the light at the end of the tunnel."

Milosevic had finally given in, allowing the opposition victories and,
comment the commentators, is much 'weakened' by the relentless demonstrations in which the people of Belgrade were showing themselves as tena-
cious, cool and controlled as the Albanians in Kosovo, and as careful not to
provoke violence.

But in Kosovo Milosevic is not giving in. One reason the Serbian
economy is still in chaos is because sanctions remain to pressure Serbia not
only to co-operate over war crimes in Bosnia but to improve human rights
in Kosovo. Now, in March 1997, that seems even more unlikely. Not just
because, as Milena says, the opposition leaders are as nationalist as the
Milosevic regime but right now there is chaos in Albania and guns flooding
into Kosovo. Today, Saturday, U. S Marines are evacuating American citizens from the capital Tirana.

At seven thirty we heard the whistles. The evening news according to Milosevic had begun.

We walked one minute up the street to Republic Square and then turned right and we could see the students setting up by the old *Fil. Fak.* in *Studentski Trg:* Students' Square. There was the music, the graffiti, the noise. No police in view; older people smiling, not minding the noise. A stone's throw away is Nada's flat. I really chose my friends well. Yes, she'd been marching too — Everybody has! The students are now intent on forcing the Rector of the University to resign. "He was against the marches." *Beogradski Univerzitet* is now on the sweat shirts: BU.

Sunday morning cold and grey. Monday will be St Patrick's Day. Posters in Celtic script: *Come To Real Orthodox Celtic Celebration — Starting 11 PM.* Popcorn is being sold everywhere; that's new.

U.S. Marines on their stomachs at the airport, chins and guns up, checking for Albanian snipers; US Cobra gun-ships overhead. Serbian television, of course, making the most of the anarchy in Albania. But you don't need to distort the news to make it seem bad. There has been a total breakdown of government. Police stations and arsenals, barracks and military camps have been raided; guns, hand grenades, rockets, tanks and even jets have been seized and are in the hands of everyone from self proclaimed rebels to small boys up side streets who should be playing hop scotch. It all started with anger over failed pyramid schemes in which the government has been implicated. Three quarters of the country lost what little money they had. Milena says "Good for Albanians! They grabbed the guns and said 'Give us back our money!' Stupid Serbs are *still* waiting! Yes and our pyramid schemers are still living in Belgrade with our money!"

Sunday noon. I'll be in the dog house. Nada wanted me to take a trip, a Sunday afternoon, early spring *ekskursija* though the weather is lousy but Milena and I play hooky and join the march instead, starting just down from Nada's flat. One of the last, against the Rector of BU and for freedom of the media.

"Nada doesn't understand! Who wants to go for a car ride when you can *march?*" Milena has always considered Nada irredeemably 'bourgeois.'

I hadn't been on a march since Aldermaston. Then I walked in the road for the first time, against the Bomb and the Cold War, having just been to stay with Young Communists Nada and Milena the summer before and, to be honest, because the Aldermaston March like this one in Belgrade had been so handy to join. It was going down the London Road, about two minutes away. Belgrade on Sunday morning is like that very first Aldermaston march, everyone in great good humor.

Milena has her whistle. So does everyone else. Some have two. A group of University professors is gathering in front of us, a golden retriever round their knees. There are two more. It seems golden retrievers are the dog of choice. Better than the guard dogs of '94 but Aleksa says it's even more dangerous in Belgrade now; not just gangs but boys who will kill for 100 DM. All the professors have their badges: *Matematika Fak.*, *Ekonomski Fak.* and the buttons with their slogans "I'm not a marcher — I'm just a pedestrian!": "I don't wear tennis shoes!" The police one night were given their orders: chase anyone in tennis shoes.

Here are the faces of older, intelligent, sophisticated Belgraders, the young too; dedicated, sharp, aware, reclaiming old Gotham City. Milena's children, that crop, have gone or like Nada's are mired in the hopelessness of half a decade of wartime and craziness. But Milosevic's ethical cleansing of Serbia has failed. A new crop, a new generation is pushing up, green and fresh, amid the old rubble. Plus the old rubble too, with their badges and golden retrievers.

We set off, heading for Republic Square, the dogs wagging their tails, the big sound speakers on a flatbed truck thumping out a rock classic, led by a one legged man with a Christ-like beard, swinging along on crutches. Across Terazije and round the corner, heading for the steep street down towards the river. A wedding party drives slowly across the square. We cheer and blow whistles for the bride and groom. They cheer us. Every car and trolley bus slows down for us, everyone smiles and waves. They're all on our side. No police in sight. The sun is breaking through. Old women are leaning out of windows, people over balconies, throwing paper down, blessing us with drifting paper.

This Sunday afternoon of course is nothing like the half-million strong marches through the sleet and snow of winter. This is a spring stroll, but everyone is for us. Down and across the bridge over the Sava. We're all wrapped up but suddenly in bright sun; still everyone waving from buses. A tug passes below sounding its horn as it goes under us. We cheer. We're making for the park on the other side of the river. There's going to be another happening. "Every day the students do something different," Milena says.

Today it's a race for twenty-year-old cars, a skit on the fact that Milosevic's son races Mercedes. We walk over the grass springy with new daisies and dandelions to the lined up cars, their innards spilling out, forsythia stuck in sagging bumpers, old *Yugos* gift wrapped in red ribbons. Each Faculty has its racing car: there are the Philological Housewives in large curlers and aprons, holding plastic spoons. Of course, Marko's car, driven by two wacky students, wins. It's covered in Marlboro ads. Marko controls the tobacco business. The student in dark glasses representing Marko, declares himself winner. We all boo. The striking thing is none of the students are drunk or raucous. There's not even much swearing, in Belgrade, one of the swearing capitals of the world, where little old ladies have only to drop a penny to sound like a sailor on Friday night. Drunkenness was certainly part of the war. Tank them up and set them loose.

"When I see a young person now, a student," Milena declares, "I feel like going down on my knees to them!"

"...*In Dublin's Fair City*" on independent radio, Monday morning; March 17, St. Patrick's Day in Belgrade. A steady rain. By nine thirty it's snow, dissolving into rain at window height, great big frilly flakes gently changing their mind. Poster in Old Church Slavonic lettering: COME SPEND THE EVENING WITH ORTHODOX CELTS. Everything Irish is so fashionable. Nada's daughter is mad on things Celtic. Celtic crosses for sale besides the Orthodox ones; another brilliant early Christian civilization on the edge of Europe marginalized by cruel fate.

Today the students are walking in single file to Hotel *Slavia*, one behind the other along the line in the middle of the road because the cry has gone up "Who is behind the students?"

I'm taking Milena to a St. Patrick's Day concert. We saw the banner when we started to march, stretched out across the central square behind the bus stops: *B. B. KING LIVE IN BELGRADE At the Sava Center*. I remember when that opened: First Non-Aligned Conference; Summit of Presidents — Nasser, Sukharno, Nkruma, Kenyatta, Nehru. It's big and filling up with middle-aged, bearded, barrel-chested men in anoraks and leather jackets; fathers and sons in jeans, a few couples. The students from those first summers in Belgrade, holding in their stomachs now, filling the spaces with a warm buzz. We all know why we're here. Not a spare seat in the house. Young men crowding the steps and aisles. But everything is late. Excitement turns to slow hand-claps and ironic cheers. On a bright, bare stage weedy young men run around bent double with cables and connections. Finally a voice roars out from the audience — "WE WANT THE KING!" and a great crash of laughter fills the hall — Belgrade still waiting for the King.

A red and black glittering tuxedo, electric blue guitar and for a moment Milena goes up further in my estimation; she can whistle like Audrey Hepburn in *Breakfast at Tiffanys*. Then I see she's brought along her marching whistle.

Right opposite Emina's building across the road and litter strewn mud is a new ten storey apartment block in raw brick, no plaster yet. For refugees, Emina says, Serbian refugees from the war. How do the Albanians treat them? They don't mix Emina says. Only the most desperate come to Kosovo.

Others who can, refuse. So here we have the most desperate, packed in tight with the most oppressed. "Yes, Yes," Agim says, "Albanians want independence now. Serbs refuse: always tension." Two *milicija* pace slowly by. Speak Serbian, Emina murmurs.

In three years so much more building — apartments — I could lose my way. No trees.

The President of Albania, Ibrahim Berisha, is going south tomorrow to talk to the rebels. Berisha is one of the names of the northern tribes; the name is common in Kosovo. The Communist regime in Albania was dominated by southerners, the Tosks. Berisha has been supported by the States; one of the reasons being that though he's a northerner like the Kosovari he hasn't encouraged Kosovo to revolt. But now it's reported guerilla activity is on the rise: The Kosovo Liberation Army. Younger Albanians are losing patience. The Serbs are conducting big show trials of alleged members of the Kosovo Liberation Army. Maybe it's just the Serbs, not Albanians at all, Agim says. Agents provocateurs. Serbs want a reason to attack.

The flat is cold, Vlaznim taller, wound tight; fifteen years old. Born 1982. One year after the crack down on Albanian Republic aspirations in Kosovo. All he's known all his life is political tension. His Serbian is perfect in the old way like his favorite Uncle Suleiman. As in the old days his parents are 'Turks,' his father working with the Serbs, his pride Albanian.

The Serbs compliment him on his Serbian. "You speak it better than our children!" "But I do it *za inat*," says Vlaznim, "to show them what Albanians can do."

We are going to visit Agim's brothers in Obilic. All the years I was in Kosovo and Agim never invited me. Obilic outside Pristina: *Termo-elektran* and open cast mining. The lignite/coal deposits are among the largest in Europe. The air is so thick the car seems to push through it. They got money for the filters, Agim says, but 'the top people' spent it.

Cows and sheep crossing a mound of garbage, up a lane and then the house behind a high metal gate. Little concrete paths cross the yard over the wet ground. The young *nuse*, the bride, greets us. The older women cluster to one side smiling at her. Agim's two brothers live together and now one of their sons, Mohammed, has got married. So the young bride of Mohammed's son only six months married is the one to bring the *slatko* and the lemonade, and then walk backwards, holding herself tightly to do it all properly. The men haven't come home yet — we are to see the video of the wedding.

The women talk gently to Emina, wiping their mouths delicately, sitting at ease in Turkish trousers, twinkling at me. More open than I remember most of the women. Must remember — I am totally out of date.

Getting really Balkan. Living in the past. They are so quiet and low key. Milena says how English her daughter Zorana has become. "'Mum!' She protests — 'Don't talk like that!'" That is, don't talk like a Serbian. "'— Everyone here thinks you're *angry* all the time!'"

The video is of the wedding last summer. The guests link hands, laughing, talking, dancing gently round and round in the courtyard; vines overhead, in the background a rusting minibus. "*Kuku*! Look how fat I was!" exclaims Emina. There's Vlaznim in shorts and American Tee shirt. Film-star-elegant young relatives from Prizen — trust Prizren. Two in long brocade dresses, the sort that dazzle in shop windows, as bright as B. B. King's tuxedo.

"We came four days, every day from Pristina to dance and celebrate" Emina says.

Now on the video the two elegant young relatives from Prizren have changed into traditional finery; the voluminous white Turkish trousers, bunched below the tiny waists, the gilt brocade boleros, the white and gold coronet of flowers. There's the tambourine player. The gypsies always used to love me at weddings. Though I was in the women's courtyard I always had lots of cigarettes to hand out like a man. The gypsy would lean forward warming the skin of the tambourine over hot ashes and then lean forward again, to light the cigarette I'd given her.

Emina is explaining how the guests in the video are putting their hands in honey to reach up and touch the lintel of the house for good fortune. There is the *nuse*, the rigid young bride taking the hand of the visitor in her white gloves, the hand to her heart, then to her forehead. More dancing. The video goes on in the same sweetly languorous way the weddings do; the dancing round and round, grave, unselfconscious, monotonous.

And there is another video we must see; not a wedding but an engagement party in an apartment in Prizren. The young girl is opening presents, hanging up lots of dresses, embracing female friends. That's how the bride price is dealt with now. One of the young Kosovars exiled in London was indignant when I joked about selling brides. Albanians never did! The Albanians of Kosovo must have no flaws, not while they're fighting for international support. The girls are singing and dancing in the tiny spaces between the couches and the coffee table; hands held high, lilting back and forth. Emina is saying a video copy went back to Belgium.

"They came from Belgium to arrange it all." An arranged marriage. "The groom will come from Belgium to marry and take his bride back."

The two brothers arrive and the son, Mohammed, in a rush of energy, taking off shoes, apologies for grimy hands and immediately we're talking politics. The women protest. Ibrahim says "It's all politics here! To get us free of this Serbian anarchy!" Mohammed was expelled from his job as mining engineer by the Serbs.

"Bad. They let production slip — their only idea throw out Albanians." Now he says he's 'freelance.'

"Serbia will never let Kosovo go," Ibrahim states. "Too much coal here. And such good quality."

Do they have enough miners? If all Albanians are boycotting —

"They use the refugees from Bosnia,"Mohammed says.

We've had *slatko*, coffee, coca cola, and now dinner. We sit on the floor around the *sofra* in the other room; chicken soup with egg and pasta, *cufta,* the little meat balls, and rice, with paprika cabbage, chicken in batter with fresh bread, pickled peppers and white cheese, yoghurt and rice pudding. Then back to the couch, back to politics, popcorn, tea, cake and apples.

What's going to happen? Where's it going to end?

Since 1990 Ibrahim says five hundred thousand Albanians have left. Yes, tension. Tension. The Serbs practice 'psychological warfare.' At night you never know when the police will come. He raises his finger and thumb up, up to his chest, his neck, level with his eyes and finally "Poof!" His hand chops the air. Any time now.

"Ah, *kuptoni?*" he asks in Albanian, suddenly, not Serbian. "You understand?"

Yes, the final straw that breaks the camel's back.

What about Albania? Albania is the first item of news everywhere on satellite. We channel hop at the news hour for any news but the Serbian: Italian, Hungarian, Turkish (18 channels!). It's all anarchy, guns, deaths... chaos... The slow shake of the head and hiss as the breath is drawn in, way in. In the south the rebels are all old communists, bandits, mafia! That seems a standard line for the Kosovari, the northern Albanians.

International efforts are under way to reopen Tirana airport. Some announcer is saying the Germans are sending old East German arms to Kosovo from Albania to make space for new Albanian weapons: "...For the conflicting interest between US and Germany to take control of Albania." Before I can try and work that out, we've hopped on. On Albanian TV there's a sedate interview with a Minister sedately announcing the handing in of arms and a shot of two polite policemen in the back of a truck accepting two rifles from two young men.

And what does the American government think about us in Kosovo? Ibrahim leans forward intently, forearms on knees, hands together.

I've been telling Milena nobody cares. All that paranoia: everyone is out to destroy Serbia! No-one gives a damn. Hey, no-one gives a damn about *England*. All that old Empire.

Mohammed has started laughing, recalling how his mother veiled herself when they first got a television: "I don't want those people looking at me!"

"You know," says Ibrahim suddenly with a sly look, "...*we* always guarded our women so that's why we Albanians have pure blood — not like the Serbs..." Sly dig at ethnic purity and racist politics. Now to be fair, I should say that's a racist remark too.

When we get home, Vlaznim asks "What did Ibrahim say?"

"Of course!" he exclaims. "He is outspoken against Serbs."

Ibrahim calls Agim. "Mary is the best guest you've ever brought! Bring her again!"

"Did you hear what they said when we left?" Emina asks me. "'Come again!' Always before they always say to my guests Goodbye."

"That's because Mary talks politics," Vlaznim says.

Called Milena Thursday morning: The Rector of BU has resigned! The students are going to make a Victory march!

Down to our little Faculty through snow spinning down; our battered center of political life, our barometer of changing fortunes. In front of the Faculty is a statue of Vuk Karadjic, the great Serbian educator, on a marble plinth. No expense spared. Some of the letters and half the numbers in one of the dates have fallen or been prized off the front. Bad workmanship? Sabotage? Some Albanian in the dead of night, some Bashkim, maybe, braving the police patrols. Further up the hill, in front of the once big new library built to celebrate the bilingual Albanian-Serbian University, a monumental statue in swirling robes frowns downs at us; Nijegos the prince, poet priest of Montenegro, finger pointing imperiously straight down at the ground. Vlaznim, on his way to classes, in his slightly faded Miami Hurricanes jacket, collar up, snow in his hair, shakes his head. Provocation. Like Israelis building in Jerusalem. That large finger straight down. Here is the sacred ground of Serbia! Bow down here you Albanians!

Girls are coming down the old Faculty steps; shiny leather boots, make up, arms full of books, turning, calling in loud, confident Serbian voices. Only Serbian. I knew it had happened. It had happened when I was here in '94. But the war was on. There was the feeling of emergency, things in flux but here it is and set in stone. Here is Vuk Karadjic on his marble slab, the concentration camp spidery man long gone. Here is Serbian Only *Fil. Fak.* Exactly thirty years on from that cold spring when Tito came to Pristina for the first time.

The new head of the English department, Fitim, is another one of my ex-students, a Montenegrin/Albanian. One of the 'half and half's.' The first student I ever talked to back in my first week, all those years ago, a very bright girl from Montenegro, had introduced herself ironically as a 'half and half.' She had a Moslem name, Albanian parents and perfect Serbian. "Here it is not good to be neither one thing nor the other," she'd said. But classes back then had been all together and everything in Serbian, so she didn't have to choose.

Fitim had to choose. He joined the Serbian group. His Serbian was so good. So was his English. The Albanian students had been disappointed, some bitter. They were ready to be so proud of him. Now, in front of his computer, Fitim looks worn out. There are no books, he says, no money.

Assistants put their head round the door; young women, elegant, bright, excellent English. No problem now, it seems getting the best from Belgrade. Yes, and our standards are so much higher, now, Fitim says. There are 600 students in the department this year from all over Yugoslavia, the old Yugoslavia. Many are from "occupied areas"; that is, war areas, from Sarajevo and 80 refugees from Krajina, Serbs from Croatia. "They work so hard and help each other. They make me feel ashamed."

Dragana, one of Fitim's year, a sweet, bright student, is now teaching too. And her daughter. Dragana says "Good! The BU rector is out! Get someone who knows something! For here too! The University council here knows nothing and is in charge of everything!"

How liberal and aware that sounds. But there is nothing about How strange no Albanians! All our old colleagues. We're this island in the middle of a sea of Albanians and what's going to happen? Where's it all going to end?

"Oh, they have an Albanian department," Dragana says breezily "but no-one goes! There are Albanian books there but no-one uses them!"

Down in the student buffet the 1997 calendar by the counter features a Serbian general from the First World War. Alex comes in, he's teaching at the Faculty full time now. "Hey! Come and see me this afternoon! Bring Emina!" But if I do, then maybe we won't talk so openly. Maybe Alex feels there's nothing much more to say.

Down to the little market with Emina buying everything she can't afford. We spend what would be a third of Agim's monthly salary on fruit, nuts and vegetables. All Albanian stall owners. It's packed. We're joking, kidding around in Albanian and Serbian up and down the narrow aisles. Everything bright, all fresh — and there are the incredibly sweet navel oranges from Turkey, much sweeter than anything I've tasted in Florida.

What's going to happen? I ask Alex. We've got packets of nuts in front of our knees, scotch, brandy, wine; good red *Kosovski Kabernet*. There's another bottle lined up on top of the wardrobe. Just like the old days.

"Hey! Five years ago I thought I knew.....I know *nothing!* Hey — some of my students haven't even heard of the Beatles!"

"You know, this journalist says, 'I've got a pretty good grasp of what's going on. I've been around for three days.'" Alex gives a great hoot of laughter.

He talks about student days. "You know how I used to hang around you and Martin — all the foreign lectors? I was under such pressure. Cops were always after me: 'They are spies! They are spies!' Tito's boys."

"Albanian or Serbian?"

"Hey! Cops are cops!"

Friday I'm taking the 8 a.m. bus to Pec. Idriz isn't a teacher. Nezir is teaching still, I heard in London from one of his ex-students, a refugee, but I don't want to walk round Prizren asking about clandestine teaching places. Rooms are raided, teachers beaten up. And everyone always knows everything in Prizren. It used to be a town of eyes. Now who knows? Emina isn't sure. Vlaznim would just be breezy: "Don't worry!" I'll play it safe. I know Idriz worked for local government, so he'll just be unemployed.

Snow still falling, not settling. Ahead, snow covered mountains. Magpies and jackdaws, their grey hoods on black shoulders, look smart and sinister. Three teenagers stride off across the fields, school bags, heads down into the swirling snowflakes. Going to private classes? Agim says there's education in Albanian now to fourteen years but nothing beyond. Milosevic agreed to restart full education for Albanians months ago but nothing has happened. That's one reason for the growing unrest.

There are still two names on the sign posts before every village; but now Serbian/Serbian: one in the Latin alphabet, one Cyrillic. Movies on TV have subtitles in Cyrillic. New gas stations are in the Moslem green of the prophet: ALBPETROL.

Mountains grey and white through the mist all around, rising up like the unacknowledged reality. Down below daily life like the Serbs at the Faculty while all around them in the mist rising up are the statistics, nine Albanians to every Serb, the Albanian reality. What's rising up behind Albanians? What reality? I remember the face of an Albanian in 1994, dismissing the idea that ethnic cleansing could ever come to Kosovo, nodding out of the flat window to a jam-packed Pristina of apartments. "There are too many of us! — They'd have to bomb us!" So? "Well, first, they'd have to evacuate all the Serbs from the towns. And then..." his voice had trailed off. Yes? And then?

Vlaznim says Serbia will *have* to come to an agreement: "There are so many of us! Serbs here are nothing! They are told by Belgrade what to say!"

The taxi driver doesn't know which street I mean. "You know, they are always changing the names!" he grumbles as we bump around Pec. All the old *Partizanskis* and *Titos* and *Days of Revolutions* are now streets of the Great Leaders and the Great Serbian People. The driver, an Albanian, had been a government employee. His son is in Canada. He worries most about education. "The Serbs say we can elementary education now in Albanian and later we'll get back the Faculty level but we want all education now."

Nezir's former student in London was bitter about the farce of pretend education, the underground system; the gallant self help of Albanians that makes a good story.

"OK for English, for languages but science? No labs, no computers — Peoples' living rooms! A whole generation lost. Really apartheid, like South Africa." Vlaznim has been under immense pressure; he has been going to Serbian classes. But now his Albanian friends are better about it, he says. "They say now I was more clever to do it."

"You know the saddest thing," Vlaznim said last night, "Serbs now, the teachers and pupils, want to be friends with Albanians, go to parties and so on, but the Albanians don't want it."

Idriz is in hospital. He was sick yesterday and taken ill in the night. Deniz, his eldest son, is just closing the gate. He and Fatma insist I come to the hospital with them. It's just outside Pec. There's a crush of young men round the doors trying to get in. Fatma and I are let in, Deniz left outside. Idriz is lying pale but calm as always, on one of two metal bedsteads in a bare room, mountains through the window. Fatma has brought everything; juice, cookies, bottled water, soap. She starts to clean the grubby little night-stand by the bed. She has brought a nail she bangs in by the door for Idriz' towel. I'm joking Idriz may be moved — Maybe they'll move him from room to room, on purpose so they'll land up with the whole hospital cleaned. Maybe that's why they only let the women in.

Young doctors, men and women, and nurses keep popping in. They all know Idriz. He'll need to take some tests — go downstairs. You see? I tell Fatma who in a new rush of tidying is picking everything out of the little cupboard. She gets the towel off but we leave the nail.

As we're saying goodbye to Idriz, Deniz and his second son come in with another boy. His best friend, Fatma says, Branko, a Serb. How do Serbs and Albanians get along? Even with Idriz sick I've got to keep on asking.

"OK." says Fatma. "It's the government we don't like."

It was Alex who said the Albanians and the refugees in Pristina, that is the Serbians from Bosnia and Croatia, get on fine together. It's the local Serbs who don't get on with anyone.

Idriz talks in the corridor under his thin blanket waiting to go in for tests. Fatma is calming down. We're saying it's just stress — stress, of course. And talking of stress, *Kosovo* Albanians lost so much in Albania, Idriz tells me. They had shops, businesses there; the frontier had been opened in 1996. They lost not just with the pyramid schemes but when the looting and shooting started. "Albanian Albanians don't like Kosovari. We work hard. Albanians sit in cafes waiting for money. Naive — So long under Stalinism."

Idriz is a good example of a hard working Kosovar; from expelled top government worker to owning two shops, with his sons. Deniz shows me on the way home: car accessories. They are small, crammed with stuff, neat and tidy.

Fatma insists I stay for lunch. Deniz says "You see how there were no medicines, nothing in the hospital? The money goes on guns." For whom? Serbs or Albanians? "Who knows? We don't have faith in anybody." The bleak shrug, just like Belgrade. And people are not talking about politics not because they are scared or cautious but because they don't think it will do any good.

Euro-news: 1.30 p.m. Tirana airport is open again. Idriz said he'd heard on the news that Albanians live in Albania but *Siptars* live in Kosmet. It must have been *Radio Beograd.* Or maybe from Macedonia. Mrs. Petrovic's first lesson for me. Poor Mrs. Petrovic is dead, Emina says, run over by a car just outside the Faculty.

Deniz' younger brother has got married and it's his *nuse*, the young bride who serves us dinner. They are building an extension to the house. And Fatma is so happy to have a daughter in law. "When I come home from work the clothes are not on the floor; the soup is cooking." To live in the traditional way for the modern Albanian woman who goes off to work, is like hitting middle-age and getting a housewife, the new daughter in law. But marriage is so expensive. Deniz has a girl friend but says they can't afford another wedding yet. Above the couch along the wall there's a strip of wood with nails in it where all the *nusc's* finery, all the brocade and satin dresses, were hung. At Prizren weddings we were always taken in beforehand and shown all the profusion of finery, like the number of cars fetching the bride, the number of dresses indicating wealth and prestige.

There's a flurry at the door. Idriz' two sisters and a sister in law have just heard Idriz is in the hospital. Outside snow is falling hard but not settling. Idriz' sisters are very like him; fair, low key. They must be in their forties too, elegant with ash blond hair, dressed in cream and oatmeal sweaters and skirts. They curl up on the sofa, sleek legs under them, worried, talking quietly, smoking, pushing a hand with gold bracelets through their tinted ash blond hair. Women like these lived in the small towns of Bosnia; Moslem Yugoslavs.

Deniz was saying over lunch people in Bosnia must all be wrong in the head after what they've seen and suffered.

"The movement in Kosovo is secessionist, not democratic."

"What will happen?"

"Albanian tolerance is very high. And Serbian arrogance is used up."

The old Serbian professor from the apartment upstairs is sitting on the couch, no front teeth, drinking some of the good whisky I brought and not a sad figure at all. "Come on! 300,000 Italians had been quietly cleansed from Istra in a few years by the Slovenes and Croats!"

Rankovic was irrelevant. "Only came to Kosovo two or three times. Kosovo had its own Rankovics."

I've promised to check out the Albanian book scene for a Kosovar in London, a refugee. Baskets of fresh bread are being unloaded from a van in front of old Hotel Bozur. It's been taken over by Serbian war refugees. Their washing is hanging from the balconies. And *Grmija*, the excursion spot outside Pristina, with its restaurant among the trees, has been taken over by refugees too. They are entitled to free bread and free transport, Agim says.

The best book shop now is just by the big mosque down near the market. Gathered outside the mosque at Saturday lunch time, dark against the white mosque walls, are scores of older men. The first time I've seen that. And I have a strange feeling as though I'm not looking at 1997 — freedom of religion again in Eastern Europe emerging from the dark Communist years into the sunlight of Democracy — but that it's prewar, that Yugoslavia here too is spiraling backwards into the shadows of the black and white world of the old photographs in Tito's Liberation Museums. That the black suits against the pale walls of the mosque belong to a pre-World War Two life and the religious and civil wars are yet to come and to go forward all the bloody battles will have to be fought all over again.

And it's strange because in every way Albanians are an improbable success story in the midst of suppression — going steadily forward as the Serbs have lurched wildly back. Looking in the little book shop, another shock. Everything is there; elegant, slim paper backs as though Albanians have not missed a beat. New Albanian translations: Seamus Heaney poems,

The Theatre of Becket, Albanians in the Arab World. Text books on Chemistry, Physics and Medicine. The latest scholarly take on The Treaty of Berlin, 1878. Heavy duty academic stuff. Murad would have loved this. Murad is dead. Dynamic head of Biology is dead. And I heard that in London from a Kosovar, a refugee who had been one of Nezir's students in Prizren. Murad had died of cancer. Smoked like a chimney. We all did. Drank too much.

"Yes, " said the young Kosovar earnestly, "Life was so hard for them all under Communism. They drank. It was so hard."

Murad drank because he drank. He was a brilliant, tense man who drank, trying to still that nervous energy, leg always tapping away under the desk. And he reveled in being a Marxist, loved Russia. He just smoked all the time and drank too much. We all did back then. Interesting to see the new myths. Tito's world sliding backwards more remote soon than the Turks. 1945-81; 36 years. In Belgrade I saw coins on sale beside the Orthodox and Celtic crosses; King Alexander cushioned in satin and next door Tito's head.

Two men leaving the shop turn when they hear English. One an old professor, an ethnographer, has just been buying a book intending, somehow to get it to the Kosovar exiled in London that I'm checking the book store for! Well, if that isn't Kismet we don't know what is. The old professor invites me round tomorrow, Sunday morning for coffee. And a young Italian student hearing English too, asks for help to find a book. He's with another professor, an Italian, whose doing research in Kosovo for peace. He invites me to meet them tomorrow night.

There's a little barracks as I turn into the small street where the old Albanian professor lives; a soldier in front of a little wooden sentry box with red and white stripes. Like something out of *The Nutcracker Suite* except for his AK47. Shoes off, up wooden stairs into a bright room. The old Albanian professor, the ethnographer, is mellow, musing aloud.

"If it weren't Milosevic it would be someone else... The Serbian Academics are anti-Albanian."

"What will happen?"

"It will get better — gradually." He quotes the old Balkan saying: "Man to man is a wolf."

Yes, under Tito everything was fine — the *Federacija*. The Serbs were so stupid they lost everything. He retraces to 1878, the Treaty of Berlin: the Serbs got Nis, Leskovac. It was then 200,000 Albanians fled as refugees. In the Balkan Wars they got Macedonia, Kosovo. Then after the First World War they got Slovenia and Croatia. Then after the *Second* World War the *Volkdeutsch* — the Germans who had been colonizing the frontier-line for

hundreds of years — they left Vojvodina, following the German defeat —
Magyars too. And Albanians went on leaving — and still the Serbs managed
to lose everything. "They are not clever," he says gently.

He gives me a copy of his newly printed scholarly paper back; Alba-
nian population changes in southern Serbia following the Treaty of Berlin.
No, it would not be published without the tithe, he says. "Albanians in
Germany contributed one DM; in England half that because there are more
Albanians in Germany."

Albanian businesses have to make money, Agim says. They are taxed
twice, by the Serbs and by the Albanians for 'The Republic of Kosovo.'

The professor says Dr. Rugovo is good, Ibrahim Rugovo, the President
of the Albanian shadow government of Kosovo. The Republic of Kosovo, is
trying to hold the pacifist line. He heard a few days ago Dr. Rugovo went to
talk to President Tudjman in Croatia who said "Start something in Kosovo
and we will give you guns!" "And Rugovo left with a bright red face: 'No!'"

This professor says Arkan, the killer Arkan of the war, was born in
Slovenia; his father was in the army. His father threw him out. His father
was a Serb from Kosovo. My other old professor from yesterday, the old
Serbian professor, said Arkan was born in Prizren. We have juice, coffee and
sudjuk, Albanian smoked sausage, and as I leave, joking about exercise and
health with the professor and his wife, we all weigh ourselves on the scale
by the door.

It is still snowing when I go out to find Hamdi late that afternoon.
Hamdi was the last Albanian head of the English department before the
boycott and the Serbian take over. There's an icy rime on the road glittering
under the street lights. The cafe *Dubrovnik* is in a whole new block, in a
scruffy little mall like a passageway. Dingy, litter strewn. A few Sunday afternoon teenagers are hanging around in the chill. They frequent these kind
of places now, Vlaznim says. There's no more *korzo* at night. Inside beyond
the crisp white tablecloths, past the sharp young waiter who knows English
there is Hamdi, back to the wall.

"And how is Martin and how are the kids?" Martin and Hamdi had
been good friends; Hamdi had been in Literature too. Wordsworth was his
Masters.

The *Dubrovnik* is empty except for three men in dark suits who smile
over at us and keep telling the waiter to bring us drinks, dinner, whatever
we want. They must know who Hamdi is, or was.

Fitim, the new head of the English department insists, like the Serbs,
that the Albanian faculty just walked out of the University, deliberately
sacrificing the education of a whole generation of Albanians for political

ends. "Child abuse!" he called it. No, Hamdi says. "They threw us out of the Faculty. And not one Serb at the Faculty, not one colleague said anything!"

As for the parallel education, the clandestine classes in Albanian. "We *had* to offer them something here as Albanians, education in their own language or we would have lost all our youth. Mary! You should have seen the buses! Pulling into Pristina from all over Europe! Whole families were leaving!" That would be before regulations were tightened against the influx of refugees from "war torn" Yugoslavia. There is the whole diaspora of bright young Kosovar Albanians in London now.

"We thought it better to keep them here," Hamdi says, " or we would have done what Milosevic wanted — cleansed away our youth; lost them."

Hamdi's face is gaunt. Now things are a little better he says. At first he would hide his books under vegetables when he went to teach in case he was stopped. But just recently he was stopped by two young soldiers outside his flat. "What do you have in the bag?" and "What do you do?" "And luckily I had a few onions in my bag and I say, 'You see I buy and sell a little in the market.' And they ask How much did you make? 'Oh... just ten dinars.' 'That's a shame' one of the young soldiers says, 'You should get a job! You are not old!' You should have seen how new their uniforms were. So I said 'Maybe I could become a soldier' and they stepped back — 'Hey! Now you're going too far!' and they let me go."

Hamdi is totally dismissive of Albania even before the present anarchy. His son left for Albania he said but came back before the recent chaos. "It's no good there." Idriz too, said his sons wanted to open a shop in Albania but he said no.

"It's been rubbish there for fifty years!" Hamdi exclaims. "No faith, no patriotism, no idealism. Stalinism smashed them. I was there a year or two ago. I went to the library at Tirana University. There was nothing! You could burn it all! Stalinist rubbish!"

Emina and her colleagues had been upset years ago when the first delegation of Albanian teachers had come from Tirana. It had been just before I left in 1971. "They were so amazed at everything we had in Pristina — our little Pristina! But they tried not to look in the shop windows because there was one in the group who was checking them."

It's a hard blow, the crisis in Albania. Albanians on the world stage are now acting out Serbians' direst predictions; wild, uncontrollable, grabbing a gun. And these are the people the Kosovari are talking about eventual union with? On paper it had all looked so tidy and reasonable. A referendum taken. The people of Kosovo, the Albanians, had spoken: autonomy for Kosovo with eventual union with Albania but all very civilized. "Total rights for Serbians and all other minorities." After all, it's trade and technology now. Economic regions. Lap top computers and sheaves of position papers handed out. But now the headlines: Albania Awash In Guns. Guns Flooding Over Border.

Now the Albanians here are all saying: "Albanians don't care about Albania. They just want to get out. There is no pride in being Albanian."

For real Albanians now you need to go to Kosovo. Or maybe London and Germany and Switzerland. For real Albanian pride.

I don't ask Hamdi what he thinks will happen. But he does say Milosevic must fall soon. "He is surrounded by death."

"Pressure every day," Hamdi says. "They stop people in front of the flats. They beat up young boys so the children can see."

Hamdi says he has to go. We walk through the grimy tunnel, up and out into the cold, the snow still trying to lie. It's quite dark. "Give my best to Martin and the kids."

Yes, he says, you could write a letter but I won't get it. Hamdi doesn't want to pause, not even the shake of the hand. He pulls his hand free and swings round in the dark. I call out something, some silly goodbye thing and he swings round one more time, gaunt, tense, his face in shadow. It's like an encounter from the earlier days of Tito's Yugoslavia. His body tense, telling me I can't stand around like this, and is gone.

The Italian professor and his wife have been out all day but can meet us at eight for coffee in *Mozart*, a new pizza place in the small cluster of private houses climbing up the hill where the American flag is flying. There is a hard won American presence now in Pristina, the American Information Room.

On the way to the *Mozart* as Emina and I paused on the kerb for a car, a column of soldiers marched up out of the dark; the first one looking both ways before he led them across. About ten, combat ready in camouflage, automatics in right hands, helmets. Their belts were hung with what could be tin mugs, hand grenades, bayonets and water bottles; festooned like tinkers. They paced past and up the other side, disappearing at a near trot through the sparse shrubbery outside the old department store.

Mozart has shiny Byzantine copper trays and pots on bright white walls and a Whitney Houston type voice belting out western songs. We all just order tea. The professor and his wife are here for two years from the University of Florence; the Campaign for the Non-Violent Solution to the Situation in Kosovo. Preparing something for the European Parliament. There's the Civil European Peace Corps, the P B I 'Peace Brigade International,' the Balkan Peace Study Center in Macedonia. Rather tired from a day 'up country' as Edith Durham would have called it, out in Kosovo and struggling valiantly with English, they are a gentle, dedicated pair. I am instantly patronizing them in my head because they are talking about peace and reconciliation. Why? I'm always the one to argue the war didn't have to happen. But I'm thinking of the Blue Books, The Carnegie Endowment: *Report of the International Commission to Inquire into the Cause and Conduct of the Balkan Wars* brought out in 1914 recording the atrocities committed by all sides. A catalogue of rapes, murders, pillage, solemnly listing page upon page of the numbers, the ethnic origin of perpetrator and victim: Greek, Bulgarian, Serb, Turk, Albanian. As though at the end you add up points and whoever commits the least crimes and claims the most victims, wins.

But after all the talk of models of other autonomous regions, the possibilities for trilateral talks, negotiations, room for maneuver, international safeguards... limited autonomy, the mild man of peace sounds very tough and pessimistic.

"The Serbs are trying to provoke a war in Kosovo."

"The Albanian Liberation Army is preparing for a big push. They have money for guns. There are arms from Macedonia."

Clouds of black birds are rising and settling as our Belgrade bus passes close by the old battle field, the Plain of Kosovo, the Plain of Black Birds. I remember that in Pristina, always the cawing in the trees, the noisy raucous settling down at dusk of the crows, jackdaws and ravens. It's still cool and snowy. The satellite dishes are worn like white flowers on every stray house. There's the little *turbe*, and the Kosovo tower. Cooling towers on one side, smoke pouring out. A boy with two cows and a stick and the clouds of birds on the Plain of Blackbirds, the ancient battlefield.

The old Albanian professor on Sunday morning said it was not just the Serbs, there was the whole coalition; Albanians, Hungarians, Bulgarians, Greeks fighting at Kosovo. They ALL lost to the Turks. And all this talk of who was stronger — Czar Dusan or Skenderbeu? "It's like fighting over whether Davy Crockett was stronger than...than..." And he's not sure who that should be. "It's *all* myth," he says.

Twenty-six soldiers in new uniforms are walking along the road below, between sodden fields, in combat gear. And a little further on at a tiny barracks six soldiers wave at the Belgrade bus behind a double fence by a sign just inside: "*PAZE MINE!*": WARNING MINES.

The snow is holding on in gullies and corners; the slopes and shadowed paths showing white behind the narrow trunks of the trees. The density of population in Kosovo; almost never a scene, never a bus window you look out of, however remote, without houses or houses being built. There's a woman sitting outside her house in the March sunlight, sewing, snow on the roof behind her.

Belgrade; Good Friday, March 29th. This year it falls on the same day as the New Day of the Republic. That was declared in 1990 after the Bosnians and Croats split, Milena says and dreams of Greater Serbia were taking flight. I've been in bed since leaving Kosovo, with flu. This is the first bright day since I came. I'm leaving Saturday, Easter Saturday and Nada and Stefan are coming round tonight. Nada has been telling me the new facts proving how far back the Serbian people go in time. Asia minor comes into it and ancient caravan routes and the word for salt in some language or other *sorobi* from which, no doubt, the word Serb comes. I get the feeling it doesn't really matter which language just so long as it's pre-Illyrian and pre any Albanian claims.

Before I leave I stroll up to Republic Square on Saturday morning and check what's being sold: always the children and young women hawking boxes of cigarettes. The CD's of the songs from the demonstrations in the Belgrade winter and postcards of the great moments are being sold. Not hidden or under the counter but out in the street. *Rilindja* is published now as *Bujku*, "The Farmer" though says Vlaznim it's not about agriculture. They report on Dr. Rugovo; say what they want. After what has happened in ex-Yugoslavia who cares any more about mere words?

All Milena and Nada's friends have stories of their marching night after night and showed me their proudest possessions; the dirty pink plastic whistles and New Year noise makers. Milena hasn't had time to translate all the great slogans and jokes from the marches. I see PUNK AGAINST COMMUNISM on a wall and a CD called not MONTENEGRINS but, two guys in dark glasses, like rap stars: MONTENIGGERS.

Milena takes me to the airport. The sky is still grey, the color of second hand smoke. Milena has said vehemently, she would not want to have to live together mixed anymore. "If I have Croat friends then let me go there if I want to see them." So Belgrade is going to be just Serbs and Monteniggers. Well, it was Milena who said Serbs don't get on with anyone. And, now, on the way to the airport, I hear Milena say that, in fact, she is all Serb — not Serbo-Croat at all. I remember her so clearly saying "Yes! I am that typical bloody Yugoslav mix." "No!" Milena is, as always, decisive. "I just grew up in Croatia."

I knew she'd lost half her family in the war, Serbs living in Croatia.

Yes, she says, my grandfather, two uncles, grandmother, cousins. They were all shot by the Ustashi, the Croat Fascists "...and thrown in the pit and my grandfather they found him the only one with his hands tied behind his back. That meant he was the one who resisted."

There are still places in Bosnia and Macedonia where you can see Tito's picture, Milena says. The first summer I came, back when we were schoolgirls, Milena was just home from the States. She'd been chosen to represent Yugoslav Youth and then was offered a scholarship at Princeton but turned it down. She was too much of a Socialist she said and she was falling in love with a young ex-Partisan. She had been the outstanding young Communist of her year: sat next to Tito at a special banquet for school leavers.

No, Tito's time was not all bad, she says. It was a time of war and revolution. Ten thousand of the intellectuals and merchants were rounded up when the Partisans entered Belgrade in 1945, rounded up and killed. And they sent young kids of Royalist officers to the Sremski Front when the Germans were retreating. "It was unnecessary; it was as punishment. You know Vera? Her husband was sent." And Milena's father was imprisoned not only by the Ustashi in the war but then in 1963 when he was told to spy on his fellow workers and had refused. He was in prison nine months for 'economic immorality.'

"That was good for us. We saw who our real friends were. And two men I'd never seen before came to the house and brought wood before the winter began, to help us. And I never knew who they were and I never asked. And when my father died there were many men at the funeral I didn't recognize."

I suggest they might be coworkers he'd not betrayed to the police and Milena likes the idea.

Sitting in the plane seat next to mine is a middle aged black man in a business suit. Some *bizniz-man* making a sharp deal. Continually in my ethnic intensive mood I have to find out where he's from. Nigeria. One corrupt militaristic regime dealing with another. No, he's from London stationed with the UN in Vukovar; getting ready for elections in April. Vukovar, the Slavonian city not far from the Croat-Serbian border, pulverized by the Yugoslav/ Serbian army for two months. In the photographs it looks worse than Berlin in 1945, more like Hiroshima. No, he doesn't live in the ruins; the UN people live with families. He's ten minutes away with a Serbian family. They are told not to talk politics. Vukovar is due to be turned over to the Croats in July — part of the deal — part of the finalizing of the Dayton Accords. "There are demonstrations every day." The Serbs are more backward looking than the Croats, he says. The Croats are opening markets... "Yes, it's so difficult. I'm asking a woman if we could open an election office in her garage; it's a building still standing and she stands there and says 'Here my husband was killed, over here my sister, here my father...'"

The sun is shining at Gatwick; the mellow end of the day sun. The passport girl is smiling, the bus driver is smiling. How bright, gentle, rich and clean England seems and so pastoral. Just outside the airport there are cows and sheep among the dandelions, three black ponies trotting down to a stream to drink, hedges white with hawthorn. Milena's children won't go back. Nor will most of the Kosovari I've met in London, I'm sure. There's a Jane Austen house on a rising slope, with high chimneys, hidden behind a grouping of trees. FOR CROYDON FOLLOW M 23. Above everything an egg-shell blue Boticelli sky.

Emina has said Suleiman goes to the mosque now in Istanbul. Well, he's living by teaching English, private lessons, and that way he looks more respectable and makes contacts. His papers are still not in order so he has no legal status. "Suleiman found it difficult after a while living with our elder brother," Emina told me. Now he has a room somewhere and because he is considered a refugee can eat three meals a day, free, in the student dining hall.

Vlaznim wants to be a bridge between Serbs and Albanians. "Ha!" exploded Milena, "Not with this lot! Impossible with this generation! — And probably the next!" She means the Serbs.

And what about Albanians?

Next to Vlaznim's Turkish calendar on his bedroom wall is a hand written sign in English that reads: "FOR LOVE AND WORK THIS WORLD IS ABOUT."

When I left Kosovo first, in 1971, I was listening to Radio Pristina as I finished packing. It was the Sunday early morning farming program. An *agronom* was talking excitedly about corn yield, a new hybrid suitable for the conditions in Kosovo. I could see his innocent face, his short sleeved white shirt, his sunburnt hands on the green baize of the broadcast booth. And all that passion about corn. He'd been speaking in Serbian but all that mattered was he was passionate about his corn. Not history, not nationality, not the Turks or the Illyrians, not the self-importance of suffering. Just the corn. And I remember thinking that it was one of the few times in five years in Kosovo that I'd heard someone really passionate about something useful.

The End

April 1999

Enver's American wife called us from the Bronx very early one morning. Enver was Agim's cousin. Vlaznim had phoned them in the middle of the night, his voice low, saying only "We are OK. We are leaving now." He wouldn't say where they were or where they were going. That was at the start of April. Now the phone was dead. Until that moment I had thought maybe they would even stay in their Pristina apartment. There was the odd report of friendly Serbians trying to protect their Albanian neighbors. And Emina had always been such a good neighbor. We had got through for the last time just a few nights before, Emina sounding like an old woman, her voice quavering: "Five nights now we are bombed..." We talked on through the night, $74 dollars worth, until we made her laugh. Vlaznim had reassured us: her voice was faint because she didn't want to wake up the couple in the other room. They were Albanians on the run — he an ex-president of something. They were not sleeping in their own apartment fearing Serbs would come to take them away.

"It's dangerous for you, Emina!"

"Yes — but they need my help so what can I do? You know us."

The NATO bombing of Yugoslavia had started on March 24, just over a year since the killing of a whole Albanian extended family in Drenica, 'Kosovo Liberation Army stronghold,' had triggered full scale violence in Kosovo. Throughout 1998 the fighting and deaths had been in the country-side and villages but it was all coming closer to the towns. A few weeks before Vlaznim's last phone call Enver's family had fled to Pristina when the fighting between the KLA and the Yugoslav Army neared Obilic. They were the family we had spent the day with, when we saw the wedding video. They had all camped out in Emina and Agim's two rooms. Now they were back home but Enver said his father would soon be dead. Albanians were being ordered to leave their homes immediately and head for Albania or be killed and Enver's father Ibrahim, the lively brother who had talked politics over the popcorn and apples, told Enver the last time they spoke that he would not leave. "He says he fought in the war he is not afraid and he will not leave his house. So I said goodbye to him on the phone."

Milena was e-mailing me. She had sold her flat in the center of Belgrade a year ago and moved to Novi Sad, north across the Danube, where on the very first night of bombing NATO had targeted the river bridges. Milena's furious e-mail was almost incoherent with outrage but she still asked about Emina and Vlaznim.

"Tell Emina to send Vlaznim to me" Milena had been demanding for months. "Get him OUT of Kosovo!" Milena still so grateful we had got her son out of Serbia when he was to be called up for the army, just about Vlaznim's age. Milena's mother told me he would have been sent to the Croatian front. At least, I said, they weren't putting Albanians in the army anymore. Serbs didn't want to teach Albanians how to use a gun. "Ha! You don't have to teach an Albanian how to use a gun!" Milena had snorted down the phone.

We had faxed an invitation/guarantee letter to Pristina for Vlaznim, last summer without much hope: ("Having been the recipients ourselves, of so much hospitality over the years...")

"I really just want to finish my exams," Vlaznim was saying.

With the Serbian rejection of the Rambouillet peace agreement, in mid-March, suddenly that world of conference tables behind chateau walls seemed as remote as the quill pens and ink stands of the Treaty of Berlin. But it appeared the Great Powers were still running the Balkans, sorting out the lesser breeds, Europe's last colonial peoples. I wondered if the League of Prizren house, the birthplace of modern Albanian consciousness, down by the river in Prizren, had been destroyed yet.

There were one or two of my old colleagues at the Rambouillet peace talks, described as the token old guard, balancing out the KLA. They were getting out of cars in drizzly weather, having umbrellas held over their heads by attentive young men in well cut suits. There was Fehmi Agani. One of the founders of the Democratic League of Kosovo and its spokesman. The colleague I remembered so vividly from our own little 1968 demonstration at the Fil. Fak. And suddenly with the breakdown of the talks, they were back in our old Kosovo and Fehmi's name was in the news again. *A voice of reason and moderation.* His body was found at Stimlje, the first town stop on the Pristina bus route to Prizren. He had been shot.

It had been the villages but now it was the towns. Pec was looted and burned. Idriz' two little shops would be gone, probably the house. All Albanian businesses were being destroyed and one night as a reprisal they were rounding up Albanian men in Pec. I was refusing to process information any more. There were reports of massacres near Djakovica. Djakovica was no surprise. I'd been waiting for Djakovica, Gjakova, the most Albanian of major Kosovo towns where even the Serbs spoke Albanian, where the best Albanian radio announcers used to come from. What an affront Gjakova must have been to any Serb nationalist.

Then Pristina; looted, burned, bombed by NATO and then just emptied by the Serbs. That was when we'd heard from Enver's wife in the Bronx about the last call from Vlaznim.

The Albanians of Pristina were routed out of their apartments, driven down those dingy apartment stairs, and out into what used to be Marshal Tito Street — and then that turn, walking down the almost straight run to Kosovo Polje railway station; that seemingly endless trundle of the old *Kosovotrans* bus down to catch the Belgrade train. They would have come in two streams, from the center of Pristina and from the south side, from the new flats where Emina and Agim and Vlaznim lived. Walking that ten miles down to the station, silently, refugees said and packed into those special trains. The sides of the carriages grey, the faces grey, the windows grey with grime — back to the black and white world of the Second World War. No Vlaznim, no Emina, no Agim through those grey train windows. Then the camps: I was looking at the camps over the border in Macedonia, with CNN, the muddy fields. They were the camps for the people from Pristina — straight south in the trains to Macedonia or along the road, the route of the *Kosovotrans* buses, down to Skopje. Rain, mud. I didn't know if Emina could survive.

Then Prizren. Albanians driven out of Prizren, walking or driving their cars, to Kukes just over the Albanian border. Prizren was spared much burning: Czar Dusan's city. Serbs would not want to destroy Prizren. At least Nezir might find some comfort in that — his beloved Prizren. Would I even recognize Nezir, or Mehmet, anymore? Nezir would be someone they would talk to, the reporters, Vlaznim too — their English was so good. Vlaznim had been asked to help translate with the UN observers monitoring the cease-fire back in the fall in Kosovo, but he didn't want to interrupt his studies. He had said some of his friends were in the KLA, but not fighting. "Mostly on the political side."

Emina had told me how the KLA had come to the door one day, asking for money. "And I said if God will grant us money then I will give some but we have none in these days. And I was a little worried. He put our name down and said he would come back."

So many Albanians being interviewed for the news. So many professionals: teachers, doctors, lawyers, students from vet school, computer science, pharmacy. A whole mini-nation with only the clothes they're standing in, crowding muddy fields.

So many ordinary people too, so many people. That's always what the Serbs hated: so many Albanians, so many large families, so many people. And so few peasants in costume, even in Turkish trousers — Bosnian trousers. It was the ordinariness of the people that was so striking, caught up in the lunatic logic of ethnic cleansing. The dazed, separated from family, walking round the tents, studying lists of names in the rain, holding pictures of their children and grandchildren, scanning lists on the wire mesh of fences. The doctor walking over the border from Prizren. There she was on CNN: at the end of her shift just told to leave the hospital. No, you don't go home. Walk to the border and go over. You are Albanian. Get out of Kosovo. Go to your Albania.

The KOSOVO REFUGEE FINDER: in English and Albanian. "If you do not find the name you are looking for in this database do not panic. (*Mos nuk frikohen!*) Remember there are over 74,000 refugees and the number is growing all the time. *Type in the first name, the surname, the town.*"

"*Sorry there were no matches to your search.*"

Emina, Agim, Vlaznim: Pristina. And Hamdi, from the English department. Nezir: Prizren. And Mehmet, of course. Idriz, Pec — and Hussein, Pec. *Sorry there were no matches to your search.*

Calling SPONSORSHIP FOR U.S: "Our voice mail is full." Emina won't remember our phone number, nor will Vlaznim. It cost so much to call, we always called them. Even if they had time to take things like the address book, it would have been torn up at the border with everything else.

Type in the first name, the surname, the town. Highlight Search (Kerkoni!) *Sorry, No match. Search again?*

Milena e-mailed: "I can't get through to Pristina anymore — What is happening with Vlaznim and Emina? In all this evil madness I am so happy my children are not here. Our friendship will NOT end because bombs are trying to do it!"

I called Nada and the family still in the center of Belgrade. At least it doesn't matter what time we call. Because of the bombs no-one is sleeping. I listen about the NATO bombing. The enlargement of NATO which means the encirclement of Serbia. I don't talk about Kosovo. "No. No electricity," Nada is saying. "We are in the dark. Last night I vowed I would make a cup of coffee over a candle — all the family collected to watch and I finally did it!"

Type in the first name, the surname, the town. Sorry, no match. Search again?

June 1999

June 1, 6.45 a.m. — "HI, MERI! THIS IS VLAZNIM FROM PRISTINA!"

"YES, we are calling from our flat! NO, we didn't go! We stayed *za inat* — for spite — this is our fatherland!"

"We stayed here and in other place, *Suncani Breg'*. We were scared to be here. You know the kindergarten behind us? The military were there with ammunition. We were scared NATO would bomb it. Now we are very safe with the British. NO SERBIAN POLICE! British soldiers everywhere. Now my mother says come The British are here. You can come through Skopje!

"We are meeting people here every day, talking English with the soldiers. But sometimes it is hard to understand them. They are talking cock-nee."

"Yesterday we had Nescafe with the British soldiers. And my mother was queuing for her pension and the people were in a muddle and she called to the British soldiers to help her make a queue and they made a queue!"

"What about everyone in Obilic?"

"They are O.K! They are O.K! Everyone is O.K!"

"Hey! Here is my mother!"

"Yes, yes. Thank god, no Serbian police. We lived on bread and milk. We were scared for Vlaznim. He didn't go out for three weeks. All the Albanian neighbors who left had their furniture and TVs taken... even the phones. Our Serbian neighbors saved us. They are wonderful people. You know the old professor of psychology? He saved everyone on his floor. He said 'I am Serb and a writer. And if you touch anyone of these people I will write it all down.'"

"But you know Suzana? The doctor? She left and they took everything. The furniture, the phones. There is nothing there. But our Serbian neighbors said to all the Albanians you can sleep here with us."

"We are telling them to register what was taken, register the loss. Tell the British. The British people are working hard to register. We will be witnesses."

"Our soldiers are all English-speaking. Thank God no Serbian police! Only the people who did these things left. I told my Serbian neighbors not to go. 'You must not go!'" Emina starts crying.

"Our neighbors were wonderful. You know Branko? He said 'Come on, Emina! Vlaznim goes to Serbian school! You must stay! He wrote Serbian names on the doors."

"They are marvelous, marvelous people," Emina is sobbing, "and I don't want them to go!"